VICTORIAN HANDS

VICTORIAN HANDS

*The Manual Turn in
Nineteenth-Century Body Studies*

~

PETER J. CAPUANO
and
SUE ZEMKA
Editors

THE OHIO STATE UNIVERSITY PRESS
COLUMBUS

Copyright © 2020 by The Ohio State University.
All rights reserved.

Library of Congress Cataloging-in-Publication Data
Names: Capuano, Peter J., editor. | Zemka, Sue, 1958– editor.
Title: Victorian hands : the manual turn in nineteenth-century body studies / Peter J. Capuano and Sue Zemka, editors.
Description: Columbus : The Ohio State University Press, [2020] | Includes bibliographical references and index. | Summary: "Focuses on the materiality of hands to show the role that the hand plays in Victorian literature and culture. Contributors to this volume discuss the hand in the works of Charlotte Brontë, Christina Rossetti, George Eliot, Wilkie Collins, William Morris, Thomas Hardy, Henry James, and Oscar Wilde"— Provided by publisher.
Identifiers: LCCN 2020020676 | ISBN 9780814214398 (cloth) | ISBN 0814214398 (cloth) | ISBN 9780814280737 (ebook) | ISBN 0814280730 (ebook)
Subjects: LCSH: Hand in literature. | English literature—19th century—History and criticism. | English fiction—19th century—History and criticism.
Classification: LCC PR468.H36 V53 2020 | DDC 820.9/3561—dc23
LC record available at https://lccn.loc.gov/2020020676

Other identifiers: ISBN 9780814257685 (paperback) | ISBN 0814257682 (paperback)

Cover design by Alexa Love
Text design by Juliet Williams
Type set in Adobe Minion Pro

CONTENTS

List of Illustrations   vii

INTRODUCTION   Handling Flesh and Metaphor
                    PETER J. CAPUANO AND SUE ZEMKA   1

PART I · HANDS: WHOLE AND PART

CHAPTER 1   The Anatomy of Anglican Industry: Mechanical Philosophy and Early Factory Fiction
            PETER J. CAPUANO   19

CHAPTER 2   Lost Hands and Prosthetic Narratives: William Dodd, Writing at the Industrial Join
            TAMARA KETABGIAN   36

CHAPTER 3   "A Fiery Hand Gripped My Vitals": Admiral Nelson, Amputation, and Heroic Masculinity in *Jane Eyre*
            KAREN BOURRIER   54

PART II · HANDS, PLOT, AND CHARACTER

CHAPTER 4   Hands and the Will in *The Woman in White*
            PAMELA K. GILBERT   73

CHAPTER 5   Hands at a Séance: Manual Evidence in Victorian Spiritualism and the Ghost Story
            AVIVA BRIEFEL   90

CHAPTER 6	Hands and Minds in *The Moonstone*	
	SUE ZEMKA	107
CHAPTER 7	The Dead Hand: George Eliot and the Burdens of Inheritance	
	JAMES ELI ADAMS	128
CHAPTER 8	Computation and the Gendering of Gestures	
	JONATHAN CHENG	148

PART III · FRAMING AND STAGING HANDS

CHAPTER 9	The Photographer's Hand	
	KATE FLINT	175
CHAPTER 10	Staged Hands in *Bleak House*	
	JULIANNE SMITH	196

PART IV · MANUAL EXCEPTIONALISM IN LATER VICTORIAN LITERATURE AND CULTURE

CHAPTER 11	Handling Private Dramas of Class and Gender in Anthony Trollope's *The Duke's Children*	
	DEBORAH DENENHOLZ MORSE	221
CHAPTER 12	Reading by Hand: Oscar Wilde and the Body in the Archive	
	DANIEL A. NOVAK	239
CHAPTER 13	Hands in Hardy and James	
	J. HILLIS MILLER	256
AFTERWORD	The Well Spoken Hand	
	HERBERT F. TUCKER	273

List of Contributors	281
Index	285

ILLUSTRATIONS

FIGURE 8.1	Distribution of Men's and Women's Hand in Nineteenth-Century Novels	156
FIGURE 8.2	Possessive Language and Men's and Women's Hands	157
FIGURE 8.3	Average Proportion of Women's Hands in Novels by Men Versus by Women	158
FIGURE 8.4	Average Proportion of Men's Hands in Novels by Men Versus by Women	160
FIGURE 8.5	Confidence of Gender Prediction in Nineteenth-Century Novels	163
FIGURE 9.1	Julia Margaret Cameron, *Lady Elcho/A Dantesque Vision*, 1865. Albumen print from wet collodion glass negative. Given by Mrs Margaret Southam, 1941. © Victoria and Albert Museum, London. PH.255-1982. Used with permission.	178
FIGURE 9.2	Julia Margaret Cameron, *The Neapolitan*, 1866. Albumen print from wet collodion glass negative. Given by Mrs Margaret Southam, 1941. © Victoria and Albert Museum, London. PH.249-1982. Used with permission.	180
FIGURE 9.3	Advertising for Folding Pocket Kodaks. 1899. Ellis Collection of Kodakiana. Duke University: K0559. ark:/87924/r43t9fz70. duke:430271. Used by permission.	190

FIGURE 10.1	"Consecrated Ground" by H. K. Browne. Used with the permission of the Department of Special Collections, Stanford University Libraries.	200
FIGURE 10.2	"Jennie Lee as Jo in *Bleak House*" by unknown photographer, circa 1876. NPG Ax7679. © National Portrait Gallery, London. Used with permission.	216
FIGURE 12.1	Photograph of Oscar Wilde. *Contemporary Portraits* by Frank Morris, 1915. William Andrews Clark Memorial Library, UCLA. Used by permission.	240
FIGURE 12.2	*The Graven Palm; a Manual of the Science of Palmistry,* by A. Robinson. New York: Longmans & Green Co., 1911, p. 350.	244
FIGURE 13.1	Two Haloed Mourners (1587–95), by Spinello Aretino. National Gallery, London. Used by permission from Art Resource, New York.	265
FIGURE 13.2	Lucrezia Panciatichi (1539–45), by Agnolo Bronzino. Uffizi Museum, Florence. Used by permission from Scala/Art Resource, New York.	269

INTRODUCTION

Handling Flesh and Metaphor

PETER J. CAPUANO AND SUE ZEMKA

WHY DO WE need a collection of essays dedicated to hands, one might reasonably ask? One answer is that hands are a compelling subject for working through the ongoing critical impasse between constructivism and materialism. The constructivist tendency is to fold the body into language; materialism, in contrast, maintains that there are aspects of life, including embodied life, which are ontologically independent of language. The literary history of the hand cannot but grapple with the fact that hands are both, that they operate in written texts both as signposts of embodied specificity *and* as figures of speech in a thousand dead and living metaphors.

The recent intellectual history many of us grew up with clarifies this issue. Literary and cultural studies of the latter twentieth century were largely dominated by Foucault's early work on discourse studies, which defined "discourse" as the linguistic practices with which a society produces its reality and corroborates its power relations. Discourse has material and political effects that exceed its status as 'just talk'—it conditions and limits the emergence within a society of what it takes to be facts, realities, veritable truths. Foucault's dynamic influence set in motion an entire program of scholarly research that treated the body primarily as a linguistic and discursive construction, subject to epistemic epochs and the systems of power they enabled. The Foucauldian body is more acted upon than acting, and, with qualifications, this is still true of his later work on biopower.

But if bodies can be convincingly situated in a Foucauldian paradigm, it is not clear that the same is true of hands. Approaching the hand requires a different frame, which yields a different set of questions. One, we exchange an investigation of power for an investigation of agency (with all the pitfalls of the presumed priority of individual actors which that entails). Two, we enter a field of data where the constitutive primacy of language over material being, or vice versa, is not only impossible to decide—its impossibility is a heartbeat that runs through the whole. Historically, the hand seems to be one place where humans have negotiated the relation between their language and their material being all along.

Both of these framing questions are demonstrated by Katherine Rowe's influential *Dead Hands: Fictions of Agency, Renaissance to Modern* (Stanford University Press, 2000). Tracing the motif of the dead hand across a transhistorical set of Early Modern plays and English and American gothic texts, Rowe argues that the common denominator is a provocative uncertainty about human agency. These literary traditions, it turns out, have long been aware that human agency is an amalgam of semiotic and corporeal habits. They have been negotiating, in other words, the dilemma of the Foucauldian legacy—that the body is not only passively written on by power structures which inhabit language, but also acts within and against them, consciously and unconsciously, its volition or lack thereof evolving representationally between discourse and embodied action. And the hand, specifically the *dead* hand, is a crucial motif through which this negotiation is thought and performed. Rowe's work shows us that human volition is at a fundamental level enacted by the hand, and that is no simple matter. For "the hand," in our cultural traditions, is an amalgam of language and flesh, as well as of determinism and freedom.

The essays collected here explore this fascinating, ambiguous zone where semiosis and "anatomy" combine to form ideas about that purported basic unit of power, the human actor, and, in addition, the second-order complex actors that humans create—industry, technology, science, ideas about God, the law, theater, the archive itself. Hands, language, and agency: the contributors to this volume utilize their expertise as Victorianists in order to understand how the unique conditions of the British nineteenth century shaped the modern emergence of our cultural relationship with our hands. This frame is more than a matter of scholarly convenience; its appropriateness is supported by lexical evidence. In *Changing Hands*, Capuano makes the striking claim that there was "a sudden but sustained spike in representations of hands in British fiction and in English culture more generally . . . a spike so marked that hands appear in nineteenth-century novels more often than any other body part including faces, heads, and eyes" (12). But why?

We offer several answers, none of them conclusive, and all of which link to yet more questions. Capuano suggests that the explosion in manual terminology in the nineteenth century was a reaction to a uniquely British "double whammy" (15) experienced within a single generation: the violent supersession of manual labor by machines and the emergence of jarring evolutionary theories, the latter corroborated by the discovery of "hand-bearing" animals (gorillas and other anthropoid apes). The cultural anxiety provoked by these radically changed industrial and scientific relations made Victorians newly cognizant of what, since time out of mind, had been a living, grasping symbol of their anthropomorphic exceptionalism. This became a crisis of enormous ontological and anatomical proportions: the divinely designed human hand as the chief agent of worldly making was profoundly jolted—and for the first time. Who or what is ultimately responsible for the productive capacities of industry, with its vast economies of scale, and its social and political ramifications that so quickly spin out of human control? Amid such complexity, humans and their hands are a respite of simplicity for the fiction as well as the non-fictional prose of the period, and yet they often wind up recapitulating the same anxieties about unintended consequences and tragically lost personal connections.

It is also worth noting that those interested in materialist conceptions of the Victorian body have long focused almost exclusively on the only other body parts open for routine inspection in the nineteenth century: the head, face, and eyes. There are many compelling reasons for this lopsided critical focus on the head, including the enduring precedence of the Cartesian mind (over body), realism's intuitive connection to sightedness, and the period's flourishing pseudosciences of phrenology and physiognomy.[1] Once the observation has been made that Victorian writings are saturated with representations of hands, however, the reasons for it start to seem obvious. Is it any wonder that the first country to move through the wrenching transformation of industrial production and shocking (to some) evolutionary theory would produce a literature that magnifies the organ that links humans to machines and animals? In the spirit of Thing Theory, after all, one does not worry or manifest anxiety about something until that thing—in this case hands—becomes imperiled. Indeed, the hand wields a figurative influence so

---

1. Realism's traditional connection to sightedness provided a basis for many exemplary studies in the 1990s: Jonathan Crary's *Techniques of the Observer* (1992), Carol Christ's and John Jordan's edited collection *Victorian Literature and the Visual Imagination* (1995), and Katherine Kearns's *Nineteenth-Century Literary Realism: Through the Looking-Glass* (1996). More recently, the legacy of determinative pseudosciences of physiognomy and phrenology inspired a bona fide sub field in Victorian studies which dealt with the face and head: Mary Ann O'Farrell's *Telling Complexions* (1997), Lucy Hartley's *Physiognomy and the Meaning of Expression in Nineteenth-Century Culture* (2006) and Sharrona Pearl's *About Faces* (2010).

pervasive that it is actually difficult to recognize. All of us, by virtue of having lived after the nineteenth century, have inherited the hand as a body part always already changed so much that its alteration has become hard to notice. The time of nineteenth-century manual crisis long past, we inhabit a world where it seems once again almost *natural* to take our hands for granted. Their functional presence in our everyday lives has dissipated, in Percy Shelley's Romantic formulation, into the mists of familiarity. In Jamesonian terms, the logic of late capitalism has produced a present culture that treats its hands so metaphorically that to do so (and not to notice it) has become second nature to both critics and general readers alike. Never mind that we now spend much of our lives interacting on screens with our fingers; it's the screens one thinks about, it's the screens that tend to break. The literal digits in digitized culture are all but forgotten.

This volume of essays, therefore, represents an ongoing effort to notice what hands have to tell us about the cultural preoccupations of the nineteenth century. Taking this period's fascination with hands seriously, which it to say taking them literally and metaphorically at their word, brings into better focus a crucial moment in the history of embodiment that has remained largely unrecognizable to us. To think critically about the multiple referential pressures this culture places on hands means reimagining the familiar outlines of what mattered to the Victorians and why.

And this reimagining helps uncover the ways in which our individual and cultural relationships to our hands continues to matter in our contemporary moment. As our contributors collectively show, a sustained consideration of the hand from multiple viewpoints and disciplines brings into focus questions about will and action, to the extent that the hand belongs to (and is sometimes alienated from) the individual and the social. The hand is the most immediate embodiment or representation of human action. And yet, in another sense, apart from the human, at its furthest point of extension. Because the hand enacts intention so singularly, it enacts the human will on the world and relates a world of objects to the human subject. But as the seat of tactile contact, it is also a primary interface between subject and object—where they encounter one another in a mode of what twentieth-century phenomenologists refer to as *sub-objectivity*.

One of the founding texts of this sweeping philosophical discipline, Edmund Husserl's *Ideas Pertaining to a Pure Phenomenology* (1928), returns again and again to the hand as the primary indicator of the body's simultaneous objective and subjective "Being in the world." Husserl prefigures the phenomenology of sensation in Heidegger, Merleau-Ponty, and Derrida by exploring the uniqueness of the hand's ability to act both as a touching and feeling organ. Husserl says that, "in the case of one hand touching the other ... we have then two sensations, and each is apprehendable or experienceable in a double way" (154). Only the hand allows for this "double apprehension" where "the same touch-sensation is apprehended as feature of the 'external' Object and is apprehended as a sensation of the Body as Object" (155). Husserl calls the hand the "real organ of touch" because the other senses offer no such subject-object "analagon" (155–56).

The hand-privileging that Husserl's most famous student, Martin Heidegger exhibits is even more compelling because of the latter's direct confrontation with Darwinian evolutionary issues. Heidegger boldly states in *What Is Called Thinking?* (1952) that "apes, too, have organs that can grasp, but they do not have hands" (16). For Heidegger, the hand is an essential—and exceptional—aspect of human being in the world; the body part crucial to human beings' understanding of historicity and meaning. The being of the Heideggerian hand is not, however, determined by its bodily operation of prehension. Rather, the hand is the essence of humanity because it "reaches and extends itself, receives and welcomes—and not just things: the hand extends itself, and receives its own welcome in the hands of others. The hand holds. The hand carries. The hand designs and signs" (16). As his title indicates, the context of Heidegger's ideas about the exceptionalism of human hands is grounded in thinking. The deep etymological connection in German between manual grasping (*greifen*) and intellectual comprehension (*begreifen*) is thus not lost on him. Perhaps Jacques Derrida puts this best in his own work on "Heidegger's Hand" (*Geschlect II*): "thinking is not cerebral or discarnate for Heidegger; [thinking, *das Denken*] is a craft, a 'handicraft,' a work of the hand in two words" (38).

Derrida's other writing on Heidegger and Jean-Luc Nancy explains how the hand arrived at what he calls its place of "phenomenological nobility" (164). Tracing the ideas of thinkers from Maine de Biran to Merleau-Ponty, Derrida discusses this "nobility" of the hand in a characteristic phrase of ingeniously germane word play. The hand, according to Derrida, has enjoyed this special status in phenomenological thought precisely because it is "at the joint of two faculties; touching and feeling" (149). In terms of touch, it "occupies an *ideal* region of effort poised between passivity and activity" (155, emphasis original). Here Derrida extends Husserl's sense of the "double-apprehension" to what he calls the "touching-touched" (159).

We have neither the space nor the inclination to rehash all the ways that Derrida's thinking aligns with phenomenological thinkers, but focusing on one place where he definitively does not—where, in effect, we see his far stronger allegiances to the deconstructive program—will help illustrate one of the foundational arguments upon which this collection of essays rests. Here, Derrida outlines the primacy of the "sub-objectivity" in Husserl's hand only to interrogate it:

> And is it also true that this cannot be said of every external part of the body. But why only the hand and the finger? Why not my foot and toes? Can they not touch another part of my body and touch one another? What about the lips, especially? All of the lips on the lips? And the tongue on the lips? And the tongue on the palate and many other parts of 'my body'? How could one *speak* without this . . . And the eyelids in the blink of an eye? And, if we take sexual differences into account, the sides of the anal or genital opening? (164, emphasis original)

These questions are valid, and each has their own connection to important work on speaking, writing, and sexuality (to name only a few related directions). The litany of questions regarding the possible importance of other body parts deserves a response; one that we hope each of the essays contained in this volume helps to answer from multiple angles. The point Derrida's questioning (which may stand in for any reader's questioning) fails to account for is the historically contingent story of how the hand's importance came to be so thoroughly altered in the nineteenth century. No other body part, let alone one so quintessentially linked to human being, underwent a radical destabilization, physically or ontologically, except the hand.

The opening section of this volume has been organized under the heading "Hands: Whole and Part," because each of its essays explores the significance of the human hand's increasingly precarious, but privileged, status in early- to mid-century writings. This section dwells on the idea of the hand as separate from but a metaphor for the whole person—as shifting in and out in terms of separability and metaphoricity. Capuano's essay, "The Anatomy of Anglican Industry" traces how an unlikely convergence of scientific, industrial, and religious discourse coalesced around 1830 to make the human hand the most generative but also the most heavily contested site in the British cultural imaginary. Multiplication of manual functions into machine functions is dangerous for hands: literally, what is most important, dangers for the appendages of those who worked with and around machines; symbolically and conceptually, a shaking up of the notion of a representational and ontological continuum between divine and human makers, and of the sacred uniqueness of their imagistically and agentially similar hands. Bell's essay on *The Hand* (1833) expresses a kind of anticipatory nostalgia for a stable past, "an original perfection" of handedness as the source of which might not ever have existed as such

(Eden seen through the gates of exile) but comes into existence now as present conditions call for an alternative, a contrast that might clarify what is wrong or threatening in the ways things are going. Hence Capuano's argument—the growing acclimation to industrialized environments, with their multiplication of mechanical acts of making, and "the factory system," with its decentralized administration, pulls Bell's attention to the hand as a something other—something that is either at the heart of this system or eclipsed by it—a divinely designed, corporally localized, and organic locus of human making.

Bell, a medical doctor, surgeon, and natural theologian, could reflect on the hand as having an autonomous or quasi-autonomous dignity, as a marvel of design in itself, before or apart from its uses. Tamara Ketabgian's essay, "Lost Hands and Prosthetic Narratives: William Dodd, Writing at the Industrial Join," moves into realms of experience and discourse where there is no such autonomy, where hands have a purely functional purpose as the point of contact between laboring individuals and factory machines. Hence the manifold meanings and valences that gather around "the join." Focusing on the life of William Dodd, a hand amputee, Ketabgian makes real for us the terrifying vulnerability experienced by the first generations of British factory workers, and for the appendage most crucial to their livelihoods. She astutely describes the situation as "a destructive coupling of humans and machines, in which the hand serves as its most densely freighted site of intersection, transformation, and vulnerability." Thus the damaged hand emerges not only *at* the industrial "join" but also as a complex prosthetic emblem for the join itself—as a deeply ramified juncture of human and mechanical hinges, straps, bones, ligaments, joints, and wounds. Such a combination of literal and figurative schemata for machine culture, in Ketabgian's argument, provides a grisly index of industrial loss and suffering, but it crucially also provides other prosthetic compensations. Dodd's lost hand enables the growth of alternative skills and subjectivities: his autobiographical narrative doubles as an account of his growing literacy, his mastery of new writing practices and technologies, and his development as a leading public voice. Because she analyzes how Dodd's writings constitute a complex alliance and complicity with the same factory system that he so powerfully repudiates, Ketabgian's essay, like Capuano's, reminds us that the battle lines of the "Industrial Question" were often not so clearly defined as we and our students often surmise. We might understand William Dodd as a type of modern subject, one who organizes himself around injury and adaptation, and for whom independence and dependence remain complexly coupled.

Accustomed as we are to the barriers of social class in the nineteenth century, it is startling to realize that maiming bridged the classes, a consequence of the industrial continuum between modern warfare and modern production. The final essay of this section, Karen Bourrier's "Admiral Nelson, Amputation, and Heroic Masculinity in *Jane Eyre*," analyzes another Victorian man who grows and evolves around an injury and adaptation, albeit this time a fictional character, and one far removed from the cotton mills in which Dodd worked. Bourrier reads Edward Rochester's maimed hand as an indicator of heroic masculinity, arguing that associations between heroism and disability were common and important for the generation after the Napoleonic Wars. Admiral Nelson, who lost an eye and an arm before losing his life at Trafalgar, was a paragon of this ideal. Having suffered with courage for a higher cause (such as Rochester saving almost everyone in the Thornfield fire), the disabilities of such men, Bourrier argues, added to their sexual appeal. This latter attribute might have reinscribed a class difference among male amputees in Victorian England, since in the cases Bourrier considers, it is bundled in with the alluring status of gentlemen and officers. Nevertheless, the focus on hands, here, as in Ketabgian's essay, suggests a different way of understanding textual characters, one that takes us away from the traditional clarities of virtue and vice, dependence and independence, and forces a recognition of the manifold and seemingly contradictory attributes that accrue around narratologically represented lives, beneath or beside other types of classification.

Part II consists of five essays that focus on the novel. They center on the human hand's complex importance for character and plot in the Victorian novelistic imagination. Several sub-factors fall under the rubric of character and plot: touch, agency, gender, (computational) evidence, intentionality, and (intentionality's reification), the will.

Continuing with the method of preceding essays of bringing hands from the background to the foreground of reading, Pamela K. Gilbert unearths in "Hands and the Will in *The Woman in White*" a fascinating linkage between key mid-Victorian political concerns: the will of individuals, the will of the body politic, women's property, and the destiny of nations. Hands in Collins's novel perform the startling instability of individual and national "wills" alike. From Anne Catherick to Marian Earle to Walter Hartwright to Count Fosco, manual action suggests that individual will is contingent, vulnerable, hard-won, and not exactly individual at all; remember that the novel starts with Catherick extracting a promise from Hartwright, which promise takes control of his life like destiny, as if Catherick's will, albeit powerless in herself, a woman, can be larger than life in others. Add to this that the promise she extracts is to by all means leave her alone, and the stage is set for a story of women gaining independence through dependence, self-determination through group effort. And all of this sealing of destiny transpires through the thrice-placed touch of Catherick's hand on Hartwright's body. As Gilbert explains, the power of that touch is buttressed by the massive importance that Victorian psychology placed on sensation and preconscious bodily feeling. All the more interesting, then, is the fact that hands do not continue to reside at this material level of existence in the novel, but garner symbolic meanings, meanings that imbricate them in philosophy's long debate about the will of the state (which Gilbert traces from Aristotle to Locke to Hegel and Mill). That a state could have a body, or be theorized as such, quickly folds right back into material, other than-metaphorical implications, such as the state's 'reach' over its constituents, its power to limit individual freedoms, whenever and wherever those freedoms impinge on its own best interests, its health and security, as a monolithic entity. In the era of nationalist revolutions, the will of a state is even more mysterious than that, as it is fundamentally incoherent, owned with violently oppositional definitions by both monarchists and revolutionaries. Collins's sympathies go with the revolutionaries, who align the will of their nations with "liberal modes of human freedom"; hence Fosco, the traitor of Italian liberty, is struck dead by "hands that could never be traced" (88). That those individual hands cannot be traced back to their source—nor individuated—seals the argument of Gilbert's essay, which demonstrates the novel's attunement to the *collective* struggle of nineteenth-century battles for liberty—both women's legal liberties and larger democratic liberties, which John Stuart Mill insists depend on each other, as does Collins's plot. The true definition of "will," like destiny, will be verified retrospectively. It will go to the victors, who *The Woman in White,* as a deeply Victorian novel, believes are those who fight, struggle, and sacrifice for the expansion and extension of individual rights.

Tactility, evidence, and the will: manual metaphors and turns of phrase impart a certainty, a concreteness, to these concepts that veils their vagueness and imprecision. Manual figures of speech often promise a simple, singular, material chain of cause and effect; the hand stands for one body, one mind, one intention, one means. It's not a necessarily comforting reduction; the age-old popularity of the dead hand horror story translates these turns of phrase and their simple promises into gothic, even campy literalness. Aviva Briefel's essay, "Hands at a Séance," focuses on spiritualism, an area of Victorian culture where the assumption that hands operate as irrefutably material evidence is marshalled *against* materialism. From the earliest séances, "the appearance of tangible spirit-hands, which came in a variety of shapes and sizes, provided palpable evidence of the supernatural" (91). That the empirical evidence of these hands was fabricated with sometimes elaborate illusions is beside the point, which is simply that the appearance or sensation of an unidentified but palpable hand was enough to convince the grieving attendees of séances of the full presence (albeit generally silent and incommunicative) of their beloved dead. Here, Briefel's main concern, as in *The Racial Hand in the Victorian Imagination*, is with the many ways in which hands were assumed to be more truthful—more revelatory of their owners—when they were separated from those owners, whether through amputation, palm-reading, fingerprinting, or, as in this essay, in séances. Victorian spiritualism represents one of the most extravagant examples of Briefel's thesis, where detached, floating hands are taken as 'physical' proof of the presence of ghosts. What they are thought to reveal, in their mute and eerie autonomy, is no more and no less than a complete human being, her soul, body, personality, and ongoing cohabitation with the still-living. So successfully and extravagantly did spiritualists lay claim to this equation, Briefel argues, they effectively shamed honest ghost story writers into disowning the dead hand trope that had been theirs for centuries. Thus the later part of the essay turns to the fiction of Sheridan Le Fanu, who reclaimed some vitality for his fictional ghosts by ridiculing the manual trickery of spiritualists and resorting to the more credible horror of invisible spirits.

Sue Zemka's essay returns to Wilkie Collins, this time *The Moonstone*, and continues with the other essays' discoveries that hands subtly deliver the opposite of what they promise; not the identificatory trace of their owners—a singular volitional person at the other end of the hand's action and marks—but rather identity's abstractness, its dispersal across a field of attributes or actants, or its merely wishful certainty (and more wishful immortality). Every Victorian hand starts to look like a severed hand. The upshot of Zemka's analysis of hands is that Collins's art of character is more accurately an art of anti-character, a method of characterization that focuses on the parts that comprise the wholes of literary character, but in so doing deactivates the enchanting verisimilitude (we used to call it "roundedness") that binds them together into seemingly living entities. Literary character, in Collins's novel, is a little like Humpty Dumpty, which, once broken apart, can't be put back together again. Less a failure than an experiment, Collins's novel devises the perfect premise for itself—Fredrick Blake's hands carry out a theft of which Frederick himself is unaware. Hands acting without minds, Zemka argues, is the novel's thesis, its staged contention not only with the Victorian desire for lifelike and loveable fictional characters, but also with the theory of agency that accompanies such art of character, one that believes in straightforward and uncontestable accountability. Hands crowd the novel with a crazy frequency that belies their semi-visibility and their surprisingly thematic coherence: manual action and manual metaphors do not uphold an Enlightenment notion of human individuals effectively imparting their will to the world. On the contrary, they suggest something else going on under the rubric of what we call volitional cause and effect. This impertinent experiment is good as far as it goes, but it is throughout haunted by a reason to retract itself. The novel's eponymous non-human central character, the moonstone, registers an appeal for the sanctity of whole living bodies, for precisely the ideas about human life that Collins's method of character seemed to challenge. Behind this appeal, Zemka suggests, are the memories of mutilation and carnage from the India Mutiny. The severed or dissociated hand, this essay contends, reaches its end point of figural play and philosophical exploration at corporeal literalization.

With James Eli Adam's essay on "The Dead Hand" in *Middlemarch,* the focus shifts away from the embodied hand to its importance as a literal *and* figurative legal mechanism for the conveyance of Victorian property. His analysis reveals how, in *Middlemarch,* the trope of mortmain complicates novelistic representations of inheritance as a fantasy of power or exemption from economic life. Adams suggests that in this most iconic of Eliot's novels there is a broadly Burkean understanding of inheritance as a force that not only enables but also restrains and regulates human agency (in an older sense of "entitlement")—that mechanism which Burke invoked as the foundation of English identity. As it incarnates the authority of the past, the dead hand becomes a focal point of radical ambivalence in *Middlemarch,* and Adams shows how it illuminates the powerfully moral psychology that is representative of Eliot's fiction more generally.

Instead of using the methods of close reading, Jonathan Cheng's essay offers a quantitative compendium to the art of close reading. His essay gets 'meta' on the questions of manual representation that concern the preceding essays in this section by asking what we may learn by counting hand gestures in fictional texts using a methodology that has come to be known as a "distant reading." The chapter bridges the research of three scholarly fields: cultural analytics (more commonly known as "computational criticism"), gender studies, and body studies. Using the methods of data science *and* literary criticism, Cheng explores how large digital collections might be leveraged in order to ask macroscopic questions about the production of gender within the depiction of characters' hand gestures. And by computationally extracting the hand gestures of fictional men and women from nearly 1,000 nineteenth-century novels, the chapter raises two central questions with critical implications for advancing our knowledge of Victorian handedness. First, proportionally speaking, do either female or male characters appear more often through the representation of their hands? Second, to what extent are particular hand motions exclusively associated with feminine or masculine characters? In demonstrating how even innocuous gestures such as "giving" or "offering" one's hand consistently get deployed along gendered lines, Cheng's analysis offers not proof but provocation for further study related to the gendering and engendering of characters in Victorian fiction. Furthermore, Cheng demonstrates how quantification does not lead to truth claims (as many critics of digital methodologies assume); instead, it creates new contexts and opportunities for *closely* reading many different kinds of social and literary forms of evidence.

Section III moves on to extraliterary sources. The previous essays studied the hand in textual representation, mostly fictional. These essays try to bring us closer to physical hands, try (if it's somehow possible) to recover hands not in semiosis but in the flesh. Not "Victorian hands" as discursive signifiers in literature, but the hands of actual Victorian men and women recorded in practices of making. Thus they turn to the archives of photography and theater.

Kate Flint's essay, "The Photographer's Hand," explores instances of nineteenth-century photographers using their hands as they fumble through the development of this chemical, machinic imaging technology. It's a fascinating story, and much of the import is unfolding, or retrospective. Photographic chemicals stained fingers and palms. The deleterious consequences for health and the environment were unknown. True to their general tendencies, Victorians were more focused on the sociology of hand stains. For early art photographers, they were badges of honor. Later in the century, they became class markers, once methods for protecting the hands from chemical stains were developed, since these were too expensive for the poorer members of the burgeoning photographic industry, commercial practitioners. It's impossible to read Flint's accounts of early photographers' cavalier use of pyro and silver nitrate without feeling some horror at their ignorance of toxicity. We can see it, but they couldn't. Nor could they see the unfolding ramifications of their hobby for the particular "permeable interface of thing and body" that is unique to the history of photography. When devising new techniques and new instruments, they were focused on the immediate ends of a better composition, or finding the right aesthetic moment, or else on how to make photography cheaper and accessible to all. But the larger implications of their activities had to do with the way that human bodies participate with tools in the art of making images. In a trajectory that is repeated several times in this volume, but through different subject matter, the role of the human hand is eclipsed by those of the eye and mind. Not forgotten entirely, and certainly not obsolete (you still need hands and fingers to work the camera), but eclipsed. The making of art photographs still needs hands for secondary, functional tasks, but creativity proceeds from somewhere else, from something that transpires between mind, eye, and machine. Considering the hand both as a physical part of an individual and as a synecdoche for photographic work allows for a new understanding of the changing relationship of technology to human agency in one of the century's most exemplary artistic mediums.

Julianne Smith then shifts our frame of reference from photography to the stage in her essay on Charles Dickens's *Bleak House* (1852–53) and its theatrical adaptations in the 1870s. While there is no dearth of scholarship dedicated to the theatricality of Dickens's prose fiction (especially in *Bleak House*), few have analyzed the "manual continuity" that connects his fiction to its staged adaptations. Smith draws our attention to how Dickens's prose, in combination with Hablôt K. Browne's illustrations, privileges gesturing hands and then traces this manual privileging to the development of popular stage adaptations such as Henry Rendle's *Chesney Wold* (1871) and J. P. Burnett's *Bleak House* (1876). Smith explores why hands matter both for how these scripts were composed and also for how they were visually presented to audiences. Ultimately, these adaptations extend our knowledge of Victorian anxieties rooted in the classed and gendered body—but crucially from perspectives where these anxieties are dramatized, and therefore, may express manual preoccupations and boundaries that remain inappropriate or ineffable in prose, illustrations, or scripts of the period.

The fourth and final section of this volume begins with a return to a "close reading" of the ways in which gender and class depend on manual interaction in one of the Victorian period's most intricate fictional choreographers of domestic life: Anthony Trollope. Here, Deborah Denenholz Morse argues that Trollope's depiction of England's highest social classes emerges in his characters' pervasive attempts to express and distinguish gradations of emotion specifically through their hands, which are staged as the bodily appendages that must negotiate the swift-changing manners and mores of civilized society in the century's later decades. In *The Duke's Children* (1880), the haptic especially marks gradations of loss and connection—in particular between lovers, but also between family members and between friends. Morse analyzes how the Duke's slow reconnection with life after the death of his wife Glencora is marked by symbolic, intimate scenes in which the embodied hand dramatizes his incremental acceptance of his children's more progressive ideas about gender and social class. She also maintains that there is an important tension with this narrative of reconnection, however, that is most prominent in the stories of Tregear's first love Lady Mabel Grex and Silverbridge's racing partner Major Tifto. The increasing isolation of both figures occurs in scenes in which representations of the hand are central in defining their losses in relation to gender and social class demarcations.

Daniel A. Novak's essay turns our focus to how a different but related strain of manual exceptionalism plays out in the archive of Oscar Wilde studies. Novak shows how, from early twentieth-century "automatic writing" purporting to channel Wilde in psychic messages, to later twentieth-century biographies promising to deliver the "real" Oscar Wilde, the literary-theoretical enterprise of Wilde studies has been particularly concerned with being in touch with Wilde's body and its desires. From within this context, Novak explores the ways in which Wilde himself uses the hand as a key site to theorize the relationship between the body, writing, and identity (authorial, sexual, and otherwise), in works like "Lord Arthur Saville Crime," *The Portrait of Mr. W. H.*, *The Picture of Dorian Gray*, and *De Profundis*. He emphasizes how Wilde's texts also offer a theory of the archive, and the Wilde archive in particular, that is often connected to hands. In this sense, Novak maintains that when we look for the hand and its trace in Wilde's texts, we often find both already archival objects and the strange temporality of the archive itself. Novak's argument ultimately posits that the writing hand and writing *on* the hand in Wilde often internalizes and presupposes the "posterity" of reading and the future of the archive in a simultaneous manner.

In the final contribution, J. Hillis Miller's essay on "Hands in Hardy and James" addresses—but from a philosophical, theoretical, and linguistic perspective—the troubled notions of manual exceptionalism that Capuano identifies at the start of this volume. Tracing how manual exceptionalism contributes to the hand's conspicuous "afterlife" in figurative language, Miller makes the parallel claim that what is most distinctive, singular, even special about a given nineteenth-century writer may be identified by way of the artist's manipulation of hand idioms. In Miller's view, despite the common conception that Hardy's work is indefatigable in inventing or discovering hopeless impasses, his focus on hands offers a surprising level of agency to both his novels and poems. Miller finds representations of the manual in Henry James to be more somewhat more abstract, but his analysis reveals how even James's abstractions reflect new tensions that arise at the end of the century from still greater alterations in human relationships to this most distinctive body part. For Miller, the body's haptic connection between selves, objects, and others is also in its cultural deployments a source of self-fashioned identity, a source of difference *from* others.

Herbert F. Tucker's Afterword is a concise meditation on some of the major themes of this volume as they appear in Victorian poetry. While he doesn't exactly say so, his discussion suggests that the relative neglect of poetry in the preceding essays is a missed opportunity, but one for which Tucker brilliantly makes amends. Where better than in poetry, with its aural rhythms, does the mysterious alliance of body and language find a vehicle of expression? And this alliance, the volume argues, concentrates itself in our hands, the first and still most important organ of human gesture. Manual gesture attenuates itself in chirography, where the alliance of body and language is less physical, but more precise—less visceral, more conceptual. Writing also has immeasurably greater social impact than gesture, because writing is capable of reproduction and dissemination. Again, as Tucker shows, poetry, perhaps Victorian poetry especially, concentrates this mysterious history of communication, insofar as poets like Hopkins, Browning, and Tennyson find ways to remember the hand in their poems, find ways to write the hand as an instance of the movement from interiority to exteriority. Generalizing from poetry to Victorian culture at large, it's possible that the nineteenth-century provided a viable context for a literary preoccupation with hands because of the culture's still-lingering awareness of the communicative power of manual activity, in all its concerning ambiguity and intractable affectivity (hence the histories of BSL and the Delsarte movement). Maybe, as Tucker's concluding discussion of *Portrait of Dorian Gray* suggests, the Victorians' literary preoccupation with the hand stems from their attunement to its untoward excessiveness of signification, to the irreducibility of manual expression's potency to motive, let alone meaning. If this is the case, maybe we have (at this late moment in the volume) discovered another way of understanding the Victorians' relationship with their hands—that they were the bodily locus of a pre-Freudian unconscious, the corporal proof of an excess of meaning, memory, and desire that makes us always, to some degree, strangers to ourselves.

In a time and a place where population, industry, and scientific discovery were growing at unprecedented rates, is it any surprise that representation would seek a counterbalance to these forces of expansion, abstraction, and confusion—and find it in the small, singular organ of a human hand? The hand militates against abstraction. Our most functionally intricate and sensorially packed appendage, the hand links us to objects, others, and non-human living in a way that can't *but* be personal, can't *but* be individualizing. What better way, then, to simplify and personalize the impersonal complexities of nineteenth-century industrial and bureaucratic existence than by bringing it all down to hands?

But it's also true that abstraction militates against the hand. The increasingly complex technological, economic, and bureaucratic systems in which Victorians (and all moderns) find themselves are comprehensible in theory only, and even then only imperfectly. The seeming impenetrability of such systems threatens the desires of manual representation with the charge that they are smitten by a nostalgic dream of human control. This predicament sets the stage for what we are attempting here, a reinvestigation of Victorian hands as sites where human agency, personhood, accountability, and care are being reconfigured, salvaged, and fought for. Our larger hope is that this shift in focus to the hand ultimately helps us reach new understandings about how embodied life is determined by the social, scientific, and institutional worlds in which it finds itself, and about the possibilities for imagining, finding, and creating other forms of freedom.

WORKS CITED

Capuano, Peter J. *Changing Hands: Industry, Evolution, and the Reconfiguration of the Victorian Body.* U of Michigan P, 2015.

Crary, Jonathan. *Techniques of the Observer: On Vision and Modernity in the Nineteenth Century.* MIT Press, 1992.

Derrida, Jacques. "Heidegger's Hand (Geschlect II)." Translated by John P. Leavy, Jr. *Psyche: Inventions of the Other, Vol. II,* edited by Peggy Kamuf and Elizabeth Rottenberg, Stanford UP, 2007.

———. *On Touching—Jean-Luc Nancy.* Translated by Christine Irizarry, Stanford UP, 2005.

Hartley, Lucy. *Physiognomy and the Meaning of Expression in Nineteenth-Century Culture.* Cambridge UP, 2006.

Heidegger, Martin. *What Is Called Thinking?* Translated by Fred D. Wieck and J. Glenn Gray, Harper & Row, 1968.

Husserl, Edmund. *Ideas Pertaining to a Pure Phenomenology,* Second Book. *Studies in the Phenomenology of Constitution.* Translated by Richard Rojcewicz and Andre Schuwer, Kluer, 1989.

Kearns, Katherine. Nineteenth-Century Literary Realism: Through the Looking-Glass. Cambridge UP, 1996.

O'Farrell, Mary Ann. *Telling Complexions: The Nineteenth-Century English Novel and the Blush.* Duke UP, 1997.

Pearl, Sharrona. *About Faces: Physiognomy in Nineteenth-Century Britain.* Harvard UP, 2010.

Victorian Literature and the Visual Imagination. Edited by Carol Christ and John Jordan. U of California P, 1995.

PART I

~

Hands

Whole and Part

CHAPTER 1

~

The Anatomy of Anglican Industry

Mechanical Philosophy and Early Factory Fiction

PETER J. CAPUANO

THIS ESSAY explores how an unlikely convergence of scientific, industrial, and religious discourse coalesced around 1830 to make the human hand the most generative but also the most heavily contested site in the British cultural imaginary. Assessing the threat posed to traditional Anglicanism by nascent evolutionary theory (emanating most intensely from France and Germany) is necessarily to consider English responses to such threats. Though there are many that fit this description, I will look more closely at one particular response—Sir Charles Bell's Bridgewater Treatise on *The Hand* (1833)—because it remains relatively unexamined and because it provides an early and rare instance of a text which struggles to address both natural philosophy and industrial expansion. In my estimation, Bell's Treatise is exemplary of how early evolutionary discourse on the hand became imbricated with grave new questions about mechanized manufacture.

The Earl of Bridgewater died in February 1829 and bequeathed £8,000 to the President of the Royal Society to publish works of natural theology on the "Power, Wisdom, and Goodness of God as manifested in the Creation" (Bell vi). The Royal Society selected Charles Bell to compose one in a series of eight publications.[1] This Treatise on the "mechanism and vital endowments" of the human hand appeared in a series that became one of the most widely

---

1. Bell's 1833 Treatise was the fourth published in a series of eight.

circulated works on science published in the first half of the nineteenth century—despite its relative obscurity today (vi).[2] Bell's Treatise takes up his subject comparatively, exhibiting a detailed anatomical overview of animal appendages descending from the human hand to the "hand-like" extremities of monkeys, the paws of bears and lions, the wings of birds, and the fins of fish. These physical morphologies are unproblematic for Bell because of his belief in the prevailing notion that "man [was] created last of all"—as "the highest and most perfect" creation of a God who had intended it to be ordered in exactly this fashion (*The Hand* 21, 34). The deeply religious Bell was the son of an Episcopal Church of Scotland clergyman and believed without hesitation that the human hand—as opposed to the eye—was "the last and best proof of that principle of adaptation which evinces design in the creation" (38). Bell was so personally and professionally dedicated to the 'Design' model that he was chosen to edit and even to illustrate later editions of Paley's *Natural Theology*. Because of this association, Bell's Treatise on *The Hand*, when it has been acknowledged, is treated almost exclusively as a distinct but unremarkable integer in the wider calculus of British philosophical thought built on "purposeful" adaptation in the natural world. However, Bell's 1833 Treatise is also a key transitional text linking nineteenth-century ideas about 'Creation,' industrialization, and representations of the factory in early industrial British fiction.

Just as *Frankenstein* took shape amid earlier debates about religious creation and design, Bell's Treatise was composed during the hotly contested 'Machinery Question' as it unfurled during the 1820s and 1830s. Labor historians associate this period with the most exponential development and implementation of mechanized production. Raphael Samuel, for example, claims that "the machinery question attract[ed] attention chiefly in the 1820s and 1830s, when Cartwright's loom was throwing thousands out of work, and when the rival merits of an agrarian and an industrial society ('past and present') were being canvassed on all sides" (9). Likewise, Francois Crouzet estimates in *The Victorian Economy* (1982) that the number of power looms increased by a factor of ten between 1820 and 1833—the year of Bell's Treatise on *The Hand* (199).[3] The rapid development and implementation of all-metal mechanisms

---

2. *The Hand*'s popularity was reinforced by more than 120 reviews that appeared in forty different periodicals during the 1830s.

3. This process, of course, does not occur overnight despite the rapid growth attested to by economic historians. As Elaine Freedgood has pointed out, the power loom, the steam engine, and the spinning frame "had not achieved the dominance in mid-Victorian imaginations that we might expect in part because they had not [yet] achieved that dominance in production" (2).

made the textile machine simultaneously both a philosophical symbol and a tangible reality. "On every hand," Thomas Carlyle famously commented in his 1829 "Signs of the Times," "the living artisan is driven from his workshop, to make room for a speedier, inanimate one" in which "the shuttle drops from the fingers of the weaver, and falls into iron fingers that ply it faster" (59). Though the inward sense of mechanization was clearly Carlyle's greatest concern for what he termed "the Age of Machinery," the tangible effects of automatic manufacture were beginning to register in unprecedented, disorienting, and, as we shall see, physically perilous ways. Bell, for his part, believed that the machinery itself posed a challenge to the "perfect," God-given human hand as the model of all productive activity (172).

Thus, if we consider these issues in conjunction with Bell's experiences during this time as a practicing surgeon who treated victims of industrial accidents at Middlesex Hospital and Leeds Infirmary, his Bridgewater Treatise may be seen not only in an evolutionary context, but also in its larger cultural one: as an important response to the era's struggle with the grim physical realities attendant upon the supersession of hand labor by automatic manufacture.

The proliferation of this new productive power quite obviously had wide-ranging effects. For the first time in history, mechanized textile equipment employed automatic appendages that functioned more productively and more efficiently than the human hand alone. Mechanical contrivances had moved worlds beyond Vaucanson's eighteenth-century automatons to accomplish significant industrial tasks. Mechanized gig-mills, shearing frames, and multi-bobbin power looms outperformed work that had been previously accomplished by skilled craftsmen for centuries. Unlike manual labor, machines began to operate with unparalleled rapidity, regularity, and tirelessness. Therefore, the body part that had been the primary emblem of human exceptionalism in the natural and economic world—the part that had been celebrated as "the instrument of instruments" from Aristotle to Galen, Shakespeare to Bulwer—began to appear physically inadequate in an inconceivably altered way. Peter Gaskell describes this process from the human worker's point of view in his *Manufacturing Population of England* (1833):

> The labourer is indeed a subsidiary to this [machine] power. Already he is condemned, hour after hour, day after day, to watch and minister to [the machine's] operations—to become himself as much a part of its mechanism as its cranks and cog-wheels,—already to feel that he is but a portion of a mighty machine, every improved application of which, every addition to its Briareus-like arms, rapidly lessen his importance . . . (183)

Another contemporary presciently noted in the 1830s that the prevalence of automatic machinery was "rendering *hands* artificially *superfluous*" (Place 171, original emphasis).

The result was not simply one of scale or degree. In fact, newspaper accounts and working-class literature reveal that the increased productivity brought on by machine manufacture was only one unsettling feature of England's rapid progression to mechanized production. The frequent injury, and often death, endured by factory workers as a result of their interactions with automatic machinery quickly became a far more immediate concern for those in closest proximity to the supposedly self-acting mechanisms. As Jamie L. Bronstein has noted in *Caught in the Machinery* (2007), crushed fingers "resulting in the amputation of one or several joints, were common" (2). So often did the new mill gearing tear off fingers, in fact, that Bronstein reports "factories were filled with workers missing parts of their hands" (96).

MANUAL 'PERFECTION' AND THE INDUSTRIAL QUESTION

By the late 1820s factory accidents attracted attention all over England. The scenes of grisly dismemberment in *A Memoir of Robert Blincoe* (which ran in *The Lion* from 25 January through 22 February 1828) helped establish and then popularize what became known as "the man-eating-machine" genre in daily newspapers. Thomas Laqueur has shown how these stories forged a "humanitarian narrative" linking those who suffered and those who read about such suffering (176). The *Times* published a representative example of this new genre in its reporting of the death of Daniel Buckley, a mill worker who died in 1830 as a result of gruesome injuries to his hand by a machine used for carding horsehair. The article recounts in graphic detail how Buckley's left hand "was caught and lacerated, and his fingers crushed" by the studded teeth of a cylinder before the machine could be stopped by his co-workers ("Coroner's Inquest"). The *Times* article also reports that Buckley died after spending two full weeks in Middlesex Hospital—the same facility where Sir Charles Bell, the future author of the Bridgewater Treatise on *The Hand*, was employed as the lead surgeon.

Other accounts of factory life from this period show the extent to which workers were constantly confronted with the specter of losing their hands to machines. The *Narrative of the Experiences and Sufferings of William Dodd, a Factory Cripple* (1841) recounts the life of a young boy who enters the factory in 1809 and leaves it with an amputated hand in 1837. Though he does not describe his own maiming, Dodd describes how his sister's right hand became entangled in a carding machine barely ten pages into the narrative:

> Four iron teeth of a wheel, three-quarters of an inch broad, and one-quarter of an inch thick, had been forced through her hand . . . and the fifth iron tooth fell upon the thumb, and crushed it into atoms . . . This accident might have been prevented, if the wheels above referred to had been boxed off, which they might have been for a couple of shillings; and the very next week after this accident, a man had two fingers taken off his hand, by the very same wheels—and still they are not boxed off! (285)

P. W. J. Bartrip and S. B. Burman have demonstrated in *The Wounded Soldiers of Industry* (1983) how factory workers had few, if any, rights to compensation from their employers after their survival from workplace accidents. This was partly because the rapidly expanding economic activity provided employers with financial incentives to ignore the law (21). It was simply cheaper for employers to pay nominal fines when there were injuries and to keep the factory equipment running as usual than to stop the machines and fence off the most dangerous parts. As a result, factory production in this unregulated era created large numbers of industrial amputations, particularly of the hands and fingers (Bronstein 2).

Furthermore, many factories maintained policies that did not allow for their engines to be shut down even during service or maintenance (Cawthon 49). *The Times* reported on the case of William Lloyd, who was oiling the cogs of an operating engine when it drew in his left hand and severed it at the wrist (24 March 1838). Surgeons consequently trained their students to operate with an awareness of their patients' chances to gain employment after hand injuries. One surgeon at St. George's Hospital cautioned his students that "a finger or a thumb, or even the stump of a finger, [would] always be more useful than any artificial appendage, particularly when the accident occurs to a mechanic" (qtd in Cawthon 59). Stories abound of workers who attempted to return to their former factory positions only to be turned away because of mangled hands. What's worse, machines existed for those who had survived lower-body injuries because these machines could be operated from a seated position. None, however, could operate without the assistance of hands. Therein lay a particularly cruel historical irony: the hand became simultaneously the most valuable *and* most vulnerable part of the human body for a factory worker.

Tending to hand injuries in the 1820s compelled Charles Bell to visit surgeons at other hospitals in England's manufacturing towns. One of the colleagues Bell visited was Samuel Smith, his former student and a surgeon at the Leeds General Infirmary, where severe injuries to the arms and hands occurred in disproportionately large numbers. Smith testified to Michael Sadler's Parliamentary Committee on Factories in July 1832 that he had "frequently seen accidents of the most dreadful kind that it is possible to conceive ... cases in which the arm had been torn off near the shoulder joint ... the upper extremity chopped into small fragments, from the tip of the finger to above the elbow ... the most shocking cases of lacerations that it is possible to conceive" (Smith, "Testimony" 503). Bell toured the region's hospitals during that summer and heard similar reports of the gruesome hand injuries sustained by the area's workers. He testified before the same Parliamentary Committee less than a month later, saying that he "was very much struck with the nature and number of the accidents received [from machinery]" both in his own hospital and in those he visited (Bell, "Testimony" 605).

The experiences of many other medical practitioners reveal similar responses. William Lutener, a Montgomeryshire surgeon, testified that he "had frequently to amputate the hands and fingers of children" who would most likely become paupers for life (Lutener, "Testimony" 179). The Sadler Committee's report was controversial with factory owners partly because its grim findings were thought to lack firm data. The Factory Act of 1833, though, required official inspectorates to keep lists of injuries with specific headings such as "Time, place and Mode of Maiming," "Distorted," and "Description or Degree of Distortion" (*Instructions* 34–35). This more formally collected data confirmed that the most common injury requiring hospitalization was the severing or pulverization of the hand by mechanized fly-wheels. In one year during this decade, for instance, severe injuries to the hand, thumb, or fingers accounted for 243 of the 261 patients (over 93%) treated at the Leeds Infirmary in cases related to mill accidents (Lee 89).

Bell's deep religious faith, combined with his experience treating victims of these kinds of factory accidents at Middlesex Hospital, undoubtedly influenced his decision to choose the hand as his topic when he was invited to contribute a volume to the Bridgewater Treatises. For him and for many Britons in the nineteenth century, "the perfection" of the human hand directly signified "the presence of the hand of the Creator" (*The Hand* 223). In two lengthy chapters of the Treatise, Bell analyzes how "the Author of nature" constructed the superior sense of touch in the hand, and Bell states the chief reason for doing so: "to show that the most perfect proof of power and design" resides in the hand's sensory apparatus (172, 175). Its flawless design reflects Bell's belief in a world quite literally wrought "pure from the Maker's hands" (220). Once jeopardized, hands become the new threshold for evaluating 'Design' in the natural world.

New with Bell, though, is a different, more timely, inflection of cultural anxiety surrounding the process and perils of industrial mechanization. As recent critics have shown, machines were often described by pro-industrialists as organic and cooperative improvements to the human anatomy.[4] Charles Babbage's *Economy of Machinery and Manufactures* (1833), for example, is principally interested in the substitution of machinery for human limbs. Published just one year before Bell's Treatise on *The Hand*, Babbage's *Economy* glorifies mechanisms that "exer[t] forces too great for human power" and that "execut[e] operations too delicate for human touch" (47). Babbage praises the "giant arm" of the engine that works "with almost fairy fingers [to] entwin[e] the meshes of the most delicate fabric" (49, 50). This focus on mechanical prosthetic improvement (and thus the limitations of the human hand) stands in direct opposition to Bell's notion of an appendage designed "pure from the Maker's hands" (220). Babbage's comments nonetheless show how critics and supporters of the factory system produced alternate and contradictory representations of body–machine relations.

This is not meant to suggest that Bell was hostile to factory production or even mechanization *per se*; we will encounter more from those on the opposition side to the 'Factory Question' later on in this essay. Nowhere in Bell's Treatise, in fact, does he criticize the productive power of automatic manufacture. Instead, he is at pains to demonstrate how *all* mechanical contrivances are themselves based on the model of anatomical perfection embodied in the divinely constructed hand. The subject matter of Bell's introduction is telling in this respect. He does not open his Treatise with a discussion of the perfection of the human hand in comparison to animal appendages as one might reasonably expect in a work of natural philosophy. This highlights why we should read Bell against the strictly evolutionist/'Design' grain. In contrast to traditional works of natural philosophy, Bell opens with an unexpected anecdote about how the perfection of the hand "makes us insensible to its use" (13) in the increasingly mechanized world of the 1830s:

> A man will make journeys to see an engine stamp a coin or turn a block; yet the organs [hands] through which he has a thousand sources of enjoyment, and which are in themselves more exquisite in design and more curious both in contrivance and in mechanism, do not enter his thoughts. (12)

Indeed, Bell's repeated emphasis on the God-given hand as the model for *all* "mechanical contrivances" becomes the dominant theme of the Treatise

---

4. See Sussman, *Victorians and the Machine*; Bizup, *Manufacturing Culture*; Ketabgian, *The Lives of Machines*.

(114). In one notable demonstration of this theme, Bell illustrates the skeletal mechanism running from the hand to the shoulder required to make use of a traditional hammer. According to Bell, the hand's use of the hammer "is, in truth, similar to the operation of the fly wheel, by which the gradual motion of an engine is accumulated to a point of time, and a blow is struck capable of crushing or of stamping a piece of gold or silver" (116). This reasoning prompts him to ask, "in what respect does the mechanism of the arm differ from the engine with which the printer throws off his sheet?" (116).

Here and throughout his Treatise, Bell focuses not so much on judging the usefulness of the new productive power offered by automatic machinery. Instead, he emphasizes the ways in which machinery achieves its productive power by utilizing a series of mechanical components originally designed by the Creator in the hand. His era's tendency to overlook what he considers the original perfection—and by extension, God's role in scientific development—often appears as Bell's chief concern regarding the era's unprecedented industrial advancements.

Looking at a meteorological analogy from the latter part of the Treatise should help illustrate this point. If "one sees the fire of heaven brought down into a phial," Bell writes, "and materials compounded, to produce an explosion louder than the [original] thunder, and ten times more destructive, the storm will no longer speak an impressive language to him" (230). In Bell's metaphor, "the fire of heaven brought down in a phial" represents the human co-option of the hand's divine construction in mechanical inventions such as Babbage's, where manmade automatic "hands" work "with almost fairy fingers" to accomplish previously human tasks (Babbage 50). Extending Bell's meteorological metaphor along these lines, the "materials compounded, to produce an explosion louder than the original thunder, and ten times more destructive" signifies the manmade, technical, and therefore more powerful improvements made to God's original design. Lastly in Bell's metaphor, man's development and implementation of this mechanized system makes God's originating manual component "no longer . . . impressive . . . to him." William Dodd emphasizes a similar point as he compares factory machinery with the human body: "[the worker] sees nothing but an endless variety of shafts, drums, straps, and wheels in motion; and though these may, at first, inspire him with a feeling of respect for, and admiration of, [the machinery] . . . this feeling will vanish, when he reflects on their power to destroy or render useless for life *that exalted piece of mechanism formed by and after the image of God!*" (312, emphasis added).

Of course, for all the mechanical implications of Bell's Treatise, given the terms of the Earl of Bridgewater's bequest, the Treatise actually *does* defend an argument for 'Design' from an evolutionary standpoint. Bell performs a sustained comparison of human hands in relation to "lower" animals for large sections of the text. But even this strategy is framed by a critique of his culture's tendency to be drawn more to "what is uncommon and monstrous" than to "what is natural and perfectly adjusted to its office" (12). Bell maintains that "a vulgar admiration is excited by seeing the spider-monkey pick up a straw, or a piece of wood, with its tail; or the elephant searching the keeper's pocket with his trunk" (13). This chiding is relatively innocuous in Bell's work, though, precisely because the imperative to distinguish humans from animals by way of the hand was not yet as urgent in the 1820s and 1830s as the one to distinguish them from the machines that were injuring and maiming them in the process of mechanical supersession.

The extraordinary sales figures for Bell's Treatise before *The Origin of Species* (1859)—and, therefore, before the full-blown debate about evolutionary adaptation—suggest that Bell's view of "manual perfection" was reassuring to a culture whose hands were being outperformed, displaced, and mangled by machines. When *The Hand* was published in June 1833, the first edition was already oversubscribed by 300 copies (Topham, "Beyond the Common Context" 244). This is impressive, considering that a successful print run at that time would have been around 500 copies. Pickering published 2,000 additional copies in September 1833, 3,000 in April 1834, and 2,500 in October 1834 (Topham, "'Infinite Variety of Arguments'" 284). Thus Bell's 1833 Treatise marks another distinct historical moment when representations of the hand sat precariously between perfection and superiority in relation to animals on the one side and between imperfection and productive inadequacy in relation to machines on the other. The 'Hand' as a factory operative therefore becomes a powerful locus for thinking about interrelations of human, animal, and mechanism. The 'Machinery Question,' as those in the nineteenth century experienced it, was ultimately a question about the limits of the human—and the debate about industrialization was the most poignant context for asking that question about human limits until Darwinian evolutionary theory.

Many cultural commentators came to the same conclusion in exactly the same year. In an article entitled "The Factory System" from April 1833, an author for *Blackwood's Edinburgh Magazine* (John Wilson) located human factory operatives in this same liminal space between machines and animals: "Though as a class they are degraded, they are yet human; they feel, though you treat them as such, that they are neither machines nor brutes" (450). The anxiety stemming from the precariousness of the body part so essential to notions of what it meant to be human helped inaugurate an intense cultural fascination with the hand for the remainder of the nineteenth century.

INDUSTRIAL DISCOURSE, EARLY FACTORY FICTION, AND THE DISCURSIVE STRUGGLE FOR DIVINE CONSENT

Andrew Ure's *Philosophy of Manufactures* (1835) was another important text built on the corporeal schema of pro-industrialist discourse. In many respects, Ure's work reads like a point-by-point response to Bell's Treatise by invoking the rhetoric of anthropomorphic and mechanical "perfection" of its own mechanical kind. Ure discusses, for instance, the "present perfection" of the self-acting machine's "automatic organs" and "mechanical fingers" (368, 32, 15). What made the debate about factory work in contemporary discourse so contentious was the manner in which both sides claimed divine consent. Ure situates the machines themselves (not the "design" upon which they are built) as Providential "*blessings* which physico-mechanical science has bestowed on society" (6–7, emphasis added). According to Ure, "the new [factory] system of labour was designed by Providence" to be "a benefaction, which, wisely administered," would "become the best temporal gift of Providence to the poor"—"a progression of improvement designed by Providence to emancipate [the poor's] animal functions from brute toil, and to leave his intelligent principle leisure to think of its immortal interests!" (14, 370).

At several junctures *Philosophy of Manufactures* operates as propaganda, or at least positive advertising, for the recruitment of factory workers described by Ure as "young persons about to make the choice of profession" (6). He makes this case for recruitment by directly comparing the difficulty of handicraft work to the relative 'ease' of automatic manufacture: ". . . the non-factory weaver, having everything to execute by muscular exertion, finds the labour irksome, makes in consequence several short pauses, separately of little account, but great when added together; earns therefore proportionally low wages, while he loses his health by poor diet and the dampness of his hovel" (7). Where Marx and others saw the factory as a monstrous and dangerous amalgam of the human body and the machines controlling them, Ure presented a view of workers as the intelligent directors of machinery within comfortable—even leisurely—conditions:

> . . . old, young, and middle-aged of both sexes, many of them too feeble to get their daily bread by any of the former modes of industry, ear[n] abundant food, raiment, and domestic accommodation, without perspiring at a single pore, screened meanwhile from the summer's sun and the winter's frost, in apartments more airy and salubrious than those of the metropolis in which our legislative and fashionable aristocracies assemble. In those spa-

cious halls the benignant power of steam summons around him his myriads of willing menials, and assigns to each the regulated task, substituting for painful muscular effort on their part, the energies of his own gigantic arm ... (17–18)

While it was no doubt true that agricultural work was difficult and strenuous, Ure perhaps overstates the salubriousness of the factory when he claims that industrial labor is punctuated by long stretches of leisurely activity: "though [the child worker] attends two mules, he has still six hours of non-exertion. Spinners sometimes dedicate these intervals to the perusal of books" (310–11).

It is not surprising that Ure treats the topic of factory injuries sparingly in *Philosophy of Manufactures*. What is surprising, though, is that when he does broach the subject, he does so by yoking injury to a failure to follow the rules of automatic labor—which he then quite boldly links to God's moral law: "Of the amount of the injury resulting from the violation of the rules of automatic labour [the factory operative] can hardly ever be a proper judge; just as mankind at large can never fully estimate the evils consequent upon an infraction of God's moral law" (279). Commentary in this Providential vein reveals how surprisingly theological pro-industrialist texts could be. Critics of factory expansion sensed blasphemy in these accounts and often met their Providential rhetoric with even stronger deistic and anthropomorphic invocations of their own. A letter from an 1835 delegate meeting of Preston cotton spinners, for example, appealed to the kind of interventionist power of God's hand in the Old Testament by calling on "the arm of Omnipotence, humbly imploring his power and approbation" on their behalf (Place 170).

Representations of factory work such as Ure's were also highly contested within established journals. In *Blackwood's*, John Wilson noted "the guilt which England was contracting in the kindling eye of Heaven, when nothing but exultations were heard about the perfection of her machinery, the want of her manufactures, and the rapid increase of her wealth and prosperity!" (420). Similar religious objections to the factory system eventually spilled over from journalism to fiction, where they provided the impetus for England's earliest industrial novels. Thus the industrial novel began as a genre that bluntly extended the continuities between non-fictional social discourse and fictional subjects that dramatized the various positions and counterpositions of the 'Machinery Question.'

Charlotte Elizabeth Tonna's *Helen Fleetwood* (1839–40) is probably the best example of fiction responding directly to pro-industrialist positions regarding the factory system. Tonna's novel is by no means a work of high artistic merit, but its uniqueness lies in its employment of official reports and inquiries as the factual basis of its narrative. As Ivanka Kovačević and S. Barbara Kanner have noted, Tonna was the first author to translate the recorded testimony of witnesses in official documents like the Saddler Committee Report, *Hansard's Parliamentary Debates,* reformist pamphlets, and even contemporary police reports into dialogue for her novel (164). *Helen Fleetwood,* first serialized in *The Christian Lady's Magazine,* is unabashedly propagandist in its dependence on government reports and ultra-Evangelical in its outward religiosity, but it remains one of the very few works of fiction to describe the actual conditions of the *inside* of factories from the perspective of the factory operatives themselves.[5] Tonna designed her fictional work to operate with the swiftness of non-fictional forms of anti-industrialist discourse but with a different target audience in mind. She wanted to expose the grim official reports to a middle-class audience of wives and mothers (who were not likely to have read them otherwise) so that they could in turn influence their voting husbands, fathers and sons (Kovačević and Kanner 156).

Helen Fleetwood tells the story of a family coerced by industrial recruiters into moving from the agricultural English coast to the city of "M.," a thinly disguised Manchester, in order to pursue a better life in the textile mills. The family's situation in their agricultural town is far from ideal. The concentration of land ownership to fewer families meant that landless laborers were forced out of tenancies by rising rents in the first decades of the century. This is exactly what is happening to the Green family at the start of the novel, and so a move to the city initially seems logical. True to the government statistics, though, the family members who acquire work in the factory in the city of M. appear in constant danger of losing their limbs to machinery accidents. A veteran factory operative admits that "the worst thing are the accidents," warning the newly arrived ("Green") family of the physical perilousness of the factory system: "You must step back, and run forward, and duck, and turn, and move as [the machines] do, or off goes a finger or an arm" (78–79). One of Tonna's main characters, a young girl named Sarah who is missing a hand from a factory accident, is a living representation of this danger from the moment the Greens arrive in manufacturing city. Sarah's crippled presence throughout the text—she often interrupts the narrative to ask others to

---

5. Critics agree that the most canonized British "factory fiction" shows remarkably little of what occurs inside the walls of the factories themselves. The lack of attention to *actual* factories in Mary Gaskell's *Mary Barton* (1848) and *North and South* (1855), Charlotte Brontë's *Shirley* (1849), and Charles Dickens's *Hard Times* (1854) are but a few examples that prove the rule. For another early example that *does* reveal the insides of factories, see Frances Trollope's *Michael Armstrong, Factory Boy* (1840)—particularly the scene where Mary Brotherton discovers a factory worker with "a little shriveled right-hand, three fingers of which had a joint deficient" (128).

write letters for her, for instance—serves as a constant reminder of the grim physical realities involved in factory labor. This reminder becomes reinforced as the reader meets other similarly maimed children and working adults who bear "the marks of bodily injuries" from their time in the factories (75, 291).

It is remarkable how well *Helen Fleetwood*'s themes and rhetoric align with the "divinely-manual" focus that we've been tracing through Bell's 1833 Bridgewater Treatise. To put the same point less abstractly, *Helen Fleetwood* is not only a novel about the maiming of human hands by factory machinery, but one that deliberately sets up this context in relation to blunt anthropomorphic references to a Judeo-Christian God figure. Regularly, for example, in this novel where workers lose their appendages to machinery, Tonna's characters reference "the unseen arm of Omnipotence" (203), "the hands of Him who is Father to the fatherless" (39), "the hand [of Christ]" who holds even "the weakest lamb" (366), "the arm of the Lord Jesus" (358), "the higher hand" that "over-rul[es] all for good" (26), "He who order all things . . . at his hand" (23), and on and on. The elaborate two-sentence paragraph with which the narrative opens could hardly be more representative in this regard:

> Who that has seen the sun's uprising, when his first bright gleam comes sparkling over the billows on a clear autumnal morning, but has felt a thrill of gladness at his heart—an involuntary, perhaps an unconscious ascription of praise to the Creator, who has so framed him that all his innate perverseness cannot bar the entrance of that thrill? The brisk wind that curls the wave, and flings its light spray abroad, does but multiply mirrors for the imaged ray to flash from; and when the mighty orb has wholly lifted his disk above the swelling outline of the beautifully-rounded horizon, and looks down upon the surmounted barrier, sending beam after beam to traverse that watery world, and to gild it with dazzling splendor, who does not accord *the palm of natural magnificence* to that of which no adequate idea can be conveyed to one who has not looked upon it—sunrise at sea? (1, emphasis mine)

Tonna establishes an important structural theme by beginning her novel in this way. As Raymond Williams has noted, "the pull of the idea of the country is towards old ways, human ways, natural ways"—and to this list in *Helen Fleetwood*'s case, we may add "Godly" ways (297). Tonna inaugurates the Creator as the entity that actively "frame[s]" the countryside with a "palm of natural magnificence." This framing device does double duty for Tonna; it frames not only the opening paragraph, but also the rural agricultural coast as beautiful and providential in contrast to the city of M., which is predictably unappealing and devoid of God. She highlights these frames throughout the narrative by combining what Janis McLarren Caldwell calls the "two-text epistemology" of Nature and Scripture in a single character who moves openly and often between the Green family's old pastoral life and its new industrial one (2). Richard, the seventeen-year-old family member, stays behind and vows to depend on the strength of his "two hands," but he makes several crucial visits to M. which allow Tonna to juxtapose an agrarian—and therefore providentially "Natural"—lifestyle with an industrial one wherein "a great many people . . . shun and even revile religion" (156).

Catherine Gallagher first pointed out how this country/city divide becomes deeply problematic for staunch Evangelical authors. Tonna and other religious reformers were torn between the contradictory components of their own propaganda; they wanted both to assert their belief in human free will and a benign Providence, and to illustrate the helplessness of individuals caught in the industrial system. "The moral consequences of industrialism aroused Charlotte Elizabeth Tonna's religious indignation against the factory system," Gallagher notes, "but they also made it impossible for her to fit the industrial world into a providential scheme" (45). Quite obviously, having a benevolent, designing, and all-seeing God who allows the disorientation and maiming of the factory operatives is a significant theological and narratological problem for Tonna.[6] Susan Zlotnick builds on Gallagher's insights by contending that Tonna accommodates the determining environment of M. with her Evangelical faith in free will and a benign providential order "by establishing M. as a separate, antiprovidential zone" in the novel (140).

In terms of my argument, it is even more salient that Tonna portrays this "antiprovidential zone" of the factory as completely man-made and, therefore, subject to all manner of antireligious accusation. For instance, the factory in *Helen Fleetwood* is figured as a "blasphemous" place where "deliberate scoffing at God's name and word, infidel jests, [and] atheistical arguments" prevail among both factory owner and worker alike (347). Tonna's phrasing explicitly locates the split between divine and human manufacture, though. In *Helen Fleetwood,* the entire factory system is resolutely "none of God's making"— from those who constructed it in the accumulation of their wealth "by this [new] species of labor" to those fallen workers who "constantly tr[y] to prove [the Bible] the vilest book ever written" (355, 204, 349). Tonna at times empha-

---

6. As Catherine Gallagher points out: "The novel contains no logical solution to this dilemma, but the narrator does find a stylistic device to cover the contradiction. She tells the events of Helen's life completely from Helen's viewpoint, filtering everything that happens in the factory through Helen's submissive and largely nonanalytical consciousness . . . most of the narrator's analyses of the factory system are thus separated from the recounting of Helen's providentially ordained experience" (46).

sizes the factory's bald irreligiousness with more nuance. In one of these instances of relative subtlety, the extreme physical disorientation new factory workers experience highlights the inversion of a "natural" religious hierarchy:

> Move, move, move, everything moves. The wheels and frames are always going, and the little reels turn round as fast as they ever can; and the pulleys and chains, and great iron-works over-head, are all moving; and the cotton moves so fast that it is hard to piece it quick enough; and there is a great dust, and such a noise of whirr, whirr, whirr, that at first I did not know whether I was not standing on my head. (96)

Here, Tonna presents the worker's world as figuratively, but also religiously, turned upside down. The traditional notion of a God situated above watching "blessed country labor" (as in the novel's opening paragraph) becomes supplanted by an iron machine that hangs "over-head" (75). The "cheerless . . . noisy monotony" of factory life represents the "unkindliness of an atmosphere such as God never made" (323).[7] This example is quite clearly a literary volley in the wider cultural debate over which side God takes in the 'Machinery Question.'

What constitutes this mechanized atmosphere as one (in Tonna's mind) that "God never made" is not only its spatial orientation with the machine operating overhead of the operative, though. The metaphorical absence of God's hand figured by the literal absence of a human hand also connotes a feeling of deep ontological disorientation for a culture that—from time out of mind—had viewed its hands as essential markers of human identity. We see this from a slightly more secularized position only a few years after *Helen Fleetwood* in a scene from Benjamin Disraeli's *Coningsby* (1844), when the eponymous character enters the factory for the first time and says: "it is the machinery without any interposition of manual power that overwhelms me. It haunts my dreams" (150). The fact that the lack of manual power in automatic

---

7. To fortify my interpretation that Tonna's noise-centered description of the factory is in direct conversation with pro-industrialist discourse, consider Ure's placid and, indeed, almost silent account of his experience on the factory floor: "The spinning-factory of Messrs. Ashworth, at Egerton, which has been at work for several years, exhibits an elegant pattern of the engineering just described: for it has some subordinate shafts, hardly thicker than the human wrist, which convey the power of ten horses, and revolve with great speed, *without the slightest noise or vibration*. The prime-mover of the whole is a gigantic water-wheel of sixty feet diameter, and one hundred horses' power. I have frequently been at a loss, in walking through several millwright factories, to know whether the polished shafts that drive the automatic lathes and planning machines were at rest or in motion, *so truly silently* did they revolve" (35, emphasis added).

manufacture induces Coningsby's "haunted" dreams recalls Shelley's inverted nightmare scenario where Victor Frankenstein's "odious handywork" mocks "the stupendous mechanism of the Creator of the world" (9). Not surprisingly, *Helen Fleetwood* ends with Richard working "like a man, not like a wheel and pulley" in a rural country scene (319). This conflict between the divine-made and the man-made has, by 1840, moved far beyond the scientific-theological debates that preoccupied *Frankenstein*. But in Bell's Bridgewater Treatise, and in manufacturing philosophies of every stripe, the human hand emerged in the first part of the nineteenth century as a site of heightened significance for a society living through unprecedented scientific and industrial change.

WORKS CITED

Babbage, Charles. *Economy of Machinery and Manufactures*. London, Charles Knight, 1833.

Bartrip, P. W. J., and S. B. Burman. *The Wounded Soldiers of Industry: Industrial Compensation Policy 1833–1897*. Clarendon P, 1983.

Bell, Sir Charles. Testimony from the Select Committee on the "Bill to Regulate the Labour of Children in the Mills and Factories of the United Kingdom." 7 August 1832, *Parliamentary Papers* (1831–32 XV), Report, pp. 604–5.

———. *The Hand: Its Mechanism and Endowments as Evincing Design*. London, Pickering and Chatto, 1833.

Bizup, Joseph. *Manufacturing Culture*. U of Virginia P, 2003.

Bronstein, Jamie L. *Caught in the Machinery*. Stanford UP, 2007.

Caldwell, Janice McLarren. *Literature and Medicine in Nineteenth-Century Britain*. Cambridge UP, 2004.

Carlyle, Thomas. "Signs of the Times." *The Works of Thomas Carlyle*, vol. 27, London, Chapman and Hall, 1899, pp. 56–82.

Cawthon, Elisabeth A. *Job Accidents and the Law in England's Early Railway Age*. Edward Mellon Press, 1997.

"Coroner's Inquest." *Times*, 12 October 1830, p. 3.

Crouzet, François. *The Victorian Economy*. Trans. Anthony Foster, Columbia UP, 1982.

Disraeli, Benjamin. *Coningsby*. London, J. Lehmann, 1948.

Dodd, William. *A Narrative of the Experiences and Sufferings of William Dodd, A Factory Cripple. The Factory System Illustrated*. Augustus Kelley, 1968, pp. 267–319.

Freedgood, Elaine, editor. *Factory Production in Nineteenth-Century Britain*. Oxford UP, 2003.

Gallagher, Catherine. *The Industrial Reformation of English Fiction*. U of Chicago P, 1985.

Gaskell, Peter. *The Manufacturing Population of England*. London, Baldwin and Cradock, 1833.

Instructions from the Central Board of Factory Commissioners to District, Civil, and Medical Commissioners. 1833. Factory Commission.

Ketabgian, Tamara. *The Lives of Machines*. U of Michigan P, 2011.

Kovačević, Ivanka, and S. Barbara Kanner. "Blue Book into Novel: The Forgotten Industrial Fiction of Charlotte Elizabeth Tonna." *Nineteenth-Century Fiction*, vol. 25, no. 2, September 1970, pp. 152–73.

Laqueur, Thomas. "Bodies, Details and the Humanitarian Narrative." *The New Cultural History*, edited by Lynn Hunt, U of California P, 1989, pp. 176–204.

Lee, W. R. "Robert Baker: The First Doctor in the Factory Department. Part I. 1803–1858." *British Journal of Industrial Medicine*, vol. 21, no. 2, April 1964, pp. 85–93.

Lutener, William. Testimony from the Select Committee on the "Bill to Regulate the Labour of Children in the Mills and Factories of the United Kingdom." 7 August 1832, *Parliamentary Papers* (1831–32 XV), Report, pp. 604–5.

A Memoir of Robert Blincoe, edited by John Brown, Sussex, Caliban Books, 1977.

Paley, William. *Natural Theology*. New York, Harper, 1840.

Place, Francis. "Hand Loom Weavers and Factory Workers: A Letter to James Turner, Cotton Spinner." *Factory Production in Nineteenth-Century Britain*, edited by Elaine Freedgood, Oxford UP, 2003, pp. 165–77.

Samuel, Raphael. "Workshop of the World: Steam Power and Hand Technology in Mid-Victorian Britain." *History Workshop*, Spring 1977, pp. 6–72.

Shelley, Mary. *Frankenstein*. Penguin, 2003.

Smith, Samuel. Testimony from the Select Committee on the "Bill to Regulate the Labour of Children in the Mills and Factories of the United Kingdom." 7 August 1832. *Parliamentary Papers* (1831–32 XV), Report, p. 503.

Sussman, Herbert. *Victorians and the Machine*. Harvard UP, 1968.

Tonna, Charlotte Elizabeth. *Helen Fleetwood*. New York, Taylor, 1841.

Topham, Jonathan R. "'An Infinite Variety of Arguments': The *Bridgewater Treatises* and British Natural Theology in the 1830s." Diss. University of Lancaster, 1993.

———. "Beyond the 'Common Context': The Production and Reading of the Bridgewater Treatises." *Isis: The History of Science Society*, vol. 89, no. 1, 1998, pp. 233–62.

Trollope, Frances. *Michael Armstrong, Factory Boy*. London, Colburn, 1840.

Ure, Andrew. *The Philosophy of Manufactures*. London, H. G. Bohn, 1861.

Williams, Raymond. *The Country and the City*. Oxford UP, 1973.

Wilson, John. "The Factory System." *Blackwood's Edinburgh Magazine*, vol. 33, no. 206, April 1833, pp. 419–50.

Zlotnick, Susan. *Women, Writing, and the Industrial Revolution*. Johns Hopkins UP, 1998.

CHAPTER 2

Lost Hands and Prosthetic Narratives

William Dodd, Writing at the Industrial Join

TAMARA KETABGIAN

IN 1844, during an impassioned parliamentary debate, Lord Ashley (Anthony Ashley-Cooper, 1801–1885) described William Dodd (1804–?) as a most "wretched object"—and object lesson—of the British factory system: "He had lost his hand, and, I may say had almost lost his shape. He hardly looked indeed like a human being" (*Hansard's* 1154–55).[1] As a self-styled "Factory Cripple," enlisted by Ashley to support the Ten Hours Factory Act,[2] Dodd presents his own disability in equally melodramatic terms. In his autobiography, Dodd stresses that he draws no "exaggerated picture of factory life:—it would be well for me [. . .] if instead of being a miserable cripple, scarcely the shadow of a man, it could be proved that I am straight, strong, and hardy as when I entered the factories" (*Narrative* 44). This essay explores how Dodd gained an influential public voice through his bent body and his injured and later amputated hand. Sensationally recounting his choice to "lose either

---

The author wishes to thank Jean Franzino, Laura Karpenko, and Daniel Youd for suggestions that aided the writing of this article. She also thanks Elaine Freedgood for graciously sharing her manuscript and granting permission to cite from it. This essay is indebted to James R. Simmons Jr.'s fine edition of *Factory Lives: Four Nineteenth-Century Working-Class Autobiographies* and to Janice Carlisle's excellent introduction.

    1. Passages from *Hansard's Parliamentary Debates* are helpfully excerpted and introduced in Simmons 334–48.

    2. Passed in 1847, the Ten Hours Act limited the working hours of women and children (13–18 years) in textile mills to ten hours a day. Lord Ashley promoted this legislation since the 1830s and most prominently in 1844, when it was briefly passed but then reversed.

my hand or my life" (44), Dodd portrays the Victorian factory as a destructive coupling of humans and machines, in which the hand serves as its most densely freighted site of intersection, transformation, and vulnerability. In *The Narrative of the Experience and Sufferings of William Dodd* (1841) and Dodd's *Factory System Illustrated* (1842), this damaged hand and body emerge not only *at* the industrial "join" but also as emblems *for* the join itself, as a deeply ramified juncture of human and mechanical hinges, straps, bones, ligaments, joints, and wounds. These misshapen bodies and parts provide a consistent figurative schema both for the mill's evolving "co-operative body" (Ure 15) and for that of greater society, subject to its own uneven waxing and waning. For Dodd, moreover, these forms express his own sense of industrial ambivalence, of *feeling torn* amid a rending process of emotional loss, division, identification, and repair.

Dodd's life writing displays the hallmarks of what Thomas Laqueur has termed modern "humanitarian narrative," with its stress on embodied detail as a "sign of truth" and an impetus for corrective moral action (177–78). Yet Dodd's *Narrative* is still far from a straightforward tale of injury and exploitation. For, along with its grisly portraits of industrial loss and suffering, his account supports alternate skills and compensations. Dodd's disability may bar him from certain forms of work, but it also supplies him with new sources of identity, vocation, and expression (as a "Factory Cripple"). The loss of his hand thus effects its own prosthetic replacement—through its restaging as narrative. Dodd's autobiography doubles as an account of his growing literacy, his mastery of new writing practices, and his development of a public voice and profession, as an outspoken proponent of factory reform. Accordingly, this essay treats not only Dodd's images of wounding industrial linkage but also the prosthetic growth of his own "experience" and writings, whose "enlarged and corrected" (*Narrative* 3) editions were faulted both for their "too highly coloured" (*Factory System* 29) tone and for Dodd's own perceived unreliability and opportunism. These strong feelings were also shared by Dodd's readers and patrons, especially toward his disputed role as an object of charity aspiring to middle-class authorship. Here, too, Dodd writes at the industrial join, revealing a complex sympathy with the same machine culture that he so powerfully repudiates, in texts that continually revise the cause and chronology of his amputation.

HUMAN HINGES: HANDS AND BODIES

Like the earlier *Memoir of Robert Blincoe* (1832), and contemporary sensational novels such as Frances Trollope's *Michael Armstrong* (1840) and Charlotte Tonna's *Helen Fleetwood* (1841), Dodd's *Narrative* dwells most pointedly upon his sufferings as a child factory laborer. Born in Kendal in 1804, Dodd began work at five, making cotton cards, and became a piecer in a local woolen mill at age six. He reports working for twenty-five years in the factory, holding various jobs there, including those of book-keeper and time-keeper. Dodd's memoir stresses his ongoing struggle to find other work with his disability (as a teacher and clerk), and climaxes—dramatically—with the amputation of his right forearm in 1840, following his brief employment as a London tailor. Dodd wrote his *Narrative* after this devastating loss, which, he argues, resulted from "the general weakness of my joints brought on in the factories" (41). The first edition of Dodd's tale caught the eye of Lord Ashley (later the seventh earl of Shaftesbury),[3] an ardent advocate of labor protections for women and child factory workers. Adopted by this Evangelical Tory MP as both a model cripple and protégé, Dodd dedicated the second edition of his *Narrative* to Ashley and, soon thereafter, published *The Factory System Illustrated*, a work of industrial reportage espousing the Ten Hours Act, and issued in the form of letters to his patron. Between 1841 and 1842, Ashley supported Dodd's travel and research throughout the manufacturing districts,[4] and praised him as "a jewel" of "unequalled" "talent and skill" who "sends me invaluable evidence" (Hodder 204). Later, however, the two men differed and parted ways, with Dodd emigrating to the United States in 1843 and Ashley deeming him "unworthy [of] my kindness" (*Hansard's* 1155), in a conflict that this essay will address in its final pages.

Dodd's *Narrative* focuses on a transformative process: the joining of the human body with the factory as a destructive system of contact. Dodd seeks "to show the *effects* of [this] system upon my mind, person, and condition" (*Narrative* 5, emphasis his). Both his memoir and his later works explore the remarkable plasticity of the human form, as it adjusts to the shape, stress, and weight of more durable industrial objects and machines. Dodd recounts how, from a vigorous boy able to outrun all pursuers, he "has been made a cripple for life" (6). His early overwork as a piecer bends and distorts his body, reshaping it much like the woolen strips that he rubs and joins together into cardings to be spun. Adapting his stance to the factory's spinning frames, Dodd must repeatedly twist "in a sidling direction, constantly keeping his right side towards the frame" (10). Placing incessant pressure on his right knee, "which is almost always the first joint to give way," child piecers like

---

3. No print copy appears to exist of this first edition.

4. According to Dodd, Ashley paid him 45s a week and coach hire while visiting manufacturing districts and 20s a week while in London (Chaloner xiii). See Boyson 163, 178; Finlayson 234–35 for different accounts of this support in Ashley's letters and diaries.

Dodd often become "cripples with the right knee in," although many also have "both knees in" or "splay-foot" (10). In Dodd's case, both knees are permanently bent in, while his "legs form a sort of arch for the support of the body" (30). His deformity follows emerging models of industrial pathology, which, as Erin O'Connor notes, defines workers' bodies as "raw material" to be manufactured and "disease as something that is made by work" (7). For Dodd, his twisted legs and weakened form are the specific products of his labor, which seeks to accommodate both factory machines and the spinners who supply them.

Industrial contact not only reshapes Dodd's body; it also makes him physically dependent upon the factory—and incomplete without it. Dodd vividly recalls his difficulty returning to the mill on Monday after a Sunday of rest from his work as a piecer:

> Even now, it makes me tremble, to think upon the sufferings of those mornings! My joints were then like so many rusty hinges, that had laid by for years. I had to get up an hour earlier, and, with the broom under one arm as a crutch, and a stick in my hand, walk over the house till I had got my joints into working order! And then, this day of the week was generally the most painful of the seven. (*Narrative* 13)

Dodd experiences his resting body as a group of dysfunctional "hinges"—a metaphor that suggests both a disused mechanism and a vulnerable point of contact, a "joint" evoking industrial forms of human and nonhuman linkage. Yet, surprisingly, Dodd's worst struggle is his own detachment from the mill. He shows how, once joined to the factory, the worker's body is technically not a body at all, but an attached fragment, part, hand, or hinge—a site of prosthetic juncture, relying on machines that both amplify and wound their users. Here, like many of his contemporaries, Dodd invokes a popular early Victorian discourse of the factory as a hybrid network of human and mechanical organs (Bizup; Ketabgian). Promoted by the industrial apologist Andrew Ure, this discourse calls into question the autonomy and structural integrity of workers, who, like Dodd, require a prosthetic crutch when removed from the factory's familiar mechanical systems. Elsewhere in *The Factory System Illustrated*, Dodd traces the extremes of this industrial dependence, in disabled former mill hands who cannot stand without crutches (54), who must "walk in irons" (133), or whose "joints are almost sure to be wrong" (113), presenting a nearly endless taxonomy of deformity.

For Dodd, these disabled hands and bodies serve as analogues for the factory's own architectural logic and structure: its various hinges, straps, and shafts. Dodd focuses, above all, on joins and joints, as transitional sites that the mill places under particular stress. Nor is it any coincidence that Dodd repeatedly sketches people who, as they repair these sites, themselves *become* such industrial joins and straps—"reduced to 'hands'" (Williams 15), to invoke the popular term, or worse. In *The Factory System Illustrated,* Dodd interviews one man who loses both of his hands after fixing the coupling of a leather strap to its power-bearing shaft. As this worker recounts, the strap "gave a twitch, and in an instant my whole body was coiled round the shaft; and in this manner I was carried round for the space of a minute. When the engine was stopped, I was suspended *by the flesh of my right arm*" (*Factory System* 75, emphasis his). Replacing the factory's strap with his own flesh and blood, this man gruesomely mimics its form with his own smashed and extended body, bent to curl around the shaft. With grisly literalism, this worker anticipates John Ruskin's famed image of factory hands as "leathern thongs to yoke machinery with" (178).

In *The Factory System Illustrated,* this worker's injured body is only one of countless others transformed into human straps and links—objects that, like Dodd's own hands and "hinge"-joints, both internalize and reproduce the mill's greater structure. Dodd describes workers growing wider rather than longer, with limbs "enlarged," "out of joint," and shaped into "bridge[s]" so broad "that a person may run a wheel-barrow between [them]" (*Factory System* 12, 8, 30). These misshapen, architectural forms offer a pointed rejoinder to industrial proponents such as Ure, who triumphantly liken the mill to a natural human body, equipped both with a "gigantic arm" of steam and with "slender shafts, like small sinewy arms," "hardly thicker than the human wrist" (18, 35). In Dodd's writings, this "co-operative body" (Ure 15) of the factory is nothing if not distorted. Shared by workers and machines, it consists of bent "arch[es]" of bone (*Factory System* 29), joints like "rusty hinges" (*Narrative* 13), and "suspended" straps of boneless "flesh" (*Factory System* 75). Here, flesh and bone learn to become iron, leather, wood, and brass; and human deformity reflects the equally disproportionate form of the mill.

Dodd's accounts of industrial "wound culture" (Seltzer) are tragic and troubling, evoking many storied melodramatic tropes of disability (Holmes). However, these same mechanical figures also express a fantasy of human durability, as Elaine Freedgood has movingly suggested. Following Freedgood, we may read Dodd's misshapen industrial forms not only as dehumanizing and objectifying, but also as voicing an "armoring" and "consolatory" desire: that by imagining "certain very ephemeral people" as inanimate and resilient things, they might gain more strength, permanence, and "weight in the world" (17).

While Dodd's workers are persistently plastic, their *hands* serve as the most distinctive emblem of this fragility. Throughout Dodd's writings, damaged and severed hands are never far from the swollen and disjointed bodies of labor. In his portraits of attached parts, straps, and hinges, hands mediate the sensitive frontier between human and machine. Representing both people and their bodily organs, these members serve as synecdoches, as parts standing for wholes in what Vivan Sobchak terms a "relationship of connection" where "two objects form an ensemble, a physical or metaphysical whole, the existence or idea of one being included in [ ] the other" (25).[5] Hands, moreover, are not only located at the industrial join; they also represent the join itself. Peter J. Capuano has persuasively shown how hands gained a "new visibility" in nineteenth-century literary and cultural discourse, in a shift that signals historical "anxieties" surrounding their changed and threatened status (2, 18). Essential for work, yet most commonly injured on the job (Capuano 48; Bronstein 2, 14), these organs gained special resonance for factory workers, as potent markers of human agency and vulnerability. In the case studies of *The Factory System Illustrated,* Dodd stresses the high proportion of accidents involving hands and fingers. His study is dotted with innumerable severed hands, and with tragic sketches where the loss of one member, caught and crushed in machinery, is commonly followed by that of another.

Whether wounded, severed, or narratively displaced, these hands combine with bodies to portray greater forms of social allegory for Dodd. According to critics David Mitchell and Sharon Snyder, disability often serves as a "metaphorical signifier of social and individual collapse" (47). Certainly, in Dodd's fallen world, "factory cripples" reveal similar forms of crisis and disorder. In both the workers Dodd surveys and his own form, these missing hands and bent bodies express a disproportionate waxing and waning of industrial society more generally. Dodd cites an anonymous interviewee from Leeds, who notes how the factory system

> is monopolized by a few hands, which are every year becoming fewer and fewer [...] As the smaller firms give way beneath the pressure, the workpeople are thrown out of employment, and thus increase the number of famishing poor, and swell the already-glutted market of labour. (*Factory System* 5)

Dodd's speaker describes a world subject to the same distortions that shape the bodies of its mill workers. Like our author's own enlarged limbs and depleted hands, this culture is either "swollen" by "glutted" markets and the "famish-

---

5. I have removed Sobchak's emphasis for clarity.

ing poor," or it is shrinking, with "few[er] hands," dwindling under the "pressure" of the marketplace (5). The resulting social body is marked by deranged growth and decline, in the fields of both production and consumption.

Mediating these expansions and contractions, hands assume a pivotal social and thematic role in Dodd's autobiography. Dismemberment prompts the very writing of his memoir, and, indeed, defines its emphasis on 'manual' damage and threat. In one such instance, Dodd recounts the strain that his hand suffers as he works as a piecer, rubbing rough wool together into cardings upon a canvas cloth. He notes:

> The number of cardings a piecer has through his fingers in a day is very great; each piecing requires three or four rubs, over a space of three or four inches, and the continual friction of the hand in rubbing the piecing upon the coarse wrapper wears off the skin and causes the fingers to bleed. I have had my fingers in this state for weeks tougher, healing up in the night, and breaking out again in little holes as soon as I commenced work on the following morning. (*Narrative* 9)

Here Dodd offers a highly granular account of damage, wear, and recovery. His fingers serve as permeable membranes, pierced and worn as they join together the stuff of manufacture.

Yet, as a narrative of his hand's labor and crisis, Dodd's text also presents a paradox. After his early sketch of work as a piecer, we rarely encounter the trauma of *his own* hand in explicit material and individual detail—that is, until we reach the brief two-page account of the amputation that closes his tale. Instead, throughout his memoir, Dodd focuses on the displaced forms of *other* endangered hands. He provides an exhaustive portrait of his sister's crushed palm and thumb, as they are caught in the iron teeth of a machine wheel and deformed into a "stiff and contracted" appendage, a "very feeble apology for a hand" (*Narrative* 16). Dodd adds, "the very next week after this accident, a man had two fingers taken off his hand, by the very same wheels—and still [the wheels] are not boxed off!" (17).[6] Finally, Dodd recounts his own "narrow escape" from death and dismemberment, as he cleans a woolen teasing machine with a broom: "if I had not had the presence of mind to let go my hold, I must have been dragged in[to the machine] with it. The broom was torn in a thousand pieces" (18).

---

6. According to interpretations of the Factory Act of 1833, exposed factory gearing was required to be fenced off for the safety of workers.

All the while, Dodd narratively defers the most singular physical experience of his tale: his own central dismemberment. It is only after his extended pursuit of work outside of the factory (most recently as a tailor) that Dodd succumbs to this final amputation. Required to halt the spread of disease from a wrist now swollen to "twelve inches round," this operation removes his right forearm from "a little below the elbow," to expose bones without marrow, resembling "an empty honeycomb" (*Narrative* 42). This loss of limb is, of course, powerfully affecting, with Dodd mourning all his hopes and plans now "frustrated and dashed to the ground!" (42). Even so, the brevity and deferral of Dodd's amputation is a striking choice for a text otherwise so intently trained on the hand as an index of modern industrial agency and suffering. Dodd narrates his memoir as a self-identified "Factory Cripple" and often invokes his disabilities, but he never explicitly reveals the absence of his right hand—and, indeed, of his *writing* hand—until we reach the last pages of his account. Dodd's loss is belated, mediated, and retrospective, and sets in motion an alternate narrative space and time, a chronotope in which he writes with a hand that is both extant and already gone.

Symbolically central yet narratively opaque, the mediated presence and absence of Dodd's hand leaves his tale open to other narrative compensations. In their study of literary disability, David Mitchell and Sharon Snyder argue that narrative often serves a prosthetic function, seeking to "rehabilitat[e] or fix [. . .] deviance" through a variety of modes, including cure, erasure, "rescue [. . .] from social censure," or "the revaluation of an alternate mode of being" (53).[7] At first glance, Dodd hardly poses such a fix. His account ends not with redemption or revaluation, but with the melancholy wish that he had never been born. "[H]ow much better would it have been for me, if I had [. . .] been so sacrificed in my infancy," Dodd exclaims, "rather than have been put to daily torture for upwards of a quarter of a century [. . .]!" (*Narrative* 44). Dodd does not seek to recuperate his disability: rather, he appears to agree with the judgment of others that he is a "miserable" object—unemployable, unmarriageable, "scarcely" human (44), and seemingly without future. Yet, in the face of this histrionic elegy, which ends with appeals to death and the eternal beyond, Dodd develops an assertive voice and vocation. He speaks of the rights and disabilities of factory workers with a vehemence and authority that would grant him a rising profile within the Ten Hours Movement. And, as literary historian Janice Carlisle stresses, the social and political impact of

---

7. Mitchell and Snyder note that this prosthetic operation is often not fully successful in narratives: "*disability also operates as the textual obstacle that causes the literary operation of open-endedness to close down or stumble*" (50, emphasis theirs). See also Quayson for a more sustained critique of the prosthetic function of narrative as posed by Snyder and Mitchell (210).

Dodd's *Narrative* was unusual. Its public discussion by Ashley and Ashley's opponent, the Whig MP John Bright, was "an extraordinary and probably unprecedented event in the history of parliamentary debate: two members of Parliament—both, presumably, gentlemen—were arguing over the reliability of a life story written about and by a former factory worker" (Carlisle 12). Dodd's dismemberment thus serves as a prosthetic locale of writing, with the narrative of one lost hand attending its replacement by another: the confident, authorial hand of William Dodd, "Factory Cripple" and vocal industrial critic.

PROSTHETIC WRITING AND VOICE

In Dodd's *Narrative*, the weakening of his body unfolds as the growth of both his literacy and public voice as a writer. For Dodd, these disabling and consolatory processes are inseparable, and even occur in the same factory where the seeds of his future disease—and amputation—are sown. Dodd describes how, in the midst of his sufferings as a fifteen-year-old, he finds an old board and piece of chalk, and, "scrawl[s] out" his initials before "turning to my work" (*Narrative* 18–19). As a defining assertion of his hand and identity ("W. D."), this act of writing spurs the kindly interest of Dodd's master, who is moved to support the factory boy's education for several years. Smiling upon Dodd's efforts, this employer allows the boy to leave the factory an hour earlier to study, provides presents of books, and supplies "two-pence to purchase papers, pens, and ink—which sum he continued weekly for several years, always inspecting my humble endeavours and suggesting any improvements which he thought necessary" (19). Dodd reports continuing his education into adulthood with borrowed books, lecture attendance at his local Mechanics' Institute, and later aspirations to teaching as a vocation. Countering the mill's erosion of his body and subjectivity, this act of literacy serves as a turning point in Dodd's memoir, paradoxically complementing the later loss of his writing hand.

How did Dodd write after his amputation? As an account of literacy, his autobiography lacks many references to specific prosthetic writing technologies—even after his final dismemberment. According to Sue Zemka, "The ability to write again is a leitmotif in nineteenth-century stories of overcoming all types of debilitating hand injuries." Here, again, Dodd is unforthcoming, although the very presence of his *Narrative* speaks for itself as a triumph over disability. Dodd may, of course, have dictated his texts to transcribers. However, in his later *Laboring Classes of England* (1847), in the chapter "Incidents in the Life of the Author" (13–26), we learn that Dodd comes to write with his non-dominant hand after his amputation.[8] Narrated in the third person as the history of "James Graham," this account describes his efforts "to teach the *left* hand the knowledge previously possessed by the *right* hand, such as the use of the pen, needle, sheers, razor, &c" (25).[9] Elsewhere in *The Factory System Illustrated*, Dodd investigates the use of other prosthetic writing practices and technologies, including a double amputee who writes with his teeth (76) and an armless girl who uses an improvised leather claw and glove, fixed to a tube for holding and moving a pen (20–21). Ultimately, however, Dodd's works do not focus on the materiality of writing, but on the growing presence of another compensation: his public voice.

Through its various textual forms, Dodd's life story realizes its own ambitious public expansion and transformation. Upon the urging of Lord Ashley, Dodd revised the earlier "brief outline" of his sufferings into the "enlarged and corrected account" (3) of his current *Narrative*, as a second edition deliberately shaped to publicize factory reform and the Ten Hours Movement. The *Narrative* also paints Dodd himself as well suited for public discourse. Dodd recalls how, after his early gains in literacy, he makes a successful public address to his local Society of Odd Fellows (24), resulting in his landslide election as the Society's secretary and, later, its district representative.

This same voice is inseparable from the greater unity and reliability of Dodd's tale, as a product of narrative framing and sequencing. In his memoir, the order of events spurs pointed questions surrounding industrial causality and responsibility. His *Narrative* presents his later amputation in London as a gradual, but also irrevocable, effect of industrial infirmity and disease. Dodd reflects, "the weakness and pain I had occasionally felt in this arm for years [...] may be clearly traced to the same cause as the rest of my sufferings—viz. the factory system" (42). While it might best serve Dodd to present his dismemberment as an immediate injury, in both his memoir and *The Factory System Illustrated*, he stresses its oblique and incremental cause: the result "not of accident—but of disease of the bone, brought on entirely by unremitting and exhausting labour" (*Factory System* iv). At the time of his amputation in 1840, Dodd had already left the factory for three years and had worked as a London tailor for a little over a year (*Narrative* 35–36, 41–42). His insistence on his disease's gradual industrial source is thus crucial for the unity and success of his attacks on the factory system. Otherwise, what would stop readers from view-

---

8. See Zemka for a substantial discussion of non-dominant hand writing.

9. In this later text Dodd also refers to his "invent[ion], with a little assistance from an ingenious machinist of London, of an artificial arm, and several instruments, whereby he has been enabled to work at his trade as a tailor" (*Laboring Classes* 25).

ing Dodd's bone disease, and subsequent amputation, as simply the effects of his overwork as a tailor—or even as produced by another source entirely?

In *The Laboring Classes of England,* published in the United States after Dodd's dismissal by Ashley and emigration from Britain, we encounter a very different chronology of industrial loss. Whereas Dodd's *Narrative* recounts his narrow escape from the grasp of a wool teaser, in *The Laboring Classes,* the right hand of the "factory cripple" "James Graham" is clearly caught in this machine, directly leading to its amputation five years later "in consequence of some of the bones being injured as is supposed, by this accident, and having still to continue to work" (22). With its distant industrial etiology, Dodd's earlier sketch of his deformed body and lost hand is certainly not as neat as the story in *The Laboring Classes,* which both conflates Dodd and his sister's injuries and moves the date of his amputation up by roughly fifteen years.[10] Dodd's revision of this sequence suggests that its earlier disjunctions and ambiguities—the long pause between his factory work and his amputation, the distracting range of his later jobs—may have jarred with the intended effect of *The Laboring Classes.*[11] Through these changes, Dodd stresses both his clear victimization by the factory and the greater narrative coherence of his identity, as a unified "self of memory and anticipation, extending across time" (Eakin 122).

Even modern literary historians commonly—and quite understandably—mistake the causal links of Dodd's *Narrative,* often claiming that the loss of his hand occurs either while he is still employed in the factory or in its immediate vicinity.[12] These critics tend to overlook portions of the autobiography that occur outside the mill or that do not involve factory work in an explicitly material sense. Regenia Gagnier, for instance, argues that "the entire text is Dodd's personal battle with the factory's literal machinery" ("Social Atoms" 339) and that it unfolds as "a narrative of actual face to face combat between man and machine" (*Subjectivities* 75). As suggested by both this critical reception and Dodd's own revisions, his autobiography may appeal more strongly to readers as a linear and clearly causal narrative—as a straightforward tale of industrial maiming and culpability. Emotionally and thematically, his memoir *does* read as Gagnier's account of embattled mechanical combat, but its form

---

10. In his *Narrative,* Dodd describes himself narrowly escaping injury from a wool teaser at sixteen years of age (18). If we rely on Dodd's stated birthdate of June 18, 1804, this event would have occurred in 1820. According to the timeline of *The Laboring Classes of England,* Dodd's amputation would then have occurred five years later in 1825. This date is fifteen years earlier than the amputation in 1840 that Dodd describes in his *Narrative.*

11. On Dodd's American lecture tour, which likely focused on topics similar to *The Laboring Classes of England,* see Boyson 180.

12. For these different chronologies, see Capuano 45; Gagnier, *Subjectivities* 75.

is mediated, circuitous, and disjointed. Like the bodies and machines that it couples, Dodd's *Narrative* displays a byzantine logic of prosthetic linkage, absence, distortion and ambivalence, in both its narrative form and the figure of its belatedly lost hand.

Through his autobiographical plot and chronology, Dodd seeks to promote the legitimacy of his public voice and viewpoint. This attempt to craft a coherent self through order and sequence is, as philosopher and cognitive linguist Mark Johnson observes, an ethical act central to "moral reasoning and explanation" (156). As Johnson notes, "a person's identity as a moral agent is inextricably tied up with her quest for synthetic unity in her life, the most comprehensive form of which is narrative" (163). In the opening of his *Narrative,* Dodd asserts the probity and integrity of his writing and character. He presents his account as "fair and impartial" (5) and emphasizes no "motive of ill-feeling to any party with whom I have formerly been connected" (5). Later, in *The Factory System Illustrated,* Dodd even more keenly stresses his objectivity and emotional restraint as an author and industrial critic. He anticipates criticism of his "statements" as "exaggerated" and "too highly coloured" (iv), and insists that while "I can speak feelingly, I have, at the same time, endeavoured to speak temperately, and to avoid, to the uttermost, every unguarded expression which would not become a humble operative (factory worker) like myself to use" (iv).

This defensive stance was prescient, since, as a prominent figure in the Ten Hours Debate, Dodd soon gained notoriety both for the questionable veracity of his writings and for the emotional intensity and presumption of his working-class testimony. A review in the *Spectator* describes him as "unable [. . .] to take a large and philosophical view of the subject, so as calmly to investigate its true nature" (545). According to the *Spectator,* Dodd cannot make acceptable public truth claims since "facts" from his local perspective "may be coloured, they may be exceptions, and even if they have an average sort of truth they only present a limited and particular view" (545). Dodd, the review implies, is unreliable because he writes from his own embodied working-class experiences and feelings, rather than from the more putatively objective vantage of another class position. Three years later, Dodd's writings and character were attacked far more conspicuously, in parliamentary debate on "Hours of Labour in Factories" in March of 1844. Lord Ashley's industrialist opponent, John Bright, accused Dodd not only of bias, but also of reprehensible excess, sensationalism, and deception. Among Dodd's writings on the factory system, Bright charges, "some [. . .] are wholly false, and most [. . .] are grossly and malignantly exaggerated" (*Hansard's* 1149). Like Dodd's swollen and distorted body, his public voice and persona are—according to

Bright—immoderate and deranged. As we will see, this parliamentary session would subject Dodd's character to damaging scrutiny, as a "Factory Cripple" whose pursuit of vocation undermines established forms of sentimental charity and disability.

FEELING TORN: CHARITY AND VOCATION

In Bright and Ashley's debate, Dodd's writings, character, and body all unite in deformity and presumption, grotesquely offending against the sympathy that they initially inspire. In his bid to discredit the Ten Hours campaign, Bright claims that Ashley has been "grossly imposed upon" by Dodd as a person "unworthy of credit" (*Hansard's* 1149). According to Bright, Dodd is equally guilty of disloyalty toward his former industrial employers: "Dodd states that from the hardships he endured in a factory, he was 'done up' at the age of thirty-two, whereas I can prove that he was treated with uniform kindness, which he repaid by gross immorality of conduct, and for which he was at length discharged from his employment" (*Hansard's* 1149–50). Bright's most damning evidence, however, comes from Dodd's own hand—from personal letters that Bright quotes at length. Acquired from the industrialists Edmund and Henry Ashworth (Bright's brothers-in-law) and dated from late 1842, these letters arguably expose Dodd's dishonesty, opportunism, and ingratitude toward his aristocratic patron. In them, Dodd claims he has been "extremely ill-used" by Ashley and Ashley's agent Benjamin Jowett, offers to serve as a counterinformant for Ashley's opponents,[13] and regrets both his unpaid work and its partisan use as "an instance of the cruelty of the manufacturers" (*Hansard's* 1155). Yet, when viewed more expansively, these same letters also express a state of profound internal division, with Dodd struggling to find vocation after the loss of his hand and employment. As part of a greater narrative of wounding and repair, these texts reveal Dodd's own ambivalent negotiation between Tory paternalism and Northern machine culture, between his role as an object of charity and his aspirations to middle-class autonomy.

However we treat Bright's revelations, Dodd's refusal to serve as a passive object of charity provoked powerful anger and indignation among his readers and patrons. His letters inspired shock precisely because they upset established sentimental responses toward his disability: instead of remaining grateful and pathetic, Dodd's voice is ambitious, and his prosthetic *writing* hand is active and resiliently careerist. According to critic Martha Stoddard Holmes, such "emotional excess" (4) typically attends Victorian disability narratives,

---

13. The Ashworths opposed the Ten Hours Act and had been targets of criticism by Lord Ashley and in Dodd's *Factory System Illustrated*. See Boyson 178–79.

both as sympathy toward deserving objects of pity and as melodramatic outrage toward "begging impostor[s]" (94). In Bright's *exposé*, Dodd assumes the latter role, prompting violent censure for his dishonesty and opportunism from Ashley and Ashley's biographers, who view the "Factory Cripple" as exactly such an "unworthy" "impostor" (*Hansard's* 1155, Battiscombe 204). In his private diaries, Ashley goes even further, describing his former "jewel" (Hodder 204) in sensationally inhuman terms: as "a fiend in the form of man" (Boyson 181).

Dodd, it is fair to say, was no fiend, although his letters paint a man determined to find work, and aware of the uneasy path he treads between exciting pity for his disability and channeling those feelings into a stable, paid profession. In one missive to the Ashworths, dated from October 1842, he regrets

> the manner in which I was taken hold of to serve party purposes, the work I was employed on, the hopes and expectations held out to me, the insignificant wages I received, and, now that they have got all out of me that they can, the manner in which I am cast off, even by Lord Ashley himself, without assigning any reason, and refusing to listen to my claims. (*Hansard's* 1155–56)

As a dependent charity case, Dodd lacks the dignity and redress of an individual able to contract his own professional labor.

Nothing reveals this tension between charity and vocation more than the heated response Dodd received when he applied directly to Ashley for payment for his labor. In a later letter cited by Bright, Dodd recalls writing to the noble Lord

> [to] request [. . .] the remittance of a small balance due to me for services rendered—and in reply I received a very angry letter saying that I [had] 'no claim upon them,['] that my employment was 'a mere matter of charity,' that I had received so much money, and even recounted the dinners I had received at his Lordship's table, and told me the condition I was in at the time he took notice of me, and other matters equally galling. It is very clear that party has all along considered me only as a tool, and having made all the use they can of me, I may now go about my business. (*Hansard's* 1157)

As this account suggests, Ashley and his fellow Ten Hours campaigners did not view Dodd as a legitimate employee, but as a beggar receiving alms— "a mere matter of charity" (*Hansard's* 1157).[14] In contrast, Dodd presents his

---

14. Dodd particularly blames his dismissal on Benjamin Jowett, a Ten Hours propagandist employed by Ashley and to whom Dodd frequently reported. See Boyson 178–80.

exchange with Ashley as a fair market transaction among equals—and as one that Ashley has forsaken. Dodd's letters thus highlight his growing insistence on an individualist narrative of vocation. Stressing his agency as a disabled writer and ideologue, Dodd aspires toward middle-class models of self-representation, which, as Gagnier notes, prioritize "creativity, autonomy, and individual freedom" ("Social Atoms" 362) over more "communal" forms of working-class identity (*Subjectivities* 29).[15] While never intended for a broader audience, his letters develop the assertive individual voice of his earlier *Narrative*, but without its melodramatic resignation and forbearance. If narrating the loss of his hand and labor is a source of prosthetic compensation, it is also, as Dodd's letters claim, a vocation in its own right.

Despite Dodd's insistent self-promotion, his vocation as a writer remains ambivalent—torn between working- and middle-class narratives of identity, between the melodramatic pathos of Tory paternalism and the liberal individualism of modern machine culture. Writing at the industrial join, Dodd displays both misgivings toward Ashley's cause and a surprising sympathy toward the factories that he so demonizes. In his letters to the Ashworths, he describes being "almost ashamed of" his earlier writing (*Hansard's* 1153)[16] and finds the Ten Hours campaign "much against my feelings, only it supplies me with a dinner" (*Hansard's* 1156). He recounts his growing disgust toward the movement, deems it "not to be relied on" (*Hansard's* 1155), and regrets his inability to expose its misleading propaganda.[17] For Bright and Ashley, Dodd's complaints were signs of dishonesty and opportunism, but this explanation does not wholly account for Dodd's conflicted affinity with—and division from—his various masters, mentors, and communities.

Like Dodd's letters, his autobiography reveals a complex attachment to the same industrial world that both breaks his body and makes his tale. His *Narrative* expresses "personal respect" (5) for his former factory masters and recalls their support of his literacy as a "kindness [. . .] as fresh to me now as if it had occurred but yesterday" (19). Dodd's praise of his masters is, of course, blended with a keen sense of injury and betrayal—by a system that "mangle[s]"

---

15. On the "triumphant individualism" that typically defines middle-class autobiography, see Carlisle 27–28. On autobiography, disability, and concepts of autonomy, see Couser 182–85.

16. It is uncertain whether Dodd's reference to his "book" in this letter alludes to his *Narrative* or to *The Factory System Illustrated* (*Hansard's* 1153).

17. In his diaries, Ashley suspects that Bright and the Ashworths have bribed Dodd to "trump up a case" (Finlayson 212) against him and Benjamin Jowett. According to Ashley's biographer Geoffrey Finlayson, "It was an accusation almost certainly without foundation, and, in making it—as in forming his association with Dodd—Ashley showed that waywardness of judgment of which he could be guilty" (212). See also Boyson 181 on the Ashworths' refusal to respond to Dodd.

the bodies of its workers while "amassing immense wealth" (26–27). Yet, the most telling sign of this attachment is Dodd's own continuing presence at his masters' mill for twenty-five years. When Dodd's disability bars him from active physical labor, he is promoted to book-keeper and time-keeper (23–25)—increasingly managerial roles that speak to his own uneasy complicity with factory operations. Dodd's *Narrative* highlights his many failed attempts to find non-factory work, but, even after his amputation, his quest for vocation still fatefully returns him to the mill: first as an anti-industrial propagandist, and later as a writer offering his services once more to new factory masters—the Ashworths.

All the while, Dodd sketches a peculiarly industrial process of emotional loss, division, and compensation: from his lost hand to its prosthetic remaking through narrative and vocation. In his letters, his autobiography, and *The Factory System Illustrated,* Dodd remains torn between cultures and identities—and *materially* torn through the very fibers of his body and hand. Present and absent, his hand both mediates this industrial join and represents the join itself, as a relationship of evolving sympathy, distance, attachment, and vulnerability. As a tale of wounding and repair, Dodd's story will likely always inspire discomfort and uncertainty—surrounding his loyalties, his veracity, his disability, his voice, and his melodramatic appeal to charity. Yet, despite Dodd's aspirations to middle-class vocation, the primary focus of his writings is not individual autonomy or wholeness. Rather, as a self-styled "Factory Cripple," Dodd more closely approaches critic Lennard Davis's view of all humans as disabled, as "partial, incomplete subject[s] whose realization is not autonomy and independence but dependency and interdependence" (275). Dodd acknowledges that he is, and always will be, torn: that industrial culture *is* wound culture, and that his hand writes at both its rupture and join.

WORKS CITED

Battiscombe, Georgina. *Shaftesbury: The Great Reformer 1801–1885.* Boston, Houghton Mifflin, 1975.

Bizup, Joseph. *Manufacturing Culture: Vindications of Early Victorian Industry.* U of Virginia P, 2003.

Boyson, Rhodes. *The Ashworth Cotton Enterprise: The Rise and Fall of a Family Firm 1818–1880.* Clarendon P, 1970.

Bronstein, Jamie L. *Caught in the Machinery: Workplace Accidents and Injured Workers in Nineteenth-Century Britain.* Stanford UP, 2007.

Capuano, Peter J. *Changing Hands: Industry, Evolution, and the Reconfiguration of the Victorian Body.* U of Michigan P, 2015.

Carlisle, Janice. Introduction. *Factory Lives: Four Nineteenth-Century Working-Class Autobiographies*, edited by James R. Simmons, Jr., Broadview P, 2007, pp. 11–76.

Chaloner, W. H. Introduction. *The Factory System Illustrated,* by William Dodd, London, Frank Cass, 1968, pp. v–xiii.

Couser, G. Thomas. "Crossing (Out) the Border: Autobiography and Physical Disability." *Recovering Bodies: Illness, Disability, and Life-Writing.* U of Wisconsin P, 1997, pp. 177–220. ProQuest Ebook Central.

Davis, Lennard J. "The End of Identity Politics: On Disability as an Unstable Category." *The Disability Studies Reader,* edited by Lennard J. Davis, 4th ed., Routledge, 2013, pp. 263–77. ProQuest Ebook Central.

Dodd, William. *The Factory System Illustrated.* London, John Murray, 1842. Google Books.

———. *The Laboring Classes of England.* Boston, John Putnam, 1848. Google Books.

———. *The Narrative of the Experience and Sufferings of William Dodd, A Factory Cripple.* London, L. G. Seeley, 1841. Google Books.

Eakin, Paul John. "What Are We Reading When We Read Autobiography?" *Narrative,* vol. 12, no. 1, May 2004, pp. 121–32. JSTOR.

Finlayson, Geoffrey B. A. M. *The Seventh Earl of Shaftesbury 1801–1885.* London, Eyre Methuen, 1981.

Freedgood, Elaine. "That People Might Be Like Things and Live." Manuscript, New York U, March 2009.

Gagnier, Regenia. "Social Atoms: Working-Class Autobiography, Subjectivity, and Gender." *Victorian Studies,* vol. 30, no. 3, Spring 1987, pp. 335–63.

———. *Subjectivities: A History of Self-Representation in Britain, 1832–1920.* Oxford UP, 1991. ProQuest Ebook Central.

Hansard's Parliamentary Debates, 3rd ser., vol. 73, 1844 Mar. 15, col. 1073–158. Google Books.

Hodder, Edwin. *Life and Work of the Seventh Earl of Shaftesbury K. G.* London, Cassell, 1893. Google Books.

Holmes, Martha Stoddard. *Fictions of Affliction: Physical Disability in Victorian Culture.* U of Michigan P, 2009. ProQuest Ebook Central.

Johnson, Mark. *The Moral Imagination: Implications of Cognitive Science for Ethics.* U of Chicago P, 1993.

Ketabgian, Tamara. *Lives of the Machines: The Industrial Imaginary in Victorian Literature and Culture.* U of Michigan P, 2011.

Laqueur, Thomas. "Bodies, Details, and Humanitarian Narrative." *The New Cultural History,* edited by Lynn Hunt, U of California P, 1989, pp. 176–204.

Mitchell, David T., and Sharon L. Snyder. *Narrative Prosthesis: Disability and the Dependencies of Discourse.* U of Michigan P, 2001.

O'Connor, Erin. *Raw Material: Producing Pathology in Victorian Culture.* Duke UP, 2000.

Quayson, Ato. *Aesthetic Nervousness: Disability and the Crisis of Representation.* Columbia UP, 2007.

Ruskin, John. *The Genius of John Ruskin: Selections from His Writings,* edited by John D. Rosenberg, UP of Virginia, 1998.

Seltzer, Mark. *Serial Killers: Death and Life in America's Wound Culture.* Routledge, 1998.

Simmons, James R. Jr., editor. *Factory Lives: Four Nineteenth-Century Working-Class Autobiographies*. Broadview P, 2007.

Sobchak, Vivan. "A Leg to Stand On: Prosthetics, Metaphor, and Materiality." *The Prosthetic Impulse: From a Posthuman Present to a Biocultural Future*, edited by Marquard Smith and Joanne Morra, MIT P, 2006, pp. 17–41.

Ure, Andrew. *The Philosophy of Manufactures*. London, Charles Knight, 1835. Google Books.

"William Dodd's *Factory System Illustrated*." *Spectator*, vol. 15, no. 727, 1842 June 4, pp. 545–6. Periodical Archives Online.

Williams, Raymond. *Culture and Society, 1780–1950*. Columbia UP, 1958.

Zemka, Sue. "1822, 1845, 1869, 1893, and 1917: Artificial Hands." *BRANCH: Britain, Representation and Nineteenth-Century History*, edited by Dino Franco Felluga, extension of *Romanticism and Victorianism on the Net*, 2016, http://www.branchcollective.org/?ps_articles =sue-zemka-1822-1845-1869-1893-and-1917-artificial-hands.

CHAPTER 3

"A Fiery Hand Gripped My Vitals"

*Admiral Nelson, Amputation, and
Heroic Masculinity in* Jane Eyre

KAREN BOURRIER

IN *JANE EYRE*, the physical feature that the heroine finds most attractive in the hero is arguably not his face or his physique, but his hands. Rochester is infamously ugly. His forehead is too square, his hair too black, his "decisive nose" is "more remarkable for character than for beauty," his "full nostrils" denote "choler" his "mouth, chin, and jaw" are "very grim" (119–20). Even his figure, while "good" in the "athletic sense of the term" is "neither tall nor graceful" (120). Such are the qualities that lead Jane to tell her master point blank at the second interview that she does not think him handsome (131). For all Rochester's infamous ugliness, however, his hands hold a certain sexual appeal. In an early courtship scene, Jane notes: "He had a rounded, muscular and vigorous hand" (279). Rochester's hands may also be central to his identity: they are what gives him away when he cross-dresses as a gypsy. It is all the more interesting, then, that he loses his left hand (along with his eye) at the end of the novel.

Following work in Victorian hand studies by Aviva Briefel and Peter J. Capuano, in this essay I take the hand as my site of analysis, arguing that Rochester's manual amputation is central to our reading of marriage and the representation of disability in *Jane Eyre*. While most readings of disability in *Jane Eyre* focus on Rochester's blindness, examining Rochester's manual amputation brings us a more nuanced picture of the historical and cultural resonance of his disabilities.[1] For *Jane Eyre*'s first readers, one of the immediate cultural references for Rochester's missing hand would have been Admiral Lord Nelson, who lost his right hand (along with most of his right arm) in the Battle of Tenerife, as well as the sight of his right eye in the Invasion of Corsica. Taken together, Rochester's missing eye and amputated hand resonate with both the biblical punishment for adultery—"And if thy right eye offend thee, pluck it out . . . And if thy right hand offend thee, cut it off" (Matthew 5:28–30)—and the iconic disabilities of Nelson (himself a well-known adulterer). In this context, we can see Rochester's manual amputation as a physical marker of both his attempted bigamy and of his heroism in attempting to rescue Bertha. The hand is often a symbol of agency; and while a missing hand may be taken to diminish Rochester's individual agency, reading from a disability studies perspective, we might emphasize instead his interdependence with Jane, who becomes his right hand as he takes her hand in marriage. In this historical context, I argue that Rochester's amputated limb and missing eye become symbols of his heroism, as well as of his Nelsonian sexual entanglements, and that Jane, like Lady Hamilton, can be read as the celebrant and domesticator of that heroism.

Jane and Rochester's union forms part of a novelistic tradition that Talia Schaffer identifies as "disability marriage." Schaffer argues that, like Jane Eyre, the heroines of nineteenth-century novels are often torn between a familiar choice of mate—a cousin, a neighbor, or perhaps a man with a disability—who offers stability, family connections, and even a fulfilling occupation (in *Jane Eyre*, this figure would be St. John), and a romantic choice, often a stranger associated with passion and sexual desire. At the beginning of the novel, Rochester is the romantic choice, and by the end, when he is disabled, Rochester embodies the best of both familiar and romantic marriage, offering Jane a fulfilling occupation in taking care of him as well as the romantic and sexual love she craves. As Schaffer notes, "by the time they marry, Rochester has been refashioned: a disabled man, who gives Jane a lifetime of meaningful work, he can enter a marriage characterized by something more like the kind of egalitarian mutual respect of the familiar marriage" (35–36). Rochester's disabilities do not negate his sex appeal, and he remains an object of desire for Jane.

Jane's desire for a disabled Rochester can be difficult to understand from our historical vantage point. In the twenty-first century, we are tethered to

---

1. See for example, the essays included in the recent collection *The Madwoman and the Blindman:* Jane Eyre, *Discourse, Disability* whose title foregrounds Bertha's madness and Rochester's blindness.

a medical model of disability, one that sees desire for disability as queer or pathologized, and the sexual practices of those with disabilities as "outlandish or kinky" (Siebers 132). This medical model of disability is reflected in twentieth- and twenty-first-century filmic adaptations of *Jane Eyre*, which typically omit Rochester's manual amputation. As Martha Stoddard Holmes notes, in almost every film version, "Rochester's hands are completely or virtually intact"; instead of showing a visible amputation, Rochester's manual impairment is typically represented through burn makeup or bandages on his left hand (170). Stoddard Holmes suggests that the filmic erasure of Rochester's manual disability suggests that "desire for an amputated Rochester is queerly outside the limits of what filmmakers expect their audiences to imagine" (155).

Examining the significance of Rochester's manual amputation in Brontë's novel allows us to see the importance of his disabilities in a broader cultural context. As Capuano notes, the significance of the hand has long been "treated only metonymically or metaphorically" in studies of Victorian literature and culture (3). This is certainly the case with Rochester's blindness and missing hand, which critics from the mid-twentieth century onward have read as representative of the hero's symbolic castration.[2] Recent work in Victorian disability studies asks us to take the hand as a hand, and Rochester's amputation as a lived physical disability rather than a symbolic one. Reading Rochester's manual amputation in the historical context of Nelson's iconic disabilities, and the fervent desire they fomented in the breasts of British women, can help us understand him not as a man who has been castrated by his manual amputation, but rather, as a man to be desired in part because of his heroic disabilities.

---

2. Critics from mid-twentieth-century psychoanalysts to second wave feminists have read Rochester's disabilities as a form of symbolic castration. In his 1948 essay, Richard Chase applied a Freudian lens to Brontë's novel, writing, "Rochester's injuries are, I should think, a symbolic castration. The faculty of vision, the analysts have shown, is often identified in the unconscious with the energy of sex. When Rochester had tried to make love to Jane, she felt "a fiery hand grasp at her vitals; the hand, then, must be cut off" (108–9). Although the terms of the argument shifted with second wave feminist interpretations of the text in the late 1970s and early 1980s, the final conclusion—symbolic castration—remained the same. Now, instead of finding that "Charlotte Brontë's spinsterish sensibilities were such that his [Rochester's] rampant sexuality had to be tamed before he could become a suitable husband for a nice early-Victorian heroine like Jane Eyre" (170), as Peter Pickrel summed up Chase's argument, disabling Rochester became an empowering move for the woman novelist that reversed the power relations between hero and heroine. Sandra Gilbert argues that there is "an element of truth" in his diagnosis of symbolic castration for "The angry Bertha in Jane had wanted to punish Rochester, to burn him in his bed, destroy his house, cut off his hand, and pluck out his overmastering 'full falcon eye'" (802).

The hand was an important marker of class and gender, and I would add, physical ability, in the nineteenth century. As Capuano notes, "the head and the hand were routinely the only two body parts open to inspection" in the nineteenth century (10); a bare hand was thus a potential site of interpretation. Surveying various modes of palmistry, chirognomy, and fingerprinting, Briefel argues that in the nineteenth century, the hand "offered privileged information about human character and identity" (3). The hand, with its associations with labor, often offers a quick index to class in the Victorian novel. In *Jane Eyre*, we might consider the "floury and horny hand" of Hannah (342), the Rivers' gruff but trustworthy servant, or the "white hands" of the "young men of the present day" so disdained by Blanche Ingram (179). In both these cases, the hand acts as a visible index of class and gender, with the traces of one's labor (or lack thereof) legible on the hand. For the Victorians, even when the hand itself remained unimpaired, there was a supposition that the weakness or disability of the rest of the body could be read on the hand. Victorian novelists frequently juxtapose the hands of two male friends as a way of delineating the strength of one and the weakness of the other.[3] In *The Mill on the Floss* Philip Wakem's hunchback seems legible in his "small delicate hand," while Tom Tulliver has a more "substantial" grasp (191). In Thomas Hughes's *Tom Brown's Schooldays*, the invalid Arthur lays his "thin white hand, on which the blue veins stood out so plainly," on Tom Brown's "great brown fist" (308). In these moments, the contrast between the boys' bodies is made apparent in the contrast between their hands.

Although the case of an amputated or otherwise missing hand has the potential to disrupt the legibility of the body, for many Victorians, a missing hand was legible as a legacy of participation in war or industrial accident. Reading the severed hand in the context of Britain's postcolonial history, as a "signifier of imperial responsibility and intervention" (25), Briefel notes that, surprisingly, as the nineteenth century progressed, "the most legible hands were those that were detached—literally or figuratively—from the acting body" (6). This may also be true on the home front. In the first half of the nineteenth century, increased industrialization and participation in warfare from the Napoleonic wars to the Crimean war meant that more Britons were losing limbs, while improvements in medicine and the prevention of infection meant that more were surviving and adjusting to their new lives as amputees (Zemka 1). As Erin O'Connor notes, the development of anesthesia and antisepsis in the mid-nineteenth century improved outcomes for amputees, such

---

3. I first made this point in *The Measure of Manliness* 9.

that "amputation became an increasingly visible phenomenon as the century progressed" (106).

Due to the increased prevalence of amputees, prosthetics were a growth industry in the Victorian period. While initial research in the nineteenth-century history of prosthetic limbs has focused on prosthetic legs, Sue Zemka argues that artificial hands, whose design oscillated between a focus on aesthetics and a focus on functionality, play "a relevant and possibly crucial role to changing conceptions of the human body, especially as they move between images of organic autonomy and images of technological hybridity" (12). Despite the increasing prevalence of amputees in the Victorian era, manual amputees, and in particular users of manual prosthetics, are fairly rare in Victorian literature. As Ryan Sweet notes, "While hook-hand users, including most famously, Captain Cuttle and Captain Hook, were occasionally represented, artificial hands—by which I mean more sophisticated prostheses that attempted to stand in aesthetically and functionally for absent limbs— were few and far between in literary texts from this period" (forthcoming). Examples of characters who are missing hands but who do not use prosthetics include Rochester, Alick Keith in Charlotte Yonge's *The Clever Woman of the Family* (1865), who has lost several fingers in the siege of Dehli, and Hatherley in Arthur Conan Doyle's "The Adventure of the Engineer's Thumb" (1892). Rochester's amputation comes at the end of *Jane Eyre,* and Brontë does not indicate that her hero is using a prosthetic in the immediate aftermath of the fire at Thornfield. However, we can see his missing hand as the signifier that places Rochester in a larger discourse about masculinity, heroism, and warfare in the mid-nineteenth century.

One of the main ways that British men lost hands in the nineteenth century was through warfare, though as Zemka points out, limbs were also lost in train and factory accidents, as well as through farm work (6).[4] For *Jane Eyre*'s first audience, the sight of Rochester's amputated hand would have called up images of the Napoleonic wars in general, and of Horatio Nelson in particular. Vice Admiral Horatio Nelson, 1st Viscount Nelson, and significantly, 1st Duke of Bronté, was, alongside the Duke of Wellington, one of the British naval heroes of the Napoleonic wars. His image loomed large in the Brontës' childhood and in the British imagination in general in the first half of the nineteenth century. Stories of soldiers and naval officers who were missing hands as a result of a canon or rifle misfiring, or direct combat, were not uncommon. As Zemka writes, "There was a world of unspoken meaning in

---

4. Although there was a strong association between war and limb loss, as Capuano notes, industrial accidents were also prevalent. In one year in the 1830s, over 93% of the cases treated at the Leeds infirmary involved "severe injuries to the hand, thumb, or fingers" (49).

the empty sleeves of the former officers of the nineteenth century's man wars" (2). George Webb Derenzy, author of the widely read *Echiridion: or A Hand for the One-Handed* (1822) (Daen 93), is just one example of a naval officer who survived the Napoleonic war as a manual amputee, having lost his right arm in the battle of Vittoria (iv). The Napoleonic wars provided a narrative framework for the British male manual amputee in the early to mid-nineteenth century. The narrative of the war amputee emphasized heroism and reintegration into civilian life through the civilizing efforts of women.

Indeed, the first half of the nineteenth century saw a spate of novels aimed at a female readership that fictionalized Nelson as naval hero. Kate Williams, Lady Hamilton's biographer, points to an archive of novels written by women in the late 1790s and early 1800s which feature a sensitive Nelsonian hero and grapple with his infamous adultery (72). Examples of novels rewriting Nelson and his circle include *The Wild Irish Girl* (1806), *A Sailor's Friendship and a Soldier's Love* (1805), *The Convict; or The Navy Lieutenant* (1806), and *The Wife and the Mistress* (1802) (Williams 72–77). Williams argues that these novels move towards imagining a man who is as physically damaged as Nelson as a hero, though they typically do not disable their heroes to the extent that the historical Nelson was wounded (80). And yet, Nelson's wounds were part of his sexual appeal; they were the "direct mark of his valour" and also emblematic of "the wounds suffered by countless sailors and soldiers during the Napoleonic Wars" (80). Part of the appeal of Nelson's wounds, Williams argues, was that they made him vulnerable: "the great warrior was also disabled" (80); he "simultaneously projected a sense of strength and weakness, appealing to the nurturing feelings of English women even while he fulfilled the role of a powerful protected" (81). While most novelists of the turn of the century may have shied away from wounding their heroes to the extent of the impairment experienced by Nelson, Charlotte Brontë is one novelist who reimagines almost the full extent of Nelson's wounds in her hero. Rochester does not lose his whole arm as Nelson did, but he does lose his hand, as well as having his eye knocked out. Both Nelson and Rochester also have significant facial scarring as a result of their heroic acts. In the disabled Rochester, then, we can see Brontë participating in a tradition of rewriting the manly, sensitive, sexually promiscuous, and disabled Nelsonian hero.

The novels by women writers fictionalizing Nelson and his circle were in vogue before Charlotte Brontë was born in 1816, but there is evidence that she too was captivated by this saga of war, adultery, and disability. Brontë's early short story, "Lily Hart," written in November of 1833 as part of the saga of the Kingdom of Angria, imagines a young woman's encounter with a disabled soldier whom she nurses back to health and then marries. As Christine Alexander notes, the name Lily Hart was likely suggested by "Emily Hart," which was the assumed name of Nelson's mistress Emma Lyon / Lady Hamilton (Brontë, "Lily Hart" 301n29). Like Lady Hamilton, Lily Hart is raised by her widowed mother. One day, mother and daughter sit in their quiet suburban home, listening to the "thunder of a distant artillery" and watching a "cloud of smoke," which gradually wanes as news arrives that the Great Insurrection has been put down (301). Soon after, the women find a wounded soldier in their garden; he has a bayonet wound on his right side, which is fortunately not deep and has not injured his vital organs. The two women bring the soldier, who calls himself Mr. Seymour, into their home and nurse him back to health after his friend Colonel Percival vouches for his character. As his health improves, Seymour becomes increasingly agreeable; like Rochester he is a charismatic conversationalist: when the subject interests him "his countenance grew very animated; his eyes sparkled; and his words flowed forth with freedom, energy and even brilliancy" (304). A year after his recovery, Lily is in financial distress after the death of her mother, and she meets the enigmatic young soldier in the street. He asks her to marry him but there is one condition: their union must be kept "strictly private" (309). Unlike Jane Eyre, Lily Hart readily agrees to a marriage under circumstances that look like she is actually to be the mistress, especially given the origin of her name. After their marriage she is whisked off to a love nest where she gives birth to a son and is generally extraordinarily happy, except that her husband only spends one month in four with her and she has never met his family (312). Just when the reader is sure there is a Nelsonian bigamy or adultery plot afoot, it turns out that Seymour has kept their marriage a secret because he is really Prince John, Duke of Fidena, and son of the King. He compels his father to accept Lily, and she graces the highest society of Verdopolis. In this story, Brontë imagines a battle injury and lengthy convalescence as leading to sexual intimacy and marriage.[5]

The Brontë family's interest in the Napoleonic wars in general, and in Nelson in particular, is well documented. Indeed, the interest can be traced all the way to their surname. According to family lore, Patrick Brontë changed the family name from the Irish Brunty to Brontë when he matriculated at Cambridge in 1802 in honor of Nelson, who became the Duke of Bronté when he annulled the Neapolitan capitulation to France in 1799 (*Letters of Charlotte Brontë* 2.279–80). Years later, a rumor that Acton, Ellis and Currer Bell, were really called Brontë and were "of the Nelson family" persisted in spite of Charlotte's assertions to the contrary (*Letters of Charlotte Brontë* 2.279–

---

5. Brontë's most extensive treatment of disability in her juvenilia lies elsewhere, in Finic, a "deaf-mute" dwarf whose disabilities are problematically racialized, and who may be a prototype of Madame Walravens in *Villette*, who stands like Finic about three feet high (Pike 120–21).

80, 303). Southey's *Life of Nelson* was a bestseller throughout the nineteenth century, and Charlotte recommended it to Ellen Nussey as important reading in biography (*Letters of Charlotte Brontë* 1.131), suggesting that she herself had read it carefully. The Napoleonic wars figured largely in the Brontë children's juvenilia, as the siblings reimagined articles about the Napoleonic wars appearing in periodicals such as *Blackwood's* and *Fraser's Magazine* in the sagas of Angria and Gondol (Butcher 470–71). The Duke of Wellington was the particular hero of both Charlotte and her father (Alexander and Smith 535), and some scholars have suggested that Wellington was the model for Rochester (Alexander 1; Colley 263). Rochester's wounds, however, would point to Nelson as an additional model for Brontë's hero. Scholars have briefly noted this resemblance, but have not fully explored its significance. As Jen Hill argues in her work on the Victorian Arctic, "Rochester's wounds are a form of national(list) stigmata that mirror those of that symbol of heroic national masculinity, Horatio Nelson, whose early experience in the polar seas is central to all narratives of character formation that follow it, including *Jane Eyre*" (109). Moving away from the Arctic and towards the home front, we can see the resonance of Nelson's disabilities in general, and his manual amputation in particular, for Brontë's hero.

More than forty years after his death at the battle of Trafalgar, Nelson was newly relevant as Brontë was writing *Jane Eyre* with the installation of Nelson's Column in Trafalgar Square in 1843. The project for a monument to Nelson in Trafalgar square had stalled for nearly thirty-five years after his death, to be revived in the late 1830s (Mace 56). There was an enormous response to a competition to design the monument in 1838 (Mace 61); Rodney Mace suggests that this renewed interest in a patriotic monument of a naval hero responsible in part for England's triumph over Jacobinism was in part a response to the Chartist movement (57). For her part, Brontë wrote Elizabeth Gaskell that she thought Trafalgar Square was a "fine site; (and sight also)" and that the view, including Nelson's Column, was "grand and imposing" (*Letters of Charlotte Brontë* 2.676). In the 1840s, then, Nelson was still very much a part of the British popular imagination, as well as of the private imaginings at Haworth parsonage. On a national scale, Nelson's Column showed the Admiral complete with an empty sleeve pinned across his jacket, immediately legible as a signal of his missing arm (though not with any discernible injury to his eye), and Trafalgar Day customs were being developed throughout the decade (White 105, 109).[6] At home, throughout the autumn of 1841, Branwell

---

6. Trafalgar Square has been a significant site of the public performance of disability. When it was unveiled in the square in 2005, Marc Quinn's marble statue Alison Lapper Pregnant, showing the disabled artist, who was born without arms and with foreshortened legs, seven months pregnant, elicited comparison to Nelson's disabilities. See Millett.

Brontë wrote three drafts of a long biographical poem on Nelson, returning to the material the following spring in a poem called "The Triumph of Mind over Body" (Barker 374, 400). Nelson was both a national and a domestic presence for the inmates of Haworth parsonage.

Nelson's disabilities were iconic. Kathleen Wilson argues that his "scarred and dismembered body made him an instantly recognisable figure" (60). For Wilson, "Nelson's fame and the iconic significance of his dismembered body marked a larger shift in the politics and practices of representation, away from the transparent and universal forms of an eighteenth-century public sphere, towards the fragmented body and body politic of nineteenth-century modernity" (49). There was also a certain level of intimacy and eroticism bound up in Nelson's amputated arm. In one widely reprinted anecdote, Nelson picked a man who had served alongside him out of a crowd in Salisbury; the officer showed Nelson a piece of lace from the sleeve of his amputated arm, which he had kept as a memento of the naval hero (Wilson 58).

Nelson seems to some extent to have embraced his disabilities as part of his heroic identity. His favorite portrait of himself, a love token for Lady Hamilton, *Rear-Admiral Horatio Nelson* (Unknown artist, c. 1805, National Maritime Museum, Greenwich), makes no attempt to disguise his missing eye or arm or his scarred face, but instead shows the hero of the battle of the Nile watching the French ship *L'Orient* ignite, and reveals him to be a "dismembered and romantic figure" (Wilson 62). Southey's *Life of Nelson* shows him to possess courage and fortitude. Every time he was injured in battle, he bore it stoically. When, during the siege of Calvi, a shot struck the ground near him, driving sand and gravel into his right eye, he spoke of it "slightly," writing the same day to Lord Hood that he "got a little hurt that morning, not much" (78). He lost the sight in his eye, but only missed one day of battle. The story of the loss of his right arm was even more heroic. Whilst engaging in hand-to-hand combat with the enemy at Tenerife, his right arm was shot. As he fell, he caught his sword in his left hand. Having put a sling and tourniquet around the wound, he called to the ship to let down a rope for him to climb up. Southey reports him as saying: "Let me alone: I have yet my legs left, and one arm. Tell the surgeon to make haste and get his instruments. I know I must lose my right arm; so the sooner it is off the better" (124). "The spirit which he displayed in jumping up the ship's side" writes the poet, "astonished everyone" (125). For the British public who devoured Southey's biography, Nelson's wounds were not indicative of an attenuated masculinity, but rather the visible emblems of his brave spirit.

Nelson's infamous affair with Lady Hamilton meant that his missing right hand and his injured eye could be read as a punishment for his sexual transgressions. Indeed, the Biblical punishment for adultery from the Sermon on the Mount commands a Christian to pluck out his right eye and cut off his right hand before committing such a sin:

> But I say unto you, That whosoever looketh on a woman to lust after her hath committed adultery with her already in his heart. / And if thy right eye offend thee, pluck it out, and cast it from thee: for it is profitable for thee that one of thy members should perish, and not that thy whole body should be cast into hell. / And if thy right hand offend thee, cut it off, and cast it from thee: for it is profitable for thee that one of thy members should perish, and not that thy whole body should be cast into hell. (Matthew 5:28–30)

Although he sustained these injuries before he met Lady Hamilton, in this context, Nelson's disabilities—the missing right hand and the injured eye—become the literal embodiment of the biblical punishment for adultery, as well as the visible symbols of his heroism.

Rochester's disabilities also embody this tension between his (attempted) adultery and his heroism. Rochester becomes an amputee in a heroic attempt to save Bertha, and the gruesome detail in which Brontë reports his dismembering is reminiscent of a battle narrative. As the innkeeper tells Jane, as the manor crashed down in flames after Rochester, "one eye was knocked out, and one hand so crushed that Mr. Carter, the surgeon, had to amputate it directly" (429). The novel's fascination with the damage done to Rochester's body suggests that his scars are the literal reminders of his heroic exploits. Rochester's disabilities can also be read as the battle scars of a man who has sinned but who sins no longer. As the reviewer for the *Spectator* wrote, he is "maimed and blinded through the heroic manner in which he exposes himself" in attempting to rescue his mad wife from the flaming manor (qtd in Allott 75). The innkeeper gives an eyewitness account of Rochester's heroism in ascending to "the attics when all was burning above and below" to wake the servants and help them down himself. He then goes back "to get his mad wife out of her cell," but too late to prevent her from leaping out of the flames to the pavement below. The scene is that of a battle: Bertha flings herself from "the battlements" on top of Thornfield (428). And, of course, Rochester emerges battle-scarred. Surely Lord Nelson could have done no better himself for valor and spirit in the same situation. As the innkeeper claims, "it was all his own courage, and a body may say, his kindness, in a way ma'am: he wouldn't leave the house till ever one else was out before him" (429). Here, Rochester imitates Nelson's famous chivalry to those below him in rank.

At the same time, as a would-be adulterer, Rochester's disabilities also reference both Nelson's adultery and the biblical punishment for adultery. As Maia McAleavey argues, although Rochester does not technically commit adultery or bigamy with Jane, much of the novel's "erotic and Gothic charge arises from the sustained period of time that forms the novel's heart—Jane's sojourn at Thornfield, where Mr. Rochester lives simultaneously with his two sequential wives" (55). Rochester's injuries are foreshadowed when Jane tears herself away from her master after finding out that he is already married, a separation that she finds as painful as an amputation. She reminds herself of the Sermon on the Mount, admonishing herself: "you shall tear yourself away; none shall help you: you shall, yourself, pluck out your right eye; yourself cut off your right hand" (297). When she determines that she must leave Rochester after discovering that he is already married, to Jane it feels as though "a hand of fiery iron grasped my vitals" (315). These biblical references prefigure Rochester's manual amputation; in this scene, Jane applies the biblical punishment to herself metaphorically: she would sooner pluck out her own right eye and cut off her own hand than become Rochester's mistress. When Rochester is maimed, there is some suggestion that it is as punishment for his attempted bigamy. As the innkeeper reports, "Some say it was a just judgment on him for keeping his first marriage secret, and wanting to take another wife while he had one living" (428). Similarly, when his son is born he inherits "his own eyes, as they once were—large, brilliant, and black," Rochester acknowledges, "with a full heart," that "God" has "tempered judgment with mercy" (451). Many bystanders also temper their judgment with the "pity" that the innkeeper confesses to feeling for the master of Thornfield (428). The novel's happy ending suggests that rather than condemning him as an adulterer, to a certain extent Rochester's injuries redeem him, enabling him to move forward and marry Jane.

It is perhaps fitting that separating herself from Rochester feels to Jane as though she is separating herself from her right hand, or as though a "fiery hand" is grasping at her vitals, as hands form some of the central imagery to Jane and Rochester's courtship. As a child at Gateshead, Jane is seen as an "underhand" thing (12, 25), or, as her Aunt Reed puts it, "such a burden to be left on my hands" (231). This imagery of the hand as burden shifts in her courtship with Rochester, with whom she experiences a tactile intimacy. The well-known scene when Rochester cross-dresses as a gypsy, telling the fortunes of the ladies of the house, gives us a sense of how central the hand is to our understanding of identity and agency in Brontë's novel. Jane understandably presumes that the gypsy will read her hand in order to tell her fortune, but she refuses to do so, arguing "I can make nothing of such a hand as that;

almost without lines: besides, what is in a palm? Destiny is not written there" (197). If Rochester refuses to read Jane's hand, she proves herself to be an expert reader of his hands. Jane recognizes Rochester at the moment that the gypsy fortune-teller stretches out her hands before the fire. "It was no more the withered limb of eld than my own;" she thinks, "it was a rounded supple member, with smooth fingers, symmetrically turned" (202).

Rochester and Jane experience a tactile courtship, in which touch rather than sight proves the most trustworthy token of affection. Indeed, their early relationship centers on a mode of communication that Kimberly Cox calls "manual intercourse," which she defines as "an extralinguistic mode of social communication conveyed through the touch of a hand" (196). Jane and Rochester's haptic relations are a consistent indicator of their passion (211). Seeing Jane is not enough for Rochester; when he endeavors to explain his first marriage to her, he implores her "Just put your hand in mine, Janet—that I may have the evidence of touch as well as sight, to prove you are near me" (304). The offers of his hand in marriage, typically a dead metaphor, is reinvigorated when one considers the significance of tactility in the pair's courtship. True to form, when he first proposes, Rochester offers Jane "my hand, my heart, and a share of all my possessions" (254). In his second proposal, the trope of the hand in marriage becomes even more significant, as Rochester's hand has now been amputated. Rochester's manual amputation literalizes the trope of taking one's hand in marriage, since Jane, in her own words, will now quite literally be his "right hand" (451). (Or, technically, his left hand, since that is the one that he loses.) Rochester's disabilities bind Jane in a new, if pleasurable, servitude as he requires her constant attendance, and they enable an erotic exchange of care between Jane and her master. Reflecting back on their first years of marriage, Jane muses that the circumstance of his continuing blind for the first two years of their marriage may have been what "drew us so very near—that knit us so very close; for I was then his vision, as I am still his right hand" (451). Jane proclaims to the blinded and maimed Rochester: "I will be your neighbour, your nurse, your housekeeper. I find you lonely; I will be your companion—to read to you, to walk with you, to sit with you, to wait on you, to be eyes and hands to you" (435). Rochester, in turn, feels that being helped by Jane as an intimate erases the shame of being helped by a hired hand. He tells her: "Hitherto I have hated to be helped—to be led: henceforth, I feel I shall hate it no more. I did not like to put my hand into a hireling's, but it is pleasant to feel it circled by Jane's little fingers" (445). Perhaps the moment that seals their union is the moment that the pair leave the wood at Ferndean, Jane leading Rochester by the hand: "Then he stretched his hand out to be led. I took that dear hand, held it a moment to my lips, then let it pass round my shoulder: being so much lower of stature than he, I served both for his prop and guide. We entered the wood, and wended homeward" (448).

Rochester's newfound state of dependence allows Jane a new level of tactility in their relationship, and softens the fiery grip that Rochester deploys earlier in their courtship. As Schaffer notes, once Rochester becomes disabled, Jane "can initiate contact, soothing and ministering to the man's body" (34). This tactility both depends on the hands, and begins with Jane taking Rochester's hand, in a reversal of their early courtship scenes in which he often imprisons her by the hand. When Jane saves him from the fire that Bertha has set in his bed, Rochester takes Jane's hand "in both his own" refusing to let go—"But he still retained my hand, and I could not free it"—until Jane pretends to hear Mrs. Fairfax (151). When Mason reveals Rochester's first wife at the altar, Rochester grips Jane's hand, and she notes "what a hot and strong grasp he had!" (289), a situation that is repeated at Thornfield as Rochester continues to make explanations and Jane notes "his gripe [sic] was painful" (317). In contrast, when Rochester gropes the air to find Jane, she comments, "I arrested his wandering hand, and prisoned it in both mine" (433). Rochester then identifies Jane by her hands: "Her very fingers! . . . her small slight fingers! If so, there must be more of her" (433). Where he once refused to read Jane's palm as evidence of her future, Rochester now identifies Jane through her hands as she did him. One might even say that Rochester reads Jane with his hands: this is fitting given that new technologies of raised print, including but not limited to braille, allowed the blind to read with their hands in the nineteenth century.[7]

If Rochester in his infirmity provides Jane with the "new servitude" that she is longing for when she first reaches Thornfield, part of her role is to appreciate his heroism. Lady Hamilton was not only the rewarder and celebrant of Nelson's victories, but also the domesticator of his fame. As Colin White argues, Lady Hamilton fulfilled her role as the "celebrant" of Nelson's "fame and the rewarder of his victories" to perfection (96). When Jane first sees Rochester after the fire at Thornfield, he keeps his mutilated left hand "hidden in his bosom" (431), or his breast pocket, in the attitude common to soldiers who have lost a hand or arm, echoing Nelson's Column with the hero's right sleeve pinned across the bosom. When Rochester draws his "mutilated limb" with "neither hand nor nails" from his breast and shows it to Jane, tell-

---

7. As Vanessa Warne notes, Valentine Hauy's system of embossed print, developed in Paris in the 1780s, was adopted by a number of British printers in the late 1820s and 1830s (46). Braille was not widely adopted until the end of the nineteenth century (57). Heather Tilley suggests that despite the rise of embossed print material in the early nineteenth century, Rochester "is identified more with the practice of reading aloud for blind people" (131).

ing her "It is a mere stump, a ghastly sight!" she agrees that, "It is a pity to see it; and a pity to see your eyes—and the scar of fire on your forehead" but not for the aesthetic reason he gives (436). Instead, she tells him that "the worst of it is that one is in danger of loving you to well for all this, and making too much of you" (436). Here, Jane could mean that she is in danger of fussing over her master too much as she waits on him, or that she is in danger of lionizing him for his heroism. The likelihood is that the passage implies both, and that in coming to be Rochester's wife, like Lady Hamilton she also comes to be the companion and celebrant of his infirmities.

Part of Jane's duty in reuniting with Rochester is to reanimate his spirits after his battle. Jane comes to her master when his infirmities are in danger of sinking him very low indeed. As she observes him unseen, she notes, "It was mournful, indeed, to witness the subjugation of that vigorous spirit to a corporeal infirmity. He sat in his chair,—still, but not at rest: expectant evidently; the lines of now habitual sadness marking his strong features" (439). Jane's duty is in part to reanimate the "vigorous spirit" that once indicated a heroic masculinity: for "It was not himself that could now kindle the lustre of animated expression: he was dependent on another for that office!" (439). Once this task is accomplished, Rochester's infirmities become part of a rugged manliness rather than indicative of a dependent femininity. As Jane remarks, despite his "cicatrized visage" (436), missing hand and missing eye, "His form was of the same strong and stalwart contour as ever: his port was still erect, his hair was still raven-black; nor were his features altered or sunk: not in one year's space, by any sorrow, could his athletic strength be quelled, or his vigorous prime blighted" (431).

In addition to permitting intimacy between the two, Rochester's disabilities provide Jane with a new duty. Jane, who has been seeking to fulfil a duty throughout the novel, tells Rochester: "I love you better now, when I can really be useful to you, than I did in your state of proud independence, when you disdained every part but that of the giver and protector" (445). Jane's claim that "there was a pleasure in my services, most full, most exquisite, even though sad" (451) allows us to read her union with Rochester as a vocation, if not quite as noble as that of serving as a missionary in Calcutta with St. John, at least not as self-indulgent as a sheer romance. In serving Rochester, as Schaffer points out (34), Jane reconciles romance with duty. If we read Rochester's blindness and manual amputation as an echo of Nelson's iconic injuries, we might also read Jane in part as Rochester's reward for his heroic masculinity at the end of the novel, just as he is her reward for her virtuous femininity.

From a twenty-first-century vantage point, we might find the sexual appeal of Rochester's amputation difficult to understand. While, in the twentieth and twenty-first centuries, Rochester's manual amputation is erased from film adaptations and not often examined in criticism, the Victorians would have read the significance of Rochester's missing hand differently. For those who remembered Nelson and the Napoleonic wars, and were to embark on the Crimean war and the Siege of Delhi in the decade following the publication of *Jane Eyre*, Rochester's missing hand was legible as a battle-scar that marked him out as in special need of female sympathy, and as an object of heterosexual desire. At least some Victorian readers found Rochester's disabilities quite stirring. Queen Victoria wrote in her diary: "The end is very touching, when Jane Eyre returns to him and finds him blind, with one hand gone from injuries during the fire in his house, which was caused by his mad wife" (qtd in Allott 390). Indeed, the Rochester that emerges, fire-scarred, at the end of the novel is a model of bravery and spirit, and one senses that Jane's duty is not to tame those qualities but to appreciate them, and to help her battle-torn master find his place in the domestic sphere after a war well fought. If Rochester's injuries are in part a punishment for his attempted bigamy, like Nelson, he has come through the punishment forgiven and rewarded for his new-found virtue. Reading Rochester's manual amputation and missing eye through the lens of Admiral Lord Nelson's iconic disabilities allows us to see his missing hand as the Victorians may have done, as an emblem of his heroism and part of his sexual appeal.

WORKS CITED

Alexander, Christine. "Charlotte Brontës, Autobiography, and the Image of the Hero." *Brontës Studies*, vol. 35, no. 1, pp. 1–19.

Alexander, Christine, and Margaret Smith. *The Oxford Companion to the Brontës*. Oxford UP, 2018.

Allott, Miriam Farris. *The Brontës: The Critical Heritage*. Routledge & K. Paul, 1974.

Barker, Juliet. *The Brontës*. Weidenfeld and Nicolson 1994.

The Bible. Authorized King James Version, Oxford UP, 1998.

Bolt, David, Elizabeth J. Donaldson, and Julia Miele Rodas, editors. *The Madwoman and the Blindman: Jane Eyre, Discourse, Disability*. The Ohio State UP, 2012.

Bourrier, Karen. *The Measure of Manliness: Disability and Masculinity in the Mid-Victorian Novel*. U of Michigan P, 2015.

Briefel, Aviva. *The Racial Hand in the Victorian Imagination*. Cambridge UP, 2015.

Brontë, Charlotte. "Lily Hart." *An Edition of the Early Writings of Charlotte Bronte, Volume II: The Rise of Angria 1833–1835, Part I: 1833–1834*, edited by Christine Alexander. Basil Blackwell, 1991, pp. 301–12.

———. *Jane Eyre*. Edited by Margaret Smith, Oxford UP, 2008.

———. *The Letters of Charlotte Brontë: With a Selection of Letters by Family and Friends, Volume II: 1848–1851*. Edited by Margaret Smith, Oxford UP, 2000.

Butcher, Emma. "Napoleonic Periodicals and the Childhood Imagination: The Influence of War Commentary on Charlotte and Branwell Brontë's Glass Town and Angria." *Victorian Periodicals Review*, vol. 48, no. 4, Winter 2015, pp. 469–86.

Capuano, Peter J. *Changing Hands: Industry, Evolution, and the Reconfiguration of the Victorian Body*. U of Michigan P, 2015.

Chase, Richard. "The Brontës, or, Myth Domesticated." *Forms of Modern Fiction*, edited by William Van O'Connor, U of Minnesota P, 1948, pp. 102–19.

Colley, Linda. *Britons: Forging the Nation 1707–1837*. 1992. Yale UP, 2009.

Cox, Kimberly. "'At Least Shake Hands': Tactile Relations in Charlotte Bronte's *Jane Eyre*." *Victorians: Journal of Literature and Culture*, no. 130, Autumn 2016, pp. 195–215.

Daen, Laurel. "'A Hand for the One-Handed': User Inventors and the Market for Assistive Technologies in Early Nineteenth-Century Britain." *Rethinking Modern Prostheses in Anglo-American Commodity Cultures, 1820–1939*, edited by Claire L. Jones, Manchester UP, 2017, pp. 93–113.

Derenzy, George Webb. *Enchiridion: A Hand for the One-Handed*. Archive.org, 30 June 2008, https://archive.org/details/enchiridionahanooderegoog. Accessed 20 Aug. 2018.

Doyle, Arthur Conan. *The Adventure of the Engineer's Thumb and Other Cases*, Penguin, 2014.

Eliot, George. *The Mill on the Floss*. 1860. Edited by A. S. Byatt, Penguin, 2003.

Hill, Jen. *White Horizon: The Arctic in the Nineteenth-Century British Imagination*. SUNY P, 2009.

Holmes, Martha Stoddard. "Visions of Rochester: Screening Desire and Disability in *Jane Eyre*." *The Madwoman and the Blindman: Jane Eyre, Discourse, Disability*, edited by David Bolt, Julia Miele Rodas, and Elizabeth J. Donaldson, The Ohio State UP, 2012, pp. 150–74.

Hughes, Thomas. *Tom Brown's Schooldays*. 1857. Edited by Andrew Sanders, Oxford UP, 1999.

Mace, Rodney. *Trafalgar Square: Emblem of Empire*. Southampton, The Camelot P, 1976.

McAleavey, Maia. *The Bigamy Plot: Sensation and Convention in the Victorian Novel*. Cambridge UP, 2015.

Millett, Ann. "Sculpting Body Ideals: *Alison Lapper Pregnant* and the Public Display of Disability." *Disability Studies Quarterly*, vol. 28, no. 3, Summer 2008, http://dsq-sds.org/article/view/122/122. Accessed 20 Aug. 2018.

O'Connor, Erin. *Raw Material: Producing Pathology in Victorian Culture*. Duke U P, 2000.

Pickrel, Paul. "*Jane Eyre*: The Apocalypse of the Body." *ELH*, vol. 53, no. 1, 1986, pp. 165–82.

Pike, Judith E. "Disability in Charlotte Brontës's Early Novellas, *Jane Eyre* and *Villette*: The Legacy of Finic's Disabled and Racialized Body." *Brontë Studies*, vol. 43, no. 2, pp. 114–24.

Schaffer, Talia. *Romance's Rival: Familiar Marriage in Victorian Fiction*. Oxford UP, 2016.

Siebers, Tobin. *Disability Theory*. U of Michigan P, 2008.

Southey, Robert. *The Life of Horatio Lord Nelson*. 1813. London: J. M. Dent & Co, 1896.

Sweet, Ryan. "Physical 'Wholeness' and 'Incompleteness' in Victorian Prosthesis Narratives." *Literature and Medicine in the Nineteenth Century*, edited by Andrew Mangham, Cambridge UP, forthcoming.

Tilley, Heather. *Blindness and Writing, from Wordsworth to Gissing*. Cambridge UP, 2018.

Warne, Vanessa. "'So That the Sense of Touch May Supply the Want of Sight': Blind Reading and Nineteenth-Century British Print Culture." *Media, Technology and Literature in the Nineteenth Century: Image, Sound, Touch*, edited by Collette Colligan and Margaret Linley, Ashgate, 2011, pp. 43–64.

White, Colin. "Nelson Apotheosised: The Creation of the Nelson Legend." *Admiral Lord Nelson: Context and Legacy,* edited by David Cannadine, Palgrave Macmillan, 2005, pp. 93–114.

Williams, Kate. "Nelson and Women: Marketing Representations and the Female Consumer." *Admiral Lord Nelson: Context and Legacy,* edited by David Cannadine, Palgrave Macmillan, 2005, pp. 67–89.

Wilson, Kathleen. "Nelson and the People: Manliness, Patriotism and Body Politics." *Admiral Lord Nelson: Context and Legacy,* edited by David Cannadine, Palgrave Macmillan, 2005, pp. 49–66.

Zemka, Sue. "1822, 1845, 1869, 1893, and 1917: Artificial Hands." *BRANCH: Britain, Representation and Nineteenth-Century History,* edited by Dino Franco Felluga, extension of *Romanticism and Victorianism on the Net,* October 2015. Accessed 16 Aug. 2018.

PART II

~

Hands, Plot, and Character

CHAPTER 4

Hands and the Will in *The Woman in White*

PAMELA K. GILBERT

THE ACTION of William Wilkie Collins's *The Woman in White* (1860) opens with one of the most famous scenes of the touching hand in Victorian literature. But there is another hand that takes prominence in the novel, one that doubles the touch of Anne Catherick's hand on the dark road from London in the novel's first installment: what Walter refers to as "the Hand [capital H] that leads men on the dark road to the future."[1] In the idealist tradition of philosophy and in law the hand is theorized as a site of the individual will's actualization of human freedom, thorough interaction both with the material world and other people. Here I'd like to think about this discussion in relation to how Collins connects the characters' individual wills and the plight of women to the metaphorical hand of an overarching political destiny.

The sensation genre focuses on the relation of sensation and action, often in place of the focus on conscious will and character development seen in many realist novels of the period—for example *Woman in White*'s focus on intuition and memory and *Moonstone*'s attention to drugged states. Its plots also tend to focus on the role and reliability of evidence in complex and often legalistic mysteries. And it was condemned precisely for "preaching to the

---

1. *Lady Audley's Secret* also contains "hand of fate" tropes. Peter J. Capuano notes that Robert Audley's repeated sense that "a hand which is stronger than [his] own beckons [him] on" is correct; in his case it is Lady Audley's hand literally, and women's capable hands more generally (221–25). In other words, women are imposing their wills on him—manually.

nerves" and evading the process of measured judgment, even while it appealed to readers to evaluate the evidence it offered up. But the sensation novel also tended to focus on aberrant and extravagant forms of wilful behavior as well as the roles of chance and mystery, as opposed to mid-century realism's cautious celebration of individual agency and its adjustment to social norms. The will and intention were particularly problematic for the materialist tradition of psychology in Britain, which focused on sensation and habit framing human actions, but had a less fully theorized model of intention as it related to larger, non-reflexive actions. But Collins is in fact perennially interested in larger political developments and is particularly so in this novel. In addition to unconscious cerebration, the novel's plot attends to wilful action: willed inheritance, deliberate fraud, marital abuse and the Italian Risorgimento. I would argue that a transpersonal historical agency transects the story of individual agencies and wills in the novel, linking the domestic rebellion of the women of the Glyde household to other revolts of the oppressed. In Collins's portrayal of this will, his treatment of hands leaves behind contemporary materialist psychology and takes up the idealist tradition of portraying the hand and will most common to the period's discussions of politics and law.

By the late eighteenth century, one of the great questions of human intention was how individual wills intersected with larger organizations, such as the state. Whereas pre-Revolutionary French thinkers posited that the state was simply an aggregate of individual wills, idealist thinkers followed Aristotle in tending to give the state its own ontological status as the embodiment or materialization of a larger idea or intention. Aristotle posits that man is a political animal given speech in order "to set forth the expedient and inexpedient, and therefore likewise the just and the unjust. . . . the association of living beings who have this sense makes a family and a state" (*Politica* 1252b). The state, however, exists prior to the family or individual, "since the whole is of necessity prior to the part; for example, if the whole body be destroyed, there will be no foot or hand, except in an equivocal sense, as we might speak of a stone hand; for when destroyed the hand will be no better than that." Aristotle conceives of the state as a complete body, which must be "a creation of nature and prior to the individual" because individuals cannot live without society (1253a). The reference to a "stone hand" is an apt metaphor: since the hand is the manifestation of the soul in the world, a stone hand is not a hand at all, as it has no agency. In his work on justice, property and the state, *The Philosophy of Right* (1820), Hegel reframes Aristotle's observation and takes it a step further:

> The state is real. Its reality consists in its realizing the interest of the whole in particular ends. . . . In so far as this unity is absent, the thing is unreal-

ized.... A bad state is one which merely exists. A sick body also exists, but it has no true reality. § A hand, which is cut off, still looks like a hand and exists, though it is not real. True reality is necessity. What is real is in itself necessary. (*Philosophy of Right* § 270,n, addition, 152)

Hegel takes Aristotle's stone hand and substitutes a severed hand, a much more violent image. In part he does so because he has an approach to the Idea of the state which sees it as an organic body that expresses Spirit. But he is also here thinking, as he often does in this particular text, of the violent fragmentation of the French state and the bodies within it.

A persistent issue in the period is the status of the state as a representation of will. Whereas Locke posited individual will as supreme, and Rousseau based his idea of a general will of the state on a kind of aggregation of individual wills, idealists insisted that the state was a kind of idea prior to and beyond the consciousness of any individual. Hegel praises Rousseau's recognition of the will as the principle of the state (§ 258,n, 133), but he insists that the "universal will" is not a rational or conscious element: he determines that this error resulted in the Terror of the French Revolution: "when these abstractions attained to power, there was enacted the most tremendous spectacle which the human race has ever witnessed. All the usages and institutions of a great state were swept away. It was then proposed to begin over again, starting from the thought, and.... To will only what was judged to be rational. But as the undertaking was begun with abstractions void of all ideas, it ended in scenes of tragic cruelty and horror" (*Philosophy of Right* § 258,n, 134). But Hegel also takes the position that the historical will causes states to evolve toward more perfect justice and freedom, and that states that fail in these aims are overthrown. The French state fell because it no longer embodied justice, its words and laws became separated from meaning and will. The great British jurist William Blackstone also mentions this conflict and explicitly refuses to take a position about the state's priority (Book 1, vol. 1, 48), but he is clear that the state has evolved to dispense justice, and that it does so by a mediation of the wills of individuals, which he suggests is not and cannot always be conscious.

Hegel's discussion of property's relation to individual freedom is often included in histories of liberal property law, in part because it provides a counterpart to traditional British liberal theories thought not to logically disallow certain social formations such as slavery (despite the general antislavery positions of most thinkers who formed them). Here I would like to focus on the exercise of freedom through property, and particularly the willed physical touch in taking control of an object or person. In *The Philosophy of Right*, principally concerned with justice and the ethical state, Hegel was in conversation with the British thinkers of his own day and earlier such as Hobbes and Locke (the most important liberal theorist on property in the British tradition, who believed life, liberty and property were related natural rights); he also read Blackstone and Parliamentary Reports on the poor Laws as well as the Scottish Common Sense thinkers (Hegel, *Philosophy of Right,* see notes of T. M. Knox, translator).[2] Hegel takes a similar position to Locke's on slavery (it is basically a state of war, if it is absolute and open-ended rather than contractual and limited) and on the person (every man has a property in his own person). But where Locke locates the person's right to property in the person's labor, Hegel locates it in the person's human nature, which is to exercise freedom in the world of objects—a more universal claim. Hegel extends this consideration in relation to the body specifically, and at length: "To grasp a thing physically is the most complete [mode of taking possession], because then I am directly present in this possession, and therefore my will is recognisable in it. . . . It is with my hand that I manage to take possession of a thing . . . What I hold in my hand—that magnificent tool which no animal possesses—can itself be a means to gripping something else. . . . . At this point positive law must enact its statutes since nothing further on this topic can be deduced from the concept" (*Philosophy of Right,* § 54–55, 12). Beyond the range of immediate manual touch is the realm of the legal property boundary—or of war.

The conversation about property and persons continues in the mid-century in Victorian Britain. John Stuart Mill poses this discussion in relation to property and human freedom in his 1859 *On Liberty* and his later work on the status of women. Of course, Marx is in the same period extending Hegel's discussion of the alienation of the worker to an analysis of industrial capitalism.[3] This debate about a collective or ideal will not fully vested in the consciousness of individuals, which underlies the impulse of history toward a just state, is also suggestive for Collins's treatment of the political back story

---

2. Paul Thomas points out that Hegel's discussion of property was a critique of Locke's Second Treatise (31), which addresses the basics of a labor theory of property. Like Hegel, Locke sees suicide and slavery as unlawful; unlike Hegel, who believes that slavery is more natural to primitive states of society, Locke suggests that earlier states of society never had true slavery, but conditions closer to indentures.

3. Mill read Hegel carefully, disliked him intensely and did not cite him as an influence, but the British tradition from Locke did not alone provide the definition of human freedom that is essential to Millsian liberalism. Nor did Utilitarianism necessarily disallow slavery, though Bentham deplored it. In fact, Mill's comments on slavery in *On Liberty* (1859) are remarkably close to the Hegelian view of an inalienable right to human freedom. Marx and Engels' *Communist Manifesto* (1847) was the first serious critique of private property in modern times, and Mill takes up Marx's thought (positively, for the most part) as well in his response. Mill's *Subjection of Women* (1859) relies on extended comparison of slavery and the situation of women.

of *Woman in White*—which was being published in *All the Year Round* side by side with Dickens's historical epic on the French Revolution, *A Tale of Two Cities,* and simultaneously with coverage of the Italian resistance to Austria.

Collins was very interested in legal rights, intention and the control of property, a theme that runs throughout his novels. In *Woman in White,* Collins links his consideration of property rights and human freedom with an exploration of intention. As several critics have noted, Collins's representation of individuals was informed by the psychological science of the day. Collins explored Alexander Bain's theories of association, as well as those of medical experts, having repeated recourse to it in several novels, including *Armadale* and *The Woman in White.* Vanessa Ryan has followed critics such as Jill Matus and Athena Vrettos in discussing Collins's use of Bain; Ryan sees Collins as referring Hartright's often non-logical insights to associationist ideas of "unconscious cerebration" (38). Her reading is persuasive in accounting for some of Hartright's intuition, but does not attempt to connect the more aleatory elements of the story to the plot—a multilevel structure encompassing the domestic story of the women and Hartright, and the oblique historical and political narrative of which Fosco is a part. For example, it is Hartright's association of the physical sensation of being touched by Anne that is revived when he first realizes that Laura resembles Anne Catherick's appearance, and that sets off the narrative's ambiguous shifting between the ineffective use of legal evidence and the effective use of the evidence of the senses. Fosco, the chief example of will that splits inner truth from outer expression on the surface of the body, is also the worst villain of the novel. As Ryan writes, "Fosco presents a horrifying vision of the materialist view of man" (45). He believes, "Mind, they say, rules the world. But what rules the mind? The body . . . lies at the mercy of the most omnipotent of all potentates—the Chemist. Give me—Fosco—chemistry; . . . and the morning draught of Alexander the Great shall make Alexander run for his life at the first sight of the enemy the same afternoon" (617). Character, consciousness, and even intention do not ultimately determine actions in this view; corporeal feeling—at a preconscious level, does. Bain, like Hume before him, largely denied the validity of free will and advanced a fully materialist physiological theory of mind and human action.[4] For Fosco, the way to exercise some freedom of intention is to be aware of how the embodied mind works and manipulate it in others.

---

4. Bain believed that will began in the body, and that muscular reflexes were a form of will, independent of or prior to consciousness. He dismissed the metaphysical side of the question with characteristic ire: "These various questions respecting the Will, if stripped of unsuitable phraseology, are not very difficult questions. They are about as easy to comprehend as the air-pump, the law of refraction of light, or the atomic theory of chemistry" (175).

However, Collins is also acutely interested in human free will and the possibility of transcending heredity or "fate" (as one sees, for example, in the ending of *Armadale*). His hero, Hartright, is an idealist; he observes that humans are not continuous with material creation, "The grandest mountain . . . is appointed to annihilation. The smallest human interest that the pure heart can feel is appointed to immortality" (53–54). Collins uses the hand as an instrument of will consistently throughout *Woman in White,* probably in part because of the general interest in the individual hand in the period as a uniquely human tool of the human will, and also as a privileged instrument in legal definitions of will. But he also links a larger, transpersonal intention to the image of a metaphorical or spiritual hand. The touching hand is used in the novel, then, not only to provide physical sensations and trigger the formation of associations, but to express intention.

Woman in White famously launches its complex plot with the thrilling touch of Anne Catherick's hand on Walter Hartright, "in one moment, every drop of blood in my body was brought to a stop by the touch of a hand laid lightly and suddenly on my shoulder from behind me" (20). Anne says she was afraid and alone, and thus, "I was obliged to steal after you, and touch you" (22). Walter wonders privately why she didn't just call out, instead of touching him, as she asks for his help getting a fly to London, adding "if you will only promise not to interfere with me, and to let me leave you, when and how I please . . . I want nothing else—will you promise?" (22). He wonders "What could I do? Here was a stranger utterly and helplessly at my mercy—and that stranger a forlorn woman. . . . no earthly right existed on my part to give me a power of control over her, even if I had known how to exercise it" (22–23). As he debates his options, she makes an incantatory third request and repeats her touch,

> As she repeated the words for the third time, she came close to me and laid her hand, with a sudden gentle stealthiness, on my bosom—a thin hand; a cold hand (when I removed it with mine) even on that sultry night. Remember that I was young; remember that the hand which touched me was a woman's.
> "Will you promise?" (23)

And of course, he does.

Although much has been made of the sensational eroticism of this touch, this scene both represents the imposition of her will upon Hartright, and suggests that her own will has been under constraint. He is bound by honor to keep his promise to a woman, and as a "young" gentleman, not able to think quickly enough to avoid so binding himself; her touch is not one of threat, but still one that invokes compulsion. Poor Anne Catherick's utmost exercise of will over another is to exact a promise for her own will not to be interfered with. Hartright is troubled in part because her query assumes that he may seize control of her, although he himself notes that "no earthly right existed . . . to give me a power of control over her" (23). One might think that would settle the matter—she is only asking for directions and a kind of negative liberty (that a stranger not interfere with her). But the query highlights the strangeness of a woman alone who is not a prostitute moving around outside at night. It begins the narrative by suggesting that women are in fact, as perhaps in law, unfree.

Once she is on her way, he finds that an asylum keeper is seeking her, and wonders: "What had I done? Assisted the victim of the most horrible of all false imprisonments to escape; or cast loose on the wide world of London an unfortunate creature, whose actions it was . . . every man's duty, mercifully to control?" (28–29). Criminals, idiots, minors and the mad: these are the traditional categories of persons under guardianship—with the addition of certain classes of unmarried women. Hartright continues to wonder long after, "Had she been traced and captured by the men in the chaise? Or was she still capable of controlling her own actions . . . ?" It is a peculiar locution—not "is she free" or "did she reach London," but "is she capable of controlling her own actions?" (29). This phrasing recalls Blackstone's definition of "capability" (Book 1, vol. 1, 19), of being held responsible in criminal law: the person must join their own will to a criminal action; moreover, the person must be in control of his actions, his will constrained neither by the actions of others nor by his own mental incapacity, defined as "the want or defect of will" (Book 1, vol. 1, 20).[5] The passage poses the question of what a man's rights and obligations

---

5. One might think of Walter's first impression of Laura: "Mingling with the vivid impression produced by the charm of her fair face and head, her sweet expression, and her winning simplicity of manner, was another impression, which, in a shadowy way, suggested to me the idea of something wanting. . . . Something wanting, something wanting—and where it was, and what it was, I could not say" (50–51). Later, he recognizes her likeness to Anne, and realizes, "That 'something wanting' was my own recognition of the ominous likeness between the fugitive from the asylum and my pupil at Limmeridge House" (57). He refers at one point to his own lack of recognition as the fault, but it seems that he recognizes "something wanting" in Anne and Laura both: a defect of will, referring in Anne's case to her status as "idiot," itself a contested term throughout the novel (55 and passim), and perhaps in Laura an effect of heredity: she is Anne's half-sister, niece of a "nervous" Frederick Fairlie (341 and passim) who dies of paralysis, and daughter of the womanizer Philip Fairlie. Blackstone *Commentaries* Book 4, vol. 2, Chapter 2, "Of the Persons Capable of Committing Crimes," defines a responsible action as an act joined to will: "ALL the several pleas and excuses, which protect the committer of a forbidden act from the punishment which is otherwise annexed thereto, may be reduced to this single consideration, the want or defect of will. . . . there must be both a will

are in relation to limiting the freedom of another who might be under certain legal disabilities: a woman, a minor, a slave, an "eccentric" or a madwoman.

Touch and its knowledge allow for the development of individual intention and action. Hartright's story is one of the development of his capacity to enact his will. He discovers his love for Laura through touch: "Not a day passed, in that dangerous intimacy of teacher and pupil, in which my hand was not close to Miss Fairlie's . . . I saw her, heard her, and touched her (when we shook hands at night and morning) as I had never seen, heard, and touched any other woman" (63–64). When Marian grasps his hand, and tells him as kindly as she is able that Laura is engaged already, that he must withdraw his will from that contact, his hand is symbolically amputated: "My arm lost all sensation of the hand that grasped it. . . . The pang passed, and nothing but the dull numbing pain of it remained. I felt Miss Halcombe's hand again, tightening its hold. . . . Her large black eyes were rooted on me, watching the white change on my face, which I felt, and which she saw" (71). When Hartright returns from South America, he is first able to exert his own will again in his own right, just as Marian loses hers. When she falls ill, she loses the capacity to unite her will with suitable action: her handwriting in the diary becomes unintelligible and she becomes unconscious—whereupon Fosco's handwriting suddenly takes the place of hers on the page. Marian's loss of consciousness and will in illness transfers agency (and narrative voice) from Marian through Fosco to Hartright, who returns from "the stern school of extremity" in which "my will had learnt to be strong, my heart to be resolute" (415). It is also through touch that Walter recognizes Laura's returning sanity after her rescue: "Our hands began to tremble again when they met" (570–71). When Walter is ready to confront Fosco, he approaches Marian: "In the days of her prosperity, Marian, I was only the teacher who guided her [Laura's] hand—I ask for it, in her adversity, as the hand of my wife!" (575). Upon preparing to approach Fosco, he takes leave of Laura: "my resolution for a moment faltered again, . . . when I saw her hand resting open on the coverlid, as if it was waiting unconsciously for mine. . . . I only touched her hand and her cheek with my lips at parting" (597). He must withhold his hand from Laura and reserve his will for the coming conflict. When he and Fosco face off, the intensity of the conflict is expressed in an identification of their hands: "his left hand slowly opened the table-drawer, and softly slipped into it. . . . My life hung by a thread, and I knew it. At that final moment I thought with *his* mind, I felt with *his* fingers—I was as certain as if I had seen it of what he kept hid-

---

and an act" (20–21). Several things may prevent a person's will from joining an act, including lack of understanding, and: "3. Where the action is constrained by some outward force and violence" (Book 4, vol. 2, Chapter 2, 21).

den from me in the drawer" (601). Having undergone his educative struggle, Hartright is able to fully read Fosco's intentions and oppose Fosco effectively: "The expression of his face changed on the instant, and his hand came out of the drawer empty. . . . His left hand trembled audibly" (603).

Women in the novel use their hands to express constraint. Like Anne, her double, Laura often wrings her hands, and hides her face behind them; Laura asserts a negative will in refusing to sign the document that would give Percival the money he wants, though she rarely raises a hand to advance her own interest. The imposition of Fosco's will upon the former feminist firebrand Madame Fosco means that her will is subordinated to his: her "dry white hands . . . [are] incessantly engaged, either in monotonous embroidery work or in rolling up endless cigarettes for the Count's own particular smoking" (218–19). Anne is the most active character besides Marian; frightened as she is, her trauma itself gives her unusual strength to act. When Walter mentions Percy,

> Her face, at all ordinary times so touching to look at, in its nervous sensitiveness, . . . became suddenly darkened by an expression of maniacally intense hatred and fear. . . . She caught up the cloth that had fallen at her side, as if it had been a living creature that she could kill, and crushed it in both her hands with such convulsive strength, that the few drops of moisture left in it trickled down on the stone beneath her. (104)

But this expression of strength exhausts her and she pleads with Walter not to speak of Percy again: "I shall lose myself if you talk of that" (104). Again, the formulation is suggestive: she does not speak of her temper or her mind, but of losing *herself*. Walter's last memory of Anne is "of her poor helpless hands beating on the tombstone" of Mrs. Fairlie (569). Women's hands are generally unable to enact their will positively in the novel, though Anne certainly tries.

The well-discussed exception, of course, is Marian—at least for the first part of the novel. Marian's hands are described as "rather large, but beautifully formed" (32). Nonetheless the agency implied by those large hands is tamed over the course of the novel. Despite her equivocal denigration of her hands as masculine early in the narrative—"My hands always were, and always will be, as awkward as a man's" (233)—they are later feminized once the narrative is transferred to the control of Hartright. "What a woman's hands ARE fit for," she said, "early and late, these hands of mine shall do," she avows to Walter, once they set out to win Laura's name back for her—but to underscore her feminine weakness, Hartright observes, "They trembled as she held them out. The wasted arms told their sad story of the past" (441).

Fosco's indecent penetration of Marian's (handwritten) diary (with his own handwriting) has often been noted, but the combat most distressing to Marian is more directly hand-to-hand. She feels sullied by the need to touch him socially, "I was . . . woman enough . . . to feel as if my hand was tainted by resting on his arm" (275), and feels as if his lips on her hand is a much more significant intimacy: "he took my hand—oh, how I despise myself! . . . and put it to his poisonous lips. Never did I know all my horror of him till then. That innocent familiarity turned my blood as if it had been the vilest insult that a man could offer me" (311). When Fosco accosts her again in London, her "hands tingled to strike him, as if I had been a man! I only kept them quiet by tearing his card to pieces under my shawl" (559). Fosco, who treats women like children or beasts—though human, they do not have a right to freedom—, violates Marian's will with a touch of his hand, as he does her diary with his handwriting. She is made powerless to use her hands in the service of her will, whereas Fosco warns her to tell Hartright he "has a man of brains to deal with, a man who snaps his big fingers at the laws and conventions of society" (561). When he leaves her, "He turned at the corner of the street, and waved his hand, and then struck it theatrically on his breast" (562), indicating both his romantic admiration for her and the unity of those brains with his actions and inner will, his hand and his heart.

As this suggests, the male villains of the novel are characterized by their aggressive hands. In fact, Dickens objected to the overreliance on hands in the novel, wondering in relation to Percy "whether any man ever showed uneasiness by hand or foot without being forced by nature to show it in his face too?" (*Letters* 97). Percy Glyde is always using his hands brutally, or thrusting them in his pockets to avoid doing so. Count Fosco's large white hands are constantly in use, whether stroking his mice (held in his palm) or making theatrical gestures. They are able to impose his will with a mere touch: "This fat, indolent, elderly man, . . . put his hand on the head of a chained bloodhound—a beast so savage that the very groom who feeds him keeps out of his reach. . . . he laid his plump, yellow-white fingers, . . . upon the formidable brute's head, and looked him straight in the eyes" (225)—and the dog is vanquished. He controls his hitherto uncontrollable wife by "never . . . [accepting] provocation at a woman's hands. It holds with animals, it holds with children, and it holds with women, who are nothing but children grown up" (330). He decries violence as a tool of the savage and the lower orders; the surest thing is not to blindly use one's hands as bludgeons, but to control them and one's will together, whereas like the brutal dog, Percy has a tendency to fly out. Though Percy is furious when he discovers Mrs. Catherick has been to the house, "the Count's persuasive hand was laid on his shoulder, and the Count's mellifluous voice interposed to quiet him" (242). And again, when Percy tries to bully Laura into signing her money away, "The Count took one of his hands out of his belt and laid it on Sir Percival's shoulder. . . . Sir Percival turned on him speechless with passion. The Count's firm hand slowly tightened its grasp on his shoulder" (248), and Percy complies "with the sullen submission of a tamed animal" (249). Privately, Fosco calms Percy by reminding him that both his wife and Marian are "under his thumb" (339). He tells Percy that he could "draw your secret out of you as easily as I draw my finger out of the palm of my hand" but he does not do it out of "self-control" (336). In all of these many examples, which become more meaningful by the force of accumulation, the hand explicitly represents and enforces the will of the character over others; Percy's is the petty violence of the domestic abuser, whereas Fosco is an example of the monstrous agency of the sensation villain who operates outside the parameters of social acceptability to larger ends.

The plight of the abused woman is central to the social-problem aspect of Collins's novel, that is, his realist approach to a typical, rather than an exceptional tale. Women lack freedom of will. In addition to Laura's lack of control over her own property and body, Anne offers a dramatic example of the power any man exercises over women, as we saw in her initial encounter with Hartright, and in her imprisonment in an asylum. Anne's status as "mad" or "idiotic" is always uncertain; Collins emphasizes that the other characters cannot decide if she is truly an "idiot"—for example, the doctor who examines her as a child thinks she will "grow out of it" (58). There is no reason to confine her except Percy's fear of disclosure. The two problems, however, are linked. Women's lack of control over property includes the lack of control over her own body. In *On Liberty*, published in the same year as the novel's serialization began, Mill defines human freedom to defy social norms in terms of property, perhaps in part because of the contemporary scandals of false commitment to asylums to which Collins is also responding. "The man, and still more the woman, who can be accused either of doing 'what nobody does,' or of not doing 'what everybody does,'" risks "a commission *de lunatico*, and of having their property taken from them" (115). He continues the thought in a footnote: "There is something both contemptible and frightful in the sort of evidence on which, of late years, any person can be judicially declared unfit for the management of his affairs; and after his death, his disposal of his property can be set aside" (115).

The liberal idealist tradition—including Locke and Hegel—has defined liberty persistently and some would argue disproportionately in terms of property. Mill here thinks of liberty in relationship to controlling and willing property. His discussion rather surprisingly elides the physical constraint of the person in favor of this discussion in part, perhaps, because (as Locke would say) the person of the person is itself the primary example of the property the person controls; physical constraint is implied by the alienation of property generally. Mill here seems to refer also to the current debate on that topic most beloved of sensation novelists and particularly germane to Collins's novel, the ease of securing an inconvenient person's (especially a woman's) commitment to a madhouse. (Lady Lytton's forcible internment in 1858 by her husband was famously the inspiration for several sensation novelists' treatment of the topic.) *Woman in White* is particularly interested in the rights of women to freedom and control of their bodies and property in marriage, and this plot is developed through Laura's status as an heiress, as well as Anne's commitment to an asylum.[6] His interest in property relates to questions of personhood and the state, freedom and justice, which were key debates in law (through Blackstone) as well as philosophy. Freedom for women in the novel is explicitly linked to the control of property (as many scholars have discussed), and marriage to a kind of enslavement that treats women as animals, without a human right to freedom vested in their own bodies and property. As Marian says, men "take us body and soul to themselves, and fasten our helpless lives to theirs as they chain up a dog to his kennel."

The first intimation that Percy will not be a good husband for Anne is his categorical refusal to allow her any ability to make a will regarding her own property: her lawyer proposes that her inheritance "was to be settled so as to give the income to the lady for her life—afterwards to Sir Percival for his life—and the principal to the children of the marriage. In default of issue, the principal was to be disposed of as the lady might by her will direct, for which purpose I reserved to her the right of making a will" (152). He blocks this reasonable request. And as Fosco does to Marian, Percy tries to force Laura to be false to herself, to falsify her own will: Laura's great assertion in the novel is in the negative; she refuses to be constrained to let Percival use her hands to enact his own will, because in refusing to explain what he wants he refuses to "treat me as a responsible being" (250). What she refuses to do is to combine voice, handwriting, and manual touch in a performative act supposedly expressing her own will. As explained by Percy's lawyer: "Lady Glyde is to sign her name in the presence of a witness—or of two witnesses, if you wish to be

---

6. Collins's novel is set in a time of discussion around the laws relating to married women's property rights (Fiorato 31), and it is of course very concerned with the critique of women's legal full personhood in relation to property (as many scholars have discussed—see Shanley, Fiorato and Wynne). This is *a priori* a question about the relation of individuals and families to the state. Collins is also interested, and particularly at the time of writing *Woman in White*, as Sundeep Bisla has argued, in questions of intellectual property, and how the iteration of language can transform intellectual property into something separate from its original.

particularly careful—and is then to put her finger on the seal and say, 'I deliver this as my act and deed'" (228). The legal formula emphasizes not only the author and action (I deliver, my act, my deed) but the intention necessary to complete a contract and convey property (a different use of the term "deed"). Collins shows us how easily a woman's intention can be subverted by "outward force and violence," as Blackstone suggests, while freedom for women in the novel is expressed through the control of property.

Percy, the petty domestic villain, is interested in securing personal property—his estate, Laura's money. But the sensational villain's outsized will is connected to the larger aims of history. The Count, operating in the service of the Austrian empire, is anti-democratic and anti-Italian independence; according to a memoir by his loyal wife, "His life was one long assertion of the rights of the aristocracy and the sacred principles of Order, and he died a martyr to his cause" (641)—at the hands of the nationalist Italian "Brotherhood." His views on women and animals align them with those of the lower orders, with what Pesca calls in his explanation of the Brotherhood an "enslaved nation" (589–90). Pesca bases his defense of the right to kill someone like the Count on a rhetoric much like Hegel's or Mill's:

> So long as a man's life is useful, or even harmless only, he has the right to enjoy it. But, if his life inflicts injury on the well-being of his fellow-men, from that moment he forfeits the right, and it is not only no crime, but a positive merit, to deprive him of it. . . . It is not for you to say—you Englishmen, who have conquered your freedom so long ago, that you have conveniently forgotten what blood you shed, . . . [to what] the worst of all exasperations may . . . carry the maddened men of an enslaved nation. (589)

The aggressor forfeits his life, property and freedom because he has failed to recognize the freedom of others' wills.

Outsized and powerful as the Count's will is, hands do not only enact individual will in the novel; there is another narrative of the influence of hands that appeals to Collins's interest in a transpersonal idea of fate or justice. This less realist narrative doubles that of Anne Catherick's hand on the dark road from London in the first installment of the novel: what Walter refers to as "the Hand . . . that leads men on the dark road to the future" (422). Hartright's transformation into the hero of his (and the women's) story takes place through a series of individuals' "hands" that do not intend what they in fact accomplish—such as Pesca's, who gets him the position as drawing master at Limmeridge and exults, "It is my auspicious hand that has given the first push to your fortune in the world" (18). Hartright goes to Central America in a typical quest to develop his manly qualities; this all happens offstage, though Marian helpfully dreams a quick summary of the three dangers through which he passes (pestilence, murderous natives, shipwreck). Marian's dream suggests that Hartright's survival is fated: all the dangers he alone escapes (three times, mirroring Anne's three requests on the dark road to London) "are steps of my journey, and take me nearer and nearer to the End" (278). This rhetoric of fatedness and the significance of dreams is the seemingly supernatural, gothic element that is partly the reason for the novel's classification as sensational.

The narrative of Italian independence never penetrates too deeply into the domestic story of Marian's rescue and Walter's pursuit of Laura. But it suggests once again the ways in which individual bodies, property and wills (in both senses) are brought insensibly into a larger narrative of history. Albert Pionke points out both that England's position on Italy was ideologically "conflicted" (104)—having just put down a threat to their own empire in India, supporting the breakup of the Austrian empire was problematic (101); on the other hand, the rhetoric of the Carbonari looked like that of the French Revolution, or the Fenians (107). Moreover, a unified Italy was both emotionally and militarily attractive as a buffer to French Power (101-4).[7] Collins was publishing *Woman in White* in *All the Year Round*, which was simultaneously featuring several articles sympathetic to unification (110-11). It appeared side by side with installments of Dickens's novel of the French Revolution; it also appeared with several journalistic pieces sympathetic to the Italian struggle with the Austrians, as well as articles on the Haitian revolution and on slavery in Turkey.

As is so often the case throughout the period in exploring questions of a larger, transpersonal will, Collins has recourse to considerations of revolution. Collins was particularly interested in the French Revolution, as William Baker shows in the survey of Collins's library, (p55); he wrote about it often, and sympathetically.[8] In "The Poisoned Meal" (first published in 1856), Collins observes that those who think of the Revolution only in terms of the Terror should perhaps "look a little further back—... and then to consider whether there was not a reason and a necessity ... for the French Revolution. ... the social good which it indisputably effected remains to this day" (171). Collins's defeat of Fosco at the "hands" of fate suggests his identification of history as

---

7. Others have also explored the connections between the Risorgimento and Collins, including Shifra Hochsburg, who makes a persuasive case for the direct influence of Ugo Foscolo's *Last Letters of Jacopo Ortis* on the plot of the novel as well as the name of its chief villain. Foscolo was a pro-unification activist.

8. For example, the novella *Sister Rose* (1855), which Dickens admired. (See Henry Milley, who attributes to it part of the inspiration for *Tale of Two Cities*).

tending to support the side of the oppressed; Fosco's will may do a great deal of damage, but ultimately, his reactionary tendencies are defeated, not primarily by the deliberate action of his opponents, but by chance.

The story's treatment of individual intention links to the international political thriller that lurks in the background of the domestic story of the women's oppression. When Hartright returns to England, the metaphorical (and capitalized) Hand appears, "From thousands on thousands of miles away . . . through peril of death thrice renewed, and thrice escaped, the Hand that leads men on the dark road to the future had led me to meet that time" (422). This hand suggests the agency of a distinctly non-individual will: destiny, fate, God? Hartright, at least, believes the latter: when Marian and Laura happen to turn and see him at the tombstone, fortuitously reuniting them, he says, "I believe in my soul that the Hand of God was pointing their way back to them" (439). Percival's death in the Church, he believes, is "ruled" by the "Visitation of God" (532). But I don't think we should see Walter's pious belief that God is intervening in the individual lives of the characters close to him as Collins's last word on the matter. Walter is in many ways one of Collins's typical upright, decent and not overly bright English heroes, whose view is narrowly concerned with domestic issues—here Laura and Marian. But Collins's vision of justice is more capacious and he is also profoundly interested in revolutions and the nature of states in ways his individual characters are generally not.[9] Here he links the story of the oppressed women to the story of an oppressed nation.

The Count has the most clearly developed will, and mostly is able to act in accordance with it. But he cannot escape his variance with what Collins sees as the larger will of history, which sometimes subordinates the will of individuals to enact its own. Ultimately, it is not through Hartright's deliberate action, but from the original push of Pesca's "auspicious" hand and the touch of Anne Catherick's tremulous one that Hartright's marriage results, as well as the death of the Count, by "hands that could never be discovered" (595): or as it says elsewhere, "The hand that struck him was never traced" (641). The untraceable hands of the Brotherhood cut an inscription—a T for traitor—effacing the original inscription on his arm, both a testimonial and a performative reinscription of his identity at the hands of an "enslaved nation," who herein ironically and angrily reclaim his body as lost property, before discarding it. The corpse is dumped in the Seine, from which it is fished out and displayed as a John Doe in the Paris morgue.

---

9. The year prior, Collins had published *Antonina*, set in fifth-century Italy, which treated the defeat of Rome by the Goths. He attributes Rome's weakness in part to Roman practices of enslavement.

There he lay, *unowned,* [my emphasis] unknown, exposed to the flippant curiosity of a French mob! . . . Hushed in the sublime repose of death, the broad, firm, massive face and head fronted us so grandly that the chattering Frenchwomen about me lifted their hands in admiration, and cried in shrill chorus, "Ah, what a handsome man!" The wound that had killed him had been struck with a knife or dagger exactly over his heart. No other traces of violence appeared about the body except on the left arm, and there, exactly in the place where I had seen the brand on Pesca's arm, were two deep cuts in the shape of the letter T, which entirely obliterated the mark of the Brotherhood. (640)

A fit ending for an aristocratic betrayer of Revolutions and opposer of liberal models of human freedom, emphasized ironically by his widow's residence "in the strictest retirement at Versailles" (641). The body, divested of its will, is not only (purposefully) unknown, but (the auditory pun emphasizing the connection) unowned, alienated and discarded. He who treated the wills and bodies of others as property is violently alienated from his own. The individual hands that could never be traced are connected to the larger force of historical will and national history (in the mid-century, of Italian nationalism) beyond the materialist construction in which Fosco trusted so resolutely. In this way the smaller domestic story of women regaining their freedom and property (the story ends with the presentation of Laura's son as the Heir of Limmeridge) is connected to the larger struggle of nations to fulfill their will to self-determination. Power is returned to the women of the family; the presentation of Laura's son as "the Heir of Limmeridge" returns her property through her own feminine labor of reproduction. (Significantly, Walter is away when she retakes possession.) The novel ends with Walter yielding his will again to theirs, and Marian's reinstatement as the author of her own narrative: "The pen falters in my hand. . . . let Marian end our Story."

WORKS CITED

Aristotle. *Politica. The Works of Aristotle*, vol. 10, edited by William David Ross and John Alexander Smith, translated by Benjamin Jowett, Clarendon P, 1921.

Bain, Alexander. "Common Errors on the Mind." *Fortnightly Review*, vol. 4, pp. 160–75.

Baker, William. *Wilkie Collins's Library: A Reconstruction.* Greenwood P, 2002.

Bisla, Sundeep. *Wilkie Collins and Copyright: Artistic Ownership in the Age of a Borderless Word.* The Ohio State UP, 2013.

Blackstone, Sir William. *Commentaries on the Laws of England in Four Books. Notes Selected from the Editions of Archibold, Christian, Coleridge, Chitty, Stewart, Kerr, and Others, Barron Field's*

Analysis, and Additional Notes, and a Life of the Author by George Sharswood. In Two Volumes. Philadelphia, J. B. Lippincott, 1893.

Capuano, Peter J. *Changing Hands: Industry, Evolution, and the Reconfiguration of the Victorian Body.* U of Michigan P, 2015.

Collins, W. Wilkie. "The Poisoned Meal" *My Miscellanies*, vol II. Sampson Low, Son & Co., 1863.

———. *The Woman in White*. With Chronology by Jenny Bourne Taylor and Introduction by John Sutherland, Oxford UP, 1996.

Dickens, Charles. *Letters of Charles Dickens to Wilkie Collins, 1851–1870, Selected by Miss Georgina Hogarth.* London, Osgood, M'Ilvaine, 1892.

———. *Tale of Two Cities.* Edited with an introduction and notes by Andrew Sanders, Oxford UP, 1998.

Fiorato, Sidia. "Women, Property and Identity in Victorian Legal Culture: Wilkie Collins's *The Woman in White*." *Pólemos*, vol. 8, no. 1, 2014, 25–50. Accessed 17 Aug. 2018, doi:10.1515/pol-2014-0003.

Hegel, Georg W. F. *Elements of the Philosophy of Right.* Translated by S. W. Dyde, London, G. Bell, 1896. *Marxists.org*, n.d. Accessed 30 Apr. 2013.

———. *Elements of the Philosophy of Right.* Translated by T. Knox. Clarendon P, 1942.

Hochsburg, Shifra. "Ugo Foscolo's 'Last Letters of Jacopo Ortis' and Wilkie Collins's 'The Woman in White': A Case for Possible Influence." *Wilkie Collins Journal*, vol. 11, 2012, https://wilkiecollinssociety.org/ugo-foscolos-last-letters-of-jacopo-ortis-and-wilkie-collinss-the-woman-in-white-a-case-for-possible-influence/. Accessed 16 Aug. 2018.

Locke, John. *The Works of John Locke Esq., Volume II.* London, The Black Swan, 1714. Google Books. Acccessed 25 Apr. 2013.

Matus, Jill L. *Shock, Memory and the Unconscious in Victorian Fiction.* Cambridge UP, 2009.

Mill, John Stuart. *On Liberty.* Edited by Edward Alexander, Peterborough, Ont., Broadview P, 1999.

Milley, Henry J. W. "Wilkie Collins and *A Tale of Two Cities*." *The Modern Language Review*, vol. 34, no. 4, Oct. 1939, pp. 525–34.

Pionke, Albert. *Plots of Opportunity: Representing Conspiracy in Victorian England.* The Ohio State UP, 2004.

Ryan, Vanessa. *Thinking Without Thinking in the Victorian Novel.* Johns Hopkins UP, 2012.

Shanley, Mary Lydon. *Feminism, Marriage, and the Law in Victorian England.* Princeton UP, 1989.

Vrettos, Athena. "Defining Habits: Dickens and the Psychology of Repetition." *Victorian Studies*, vol. 42, 1999/2000, pp. 399–426.

Wynne, Deborah. *The Sensation Novel and the Victorian Family Magazine.* Palgrave Macmillan, 2001.

CHAPTER 5

Hands at a Séance

Manual Evidence in Victorian Spiritualism and the Ghost Story

AVIVA BRIEFEL

FROM THE TIME it exploded on the British scene in the early 1850s, the spiritualist movement sought increasingly tangible ways of "materializing faith" (Tromp, "Eating" 288). The initial phase of spirit-rapping, in which supernatural forces animated furniture, gave way to verbal communication through the intervention of the planchette; to the "apport" séance, in which spirits brought material objects, such as fruits and flowers, to sitters; to the visual proof of spirit photography; to the materialization of complete spirit forms in the 1870s, most famously under the mediumship of Katie King.[1] With each new manifestation, spiritualists sought verification of an afterlife and of their ability to establish contact with it. Despite their insistence on the immateriality of ghosts, they measured the value of spectral evidence based on the material proof it offered. As Karl Bell writes, "Given the ethereal nature of spirits Victorian spiritualism made a somewhat paradoxical appeal to a contemporary emphasis on empirical evidence. To bolster their credibility spirits were requested to provide tangible proof of their existence, be it by rapping on or moving tables, leaving impressions in hot wax, writing on slates, or leaking ectoplasm from the medium's body" (83). This need for material evidence becomes more plausible with a closer study of Victorian spiritualism, which

---

1. There are numerous useful accounts on the history of spiritualism in Great Britain. See, for instance, Barrow, Brandon, Galvan, Gilbert, Kontou and Willburn, McCorristine, *Spectres of the Self,* Oppenheim, Pearsall, Smajíc, Tromp, *Altered States,* and Willburn.

developed a supernatural corollary to the materialism of contemporary mainstream society.²

Beginning with the earliest séances, the appearance of tangible spirit-hands, which came in a variety of shapes and sizes, provided palpable evidence of the supernatural. One spiritualist, who assumed the pseudonym Verax, describes encountering such a hand during a séance with the famed medium Douglas Home: it was a "soft, warm, fleshy, radiant, substantial hand, such as I should be glad to feel at the extremity of the friendship of my best friends" (5). While in some cases these hands were anonymous, in others sitters recognized them as belonging to deceased relatives or acquaintances, as seen in the following account of a man identifying the hand of his dead wife during a séance:

> I advanced my own hand, when the spirit-hand was placed in it, grasping mine; and we again grasped hands with all the fervour of long-parted friends, my wife in the spirit land and myself here. The expression of love and tenderness thus given cannot be described, for it was a reality which lasted through nearly half an hour. I examined carefully that spirit-hand, squeezed it, felt the knuckles, joints, and nails, and kissed it, while it was constantly visible to my sight. . . . Nothing in all these manifestations had been more real to me, or given me greater pleasure, than thus receiving the kindly grasp of a hand dearer to me than life, but which, according to the world's theory, has long since with all its tenderness and life mouldered into the dust of the earth. ("Spiritualism in America" 25)

In contrast to the sentimentality of this reunion scene, and others in which parents once again experienced the "rosy, dimpled hand" of a deceased child (De Morgan 220), spirit-hands could initiate more transgressive forms of touching. They grabbed sitters' bodies indiscriminately from under the table, breaking rules of personal space and decorum. Home's explanation for these below-board dealings was that "the upper part of us, or the brain and senses, were more opposed to spiritual truth than the vital, visceral, or instinctive part, which in this case is conveniently separated from the other by the table" (Verax 6). These interactions laid bare the kinds of physical freedoms enabled by the darkened séance room.³

---

2. This is the focus of my current book project, "Impossible Ghosts: Material Culture at the Limits of Evidence."

3. As Owen writes, "Physical intimacy was a legitimate aspect of spiritualist practice, whether it was the healing touch or the linking of arms and hands around the séance table" (218).

Michelle Morgan ascribes this fascination with hands to the importance spiritualism placed on the tactile, as it "demonstrates the relationship between sensory practices and materiality in the nineteenth century" (49).[4] Besides tactility, there was another reason for spiritualism's manual fixation. As the recent critical interest in "hand studies" has displayed, the hand in the nineteenth century became a privileged signifier of various kinds of truth: of the superiority of the human over the animal, of evolution, gender, character, personal identity, and so on.[5] In *The Racial Hand in the Victorian Imagination*, I argue that the hand was most informative when it was detached from the body, whose characteristics it would then disclose or even betray. The hand-reading practices of chirognomy, chiromancy (palm-reading), and later fingerprinting analysis all operated under the assumption that the hand could reveal most when it was distanced—either figuratively or literally, through amputation—from the human form. Victorian literary texts, ranging from the gothic tale to the imperial novel, took advantage of this association by narrating the kinds of truths that the severed hand might reveal.

A contemporary review of the palmistry manual *The Book of the Hand* (1867) links spiritualism to hand-reading through their shared implausibility:

> A man who believes that the spirits of his grandmother and Plato are alternately rapping ungrammatical remarks to him out of a table cannot, one would say, be very wise; yet his mental confusion is exceeded by that of a gentleman who believes that, by looking at the crease on a lady's hand, you can tell that twenty-two years before she was in danger of a violent death, and twelve years before in danger of death by poison—to say nothing of elaborately predicting her future. ("*Book of the Hand*" 760)

Both spiritualism and palmistry were notable for the conflict between their self-proclaimed intimate relationship to the truth and their susceptibility to being targeted by the wider public as nonsense. And yet, there was an important difference in the nature of the evidence they proffered, especially when it came to hands. While writings on palmistry and chirognomy asserted that manual literacy could provide information about the hand owner's identity,

---

4. Although Morgan's essay focuses on American spiritualism, the argument she makes about tactility and spirit-hands is also applicable to Britain.

5. For this recent interest in Victorian hand studies, see Capuano's *Changing Hands* and my own *The Racial Hand in the Victorian Imagination*. Other recent work on the topic includes Cox's essays on the significance of the hand in Anne Brontë's *The Tenant of Wildfell Hall* and Charlotte Brontë's *Jane Eyre*, and her roundtable "A Hand in It: Hand Studies in the Long Nineteenth Century" for MLA 2018, as well as Stainthorp's recent essay on prosthetic hands.

past, or future, spirit-hands were capable of communicating only one principal thing: their presence in the séance room. As one skeptical article for the *National Review* observes, these manifestations are limited in that "they are only general indications of the power of the spirits to make known their presence to men, and do not give any special information" ("Literature of Spirit-Rapping" 137). In what follows, I first examine the ways in which believers and skeptics addressed the redundancy of spirit-hands and then move on to discussing a mode of writing that took advantage of this redundancy to assert its own original approach to the supernatural: the ghost story. I read Sheridan Le Fanu's 1863 narrative "Ghost Stories of the Tiled House" as one example of the genre's use of spectral hands to preserve its literary integrity when confronted with the "real" ghosts of spiritualism.

PALPABLE HANDS

Written accounts of spiritualist encounters with spirit-hands provide in-depth descriptions that rival the chiromantic and chirognomic manuals of the period. As Adin Ballou describes the range of manual encounters he experienced during a séance, "Some hands are soft and velvet-like, and some of a harder consistence, marked by the peculiarities which distinguished the person's mortal hand. Some hands are warmer and others cooler. Some moist, and others comparatively dry. In a single instance the hand was absolutely cold to chilliness" (192). He quotes a sitter's description of his tactile encounter with his deceased wife's hand in terms that prioritize descriptive accuracy over sentimental affect:

> "I felt a hand as perfect as that of a living person, the touch and separation of the fingers was plainly perceptible. It purported to be the hand of my former wife. One of her hands was deformed by being badly burnt when a child. Two of her fingers were bent inward toward the palm, and the nail on one finger was very short and thick. I then asked her to put her deformed hand into mine, which she immediately did; and then passed her finger with the thick nail over the palm of my hand, as if to convince me of her identity." (Ballou 195)

Were it to refer to a living person, this description of a "deformed" hand would most likely be found in a scientific manual, such as Casimir Stanislas D'Arpentigny's *The Science of the Hand* (1857), rather than in the writings of a mourning husband. But because tangible proof is granted the highest priority in spiritualist accounts, the widower must adopt the technical specificity of the scientist.

The term "palpable," which encompasses both touch and evidentiary certainty, frequently appears in spiritualist descriptions of encounters with spirit-hands.[6] We find, for instance, references to the manifestations of a "soft, palpable hand" (Verax 6); fingers demonstrating a "spiritual palpability never dreamt of in ghostology, where form without substance was the most that was ever claimed" ("Spiritual Manifestations" 89); and a hand that remained invisible, despite the fact that it "was palpably touching" the hand of the medium (Home 90). The repetition of the discourses of palpability and palpations acts as a textual poke to remind readers that things *are* being felt—and sometimes quite persistently—within the realm of the séance. Indeed, these reiterations, along with the countless descriptions of spirit-hands in spiritualist publications, try to challenge the "you had to be there" effect of the spiritualist experience. As Alison Winter writes, "Plausibility is one of the hardest things for historians to reconstruct in a satisfying manner, perhaps because it involves not merely a set of logical propositions but also a visceral response to sensory phenomena" (353). Accounts of spirit-hands seek to reproduce these visceral sensations through their often painstakingly thorough descriptions.

Such accounts depict spirits themselves as recognizing the evidentiary importance of their hands, which they offer up for visual and tactile inspection. In his *Experimental Investigation of the Spirit Manifestations,* Robert Hare writes that when he requested "the spirits to shake hands with me . . . they did so almost instantly," and when he "asked them to let me examine their hands, . . . they placed them in mine, and I looked at them and felt them until I was entirely satisfied" (306). In more aggressive moods, spirits manifest themselves by grabbing and fondling sitters, as in the following example from an 1856 séance:

> The party then assembled about the table, when, after a few moments' conversation with the invisibles, one said to his neighbour, "Did you touch me?"—a question that several about the board asked. . . . All at the table felt the touch of hands. One of the party, who wore a wig, had a grasp made at that article, and came nigh being scalped. One gentleman, whose hand was resting upon the medium's, was taken by the wrist, and his hand thrown aside. Several were violently seized. The writer hereof had a grasp, like a vice

---

6. The *OED* defines "palpable" as: "That may be touched, felt, or handled; perceptible by the sense of touch; tangible" (1a); and "Of a fact, idea, quality, characteristic, etc.: easily perceived by the mind; manifest, obvious, clear" (4).

upon his knee, and came nigh being drawn from his chair by a sturdy pull at his foot. ("Spiritual Manifestations" 89)

These manual hijinks represent an effort on the part of spirits to have their presence recognized. This is how the spiritualist William Howitt would explain the often irritating behavior of poltergeists: "They have a strong spice of malice in them, and knock things down, fling down your crockery and your kettles, cut your clothes, pull the quilts and blankets from you in bed, and let you know to a certainty that there is a spirit world" (4). While spirit-hands do not generally belong to poltergeists, they demonstrate a similar aspiration to be known and felt.

In other cases, spirits make use of available resources and technologies to announce their presence. During a séance with Home, for example, a spirit responds to one sitter's expression of doubt by rapping out the message, "OURHANDSAREASREALASYOURS" (Jones 86). The emerging medium of spirit photography offered another platform for spirit-hands to appear, often in cryptic ways. One account tells of a young (living) girl who, while her photograph was being taken, "'was smitten with partial blindness.' . . . She spoke of it to the artist, who told her 'to wink and sit still.' In developing the plate, he noticed an imperfection, but did not observe it closely. He sat the girl again, and took a sheet of eight tintypes. She felt no blur over her eyes, and there was no blur on the pictures. The artist *now examined the first sheet, and found hands on the face and neck of every tintype, eight in all!*" (Sargent 139). In another account, upon looking at his photograph, a male subject discovers that his head on the image "was obscured by the thumb of a monstrous hand which hovered o'er him. In comparison with the other figures, the longest finger of this hand, as a natural object, must have been about 2 ft. long." When, during a séance, the man asks, "What is the philosophy of that big hand?" the spirit responds with a pun: "What! feel-osophy of the big hand?" ("Another Spirit-Photographer" 192). Whatever its deeper significance, if it has one, the photographed hand represents this body part's overwhelming—and overdetermined—power in establishing evidence of the supernatural.

The fact that these spirit-hands appear in isolation from the rest of the body enhances their evidentiary power. Spiritualist accounts recurrently emphasize the severed nature of these hands, as seen in Home's account of this phenomenon in *Incidents in My Life* (1863). Describing a séance in which a woman's hand appears and performs a variety of actions, he writes:

> The fingers were of an almost preternatural *length,* and seemed to be set *wide apart.* The extreme *pallor* of the entire hand was also remarkable. But per-

haps the most noticeable thing about it was the shape of the fingers, which, in addition to their length and thinness, were unusually *pointed* at the ends; they tapered rapidly and evenly toward the tips. The hand also *narrowed* from the lower knuckles to the wrist, *where it ended*. (93)

After the hand picks up a pencil and begins writing, Home further draws attention to its detached state: "Being the nearest one to the hand, I bent down close to it as it wrote, to see the whole of it. It extended no farther than *the wrist*. . . . The hand afterwards came and *shook hands* with each one present. I felt it minutely. It was tolerably well and symmetrically made, though not perfect; and it was *soft* and slightly *warm*. IT ENDED AT THE WRIST" (94). Home combines his repeated emphasis on the hand's detachment to a mode of manual analysis that could be taken from any number of hand-interpretation manuals of the period, which also detail aspects such as hand texture, shape, finger length, and temperature to determine anything from national identity to personal temperament. These disciplines, as well as fingerprinting later on, represent a transition from "holistic to fractional models defining the hand's relationship to the rest of the body" (Briefel 7) and urge that hands are at their most truthful when viewed apart from their owners. In his account, Home draws on these approaches to lend further authenticity to floating spirit-hands. The difference is in the absence of any kind of hand-reading in Home's account; rather than linking the woman's tapered and long fingers to her character or nationality, he leaves these details to speak (or not) for themselves. The importance in presenting such specific information about the hand, both for Home and other mediums, is to emphasize that a spirit-hand has been seen.

Skeptics turned this redundancy into absurdity, reconfiguring the evidentiary function of the detached hand into proof of the ludicrousness of the spiritualist mission. Responding to the claim that Home had produced a spirit-hand for Emperor Louis Napoleon at the Tuileries, *Punch* featured a humorous caricature of the event, in which a spectral hand, clearly held up by a fraudulent mechanism, makes a rude gesture on the emperor's nose. The *Spiritual Magazine* countered with a defensive piece, insisting that spirit-hands had been witnessed as long ago as the Feast of Belshazzar in the Bible and returning yet again to an argument based on tactile proof: "The possibility being then established, the fact itself is reduced to a question of ordinary evidence, and we assert, that spirit-hands have within the last few years been seen and felt by hundreds of persons, perfectly competent to settle the question once for all" ("*Punch*'s Cartoon" 245). Not surprisingly, this argument did not deter *Punch,* which continued to publish offensive images and accounts of spiritualist practices and noted that although spiritualists "have no objection to be called blasphemous, or audacious, or wicked, they cannot bear to be laughed at. Ridicule has been called the test of truth, but it is a test which Rappery declines to undergo" ("Mr. Punch a Spirit-Rapper").

Another approach taken by skeptics to disprove the evidence of spiritualist hands was to demonstrate how easily this phenomenon could be faked. They typically portrayed mediums as charlatans, as seen in Robert Browning's lengthy dramatic monologue satirizing Home, "Mr. Sludge, the Medium" (1864):

> Manage your feet, dispose your hands aright,
> Work wires that twitch the curtains, play the glove
> At end o' your slipper,—then put out the lights
> And . . . there, there, all you want you'll get, I hope!" (l. 446–49)

The illusion of spirit-hands, critics contended, could be produced by mediums' strategic manipulations of their own hands or feet—what one critic ludically referred to as "toe-ology" (Chapman 179)—or by the deployment of various mechanisms, such as stuffed gloves extending from the end of lazy-tongs or dangling from a string. These attacks challenge the detachment of spirit-hands as proof of their authenticity by showing how this effect is manufactured; the hands themselves are clearly operated by a human body residing just beyond the frame. In doing so, they contrast the fictiveness of spirit-hands to the reality of the human ones in terms that appropriate the imagery of manual detachment deployed by spiritualists. Critics sometimes provided illustrations to demonstrate the deceptive manual dexterity of mediums. By foregrounding images of isolated human hands, these critics tried to beat spiritualists at their own game. The evidentiary function shifts from one hand to another: the deceptive hands of mediums now expose the realities of the séance.

REVENGE OF THE PUFFY HAND

There was another mode of writing, whose own pages were filled with spectral body parts, that treated spiritualism distrustfully: the Victorian ghost story. The literary genre predated the spiritualist revival of the 1850s and afterwards rarely depicted the repetitive rituals of the séance. Instead, a number of ghost stories mocked the table-rappings and furniture moving that marked the early days of the movement. The Anglo-Irish writer Sheridan Le Fanu begins his novella *All in the Dark* (1863), for instance, by reminding readers of a time in the preceding decade when "hats began to turn and heads with them, and tables approved themselves the most intelligent of quadrupeds; chests of drawers and other grave pieces of furniture babbled of family secrets" (199). Despite these dismissals, the spiritualist movement did inform the ghost story in important ways. As Jennifer Bann argues, this influence is especially visible in the literary representation of spirit-hands, which provides a "literal metonymy for the spiritualist movement as a whole" (670). The ghost story drew from the agency and power that spiritualism ascribed to spirit-hands, traceable in "developments of the ghostly hand, from the powerless hand-wringing of Marley's ghost to the controlling, guiding, or demonstrative hands of later ghosts" (Bann 664).

This agency is often violent and aggressive in nature, as seen in the number of vengeful spectral hands that emerge in the Victorian ghost story. In narratives like Le Fanu's "Ghost Stories of the Tiled House," Mary Elizabeth Braddon's "The Cold Embrace" (1862), and Henry James's "The Romance of Certain Old Clothes" (1867), the hand of a deceased individual typically returns to impose its fatal mark on the living. For example, in Braddon's story, a woman commits suicide after she is left by her lover, an artist who had given her a ring as a token of his (temporary) affection. The woman returns in spectral form as a pair of hands that ultimately strangles him to death: "Suddenly some one, something from behind him, puts two cold arms round his neck, and clasps its hands on his breast. And yet there is no one behind him. . . . It is not ghostly, this embrace for it is *palpable* to the touch—it cannot be real, for it is invisible. . . . On the third finger of the left hand he can feel the ring which was his mother's—the golden serpent—the ring which he has always said he would know among a thousand by the touch alone. He knows it now!" (48, emphasis mine). The story picks up on the language of palpability and paradoxical materiality that is so pervasive in spiritualist accounts of spectral hands. This understated appropriation of the language of spiritualism is common in the number of stories of vengeful ghost hands that haunts the popular press of the period, even when they reject the tenets of spiritualism outright.

It is the vengefulness of the hands in these stories that marks an important break from those that emerge during the séance. "Actual" spirit-hands are rarely—if ever—vindictive. Instead, as we have seen, their main purpose is to reconnect with the living to prove the existence of an afterlife. Unlike the human victims in stories like Braddon's, séance sitters do not encounter the hands with fear or loathing; as one writer recounts touching her father's hand at a séance with Home, "I was not in the least frightened, like Lord Nelson, I never saw *fear*" (Brancker 431). A writer for the *National Review* expressed surprise that anxiety should not be felt by more séance participants, noting that "It is creditable to the nerves of the spiritualists that no one seems ever to have been alarmed by these odds and ends of human bodies turning up amongst the circles" ("Literature of Spirit-Rapping" 137). In contrast, the ghost story relies on fear and revenge as necessary literary devices that offset the tedious repetitions of the séance. There is very little narrative suspense or drive in the numerous accounts of disembodied hands emerging from the table; the repetition of the same event and image is an essential part of the evidentiary process. While one might argue that the recurrence of revenge in spectral hand stories invites its own readerly fatigue, the variety in these stories comes from the assortment of motives for revenge (betrayed loves, double-dealing siblings, etc.) and the violent deaths that ensue rather than from the persistent descriptions of the kinds of hands (young, old, wrinkled, soft) that can emerge around a séance table.

Le Fanu's "Ghost Stories of the Tiled House" delivers a subtle but forceful critique of the self-referentiality of spirit-hands. A few years later, Le Fanu would deploy a more obvious attack on the movement in his novella *All in the Dark,* which Stephen Carver describes as taking "ghosts out of the gothic and into the real world of charlatan celebrities and their credulous converts." In this narrative, we witness a séance directed by a dubious medium who tries to convince sitters that they are "feeling" the supernatural while performing his own brand of toe-ology; one attendee "felt the pressure of a large foot in a slipper—under the table" (209). Rather than explicitly depicting a fraudulent séance, "Ghost Stories of the Tiled House" relies on the readers' recognition of spiritualist tropes, especially around spirit-hands. In particular, the story reconfigures the movement's focus on the material and evidentiary value of hands, suggesting that this significance leads to a persistent, redundant, and ultimately illegible hand.

Le Fanu's story was originally published as part of the novel *The House by the Church-yard* (1863), from which it was later detached and turned into a self-standing piece. It takes the form of a frame narrative, in which a servant, Old Sally, tells her mistress an old story about hauntings that had befallen a nearby estate, the Tiled House, in the mid-eighteenth century. The tenants of the house, Mr. and Mrs. Prosser, were subjected to the repeated hauntings of a "handsomely formed, and white and plump" hand (402) that materializes in various parts of their estate. It initially appears to Mrs. Prosser as she looks outside her "back parlour window," where she "plainly saw a hand stealthily placed upon the stone window-sill outside, as if by some one beneath the window, at her right side, intending to climb up" (402). Following this first manifestation, it becomes visible to the cook—"an honest, sober woman"— against the kitchen window, "this time moving slowly up and down, pressed all the while against the glass, as if feeling carefully for some inequality in its surface" (403). The hand then undertakes a series of annoying intrusions, from loudly "rapping" on the back door (403), to pushing its finger through an "auger-hole" in a window frame (403), to leaving an impression of itself in the "dust of the 'little parlour' table" (405). This material trace truly alarms the household, especially a housemaid about whom the narrator explains, "The print of the naked foot in the sea-sand did not frighten Robinson Crusoe half so much" (405). Eventually, the hand behaves according to the generic requirements of the ghost story and begins to threaten the occupants. It tries to attack Mrs. Prosser; lying next to her head on the pillow is "the same white, fattish hand, the wrist resting on the pillow, and the fingers extended towards her temple with a slow, wavy motion" (406). Later on, it threatens the Prossers' young son, as the parents see the "fat white hand, palm downwards, presented towards the head of the child" (407). The story ends without any clear resolution, besides the repeated account of a relative of the Prossers who describes the family's plight as "an instance of a curiously monotonous, individualized, and persistent nightmare" (407).

One of the strangest aspects of this altogether peculiar story is the absence of any motivation for the haunting of the hand. Critics have tried to ascribe meaning to the hand, usually by interpreting it as a metaphor for class conflict. Katherine Rowe, for instance, argues that although it "absolutely resists rational explication" (154), it can be read "as an allegory of Irish dispossession and disenfranchisement: the working Irish hand, its estrangement figured in a ghostly synecdoche, retaliates against those who exploit its labor and alienate its possessions" (156), while its "fatness and puffiness suggest an unwholesome sensuality" implicating the aristocracy (157). Shane McCorristine identifies a similar duality in the aggressive hand of the story, viewing it at once as evidence of "dread that the disembodied hand of the subaltern would return to the Big House" and the presence of "a powerful and elite owner—the hand of a master" ("Ghost Hands" 278). In other readings, the resemblance of the ghostly hand to Cathy's in *Wuthering Heights* (1847) evokes various hauntings from the past, both literary and historical (Rowe 154, Walton 74). These interpretations aside, however, what makes this story "stick[] out like a sore thumb" (Sage 53) is its ultimate refusal to explain itself. Unlike other ghost stories—including Brontë's—it omits any revelation of betrayal or wrongdoing that would explain the presence of the pesky hand. It's just always *there*.

The only thing we have to hold on to in this story is repeated reference to the materiality of the hand. It is "short, but handsomely formed, and white and plump" (402); "fat but aristocratic-looking" (403); has a "white pudgy finger" (403); and is a "white fat hand" (407). There is not much variety in these descriptions, just the kind of repetition of manual characteristics we might find in spiritualist accounts. What is more, like the hand in the séance, this one expends most of its energies trying to be noticed. Apart from the instances in which it seems to menace members of the Prosser family—instances that show the story's allegiance to the tropes of the ghost story—it strives for recognition with its "angry rapping" on doors and walls, "sometimes very low and furtive, like a clandestine signal, and at others sudden and so loud as to threaten the breaking of the pane" (403), replicating the kinds of noises that might be heard in a spiritualist séance. Like the spirit-hands that offer themselves up for inspection, it positions itself for utmost visibility, pressing against the glass and cramming its finger into the augur hole: "first the tip, and then the two first joints introduced, and turned about this way and that, crooked against the inside, as if in search of a fastening which its owner designed to push aside" (403). The hand acknowledges the importance of evidence by leaving traces of itself in the dust; after Prosser asks each of his servants to fit their hands in the imprint, "his 'affidavit' deposed that the formation of the hand so impressed differed altogether from those of the living inhabitants of the house, and corresponded exactly with that of the hand seen by Mrs. Prosser and by the cook" (405). As Rowe argues, this focus on identifying the hand recalls the "increasingly popular forensic practice of manual identification" (154) from which spiritualist accounts also drew. All in all, the evidence of this story only works to confirm the materiality of the hand and the fact that it did haunt a set of people at a particular time.

Le Fanu's emphasis on the self-referentiality of the hand culminates in a passage that further satirizes the conventions of spiritualism. After describing the dramatic scene in which the hand almost strangles the Prossers' child, the narrator comments,

> There is a great deal more, but this will suffice. The singularity of the narrative seems to be this, that it describes the ghost of a hand, and no more. The person to whom that hand belonged never once appeared; nor was it a hand separated from a body, but only a hand so manifested and introduced, that its owner was always, by some crafty accident, hidden from view. (407)

The hand, it turns out, is not actually detached, but part of someone's body. This initially seems to bring the story closer to *Wuthering Heights*, in which Lockwood views a "child's face" accompanying the ghostly "little, ice-cold hand" that grabs him through the window, an image that humanizes the hand by linking it to Catherine Linton and her past (Brontë 56). In Le Fanu's story, however, the presence of a hidden figure embeds the hand in greater mystery and absurdity. The next paragraph provides a clue of the hand's owner, as the Prosser child reports having been haunted by "a certain gentleman, fat and pale, every curl of whose wig, every button and fold of whose laced clothes, and every feature and line of whose sensual, malignant, and unwholesome face, was . . . minutely engraven upon his memory" (407). But nowhere is this description immediately linked to the hand, nor is it contextualized by any sense of historical or personal specificity. Instead, we are left with the ludicrous image of an entity going through all sorts of contortions and concealments to hide its (ghostly? human?) body from viewers, all for the objective of presenting the image of a detached spectral hand. We catch a glimpse of this effort when, after the hand is caught trying to harm the sleeping Mrs. Prosser, we read, "Mr. Prosser, with a horrified jerk, pitched the leger right at the curtains behind which the owner of the hand might be supposed to stand. The hand was instantaneously and smoothly snatched away, the curtains made a great wave, and Mr. Prosser got round the bed in time to see the closet-door, which was at the other side, drawn close by the same white, puffy hand, as he believed" (406).

This description of a form hiding behind a curtain evokes the cabinets that, from the 1850s onward, were often used by mediums in the materialization of spirit-hands and, later, full spectral bodies. These usually involved curtains or sheets that would conceal what was going on inside the cabinet, from which different manifestations would reach into the audience. As one sitter described a séance with the famous mediums the Davenport Brothers (who were later deemed to be frauds), "I placed my hand in the small window of the cabinet, when I felt each of my five digits tightly grasped by a distinct hand, and while my own was thus held down, five or six other hands protruded from the hole above my wrist" (Damiani 414). Not surprisingly, the cabinet became one of the favorite targets of skeptics, who accused mediums of taking advantage of the darkness and distance from the audience to perform their deceptions: "Sometimes ladies' and children's gloves are covered with phosphorus and cleverly connected with a rubber tube, by blowing into which the hands of spirits are made to appear. The Davenport Brothers used to put them through the holes in their cabinet, sometimes a dozen at once, and then let out the air and conceal the gloves in their pockets" ("At a Spiritual Séance" 525). Le Fanu's description of a body hiding behind a curtain and exposing a "puffy" (fraudulently inflated?) hand provides a literary version of this subterfuge. By adding a body to the specter, Le Fanu also undermines the hand's evidentiary function. It no longer lays claim to the authenticity associated with severed hands during this period, or the wonder of the spirit-hands extending "no farther than the *wrist*" described by spiritualists like Home. While readers are not expected to believe that the hand in question is being held up by a pair of lazy-tongs, they are compelled to associate the ghostly hand with these acts of subterfuge and deception, thus undermining its spectral power in the story. Mr. Prosser, we read, "was privately of opinion that the whole affair was a practical joke or a fraud, and waited an opportunity of catching the rogue *flagrante delicto*" (404).

Prosser never does find the culprit, nor is there necessarily one in this ghost story. But, if as Bann tells us, spirit-hands functioned as a "literal metonymy for the spiritualist movement as a whole" (670), then we can take the offender to be spiritualism itself, which comes to stand in as a large, clumsy, and redundant hand in Le Fanu's narrative. Its pervasiveness and self-referentiality are reminiscent of the large hands that hovered above subjects in photographs, leading to one spirit joking about "feel-osophy." The hand in Le Fanu's narrative also seems out of place and conducive to humorously dismissive readings, turning it, as McCorristine writes, into a "bloated symbol" ("Ghost Hands" 279). By the end of the story, the narrator apologizes for the redundancy in telling the story of the hand in terms that concurrently dismiss the spiritualist movement's repetitions: "I hope the reader will pardon me for loitering so long in the Tiled House, but this sort of lore has always had a charm for me; and people, you know, especially old people, will talk of what most interests themselves, too often forgetting that others may have had more than enough of it" (407). This apology mirrors other ghost stories' attempts to position spiritualism as belonging in the past, as Le Fanu would do at the beginning of *All in the Dark*. The ending also warns against the repetitions of this movement, whose ability to convince is predicated on ever-proliferating descriptions of supernatural phenomena; Le Fanu signals that its critics "may have had more than enough of it."

In crafting this ending, Le Fanu in no way dismisses the significance of ghosts within a literary context. What "Ghost Stories of the Tiled House" does instead is to emphasize the distinction between the fictional ghost story and the real ghosts that were supposedly haunting Victorian parlors during the same period. While expressing a disbelief in this movement, Le Fanu perhaps more crucially signals that the ghost story should not, indeed cannot, take up spiritualism's narratives without altogether dampening its own literary genre. In *Apartment Stories,* Sharon Marcus reads the story as an allegory of the threats posed to middle-class domestic privacy and property through a spectral hand that insists on breaking into the sanctity of the home. Like other Victorian ghost stories, this one concludes with a restoration of "the privacy whose invasion they had depicted—a privacy that could never be documented, because it excluded the presence of any recorder or observer" (Marcus 127). Another way to read this return to privacy in Le Fanu's story is as an expulsion, or exorcism, of the hands of spiritualism from literary narratives, which can then regain their proprietorship over a representation of ghosts distinct from those of the spiritualist movement. Through his elimination of the absurd and useless hand, Le Fanu reestablishes the parameters of the ghost story, delineating the differences between spectral body parts that belong on the page and those that should be left to hover over a darkened séance table.

WORKS CITED

"Another Spirit-Photographer." *Medium and Daybreak*, 24 May 1872, pp. 191–93.

"At a Spiritual Séance." *Leisure Hour*, 18 Aug. 1877, pp. 524–26.

Ballou, Adin. *An Exposition of Views Respecting the Principal Facts, Causes and Peculiarities Involved in Spirit Manifestations: Together with Interesting Phenomenal Statements and Communications*. Bela Marsh, 1852.

Bann, Jennifer. "Ghost Hands and Ghostly Agency: The Changing Figure of the Nineteenth-Century Specter." *Victorian Studies*, vol. 51, no. 4, 2009, pp. 663–86.

Barrow, Logie. *Independent Spirits: Spiritualism and English Plebeians, 1850–1910*. Routledge & Kegan Paul, 1986.

Bell, Karl. *The Magical Imagination: Magic and Modernity in Urban England, 1780–1914*. Cambridge UP, 2012.

"*The* Book of the Hand." *Saturday Review*, 14 Dec. 1867, pp. 760–61.

Braddon, Mary Elizabeth. "The Cold Embrace." *Victorian Ghost Stories by Eminent Women Writers*, edited by Richard Dalby, Running P, 1993, pp. 43–50.

Brancker, Ann. "To the Editor of the 'Spiritual Magazine.'" *Spiritual Magazine*, Sept. 1861, pp. 431–32.

Brandon, Ruth. *The Spiritualists: The Passion for the Occult in the Nineteenth and Twentieth Centuries*. Prometheus Books, 1984.

Briefel, Aviva. *The Racial Hand in the Victorian Imagination*. Cambridge UP, 2015.

Brontë, Emily. *Wuthering Heights*. Edited by Beth Newman, Broadview P, 2007.

Browning, Robert. "Mr. Sludge, the Medium." *Robert Browning: Selected Poems*. Penguin, 1989, pp. 204–46.

Capuano, Peter J. *Changing Hands: Industry, Evolution, and the Reconfiguration of the Victorian Body*. U of Michigan P, 2015.

Carver, Stephen. "'Addicted to the Supernatural': Spiritualism and Self-Satire in Le Fanu's *All in the Dark*." *Ainsworth & Friends*, 13 Feb. 2013, https://ainsworthandfriends.wordpress.com/2013/02/13/addicted-to-the-supernatural-spiritualism-and-self-satire-in-le-fanus-all-in-the-dark/. Accessed 24 Oct. 2019.

Chapman, Alison. *Networking the Nation: British and American Women's Poetry and Italy, 1840–1870*. Oxford UP, 2015.

Cox, Kimberly. "A Touch of the Hand: Manual Intercourse in Anne Brontë's *The Tenant of Wildfell Hall*." *Nineteenth-Century Literature*, vol. 72, no. 2, 2017, pp. 161–91.

———. "'At Least Shake Hands': Tactile Relations in Charlotte Brontë's *Jane Eyre*." *Victorians*, Fall 2016, pp. 195–215.

Damiani, G. "Experiences of Spiritualism." *Human Nature*, Aug. 1869, pp. 410–18.

De Morgan, Sophia Elizabeth. *From Matter to Spirit*. Longman, Green, Longman, Roberts, and Green, 1863.

Galvan, Jill. *The Sympathetic Medium: Feminine Channeling, the Occult, and Communication Technologies, 1859–1919*. Cornell UP, 2010.

Gilbert, R. A. Introduction. *The Rise of Victorian Spiritualism*, vol. 1, edited by R. A. Gilbert, Routledge, 2000, pp. v–xix.

Hare, Robert. *Experimental Investigation of the Spirit Manifestations*. Partridge & Brittan, 1855.

Home, Douglas. *Incidents in My Life*. 5th ed., A. J. Davis, 1864.

"Home, Great Home!" *Punch*, 18 Aug. 1860, p. 63.

Howitt, William. *Throwing of Stones and Other Substances by Spirits*. T. Scott, 1865.

Illustration of Napoleon III, *Punch*, 12 May 1860, p. 189.

Jones, Jno. "Report of a Sitting with Mr. D. D. Home on Wednesday, July 21, 1869." *Human Nature*, Feb. 1870, pp. 82–88.

Katerfalto. "Spirit Rapping Made Easy; or, How to Come out as a Medium." *Once a Week*, 6 Oct. 1860, pp. 403–7.

Kontou, Tatiana, and Sarah Willburn, editors. *The Ashgate Research Companion to Nineteenth-Century Spiritualism and the Occult*. Ashgate, 2012.

Le Fanu, Sheridan. *All in the Dark*. Dublin University Magazine, Feb. 1866, pp. 198–218.

———. "Ghost Stories of the Tiled House." *Best Ghost Stories of J. S. Le Fanu*, edited by E. F. Bleiler, Dover, 1964, pp. 397–407.

"The Literature of Spirit-Rapping." *National Review*, Jan. 1857, pp. 131–51.

Marcus, Sharon. *Apartment Stories: City and Home in Nineteenth-Century Paris and London*. U of California P, 1999.

McCorristine, Shane. "Ghost Hands, Hands of Glory, and Manumission in the Fiction of Sheridan Le Fanu." *Irish Studies Review*, vol. 17, no. 3, Aug. 2009, pp. 275–95.

———. *Spectres of the Self: Thinking about Ghosts and Ghost-Seeing in England, 1750–1920*. Cambridge UP, 2010.

Morgan, Michelle. "'Soft Warm Hands': Nineteenth-Century Spiritualist Practices and the Materialization of Touch." *Sensational Religion: Sensory Cultures in Material Practice*, edited by Sally M. Promey, Yale UP, 2014, pp. 47–66.

"Mr. Punch a Spirit-Rapper." *Punch*, 9 June 1860, p. 231.

Oppenheim, Janet. *The Other World: Spiritualism and Psychical Research in England, 1850–1914*. Cambridge UP, 1985.

Owen, Alex. *The Darkened Room: Women, Power, and Spiritualism in Late Victorian England*. U of Pennsylvania P, 1990.

Pearsall, Ronald. *The Table-Rappers: The Victorians and the Occult*. New ed., Sutton, 2004.

"*Punch*'s Cartoon of the Spirit Hand: Illustrated by the Past and Present." *Spiritual Magazine*, June 1860, pp. 241–48.

Rowe, Katherine. *Dead Hands: Fictions of Agency, Renaissance to Modern*. Stanford UP, 1999.

Sage, Victor. *Le Fanu's Gothic: The Rhetoric of Darkness*. Palgrave Macmillan, 2004.

Sargent, Epes. *Planchette; or, The Despair of Science*. Robert Brothers, 1869.

Smajić, Srdjan. *Ghost-Seers, Detectives, and Spiritualists: Theories of Vision in Victorian Literature and Science*. Cambridge UP, 2010.

"Spiritualism in America." *Spiritual Magazine*, Jan. 1862, pp. 21–28.

"Spiritual Manifestations." *Spiritual Herald*, Apr. 1856, pp. 88–90.

Stainthorp, Clare. "Activity and Passivity: Class and Gender in the Case of the Artificial Hand." *Victorian Literature and Culture*, vol. 45, no. 1, 2017, pp. 1–16.

Tromp, Marlene. *Altered States: Nation, Drugs, and Self-Transformation in Victorian Spiritualism*. State U of New York P, 2006.

———. "Eating, Feeding, and Flesh: Food in Victorian Spiritualism." *The Ashgate Research Companion to Nineteenth-Century Spiritualism and the Occult*, edited by Tatiana Kontou and Sarah Willburn, Ashgate, 2012, pp. 285–309.

Verax. "Evenings with Mr. Home and the Spirits." *Spiritual Herald*, Feb. 1856, pp. 4–11.

Walton, James. *Vision and Vacancy: The Fictions of J. S. Le Fanu*. U College Dublin P, 2007.

Willburn, Sarah A. *Possessed Victorians: Extra Spheres in Nineteenth-Century Mystical Writings*. Ashgate, 2006.

Winter, Alison. *Mesmerized: Powers of Mind in Victorian Britain*. Chicago UP, 1998.

CHAPTER 6

Hands and Minds in *The Moonstone*

SUE ZEMKA

THE SEMI-VISIBLE HAND

There are hands on every page of Wilkie Collins's 1868 *The Moonstone*. In itself, this is unremarkable—almost everyone has hands, after all—and the English language, circa 1860, is littered with dead and nearly dead manual metaphors, such as "try her hands," "with my own hands," "show your hand," etc., all of which are common in Collins's vocabulary. But what the hands of *The Moonstone* do! More than most novels, they are engines of plot and character. First Herncastle steals the diamond, which adorns the handle of a dagger. Then Franklin Blake steals the diamond a second time, and a third time, with hands that act independently of his conscious mind. Then there is Rosanna Spearman, who tries to exculpate Franklin by sewing a nightgown, the product of a long night's handwork. Then there is Sergeant Cuff, called into to solve the crime, his sly personality conveyed by large claw-like hands that he shoves in his pockets (155; 165). Finally, there are the hands of Hindu jugglers (juggling: a stereotype of Asian agility and legerdemain), who strive to return the moonstone to the forehead of their statuary god—who, by the way, has four hands.

But the most impressive thing about the hands of *The Moonstone* is that no one seems to notice them. In criticism of the novel, its hands have been subsumed by other topics, which are often analyzed via a "hermeneutics of suspicion," as befits a detective novel like *The Moonstone,* where something is hidden, secreted away, thus provoking in readers a forensic search for meaning akin to the plot's forensic search for a criminal.[1] Thus when D. A. Miller quips that in *The Moonstone* "power is staged like an invisible hand" (58), he either forgets or ignores the preponderance of literal hands in the novel and succumbs to their deflective effects, the way they appear everywhere but never make their import clear, so that instead of asking what hands mean, we take them as similes for other things. Power may be staged *like* an invisible hand, but the hands of the novel stage themselves semi-visibly, at once screaming for attention and turning that attention elsewhere. In this regard, it's as if the novel is playing a joke on its readers, since it's precisely the hand that did it, Franklin's hand, albeit not his conscious mind. Our inurement to the ubiquity of hands allows the culprit to hide in plain sight.

The purpose of this essay is (one) to demonstrate the unusual abundance of hands in *The Moonstone* and their importance to its plot. That much is easy enough, but the second purpose, which I find much more difficult, is to account for their neglect—to figure out why the vast semantic proliferation of hands and manual figures of speech are routinely either overlooked or metaphorized by readers and critics of the novel.

If it wasn't for the first factor—the preponderance and importance of hands in the novel—the second would be a non-issue. Hands are easy to overlook because it is their nature to be either instrumental or symbolic—in either case, not simply themselves. There is no possibility of a being "in itself" for the hand. It is a natural synecdoche and the casebook example of synecdoche, the emblematic part that signifies a greater whole. Thus the hand cannot *but* lead away from itself, cannot *but* be a pointer and not the point, and in this way its destiny as an object of thought mimics its anciently ascribed purpose, which is to mediate—to make, signify, or point to other things. The weight of philosophical, religious, and scientific tradition repeats this pattern, for the reason that by and large these traditions assume that the hand serves the mind, that mind is what the hand mediates. Thus, to imagine the hand differently, to make it a center of attention and an object of investigation in its own right, is to upend an ancient hierarchical system that places the hand in a subservi-

---

1. The situation is ripe for change now that two books on hands in Victorian literature appeared in 2015: Peter J. Capuano's *Changing Hands: Industry, Evolution, and the Reconfiguration of the Victorian Body* and Aviva Breifel's *The Racial Hand in the Victorian Imagination.* Predating these studies, and still crucial reading for anyone interested in hands in literature, is Katherine Rowe's *Dead Hands: Fictions of Agency, Renaissance to Modern.* Consistent with the interests of this essay, Rowe argues that the dead hand trope has been a vehicle for exploring the uncertain continuity between character and intention at least since the early modern period.

ent relationship to the rational powers that direct it. And yet, to return to the point that continues to amaze me, "imagining the hand differently" is exactly what Collins does when he makes Franklin Blake's right hand the perpetrator of a crime of which Franklin is unaware.

My operative term for manual phenomena in *The Moonstone* is "semi-visible." It is the best term I can come up with for something that slides between salience and erasure. Years ago, in an earlier, unfinished version of this essay, I was struck by a pattern that I saw in the novel of emphasis and deflection in its use of hands. As an experiment, I tried thinking of the novel's hands as characters, or substitutes for character. This method of reading, especially relevant to *The Moonstone*, I refer to as manual-centrism.

While a manual-centric reading proved to be a satisfying experiment for this novel, I never finished that essay because I couldn't find a good answer to the 'why' question—why the novel would plant a hundred hands in its narrative and never make their import clear. Having unearthed some surprising patterns, useful, I felt, for understanding Collins's unconventional approach to action and character, I still couldn't see why the novel would simultaneously broadcast and bury its interest in the hand. This essay, the one you are reading, believes it finds an answer to the question of the hand's semi-visibility in the horror of mutilation, a horror that reverberates quietly underneath the novel's ludic delight in bodies and characters that are comprised of parts (especially hands) which do not easily form wholes. That reverberation, I wish to suggest, emanates from the India Mutiny, the lingering memory of which (in novels, histories, and images) continually reminded Britons that literal fragmentation is a deeply disturbing state. The literal hand, in other words, is hard to isolate, hard to focus on, hard to remember beneath its many similes, because its stark, isolated visibility triggers a reminder of its potential thingness as an object separate from the body. The literal hand traumatizes.

No sooner does the literal hand traumatize with the thought of mutilation or any other atrocity than it folds into another metaphor: *by whose hand was such a thing done?* And *that* metaphor raises questions of personal responsibility. Is doing something "by my own hand" an unequivocal ownership of responsibility, or the reverse? Normally we say yes, but remember that we are approaching the question via *The Moonstone*, which dissolves such clarity in a climate of double entendres. When Rachael Spearman writes, "*the hand which has taken Miss Rachel's jewel could by no possibility be any other hand than [Franklin's]*" (387), she speaks more truly than she is aware; Franklin's hand did it, but not his mind. Hence *The Moonstone*'s fabulous concoction of a manually disassociated theft poses a question about our common parlance of figuratively attributing agency to hands. Instead of signaling a concentration of volition in the hand, an uninterrupted pathway between mind and hand, might it not be the case that such figures also suggest the opposite, conveying a sneaking suspicion that there is no individual agency anywhere, or at least not in the way we are accustomed to think of it?

Certainly not in India, the novel might add, which shares with Seeley the opinion that the British conquered the sub-continent "in a fit of absence of mind" (34). This relates to the shock of a dismembered hand in the following regard: the literal hand traumatizes, not only and most powerfully with its unthinkably inert thingness, but also with the less visceral, equally disconcerting suggestion that the nearly ubiquitous metaphoricity of manual activity is in fact an abrogation of personal responsibility. It deflects a human cause into complexity, context, extenuating circumstances, or in other words, into a general vagueness. In this regard, the dismembered hand reveals a disturbing ambiguity in its metaphorical double—that agency itself is not discrete and whole, but rather fragmented.

Far away from sights of mutilation and fraught questions of responsibility, *The Moonstone* stages and dissects a crime for which the responsible party is a semi-visible, semi-autonomous hand.

"I WILL LAY MY HAND ON THE THIEF WHO TOOK THE MOONSTONE!" (FRANKLIN BLAKE, 361)

Nineteenth-century science corroborated the ancient hierarchy of the senses by relegating the hand, the haptic center of the body, to the governance of the mind. Subsequent discoveries in the fields of evolutionary anthropology, linguistics, and neurology promote a more complex view of the interdependence between the hand and the brain. But for much of the nineteenth century, the hierarchical view was ascendant. Darwin, in 1871, endorses the traditional view:

> Man could not have attained his present dominant position in the world without the use of his hands which are so admirably adapted to act in obedience to his will. As Sir C[harles] Bell insists, "the hand supplies all instruments, and by its correspondence with the intellect gives him universal dominion" (1:141–42).

Not just Bell, but a prodigious list of other scientists—Tylor, Renegger, Cranz, and Schoolcraft—testify to the evolutionary advantages bequeathed to the human species (a.k.a. "man") by the "tool" of the hand. The mind is master and the hand its servant, and so deeply engrained is this classical hierarchy of the human body that even Darwin, the most important scientific revolutionary of the century, cannot not see the matter otherwise.

Enter *The Moonstone*, which centers on the theft of a centuries-old diamond. Rachel witnesses the crime but withholds her knowledge of the perpetrator until an uncomfortable conversation with Franklin leads her to declare (in half a page of dialogue, where the word "hand" is repeated seven times) that it was Franklin who "put [his] hand in, and took the Diamond out" (416). Reading the scene as detective fiction, which of course it is, we should note the following; literally, it is Franklin's hand that took the diamond, and not the opium coursing through his system, or his unconscious, or his displaced desire to enter Rachel's vagina, or his symbolism of colonial theft. Undoubtedly readers make some of these connections, all of which are plausible, but in so doing, they leave behind Franklin's seven-times repeated hands. Franklin Blake doesn't know he did it. He sleepwalks through the most sensational crime of the 1868 season. His act of theft stems from a disruption in the sensorimotor hierarchy, such that his hands act out subconscious fears, while the governor of his mind is on holiday.

This mind-to-hand dissociation warrants closer examination, which is exactly what the novel does by staging the theft twice. In the staged reenactment of his crime, the lexical emphasis on hands is repeated, albeit to no end, since Ablewhite is not there to catch the diamond when it falls from Franklin's hands, as he was in the original scene (498). In neither staging of the crime can we say that an individual actor is singularly responsible. Agency is either unconscious, insofar as Franklin is asleep, or dispersed between characters, insofar as Abelwhite must be present to complete the crime.

Victorian critics were baffled by the lack of dimension in the novel's characters, and the absence of a traditional villain no doubt contributed to this reaction. A villain is a person, cunningly volitional, not a pair of hands. Not, as the reviewer for the *Nation* complained, "ingenious pieces of mechanism," "puppets" or "conundrums," which is to say, "not characters at all" (235). The reviewer for *The Spectator* put the issue more pointedly, saying that Collin's experiments give the reader "no person who can in any way be characterized as a character, no one who interests us, no one who is human enough to excite even a faint emotion of dull curiosity . . ." (881). By the criteria of human interest, Collins's experimental dissection of human character fails. Fascinated with separating out the various parts that compose human character—the jarring German and French parts of Franklin's personality (98), for example, or the "piebald" affair of Ezra Jennings's hair, one half fair and the other dark (390)—Collins seems incapable of fusing them into believable wholes. Incapable or unwilling, that is, since it is unclear if his failure to put the pieces back together again is a consequence of his experiment, or its point.

Contemporary theory offers a more sympathetic approach to Collins's art of character in ACT. Originally formulated by Bruno Latour, ACT, or actor-network theory, models action as "a distributive network, divorced from heroic individual agency" (Citton 310). One objective of ACT is to escape interpretation's "narrow" focus on human characters, defined as those endowed "with a psyche, a soul, a consciousness, and a small amount of morality" (Latour 474). The critique of character is integral to ACT's primary aim, which is to remodel conventional ideas about agency. Hence the network: agency distributed across a network is not consolidated in a "solitary, self-governing subject," but rather flows through multiple participants or "actants," human and non-human, animate and inanimate, all of them linked "in extended constellations of cause and effect" (Felski 164). For example, with our novel: Franklin's hands, his opiated brain, Rachel's cabinet, the gem, the layout of the room, Godfrey's hands—all must be positioned just so in time and space for the theft to take place; all are equally crucial to the outcome. From the perspective of the outcome, all occupy the same ontological plane. Thus we might say that the theft *precipitates* from a network. It is less a function of premeditated planning than of a circuit of movement across a field of actants. Agency does not cohere but extends, blurring the categories of human and non-human, subject and object.

What better way to realize ACT's intentions than with a narrative that focuses on hands, those appendages that *already* mark an ambiguous border between self and non-self, subject and object, body and tool? Or, to up the stakes, what better way to trouble the waters of our "narrow" and thus arguably simplistic notions of human agency than to redirect emphasis from minds to hands? For in the assembly of parts that make up character, the hand is the part that translates thought into action, intention into effect. Thus the hand marks the precise point at which personal responsibility enters into a multi-agential and never wholly predictable network.

ACT provides a perspective and a vocabulary that allows us to see and name the layers of irony packed into Franklin's determination to "lay [his] hand on the thief who took the Moonstone!" (361). It offers a defense for the relative weakness of plot and character in *The Moonstone*: the thief, i.e., Franklin, is not a thief, if thief implies a whole, integrated, and singular identity, but instead something like a network, and a not very smooth-running one at that—an assembly of parts, one part being Franklin's mind (or rather two parts being his mind, since Gabriel tells us it has two halves), and another part being Franklin's hands—and then there are his other parts as well. In this regard, ACT would not see Franklin as exceptional, but rather as hyperbolizing the non-exceptionally composite nature of all human characters, and perhaps human persons. Similarly with the plot: the crime in the novel is not, strictly speaking, a crime, if crime implies an agent or agents executing a premeditated plan. Rather it is the kind of plot that generates a complicated flow chart, a flow chart like a spider's web, which is one way of visualizing distributive agency. By dissociating Franklin's mind from his hand, and by staging the theft twice (to no forensic avail), the novel devises a hyperbolic version of what ACT claims is normal operating procedures. By arguing that the interpretive fascination with rounded human actants is part of our anthropocentric conditioning, ACT provides a partial explanation for the semi-visibility of hands in *The Moonstone*. Critics, starting in 1868, go on a search for soulful characters they can latch onto, and so they overlook the narrative's redistribution of agency into what we now term "networks"—a redirection of energies that passes through many restive hands.

But this is about as far as ACT takes us. Its rational approach does not accord with the novel's not-so-rational world, where distributive networks are animated by semi-magical things. In Victorian fashion, *The Moonstone* prioritizes invisible energies that circulate and bind, disperse and dissolve—powers of love, attraction, and life itself. Even a network is too sober and static to encompass actants such as these.

"I STOOD BEWILDERED WITH MY HAND IN HIS." (MISS CLACK, 316)

When Roseanna Spearman holds Gabriel Betteridge's hand at the Shivering Sands, she implants a tactile memory so strong it is *almost* supernatural. After her death, Gabriel is haunted by Rachel's touch, the first sensation of her ghostly presence: "I declare I *almost* felt the poor thing slip her hand into mine, and give it a grateful squeeze to thank me for speaking kindly to her. I declare I *almost* heard her voice telling me again that the Shivering Sand seemed to draw her to it against her will" (183). *Almost* holding hands finalizes a relationship that is *almost* like that of a father or a lover, although Gabriel never acknowledges it. His reticence before the powers of touch is consistent with his refusal to take a supernatural leap: "if I could only have looked a little way into the future," he says, after her suicide, "I would have taken Rosanna Spearman out of the house, then and there, with my own hand" (114). If Gabriel was clairvoyant, in other words, he would have done something different, and the novel's devotion to the idea that this tragically incomplete affection devolves on the sense of touch forces an otherwise unnecessary completion to the sentence: Gabriel would have done something different with his hands.

Affection flows through the hands and concentrates in sexual attraction. Haptic congress eludes censorship, for the reason that it eludes full awareness. When Rachel tells Franklin that she knows he's guilty, much of the information is conveyed by an erotic hand dance. Franklin takes Rachel's hand, "powerless and trembling"; she pleads with him to let it go, but he knows that "while her hand lay in mine I was her master still!" Rachel momentarily succumbs; "'let go of my hand,'" she says, as she sinks her head on his shoulder, "her hand unconsciously closing on [his]" (413). But the haptic circuit is mercurial, and Rachel soon turns on him; "'I can't tear you out of my heart,'" she yells, then "threw up her hands, and wrung them frantically in the air." Pushed to the impasse of what her hands can't or won't do, Rachel flourishes them like weapons diverted from their target. Franklin, defeated, makes an emasculated exit; "I turned, and waved my hand . . ." (422). Rachel and Franklin have their comic doubles in the mixed signals of manual courtship; Miss Clack and Godfrey Abelwhite perform it as well. The whole charade proceeds through furtive hand holding and hand kissing, until Clack is "overwhelmed" by her "exquisite triumph," and "let [Godfrey] do what he liked with my hands" (318).

Hands unite lovers, but the affective currents transmitted by manual connection are wayward and amoral; they can result in enthrallment. After Roseanna's suicide, Gabriel recoils from Detective Cuff, and his intuition of how Cuff might better him makes him cry out, "Don't touch me." Cuff perseveres: "'Mr. Betteredge,' he said, 'have you any objection to oblige me by shaking hands? I have taken an extraordinary liking to you'" (175). Gabriel concedes to Cuff's touch, and immediately moves back into the camp of his admirers. If Gabriel wanted to maintain his independence from Cuff, he should have known better than to shake his hand. Gabriel is, after all, the novel's only explicit spokesperson on the supernatural powers that flow through manual life, twice opining that "idle hands" make one vulnerable to Satan's "mischief" (106). He is right, but for the wrong reasons. It's not their idleness *per se* that is the problem, but the extrarational haptic powers that they transmit, powers of which the novel's characters are only dimly or silently aware, and to varying degrees. Betteredge, Rachel, Franklin, Ablewhite, Miss Clack, Cuff: all experience the forces that pass through hands, but they do not make it a subject of focus. Everyone is either unwilling or incapable of bringing the mysterious energies of manual contact into full awareness.

Everyone is doing it but no one talks about it, and this tacit agreement ensures that manual intimacy enjoys license. It also invites misuse. Manual power circulates between charismatic and vulnerable characters, and in ways that stem from its semi-visibility among the characters and among Victorians. The situation comes to a head in mesmerism, a nineteenth-century cultural practice that centered on supernatural prehensility—again, only implicitly—and carried associations with India, the novel's other geographical node.

EVERY TIME WE MOVE A FINGER, IT IS BY TRANSMITTING *SOMETHING* UNDER THE CONTROL OF THE WILL TO THE ENDS OF THE FINGERS, AND WHY SHOULD IT NOT GO FARTHER?" (ESDAILE 133)

Franklin is not the only character in the novel to experience abnormal hand-mind circuits; the mesmeric English boy who serves Brahmin priests is another. Mesmerism, for the Brahmins, serves the purpose of surveillance. One of the priests pours some black stuff, like ink, into the palm of the boy's hand and it becomes a screen for visions. In the words of Murthwaite, the novel's Orientalist, the Brahmins believe the boy to be "a Seer of things invisible to their eyes" (351). What I wish to stress is that the boy's hands and eyes are his most active features while he in a mesmeric state, and in this regard he recalls Franklin in his opiated trance, when he executes with his hands a theft guided by a dream.

Most readers will be familiar with Victorian mesmerism, so I will provide only a short gloss.[2] For several decades in the nineteenth-century mesmerism grew alongside legitimate clinical medicine as a dubious but popular alternative therapy, enjoying advocates in high places (e.g., Dr. James Esdaile, Dr. John Elliotson, Alfred R. Wallace, Harriet Martineau, Dickens, and Collins himself). The idea of a vital principle or fluid is central to all mesmeric theory. It exists in a fraught conceptual synapse between mind and body; it is both of the body and corrupted by it. As Esdaile explains, the vital principle is "inherent . . . implanted, as I conceive, in the human being, for the solace of his suffering fellow creature." But is has been crusted over by "the bodily part," stretching into carnal desires (19). Esdaile maintained that Indians were more susceptible to mesmeric influence than Europeans, and for this reason he chose Hooghly as the locale for a mesmeric clinic that he established in the 1840s. For Esdaile, the "vital fluid" activates a paranormal and beneficent

---

2. For mesmerism in Victorian culture, see Winter; for mesmerism as an element of the exchange of "Orientalized" knowledge between Britain and India, see Prakash, who attends to Esdaile, 33; 188.

intersubjectivity; "Man is not, as commonly supposed, shut up in his penthouse, his body, isolated and impotent to affect his fellow-creatures beneficially by a benevolent will" (3). The vital fluid saves us from such isolation; it can be poured from "one person . . . into the system of another" (3). Not all Victorian observers shared Esdaile's premise that mesmeric motives were generally benevolent, and Esdaile himself confessed that the outcome of any mesmeric session was dependent on the mesmerizer's choice to "use the power for good, or evil" (24).

Victorian descriptions of mesmerism—those of Esdaile and Collins as well as others—zero in on the hand as the most crucial body part for the excitation of the vital fluids. Techniques for activating this invisible substance involve the magnetizer moving his hands above the subject, a gesture that is a called "a pass." Magnetic relations are established by bringing the hand into proximity with the body of the mesmerized. Neither Esdaile nor John Elliotson says why, as in the quote that begins this section: Esdaile, a medically trained doctor and a mesmerist, does not explain why the fingers would be the body part uniquely equipped to transmit the invisible "something" of the will, nor why hands would be the primary vehicle of mesmerist technique. Hands disappear into general terms for what occurs; patients are "mesmerized," "catelepsed," and "entranced" (137–39).

Collins also gives an unacknowledged prominence to the hands in the articles he wrote on mesmerism for *The Leader*. Unlike Esdaile, the Count who Collins investigated used mesmerism as a sadistic party trick. Hands fly all over Collins's reports. One guest describes "a painful sensation of heat in the head—a red-hot pouring, as it were, into his brain from the Count's hands" ("Magnetic," Letter III, 184). On another evening, Collins watches the Count subject a young woman to the symptoms of strychnine poisoning with a pass of his hands ("Magnetic," Letter II, 160). In another installment, Collins relates his own encounter with a mesmerized young woman:

> . . . the magnetizer made one 'pass' over V—'s hand, when she took mine; and immediately after it began to close—tighter! tighter! tighter!—until . . . I fairly begged to be released from a sensation which most men agree to be a remarkably agreeable one—the squeeze of a young lady's hand! ("Magnetic," Letter IV, 256)

Despite mesmeric desires for a merger of souls in an oceanic bliss of vital fluid, the annals of the movement are full of such accounts of estrangement and manipulation.

Estrangement is also felt by the Brahmin's English boy, who reluctantly succumbs to his masters' demands. Other than that, the ritual is historically anomalous. Looking into a puddle of ink in the palm of one's hand—nothing like that occurs in the annals of Victorian mesmerism. Nevertheless, the scene brilliantly condenses some of Victorian mesmerism's dreams and problems. One, it repeats the semi-visibility of the mesmeric hand—mesmerism's elaborately described manual techniques, and its theoretical oversight of just this fact. Two, it connects paranormal embodiment to India, and provocatively so, inverting the usual hierarchy of a magnetizing Englishman over a magnetized Asian. Three, it reflects a mesmeric desire to communicate without language. For it is a general attribute of Victorian mesmerism that whatever the vital fluids communicate—whatever powers or emotions pass along its vapors between and into others—they defy verbal translation. The content of the vital fluid is stubbornly asemiotic. As with the woman who exerts a vice-like grip on Collins's arm; its import, affective or otherwise, is unclear. Similarly with the trance boy; his hand is made into a differently abled writing instrument, albeit one that might be valued below others, because this hand doesn't write. With its off-label use of ink as a pool for visions, the boy's hand does not produce a reproducible, textual record. Thus, while the cohort of Hindu jugglers and their clairvoyant boy can access the paranormal, their access comes with a price. Their esoteric method of linking hands with ink does not enable them to write their version of things.

In the interconnected web of *The Moonstone*'s plot—tight in its causal links, wildly eclectic in its materials—the investigation of hand-mind circuits intersects with the subject of the semiconscious powers of touch, which intersects with mesmerism, which intersects with the subject of India, which in turns intersects with the subject matter of writing. Late in the novel Collins hits upon a device for consolidating this far-flung subject matter. The device is a character and a denouement. His name is Ezra Jennings.

"A LONG, WHITE, BONY HAND STEALED AROUND THE DOOR . . . THE HAND WAS FOLLOWED BY A MAN." (COLLINS, "THE DEAD HAND")

It's Ezra's Jennings job to tie up the loose threads of the domestic plot, one thread being the novel's thematization of writing, that singularly important manual activity, which, prior to Ezra, is performed solely by white Britons—Gabriel, Miss Clack, Roseanna, Franklin—the list is long. As is often remarked,

Ezra combines Asian and European physiognomies. In addition to his piebald hair, his face reminds Franklin of those "so often found among the ancient people of the East, so seldom among the newer races of the West" (390). Ezra, our harlequin of East and West, accomplishes exactly what the other amalgam of Indian-English character parts—the trance boy and his Brahmin superiors—can't do: he converts mesmeric intuitions into a linear text.

Hands make an important and once again overlooked contribution to Ezra's consummate achievement, his "stitch[ing] together" of Mr. Candy's incoherent ramblings, which is a kind of mesmeric writing (because intuitive, intersubjective). Ezra's method of decoding involves transcribing Candy's utterances and leaving blank spaces around them, which he later fills in with his own ideas of what they suggest, then altering the order of these fragments until he has "[put] the broken sentences together" into a "more or less" meaningful whole (442). The importance of Ezra's use of his hands in this exercise is not lost on Franklin, who likens Ezra to a tailor, commending "the ingenuity which had woven this smooth and finished texture out of [a] raveled skein" (456).

Several cultural associations come together in this act: the orientalized arts of mesmeric telepathy; the novel's identification of writing with European culture; and the European association of Indian hands with skills requiring manual dexterity—with textile work to be certain, but also pottery, which, as Aviva Briefel demonstrates, was increasingly associated with Indian crafts, as machine production began to replace craftsmanship in Britain (51–77). This string of associations is strengthened by the Brahmins' other identification as jugglers. William Hazlitt had seen a troupe of Indian jugglers perform in London around 1820 and commemorated their dazzling performance, which he attributed to their marvelous hand to eye coordination. Commemoration segues into patronization, along lines echoed in the Brahmins' asemiotic ink; Hazlitt speculates that the jugglers are capable of perfect manual dexterity but incapable of acts of literary genius, such as the ones achieved by the hands of European writers (137–38). Similarly, by likening Ezra to a weaver, Collins invites us to remember the manual skill involved in writing itself. By likening him to an ingenious weaver, really a mind reader, he invites us to see him as a writer whose handiwork and creativity are equally important, and moreover collaborative, since Ezra does not relay his own thoughts but rather those of another. Ezra thus concentrates several stereotypical Asian and European talents—the purportedly Asian talents of paranormal insight and manual dexterity in crafts, and the purportedly European talents of chirography and linear thought. When he deciphers Mr. Candy's ravings, these talents are wedded together in an idealized moment of interpersonal embodiment. Ezra allows

Candy's disorganized mind to channel his organizing hands. That is, Ezra's hands are telepathically embodied by Candy.[3]

Appearing as he does late in *The Moonstone*, Ezra Jennings crystallizes the manual-centric approach to character that runs throughout *The Moonstone*: not all action emanates from mind, understood as the individuated, rationalizing seat of personality. There is a world of other activity which slips along the transitional boundaries that are the provenance of the hand—boundaries between self and other, inside and outside, thought and intuition, reason and feeling, intention and outcome, the human and its instruments. Sometimes behavior begins with a mental decision, but more often it arises from the kinetic and extrarational connections between minds and hands and hands and others. Sometimes the constituent parts of a character interface efficiently and sometimes they don't. The outcome is vexingly unpredictable. Ezra, a composite character, forms a temporary whole with Candy—whole enough, that is, to construct the textual record of a purportedly single consciousness. But Franklin, also a composite character, gets stuck in a communication breakdown between his mind and his hands.

In these emphases on contingency, we can see that another boundary which the novel's manual-centrism elides is the one between action and character. Action and character are both precipitates of complex causes—networks if your will—in which a solitary consciousness is seldom determinative. Again, the resemblances to ACT are obvious, but with an important Victorian distinction. *The Moonstone*'s networks are enchanted. Although analyzable along the lines of impersonal instrumentalism, or de-spirited affordances, they are not reducible to those terms. Ezra's hands are effective because they tap into a sympathetic intuition that proceeds from his reason and his heart—and his memories, and his quasi-magical use of pen and paper. Franklin's hands are less effective than Ezra's but similarly in touch with extrarational and telepathic intuitions, some of which are his, some the Brahmin's, and some perhaps the diamond's. Hands manifest an alternative paranormal epistemology. Enchantment governs them like an elusive god in their machine.

Collins seemed to find the conceit so giddily alluring, he extended it into his own mythology of writing *The Moonstone*, claiming to have dictated the denouement of the novel to a series of overwrought female amanuenses while

---

3. Collins first developed the character Ezra Jennings in an 1857 short story titled "The Dead Hand." The title summarizes the story's conceit; Ezra's precursor, an impoverished medical student who goes by the name "Mr. Lorn," appears to die (but doesn't) in a Doncaster inn. Another man winds up spending a night in the room with his corpse, a macabre arrangement that reaches a climax when the man sees Lorn move his "long white hand" out from under his makeshift shroud (265). He wasn't dead after all, and after the incident of this winter night reveals his odd illness.

he was high on laudanum. Hands not his own, busily aghast, wrote the end of the *The Moonstone*—or so he said—transcribing the final chapters that he claimed not to remember when, sometimes afterwards, he read the completed manuscript.[4] According to the myth, the end of the novel would thus be the product of collaboration between a semiconscious drug addict and a group of hired hands. It echoes the image of the Jugglers' boy, whose visionary powers were called into action by the sight of ink, short-circuiting his normal mental activity. But for Collins, vision flows the other way, from an already short-circuited mind to hands not his own. Even better, it echoes Ezra's role as *amanuensis* to Mr. Candy's delusional ramblings, and as a *tailor* of the resulting fragments—transcribing and sewing, both relatively mindless tasks, by and large carried out historically by women. In all cases, a decentralized writing collective manages to achieve something extraordinary by putting a mental netherworld into direct communication with the appendage of the hand.

In all of this, it is easy to forget Ezra's Asiatic features. If there is symbolization of India at work in his character, it is sublimated by his quasi-mesmeric susceptibility. Which brings us to a final question for the novel, which the above suggestions about racialized bodies and their attendant talents and propensities only begin to answer: why does a novel that foregrounds hands also develop a politicized Indian subplot? Why hands *and* India?

"I WAS NOW TO CONSIDER WHICH WAY TO STEER MY COURSE NEXT, AND WHAT TO DO WITH THE ESTATE THAT PROVIDENCE HAD THUS PUT INTO MY HANDS." (DEFOE 456)

Long before Franklin Blake stumbles around in a Yorkshire country house and steals a diamond in his sleep, his dissociated predicament is anticipated by the god who is the diamond's proper owner. The "family paper" that prefaces the novel recounts a myth of Vishnu placing the moonstone on the forehead of his statuary avatar in the Somnath temple and "breath[ing] the breath of his divinity" into it (54). With its suggestion of an *anja,* or third eye, the diamond becomes the locus of the avatar's divine consciousness; mind, eye, and stone

---

4. The real story is less fantastic. John Sutherland reports that an inspection of the manuscript for the novel reveals it to be a holograph, composed in Collin's usual "scissor-and-paste method" (xxxvi–xxxvii). There were no amanuenses, and no signs of cognitive dissociation; Collins was a sober Ezra to his own literary process. The anecdote about composing *The Moonstone* appears to be an extension of its fiction, and specifically of its images of unusual emotional and mental states that are activated by mind-to-hand circuits.

are nearly synonymous. But the sacrilege of Moghul conquerors disrupts this sublime wholeness when Tippoo Sultan "caused [the diamond] to be placed as an ornament in the handle of a dagger" (55). Thus the importance of Franklin's hand-to-mind disorder is reinforced by the fact that he shares it with the Hindu statue to whom the moonstone belongs.

The fact that the diamond first occupied the place of the *anja* cannot be overstressed. The Body Politic of India, we might surmise, has been wrongly robbed of its governing mind, with the result that its sovereignty is rerouted through a bloody path of foreign misrule. The signifiers in this symbolic history condense a denunciation of colonialism, starting with the desecration of the statue by Moghul invaders. Tippoo Sultan confuses sacred body parts; by emblazoning the *anja* onto the handle of a dagger, he wrenches it from worship to weaponry, from a serene mind to desperate appendages. Enter the British, the next wave of conquerors, and with them John Herncastle, who steals the diamond with "a torch in one hand, and a dagger dripping with blood in the other" (56). From here on, the diamond pursues a path of indiscriminate revenge. All of its subsequent appearances align it with hands that act in amazingly bad judgment—that is to say, with the hands of characters whose minds are oblivious, impassioned, panicked, opiated, dissociated, or conniving—from the moment that Herncastle steals the diamond, to the moment that Franklin fixes it in a brooch for Rachel's dress, to the moment that Franklin unconsciously steals it and drops it into Godfrey Ablewhite's waiting hands, to the moment that Luker furtively passes it to Godfrey in the lobby of the bank. In all cases, the diamond's curse operates in ways that exceed or elude the intentions of the characters who have the misfortune to hold this precious stone. For neither Vishnu, nor Tippoo Sultan, nor Herncastle, nor Franklin, nor Rachel, nor Godfrey control the specific effects of the moonstone on others and the world. Its karma is contextual mayhem.

The political allegory is simple, actually simplistic. Colonialism occasions a disturbance in the hierarchy of the sensory organs for all involved, conquerors and conquered alike. Invaders rob and murder and without check from a governing conscience, and a desecrated and mutilated Indian Body Politic retaliates with fury, its enlightened mind reprogrammed for violence. In both cases, the loss of governance results in a rule by the hand, here operating as the vehicle of unchecked emotions and desires—the dark side of manual-centrism. Understood in this way, Collins's allegory has the ulterior effect of casting a suspicious light on all kinds of extratextual hands in Anglo-Indian colonial history. The story of sepoys ordered to commit religious violations by imbibing the animal grease on the cartridges of Enfield rifles is in effect a story of mouths made to do the job of hands. Then there is the subsequent history of the rise of fingerprinting, which Sir William Hershel developed as a forensic technique in the aftermath of the Indian Rebellion, as if the task of surveilling South Asians should naturally gravitate to their hands.[5]

Indeed, one could tell the whole story of colonial beginnings, abuses, and failures manual-centrically, starting with *Robinson Crusoe* (what better place to start than Gabriel Betteridge's scriptural text?), a hand-heavy novel if ever there was one, including Crusoe's question to himself about the future management of his God-given island estate, which question serves as the epigraph that heads this section of the essay. Now that hands have lost their innocence, Crusoe's pious reflection sounds like an omen of bad things to come. One could answer him by turning to David Wilkie's 1843 painting "Sir David Baird Discovering the Body of Tipu Sultan," which on the one hand presents a classical composition of military heroism, an ode to British colonial expansion, but on the other presents a chaos of hands pointing in all directions. A manual-centric perspective sees these images of colonial confidence as Janus-faced, where the flip side of order is confusion; of intention, obliviousness; of victory, slaughter.

"[THE MOONSTONE] WAS TO BE DEPOSITED IN [AMSTERDAM] WITH A FAMOUS DIAMOND-CUTTER, AND IT WAS TO BE CUT UP INTO FROM FOUR TO SIX SEPARATE STONES." (93)

With its copious hands, *The Moonstone*, I have argued, calls for a method of reading that focuses on just this feature, retelling and rethinking the story with hands as actants. Manual-centrism, the term I've used for this method of reading, seeks to correct the semi-visibility of hands in the novel and its criticism—the simultaneous salience and erasure of its manual motifs. With this method, we have seen that hands and minds in the novel have different realms of experience. The hand is intuitive, haptic, affective, erotic, illiterate, meditative, thieving, and amoral; the mind is analytic, visual, egocentric, literate, policing, and moralistic. We have also glimpsed the attractions of this model. It inspirits life in the spaces between selves, and it centers action and agency there. It decenters subjectivity from its purportedly singular, conscious core, and frees it from the isolating autonomy of organic wholes. In doing all this,

---

5. See Briefel 27–31.

it maximizes faculties that rational individualism denies or keeps in check: haptic, intuitional, subconscious, and intersubjective.

In the domestic plot, the rules of melodrama control the results of Collins's experiment with manual-centric character and action. Suspense, danger, and romantic tension are ultimately dispelled by poetic justice and sentimental victories. In the Indian scenes, in contrast, aberrant mind-to-hand circuits are less a literary experiment than they are a condition in need of remedy. The closer we move to India, the more ominous things become. The stakes of manual-centrism get serious; they get political. Ultimately, they get violent.

In its Indian plot, the novel's manual-centrism promotes a reading of colonialism as a happenstance of human greed, irrational and uncontrollable beneath the veneer of governance and design. Colonialism is figuratively enacted by the hands as organs that are and are *not* governed by minds. Instead, they are ambiguously driven by erratic and unpredictable factors. In other words, in its political deployment, the manual-centrism of *The Moonstone* interprets colonialism as chaos, intermittently harnessed to short-term ends, but ultimately incompatible with an analysis of geopolitics as a rational design. On the world stage, the concept of volitional human action is a ruse. The politics of manual-centrism dispute the premise that humans control the ramifications of their actions, either locally or globally.

All interpretive paths through *The Moonstone* lead to Colonial India, and all paths through late Victorian perceptions of Colonial India lead to the Mutiny, either as explicit or buried subject matter. In its Indian subplot, having recognized the down side of *metaphorical* manual-centrism—the greedy chaos of colonial governance—the novel also glimpses its *literal* downside. A manual-centric body is a body without hierarchy, a body in disorder; ultimately, it is a body in fragments.

By the time of Collins's writing, a number of mostly jingoistic histories had publicized the atrocities of the Rebellion, centering on the mutilations at Cawnpore above all. Charles Ball's scurrilous account is the most graphic; as Christopher Herbert writes, it is propelled by a "repetitive, compulsive-seeming, redundant, exorbitant retelling," symptomatic of trauma narrative (274). Women and children are "frightfully mutilated," "grievously mangled," and "cut to pieces," (Ball vol. 1, pp. 63–65); a man and wife are murdered after portions of their children's bodies are "crammed down" their throats (vol. 1, p. 97); and, at Cawnpore, "such ladies as had children had to see them cut in halves before their own turns came" (vol. 1, p. 274). Visual images were 'retold' as well—certain drawings, woodcuts, and photographs of the mutiny were reprinted in books and periodicals for years. One such image, originally one of seven in W. J. Sheppard's *Personal Narrative of the Outbreak and Massacre at Cawnpore*, shows a ransacked, bloody interior, corpses and body parts removed, except for a bloody handprint on a column, which operates like an afterimage of carnage.

The troubling literalism of mutilation that haunted Indian and British memories of the Mutiny might explain why, whenever *The Moonstone* approaches its Indian subplot, it abrogates its experimentation with characters as composites of parts and networks and reverts to the sanctity of the whole body. In this world, there is one special, indivisible whole—the diamond itself. A very special whole, its reconstitution drives the whole story. But wholes devolve to other wholes, in a process of regress. The novel's one sacralized whole is not a living human body but a thing, a diamond, and the diamond is in fact a part of another greater whole, that of the statue. The one point of commonality shared by all of these 'wholes' is the potential trauma of breaking them apart. Any mention of dividing the diamond is met with horror or disdain, since the Brahmins need to return it to the statue, in order to restore the statue's anthropomorphic holism, which has been violated by colonial plunder. Human dismemberment, it's true, is not represented in the novel. My argument is that it is present, but left out. It hovers in the extratextual content of those 'histories' of the Mutiny, scurrilous or legitimate, which intensify the novel's generative interest in fragmentation, with parts that make wholes, and with wholes that cannot be broken down into parts without the loss of their animating principle, their vital fluid—call it life.

Thus the Indian statue, an anthropomorphic effigy, haunts the novel like a constant, silent caveat to its fascination with the mechanics of character. The moral seems to be that while experimentation is nice, there are certain wholes that should not be taken apart, certain parts that will never again form a whole. The plight of the Hindu statue is a symbolic displacement of the literal horror of a violent dismemberment of the human gestalt.

There's some more information about this statue that further complicates but also strengthens this reading. Collins divulges in the Family paper (53) that the actual statue in the temple of Somnath was of the moon god, hence Chandra. But Chandra (also Soma, hence Somnath) is associated with Shiva, not Vishnu, as the novel claims. In addition, the statue (as Collins would or could have known) was a *lingam*, not a human image at all, and specifically one of twelve *Jyotirlinga* in which Shiva is said to abide. Elphinstone, who Collins probably consulted, since his works on India were in the Athenaeum library, reports that the statue at "Somnat . . . was a simple cylinder of stone"— in other words, a *lingam* (vol. 1, p. 554n850). British and European commentators of the nineteenth century understood the *lingam* to be a phallic symbol, and thus expressed a requisite degree of moral horror, as Macaulay's 1843 statements on the Somnath *Jyotirlingam* make clear; *lingamism* is "idolatry in its most pernicious form," Macaulay writes, and thus Ellenborough, by seeking to restore the Somnath temple, was "paying reverence" to a "god of destruction, whose images and whose worship it would be a violation of decency to describe" (189). Thus, the *lingam* is yet another inviolable whole, now the whole of a phallic symbol, whose fragmentation provokes horror. With this association, or rather its buried memory in Collins's tale, the breaking-apart of the statue signals castration, a mutilation of the *lingam*. And the fear of castration, so we are told by all schools of psychoanalysis, is the origin, in a male or male-dominated imaginary, of subject-formation, understood as an ongoing psychic oscillation between the ego and its threats, between a wished-for wholeness of the self and its tenuous possibility.

At the start of this essay, I wrote that the literal hand traumatizes with the thought of mutilation, but then, invariably, folds back into metaphor. That statement was admittedly opaque early on, but hopefully now starts to become clear. Every foray into the literalism of mutilation gets pulled back, as if by a magnet, to figural speech. For example: by trying to build the case that literal fears of mutilation are behind *The Moonstone*'s tale of a sacralized Hindu statue, I am led back to a phallic substitution, which, via certain unavoidable theoretical echoes, folds back into the symbolism of a particular kind of mutilation, i.e., of castration. A Lacanian gloss on this movement would say that the conflation of symbolism and literalism has to end here; the theory of the castration complex establishes this particular mutilation as the vanishing point of all subsequent linguistic substitutions, indeed of language itself.

Central to this male-authored myth of the formation of human subjects and human civilizations is a violence that cannot be remembered, which maybe never happened. But that hardly matters, as this and other types of mutilation happen in real life all too often, happen in history even if not in the bourgeois homes of fin-de-siècle Vienna or mid-twentieth-century Paris. Something about the horror of mutilation (as I also tried to say earlier in the essay), whether we know it personally or through rumor and representation, is so attention-grabbing, so mentally stupefying, that it overwhelms questions of responsibility, either buries or hystericizes the question of a culprit. The perpetrator of a mutilation is almost as unthinkable as the act itself.

Parts that stand for wholes, from *lingam* to statue to *anja* to hand: these chains of figural association in *The Moonstone* (I have argued) are in partial but significant ways generated by repression. They repress mutilation as figuration's unthinkably, impermissibly literal other. Such literalization is a cold retort to the novel's own clever games with character, which we understood via

ACT as a dissolution of singular human agency into a splattered windshield of actants. The many hands of *The Moonstone* perform this double movement. They repeat themselves, almost *ad nauseam*, in an impasse between figuration and repression. They reduce to two, diametrically opposed but inseparable possibilities: on the one hand, a breaking-down of the subject into multiplicities, into others and into ludic fragmentation; on the other hand, the claims of a living body's desire for an indwelling wholeness, its prerogative to live without violation and pain.

WORKS CITED

Ball, Charles. *The History of the Indian Mutiny*. 1858. New Delhi, 1981. 2 vols.

Briefel, Aviva. *The Racial Hand in the Victorian Imagination*. Cambridge UP, 2015.

Capuano, Peter J. *Changing Hands: Industry, Evolution, and the Reconfiguration of the Victorian Body*. U of Michigan P, 2015.

Citton, Yves. "Fictional Attachments and Literary Weavings in the Anthropocene." *New Literary History*, vol. 47, no. 2/3, Summer 2016, 309–29.

Collins, Wilkie. "The Dead Hand." 1857. *Wilkie Collins: The Complete Short Fiction*, edited by Julian Thompson, New York, Carroll & Graf, 1995, pp. 436–51.

———. *The Moonstone*. 1868. Edited by Steve Farmer. Orchard Park, NY, Broadview P, 1999.

———. "Magnetic Evenings at Home," Letter II. *The Leader*, 14 Sept. 1852, p. 160.

———. "Magnetic Evenings at Home," Letter III. *The Leader*, 21 Feb. 1852, pp. 183–84.

———. "Magnetic Evenings at Home," Letter IV. *The Leader*, 15 Mar. 1852, pp. 256–57.

Darwin, Charles. *The Descent of Man*. 1871. Penguin Books, 2004.

Defoe, Daniel. *Robinson Crusoe*. 1719. Edited by J. M. Coetzee, Oxford UP, 1999.

Elphinstone, Mountstuart. *History of India*. 1841. New Delhi, Atlantic, 1988. 2 vols.

Esdaile, James. *Mesmerism in India*. London, Longman, Brown, Green, and Longmans, 1846.

Felski, Rita. *The Limits of Critique*. U of Chicago P, 2015.

Hazlitt, William. "The Indian Jugglers." 1821. *Collected Essays*, edited by George Sampson, Cambridge UP, 1917, pp. 127–40.

Herbert, Christopher. *War of No Pity*. Princeton UP, 2008.

Latour, Bruno. "Life Among Conceptual Characters." *New Literary History*, vol. 47, no. 2/3, Spring–Summer 2016, pp. 463–76.

Macaulay, Thomas Babington. "The Gates of Somnauth," a Speech delivered in the House of Commons on the 9th of March, 1843. *Miscellaneous Writings and Speeches of Lord Macaulay*, vol. 4, London, Longmans, 1880, pp. 187–90.

Miller, D. H. *The Novel and the Police*. U of California P, 1989.

Prakash, Gyan. *Another Reason: Science and the Imagination of Modern India*. Princeton UP, 1999.

Rowe, Katherine. *Dead Hands: Fictions of Agency, Renaissance to Modern*. Stanford UP, 2000.

Seeley, John. *The Expansion of England.* 1883. London, Macmillan, 1914.

Sutherland, John. "A Note on the Composition, Reception, and Text." *The Moonstone,* by Wilkie Collins, edited by John Sutherland, Oxford UP, 1999, pp. xxx–xxxix.

Unsigned review. *Nation,* 17 Sept. 1868, p. 235.

Unsigned review. *The Spectator,* 25 July 1868, pp. 881–2.

Winter, Alison. *Mesmerized: Powers of Mind in Victorian Britain.* U of Chicago P, 1998.

CHAPTER 7

The Dead Hand

George Eliot and the Burdens of Inheritance

JAMES ELI ADAMS

> [...] to be not only a descendant but also an heir,
> denotes the superiority of man over animals.
> [...] The emergence of economic individuality
> begins at the point where inheritance ends.
> —GEORG SIMMEL (453, 354)

MOST READERS will recognize "The Dead Hand" as the title of Book Five of George Eliot's *Middlemarch*. Partly owing to that context, the phrase has gained wider currency as a byword for oppression, whether it be the power of wounded male vanity over a young woman's life, or the more diffuse constraints that the past imposes on the present. In this context, the dead hand is one of many triggers of the "dread" that pervades the latter half of Eliot's novel, and much of her fiction, a torment whose effects are often evoked in gothic figurations, including dungeons and torture. Much less often noted is the meaning of "the dead hand" as a legal mechanism for the conveyance of property: the dead hand is *le mort main,* mortmain.[1] That significance, I'm going to argue, complicates our familiar understanding not only of the phrase but of Eliot's novel, and indeed her fiction generally. As a mechanism of inheritance, the dead hand in *Middlemarch* is not simply a form of tyranny; it provokes reflections on the authority of the past, the ways in which it shapes our present, and the forms of duty we owe to the past. And given the extraordinary insistence with which the authority of the past is evoked in Eliot's fiction, we might come to see the dead hand as an object of fascination, eliciting desire as well as dread.

---

1. Exceptions include Beer, who discusses the term in relation to debates over women's property rights, and Rowe, whose analysis of the trope I note below.

The dead hand thus underscores and clarifies the powerful asceticism informing the moral psychology of Eliot's fiction. Of course to stress the austerity of Eliot's moral imagination is hardly a new emphasis, but it does work against the grain of much recent reflection on Eliot, and on *Middlemarch* in particular, which has tended to subordinate ethics to erotics. Catherine Gallagher, in a richly suggestive article, "George Eliot: Immanent Victorian," argues that "Eliot's ethics are preceded and animated by an *erotics* of personalization," and sets this view against a persistent "caricature" of Eliot "as a lugubrious author who gives her novels gravity by weighing down the exuberance of narrative curiosity with moral strictures" (70). One might object that this characterization is itself a caricature, but I'm running the risk of seeming to embody it, in the interests of something beyond a revisionary reading of *Middlemarch*. I want to argue that "the dead hand" in *Middlemarch* reflects a larger preoccupation across nineteenth-century culture with what I have called "the burdens of inheritance," which is articulated with special force in Victorian fiction, and speaks to fundamental conflicts within modern economic life.

Mechanisms of legal inheritance, and the fantasies bound up with inheriting and bequeathing, are so prominent in Victorian fiction that avid readers tend to become dabblers in English property law. The appeal of the motif is not hard to explain. Most obviously, inheritance functions to secure or reinforce a sense of identity and social possibility; its power is most vivid when it falls on an heir unaware of those prospects—as in *Oliver Twist* or *Jane Eyre*. That same potential generates a host of conflicts bound up with the anticipation of inheritance: the capacity to bequeath gives the testator a power that he (it usually is a he) may use to encourage, cajole, torment, or disappoint potential heirs, as if the power to bestow property were a person's final, culminating claim to human recognition. Victorian fiction thus bears out Catherine Frank's contention that in the wake of the Wills Act of 1837, which merged the devise of land (the will) with the bequest of chattels (the testament) into a single document, "the will—that catalog of one's possessions and expression of a right in things—became synonymous with a sense of personal agency and selfhood" (6). Potential heirs in turn typically look to inheritance as a rescue or exemption from modern economic life, and that increasingly nostalgic fantasy is played out in staple episodes of Victorian fiction: scenes of wheedling relatives gathering outside an old man's sick-room, or anxiously assembled for the reading of the will.

But inheritance transmits more than possibility; it conveys obligations and bonds that may seem to constrain agency as much as they enable it. This dimension of inheritance animates the most influential political understanding of the concept across the nineteenth century. In *Reflections on the Revolu-*

tion in France* (1790), Edmund Burke famously declared that English identity, both individual and collective, is a form of inheritance. Inheritance, Burke argues, is the foundation of a distinctly English freedom, but he invokes it most immediately as a rebuke to what he called "upstart insolence," those energies of self-determination and self-fashioning that he saw unfolding in terrifying fashion across the Channel:

> The very idea of the fabrication of a new government, is enough to fill us with disgust and horror. We wished at the Revolution, and do now wish, to derive all we possess as *an inheritance from our forefathers* [. . .] Always acting as if in the presence of canonized forefathers, the spirit of freedom, leading in itself to misrule and excess, is tempered with an awful gravity. This idea of a liberal descent, inspires us with a sense of habitual native dignity, which prevents that upstart insolence almost inevitably adhering to and disgracing those who are the first acquirers of any distinction . . . (117, 121; emphasis original)

Burke's appeal to inheritance is first and foremost a means of regulating individual agency—as Thomas Paine underscored in his furious response to Burke, *The Rights of Man* (1791): "I am contending for the rights of the *living*, and against their being willed away, and controlled and contracted for, by the manuscript assumed authority of the dead; and Mr. Burke is contending for the authority of the dead over the rights and freedom of the living" (42). Of course Burke would have contested this stark dichotomy, but in *Reflections* the ideal of inheritance clearly is most appealing as a constraint on those who inherit. Its authority punctures any dream of a new beginning in human affairs.

Across the long nineteenth century, we often glimpse this function of inheritance by way of negation—perhaps most notably in the fantasy of the self-made man. Josiah Bounderby, the self-made banker and industrialist who presides over the economy of Coketown in Dickens's *Hard Times* (1854), is a quintessence of the "upstart insolence" Burke decries. The very surname of this "bully of humility" types the character as a narcissistic bounder, whose life is devoted to blustering ambition and craving for social recognition. But as so often in Dickens, the comedy throws into relief far-reaching cultural logics. Bounderby is most suggestive as he is most preposterous. He goes further than merely stressing the social distance he has travelled, the gap between past and present; he literalizes the idea of the "self-made," and instead of recalling his parents, he erases them altogether, insisting that he was born in "the gutter I have lifted myself out of" (128). This fiction might seem merely another expression of his insecurity, but it amplifies an ideal of self-determination that is writ large in the icon of the self-made man. Bounderby's repeated insistence that he was abandoned suggests that the reality of a loving and eminently respectable mother would compromise his fantasy of heroic autonomy, would explode his dream of something like immaculate self-conception.

Bounderby is far from eccentric in this regard. At mid-century the self-made man is typically evoked through a muffling or even erasure of inheritance. Just two years after *Hard Times*, Dinah Muloch produced one of the best-selling novels of the Victorian era, *John Halifax, Gentleman* (1856), whose protagonist, as the admiring narrator puts it, "was indebted to no forefathers for a family history: the chronicle commenced with himself, and was altogether his own making . . . his pedigree began and ended with his own honest name—John Halifax" (11). The ideal continued to resonate in the praise of the Reverend Thomas Binney, in a self-help manual from the 1860s: "Unquestionably, the greatest thing that can be said of a man is, that he had no father; that he sprang from nothing, and made himself; that he was born mud and died marble" (Travers 250n).

In such tributes, self-invention hints at a dream of parricide. But the praise is curiously equivocal. The fantasy of originating one's own "chronicle" of family history, of transforming oneself from mud into marble, would sweep aside inheritance only to reinscribe the heroic individualist in a new dynastic fantasy. There seems an irrepressible impulse to imagine the life of the self-made man not merely as a moral triumph in its own right, but as a myth of origin, the beginning of a new family history. That genre in turn is redolent of the dynastic chronicle, which conjures up the very authority of tradition and inheritance that the self-made man ostensibly resists. Indeed, *John Halifax* calls on this very term: "the chronicle commenced with himself, and was his own making." And the Rev. Binney is recalling the famous tribute to Caesar Augustus's transfiguration of Rome, which Johnson applied to Dryden's transfiguration of English poetry: "he found it brick, and left it marble." Such gestures suggest the persistent hold of an aristocratic ethos even on the most fervent apologists of middle-class self-determination. Even as they derogate the power of inheritance, they register its continuing fascination not merely as a legal and economic mechanism, but as a structure of personal and cultural identity that withstands the volatility of markets and the vicissitudes of history. Perhaps the dreams of a parricidal son are always those of a thwarted patriarch. But in the nineteenth century this struggle seems unusually manifold, urgent, and central to the life of European culture—which may help to explain why this era gave rise to our greatest analyst of parricide.

These tributes to the self-made man, I'm suggesting, capture a far-reaching tension that is encapsulated in the epigraphs to this essay, two claims from

Georg Simmel's magisterial *Philosophy of Money* (1907). "To be not only a descendant but also an heir," Simmel pronounces, "denotes the superiority of man over animals." And yet, "The emergence of economic individuality begins at the point where inheritance ends" (453, 354). On the threshold of the modernity that is economic individualism—a state of which the self-made man might seem the logical zenith—inheritance is at once a privilege and an embarrassment. It is an ennobling affirmation of the human capacity to shape and sustain tradition, but as such it also obstructs new ideologies and projects of self-determination. Of course Simmel's conception of "economic individuality" might itself be in thrall to the myth of the self-made man, inasmuch as it, too, seems to rest on a fantasy of perfect autonomy. One might plausibly respond, with Derrida in *Specters of Marx*, that there is no point "where inheritance ends," that "all the questions on the subject of being or of what is to be (or not to be) are questions of inheritance" (54). In Derrida's reflection, ontology is subsumed under what he calls "hauntology," the persistence in the present of specters of the past. To be sure, one might extend this analysis at least as far back as Jacob and Esau; reflection on inheritance and its burdens is hardly an invention of the nineteenth century. But the peculiar claims of inheritance are brought into focus by the very effort to resist them, in a liberal dream of unconstrained autonomy that is popularly blazoned in the self-made man. As that agent seemed to repudiate any form of obligation beyond self-interest, it also reanimated appeals to inheritance as a countervailing moral restraint. "There is no inheritance," Derrida proclaims, "without a call to responsibility" (91–92).

This maxim resonates through a good deal of George Eliot's fiction, and brings home the ongoing force of inheritance as something more than a fantasy of recognition or power. In modern economic life, as the ascendancy of the market subjects human relations to the corrosive force of unbridled self-interest, one might well look to a many-faceted sense of inheritance as a call to responsibility, a guide and restraint of human desire. "If the past is not to bind us, where can duty lie? We should have no law but the inclination of the moment" (Eliot, *Mill* 496). Maggie Tulliver's appeal in *The Mill on the Floss* is one of many passages in Eliot that invoke the authority of the past as something akin to that of a Burkean inheritance, in which present-day action is understood to be not only responsive to, but entailed by, prior actions, as succession is aligned with the force of law. Bernard Semmel among others has explored the prominence of inheritance in Eliot's later novels as a political structure, in which personal and collective identity are anchored in the sympathies of "national inheritance"—most notably in *Daniel Deronda*. More recently, scholars have explored Eliot's interest in the forces of biological inheritance, which were increasingly prominent in Victorian physiology and an emergent cognitive science. In focusing on the dead hand, I'm interested in Eliot's alignment of moral authority with mechanisms of legal inheritance.

It is hard to overstate the prominence of legal inheritance in *Middlemarch*. The novel opens with Celia and Dorothea Brooke contemplating the jewelry they have inherited from their mother, and concludes with Dorothea renouncing her inheritance from Casaubon. Throughout the novel Dorothea dwells incessantly on how to dispose of her inherited income of 700 pounds per annum. The Vincy family, along with a host of relatives, is transfixed by the approaching death of Featherstone, from which they anticipate a bequest that will enable Fred to live the life of an idle gentleman. In frustrating that expectation, Featherstone underscores not only his own vanity but the power of the will to both whet and thwart human desire. Meanwhile Casaubon provides financial support for a young relative whose grandmother had been disinherited for making a bad marriage—and whose mother, it turns out, was herself deprived of a rightful inheritance by Bulstrode, who in his desperation to avoid exposure offers to restore that inheritance. Most momentously, Casaubon attaches a codicil to his will depriving Dorothea of any inheritance should she choose to marry Ladislaw—a stricture she of course ends up defying, which prompts her uncle to wonder if he should try to cut off the entail of his estate.

On this quick survey, legal inheritance seems above all a mechanism of greed and spite. ("I wish there were no such thing as a will," Caleb Garth remarks [338].) But the novel also sustains ongoing reflection on the ethical grounds of inheritance. This is often comic—as in the laments of Featherstone's relatives over what they imagine to be his obligations to family—but it becomes more somber and sustained in the figure of Dorothea, as she muses over what strikes her as the injustice of Will's predicament, and that of his mother. "Was inheritance a question of liking or responsibility? All the energy of Dorothea's nature was on the side of responsibility—the fulfillment of claims founded on our own deeds, such as marriage and parentage" (371; chap. 37). The implicit tension between "marriage" and "liking" hints at Dorothea's increasingly grim life with Casaubon, but it more importantly insists on the conflict rehearsed in reflections on her own responsibility to Casaubon, which are thrown into sharpest relief in "The Dead Hand." This figure, as I've noted, typically is presumed to refer narrowly to Casaubon's influence over Dorothea's life (a usage echoed earlier in the novel in the reference to Featherstone's "chuckling over the vexations he could inflict by the rigid clutch of his dead hand" [324; chap. 34]). As such, the phrase typically is received as a byword for tyranny and sheer negation, even by some of Eliot's best readers.

Suzanne Graver, for example, takes the phrase to be "a synecdoche for organic perversion, for life become moribund" and thus presides over "all the events in Book Five" (204). But the significance of the dead hand as mortmain complicates this association.

Mortmain, the *OED* tells us, signifies "the conditions of lands or tenements held inalienably by an ecclesiastical or other corporation," but it is figuratively extended to denote "the posthumous control exercised by the testator over the uses to which the property is to be applied." This legal sense was clearly alive when Eliot was composing *Middlemarch*: during this period, a series of lectures "On the Subject of Endowments and Settlements of Property" was being offered at the Social Sciences Association, and the lectures were later collected in volume form under the title, *The Dead Hand*. This volume, by Arthur Hobhouse (later raised to the peerage for his services to British law) offers an arresting vantage on Dorothea's wrestling with Casaubon's legacy, which engages distinctly topical debates over the limits of a testator's powers. In language that uncannily parallels Eliot's rendering of Casaubon's ghoulish authority, Hobhouse probes discrepancies between charitable endowments and social good, conflicts in which inheritance may pit past against present, individual against collective, public against private interests, tradition against change. In effect, Hobhouse explores conditions under which mortmain might be contested or broken. A good deal of *Middlemarch* can thus be aligned with contemporary liberal reflection about individual agency. At the same time, however, Hobhouse's arguments also underscore Eliot's potent divergence from classical liberalism; in Dorothea's reflection, inheritance becomes a particularly powerful means for understanding moral obligation generally. Inheritance has for Dorothea "a peculiar fascination," as the narrator puts it, not merely as a mechanism of philanthropy, but as a model of duty, of submission to authority even when—perhaps especially when—it is at odds with one's desires. In this light, the dead hand is a deeply equivocal emblem, an object of desire as well as dread, in which a seemingly tyrannical hold over Dorothea's life in fact mimics basic structures of moral obligation throughout Eliot's fiction. Ultimately, I'll suggest, Dorothea's agonized response to Casaubon's last wishes condenses an ascetic morality that is itself readily figured as a mechanism of inheritance.

Dorothea herself is an epicure of renunciation. Her asceticism is evoked from the very outset of the novel, when we see her disdaining Celia's delight in their mother's jewels, then attempting to disown her own sensuous pleasure in their beauty. The pursuit of austerity of course animates her decision to marry Casaubon, which bewilders those around her, who see in it a perversion of her youthful beauty and vitality. "I wish her joy of her hair shirt,"

Mrs. Cadwallader remarks (61; chap. 6). But the ascetic strain may be most suggestive in Dorothea's preoccupation with the burdens of her wealth. "There was a peculiar fascination for Dorothea in this division of property intended for herself, and always regarded by her as excessive" (408; chap. 37). As Celia notes, with more insight than she perhaps realizes, "She likes giving up" (18; chap. 2). Some commentators have suggested (in part following the narrator's promptings) that this longing is a naive one, partaking of both an impulsive idealism and a feudal paternalism that the novel subjects to ongoing scrutiny. As Jeff Nunokawa puts it in *The Afterlife of Property,* Dorothea's schemes are gestures of "impractical nostalgia and ethical extravagance" (80). But this assessment seems inadequate, in part because it so strikingly echoes that of her wayward uncle, Mr. Brooke, who glibly pronounces, "Young ladies don't understand political economy" (17; chap. 3). In fact, Dorothea's ambivalence towards her own wealth rests on a conception of property, more obviously grounded in ownership of land and the duties of stewardship attached to it, that revises Nunokawa's suggestive reading of what he calls "the afterlife of property" in Victorian fiction. Nunokawa works out the reverberations of a view of property under which "absolute possession" resides in the power to alienate property. Hence arises the paradox, he suggests, that ownership of property is always fraught with a melancholic premonition of its dispersal—a sort of *tristesse d'argent,* one might say. But Dorothea reminds us of a very different possibility: far from being saddened by such surrender, a property owner might savor the prospect of alienation as a means of renunciation—while at the same time clinging to the property so as not to lose the pleasures of imagining that renunciation, or of fulfilling the "duties" attached to its possession. Hence Dorothea's perpetual vacillation over her own wealth, busying herself with charitable schemes from which she repeatedly steps away. To be sure, such vacillation recalls the Prelude, with its emphasis on Dorothea's lack of an adequate medium for her piety. But what wealth offers Dorothea is in no small part the constant pleasure of its prospective renunciation. When she vows near the novel's end, "I will learn what everything costs" (812; chap. 83), the remark may seem puzzling, inasmuch as she is falling back on an income of 700 pounds per annum—the modern equivalent of perhaps $100,000 per year, hardly a regimen of poverty, particularly for a character who throughout the novel has been exclaiming that her wealth is a burden, that she has more than she needs. One might read the exclamation as an austere commitment to a different kind of arithmetic, but surely Dorothea by this point has learned just about all there is to know in the realm of moral and emotional accounting. The remark does hint, however, at a regret attached to the curtailment of further material renunciation. She has surrendered the possibility of bequeathing anything more substantial than influence, the "incalculably diffusive" "effect of her being on those around her" (896).

There is a more particular cultural resonance attached to repudiating an inheritance of landed property. On the one hand, with her ultimate surrender of Casaubon's property Dorothea reenacts, in Simmel's terms, the emergence of economic individuality, which makes possible the distinctive freedom of the modern intellectual: "any possession other than money places more definite demands upon the individual . . . in such a way that it appears to the individual as a determination or shackle upon his life" (Simmel 312). Dorothea's ultimate destiny, however unsatisfying it may be to most readers, in this light broadly parallels that of George Eliot's own career: released from the "more definite demands" of landed property into an "incalculably diffusive" moral influence, Dorothea recalls Eliot's own move away from the confinements of provincial life into a wider, cosmopolitan world in which her writing would exert its own incalculably diffusive influence. On the other hand, such freedom may readily seem a mode of deracination, a thorough-going and morally corrosive disengagement from community, which resists the obligations epitomized in the claims of sympathy. If the past is not to bind us, where can duty lie? Dorothea's new-found freedom from property opens onto a more cosmopolitan existence, but it also places her on the threshold of the world of Joshua Rigg. Rigg is the emblem of a modernity seemingly divorced from all ties to the past, a man who sells his inherited Stone Court to pursue his dream of "a money-changer's shop on a much-frequented quay" (520; chap. 52). Alone among the novel's characters, Rigg and Raffles—"I've no particular attachment to any spot," the latter remarks (526; chap. 53)—remain outside the pale of the narrator's sympathy, insistently described as sub-human animals and "monsters." How might Dorothea, or her creator, securely distinguish herself from these nomadic creatures cut adrift from the past? (This question obviously opens onto the peculiar functions of national inheritance in *Deronda*.)

In regarding Dorothea as something of a female Quixote, we also overlook the sometimes cutting edge of her austerity, as in her early exchanges with Chettam: "I think we deserve to be beaten out of our houses with a scourge of small cords—all of us who let tenants live in such sties as we see round us" (31; chap. 3). Such fervor deeply disconcerts the world around her—"It is troublesome to talk to such women," Lydgate thinks at their first encounter (93; chap. 10)—and the anxiety aroused by her affronts to convention is reflected, as D. A. Miller points out, in the storytelling that she incites (113). To be sure, the threat is muted by her inability to shape her philanthropic desires into something substantial, but that speaks less to her own failings than to the social and ethical dilemma that brackets the novel, which begins and ends with Eliot lamenting the passing of an adequate modern medium for "heroic piety" (896). But Dorothea's "fascination" with the division of property also suggests a motivation more elusive and volatile than either noblesse oblige or liberal guilt.

The intersection of private motive and social conditions is a central concern of Hobhouse's book on inheritance, which stresses (among other things) how difficult it is to codify public endowments that do not seem "extravagant"—not so much ostentatious as eccentric, because not responsive to a genuine public need. Hobhouse's volume, *The Dead Hand,* collected lectures that were for the most part delivered to the Social Science Association during the years 1869–1872—precisely those years during which Eliot was composing *Middlemarch*. I don't know whether Eliot ever came across these lectures in her voluminous reading or by report, but it is notable that Hobhouse draws heavily on Sir Henry Maine's recent, pioneering volume on *Roman Law*, with its famous account of the epochal transition from status to contract. Eliot read (and took notes on) Maine's volume in the fall of 1869, about four months after Hobhouse delivered a lecture to the Social Science Association, "On the Disposition of Property to Public Use." Hobhouse's preoccupations, even his language, are remarkably close to Eliot's own. The reprinted lecture reads almost as a barrister's precis of the moral and social issues surrounding the forms of charitable bequest that Dorothea envisions for her own property, forms that assume comic overtones in Featherstone's bequest, and a more sinister edge in the codicil to Casaubon's will—and in Dorothea's sense of obligation to the more informal wishes he expresses in his lifetime. Although Hobhouse specifically addresses public bequests, his largest concern is with adjusting or breaking the terms of bequests that at best have no utility, and at worst may be positively inimical to the public good. "Property is not the Property of the Dead, but of the Living," is his refrain (strikingly echoing Paine's rebuke to Burke, with "Property" standing in for the state). And yet, he points out, "the cold and numbing influence of the Dead Hand is constantly visible" (114). That influence is especially marked in what he calls "Founder-worship, our slavish and literal adherence to the directions of Founders" even when those may be eccentric to the point of absurdity (118). Against this devotion he urges—rather like Will Ladislaw—"If people will not give freely and generously [. . .] then, say I, let their money perish with them! It is such false gifts [. . .] [that] are like the gifts of malignant spirits of which the old fairy tales tell us [. . .] They are fatal" (123).

As in *Middlemarch,* Gothic figuration here evokes a tyrannical abridgement of human agency. Katherine Rowe has traced such figures across a long historical arc, arguing that "dead hand stories pose the Augustinian problem of what it means to alienate some part of the self by submitting it—in faith, marriage, service, or sale—to another" (12–13); "the testamentary clutch of the past on the present" in mortmain, she notes, is one particularly vivid instance of such alienation. Of course Hobhouse's aim is not to attack mortmain as such, let alone the ideal of charitable settlements such as Dorothea vaguely envisions. Hobhouse stresses instead the need to modify endowments that are—or have become—vehicles less of disinterested giving than of vanity or spite. His arguments echo many a reading of the will in Victorian fiction; they also hint at the challenge Dorothea faces in instituting a charity more effectual than Featherstone's almshouses. But Hobhouse's diagnosis speaks most pointedly to the experience Dorothea undergoes even before Casaubon dies, when he solicits her pledge to carry on his labors toward "The Key to all Mythologies."

It's important to grasp the exorbitance of this request: Dorothea understands it as an "indefinite promise of devotion to the dead" (521; chap. 48). That "indefinite promise" would entail a degree of moral commitment—a pledge of unwavering devotion—beyond any obligation that could be enforced by the letter of the law. (Although the characters of the novel repeatedly distinguish between moral and legal obligation—most obviously when Bulstrode tries to fend off exposure of his past—this may be the most subtle and consequential instance of that distinction.) On what grounds might one repudiate a "pledge" requested by a dying man? Clearly, in Hobhouse's terms, the pledge is "applied not to meet the real needs of society, but with superstitious regard to the behests of the dead" (46). Thus, for example, Hobhouse argues that a legator "making provision to perpetuate his own name or arms or tomb" (18) is not engaged in a charitable endeavor. Eliot tellingly invokes this very figure to describe Casaubon's plans for the future of the Key: "he had come at last to create a trust for himself out of Dorothea's nature . . . and he willingly imagined her toiling under the fetters of a promise to erect a tomb with his name upon it. (Not that Mr. Casaubon called the future volumes a tomb; he called them the Key to all Mythologies.)" (493; chap. 50). Of course the sense of private obligation to one's husband might seem to override any consideration of public utility, but Dorothea has come to recognize that Casaubon's "Key" is a phantasm rather than a storehouse of wisdom, "questionable riddle-guessing" rather than "fellowship in high knowledge" (479; chap. 48). She thus feels emboldened ultimately to repudiate Casaubon's "trust" as a private delusion, which could never be successfully realized. That "trust" would have Dorothea mortgage herself in perpetuity, to live under a dead hand that would never die.

But this is *not* Dorothea's initial reaction. Instead, she undergoes an agonizing ordeal, which culminates in her acceding to his request: "I am come,

Edward; I am ready" (482; chap. 48). That vow confounds Hobhouse's liberal individualism—as well as the more inchoate sympathies of nearly all readers of the novel today, who tend to see in Dorothea's gesture something like a self-immolation. But the reflection leading up to it is something more far-reaching than the submission of a dutiful wife:

> [...] she simply felt that she was going to say 'Yes' to her own doom: she was too weak, too full of dread at the thought of inflicting a keen-edged blow on her husband, to do anything but submit completely. [...] she dreaded going to the spot where she foresaw that she must bind herself to a fellowship from which she shrank. Neither law nor the world's opinion compelled her to this—only her husband's nature and her own compassion, only the ideal and not the real yoke of marriage. She saw clearly enough the whole situation, yet she was fettered: she could not smite the stricken soul that entreated hers. If that were weakness, Dorothea was weak. (481; chap. 48)

Initially, submission seems a form of weakness, a faltering of the impulse to affirm her independence. But as the passage unfolds, compassion energizes something akin to a heroic self-suppression. Out of sympathy Dorothea resolves to bind, yoke, fetter herself to an object of dread—an object, moreover, to which she already is in some sense fettered (I'll return to the prominence of that word in the novel). The nature of this connection is complex, beginning with the meaning of the word "must." That modal might suggest a form of coercion, something to which Dorothea is "fettered" by a force imposed from without on an unwilling agent. But she can only "bind herself" to a fellowship through her own free moral assent; only thus could she transform her agency from that of an instrument into that of an active power. She accordingly feels "compelled" to do this, the passage suggests, not through external constraint but through a moral understanding that recognizes two forms of fellowship. The fellowship stipulated by law and reinforced by "the world's opinion" fetters her as "the real yoke of marriage." But the prevailing imperative, that to which "she foresaw that she must bind herself" (the prospective mode suggests the solemnity of the occasion) enacts and affirms "an ideal yoke" freely embraced in response to "her husband's nature and her own compassion." ("Might, could, would—they are contemptible auxiliaries": so remarks Mary Garth, chiding Fred for his irresponsibility [138; chap. 14].) The dead hand is thus given renewed vitality as a moral as well as a legal obligation, as the "fetters" of a seemingly tyrannical obligation are understood as allegiance to an "ideal yoke." "If that were weakness, Dorothea was weak," but when the narrator casts back to Dorothea's initial dread it has been transfigured as a paradoxical strength. As Dorothea's ordeal rehearses the burdens of moral obligation, it transforms mere submission into an active assertion of will: Dorothea concludes that she "must bind herself" to that which already fetters her.[2]

If this deliberation reflects Dorothea's ascetic imagination, it also enacts an exemplary dilemma in Eliot's fiction, as it recognizes the moral effects of past actions in the present. The dynamic is frequently evoked as a form of *nemesis*. In her notes on the *Spanish Gypsy* (1867), Eliot remarks that "the collision of Greek tragedy is often that between hereditary, entailed Nemesis, and the peculiar individual lot, awakening our sympathy, of the particular man or woman whom Nemesis is shown to grasp with terrific force" (Cross vol. 3, p. 32). Here we see the familiar Burkean strain in Eliot's thought—nemesis is something "hereditary, entailed"—linked to an emphasis more distinctly her own: this hereditary, entailed structure "grasp[s] with terrific force." Eliot's moral psychology often conjures up the influence of the past as a form of violence. In *Adam Bede,* for example, Reverend Irwine pronounces that "consequences are unpitying" (171; chap. 16) and in the same novel the narrator remarks, "There is a terrible coercion in our deeds," even if "Nemesis can seldom forge a sword for us out of our consciences" alone (315, 313; chap. 29). As Stephanie Markovits points out, the first chapter epigraph of Eliot's own invention, in chapter four of *Middlemarch,* declares "Our deeds are fetters that we forge ourselves" (Markovits 90). And the scandal surrounding Lydgate prompts Dorothea to remark on "the terrible Nemesis following on some errors" (734; chap. 72). On this view, the consequences of every human action enforce a binding, inescapable connection to the past, under which no pledge can be revoked, no decision reversed, without great and manifold cost. A reflective moral agent thus must recognize that every action establishes binding conditions for the future that cannot be altered by the agent's will—"will" in the sense of both volition and legal disposition, a pun which reverberates throughout *Middlemarch.*

But Eliot's moral agents, unlike the landowner bound by entail, in effect inherit their own legacies, bound as they are by the consequences they bequeath to themselves (and others) through their own freely chosen deeds. In this regard, much of Eliot's commentary urges on the sympathetic reader

---

2. William Myers's account of this passage is closest to my own: "the happily preempted decision to continue Mr. Casaubon's work after his death can be read as a tragic but intensely personal attempt by Dorothea to wrestle herself out of the obscurity of confused feelings into a clear sense of a unique vocation, to which she is called not by 'law,' not by 'the world's opinion,' but rather by 'the ideal ... yoke of marriage'" (199). But Dorothea's inner resistance makes plain that she has come to experience her marriage principally as a duty; the early optimistic vision of it as a vocation is irretrievably lost.

a moral attentiveness like that informing Dorothea's thought on that "indefinite promise." A fully reflective moral actor will aspire, like Dorothea, to "the freedom of voluntary submission" (51; chap. 3). In its immediate context this phrase seems to refer to a prospective husband—"voluntary submission to a guide who would take her long the grandest path." Ultimately, however, Dorothea seeks submission not to some particular person or institution, but to the operation of moral law generally. And the operation of that law is repeatedly likened to forms of inheritance, within which past actions loom over the present like stern law-givers, who cannot be placated or mollified. As the narrator of *Romola* strikingly puts it, "our deeds are like our children that are born to us; they live and act apart from our own will. Nay, children may be strangled, but deeds never . . . and that dreadful vitality of deeds was pressing hard on Tito for the first time" (171). It certainly is a dreadful vitality that would prompt one to liken the repression of consequences to the strangling of children, and find it a task less easily accomplished. As "deeds" themselves are personified, Eliot suggests that human action generally always brings with it something akin to nemesis—but a nemesis "hereditary and entailed" through our own actions.

The burden of this "dreadful vitality," along with its suggestive ambiguity, is closely akin to what is evoked in *Middlemarch* under "The Dead Hand." The sense of subjection to a tyrannical past is hard to disentangle from the claims of duty and exemplary moral discipline. Dorothea's ordeal under the burdens of Casaubon's manifold "will"—both his desire that she continue his scholarly labors, and then the degrading stipulations in the formal will regarding her remarriage—is being generalized into an exemplary wrestling with the past understood as a sort of moral entail on the present. In "the dead hand," tyranny is very complexly interwoven with duty. Dorothea has any number of reasons to decline "that indefinite promise of devotion to the dead," and of course she ultimately does so. But what is most striking in this process is the rigor of the self-scrutiny that precedes her decision.

"To say 'Yes' to her own doom" will not be an alluring prospect to most readers, and the exemplary significance I assign to this passage may seem to reinstate that "lugubrious" moral teacher of which Gallagher complains. Surely, one might object, the deliberation tells us far more about the particulars of Dorothea's character, reflecting the misplaced idealism that led her to marry Casaubon in the first place? Moreover, the moral import of her hard-won conclusion is blunted by the seeming ease with which it is overturned. As Suzanne Graver points out, if this meditation argues for renunciation, the plot of the novel promotes freedom. And that affirmation is in turn faithful to Eliot's aversion to "the men of maxims," as a famous passage from *Mill on the*

Floss has it, those minds that are "guided in their moral judgment solely by general rules" (518). To reiterate the burdens of duty and the nemesis of past action is always liable to efface those particularities of the individual life and moral judgment that Eliot's fiction, and indeed the nineteenth-century novel generally, claims as its distinctive province. And yet the sympathetic understanding, as well as the force of a casuistry attentive to moral nuance, effects its individuating discriminations within a field of moral generality and rigor, whose authority it ultimately may be unable to dislodge.[3] This is the irresolvable dilemma enacted in *Mill on the Floss*. *Middlemarch* to a degree fights free of this impasse. But my goal is to stress the peculiar *vitality* that the novel finds in excruciating mental division—an energy that ultimately, I think, helps to unsettle an easy hierarchy of "ethics" and "erotics."[4]

The passage on which I've been dwelling of course hinges on the countervailing pull of a longing for freedom, which Dorothea embraces soon after Casaubon's death, when she inserts within the "Synoptical Tabulation" a note declaring her refusal of his request and reframing her life accordingly: "Do you not see now that I could not submit my soul to yours, by working hopelessly at what I have no belief in?" (539) This "little act of hers may perhaps be smiled at as superstitious" (539; chap. 54), the narrator remarks, but as such the gesture underscores the ongoing power of Casaubon's agency—even in her defiance of his wishes, the dead hand remains alive—and also the characteristic solemnity with which "the little act" invests Dorothea's new understanding. The declaration is tellingly cast less as a (vaguely ghoulish) disclosure to Casaubon than as a revision of Dorothea's earlier stance—notably in the peculiar emphasis of "now," which seems addressed as much to her own transformed awareness as to Casaubon's. "Dorothea's native strength of will was no longer all converted into resolute submission," the narrator remarks (536). And yet the effect of the earlier mental struggle, which so thoroughly affiliates submission with strength of will—both are "resolute"—is to make her refusal of Casaubon's request seem less a gesture of defiance than a slackening of will, a yielding to the desire for freedom that she had earlier resisted. The same association helps to explain the peculiar flourish near the close of the novel, when Dorothea, in declaring her desire to marry Will, almost in the same breath

---

3. Andrew Miller offers a suggestive account of the importance of casuistry in Victorian moral reflection, including Eliot's.

4. In this emphasis, my reading has much in common with John Kucich's suggestive account of Eliot's "dialectical inwardness," which resists Gallagher's disjunction by stressing Eliot's "deep-seated, contradictory conviction that human desire can be sustained only by a certain tension within personality" that is the work of repression (117). However, Kucich's stress on the radically asocial character of such desire tends to reduce moral law to a mere phantasm, and makes Dorothea's initial submission to Casaubon's request a form of "enslavement" (151).

also declares, "I will learn what everything costs." I've suggested that the tacit referent of "costs" has less to do with actual financial constraints that with the surrender of prospects for renunciation bound up with her wealth. But the slightly histrionic gesture also encourages us to see Dorothea's defiance of the codicil as a resistance more costly than it actually is. Both episodes, that is, subtly transpose Maggie's ordeal in Book VI of *Mill on the Floss,* where the narrator remarks, "All yielding is attended with a less vivid consciousness than resistance—it is the partial sleep of thought . . ." (487; Book VI, chap. 13). The inner division prompted by wrestling with the dead hand ultimately instantiates a more vivid consciousness, a more fully wakeful moral awareness, than the gratification of her baffled longing.

This reading might seem merely to redescribe a fundamental structure of narrative (and much of life): conflict always feels more engrossing and more energetic than the relieved calm brought about by its resolution. But the peculiar forms of mental agony that Eliot's novels so insistently evoke tend to have a more pointed bearing on questions of agency.[5] Here, as William Myers has suggested, Eliot's fiction can be illuminated by Nietzsche's critiques of "ascetic morality."[6] Nietzsche knew of Eliot's fiction, and paid her the compliment of referring to her in *Twilight of the Gods* as "a little moralistic female" (a barb somewhat softened by the suggestion that she perhaps could not help the moralism, since she was English). That moralism is addressed more pointedly, albeit implicitly, in *The Genealogy of Morals,* where Eliot might seem the very epitome of what Nietzsche decries as ascetic morality. Her reflection insistently invokes the authority of the past, and her appeals to a form of moral law certainly suggest what Nietzsche called the "crass causality" of English thought, which relied on "the *vis inertiae* of habit" or . . . "something purely passive, automatic, reflexive, molecular, and thoroughly stupid" (24). But this denigration inadvertently illuminates what is at stake in Dorothea's moral drama: it is precisely "the inertia of habit" that the ordeal seems designed to unsettle. In this emphasis, moreover, Eliot shares with Nietzsche the effort to recover a place for the will in a world that might seem to confound human volition. As she wrote in a letter of 1875, "I shall not be satisfied with your philosophy until you have conciliated necessitarianism—I hate that ugly word—with the practice of willing strongly, of willing to will strongly,

---

5. This is in keeping with a distinctive pattern of Eliot's fiction nicely distilled by Markovits, "the relocating of heroism from its usual manifestation in action to the internal process of decision that precedes action," which is reinforced by Eliot's "emphasis on passive endurance and suffering as a form of activity" (96, 99).

6. I am indebted in this paragraph to Myers 119–32, which examines "malady of conscience" in Eliot, principally in regard to *Adam Bede* and *Mill on the Floss.*

and so on" (Eliot, *Letters* vi, 66).⁷ Nietzsche's critique of the "ascetic ideal" culminates, on the final page of the *Genealogy*, in a discovery within that very ideal of the redemptive power of will:

> [. . .] all this means—let us dare to grasp it—*a will to nothingness,* an aversion to life, a rebellion against the most fundamental presuppositions of life; but it is and remains a *will!*. . . . And, to repeat in conclusion what I said at the beginning; man would rather will *nothingness* than *not* will. (163)

Dorothea's meditation on Casaubon's request expresses an ascetic psychology pushed to the threshold of moral masochism, wherein one strives to master forms of subjection by, in effect, willing them on oneself—embracing what might seem otherwise a mere surrender to law.

If Eliot's interests thus clearly intersect with Nietzsche's, they also address the peculiar burdens of agency inherent in the Burkean tradition. Burke, as I've noted, invokes inheritance as a profoundly ambiguous form of "entitlement," which both enables and constrains human agency. If English identity is a form of entailed inheritance, what freedom does it offer the heir to resist or transform that legacy? Burke finesses this question (which is the burden of Paine's attack) when he famously refers to English identity as a "choice of inheritance," as if an heir could bring into being the mechanisms of transmission that had already determined his very identity. But crises of moral awareness in Eliot typically dramatize just such a paradoxical choice, which affirms a kind of freedom in the midst of what might seem a thorough-going submission to law. This is most literal in *Daniel Deronda,* where Eliot's hero is allowed to "consent" to be a Jew—which, by virtue of biological and cultural inheritance, he already is. What might seem mere submission to irrefutable fact becomes a profound gesture of willed self-determination. (This paradox lies at the heart to Cynthia Chase's well-known deconstructive reading of the novel, although she overlooks the relevance of the Burkean tradition.) But forms of affirmation akin to Deronda's are at stake throughout Eliot's fiction, in similar structures of inheritance. On the one hand, a reflective moral character comes to recognize that every action establishes binding consequences that cannot be altered by the agent's subsequent will—"will" (again) in the sense of both volition and legal disposition. At the same time, Eliot's moral agents, unlike the landowner bound by entail, must recognize that they have in effect chosen their own inheritance—they have bequeathed to themselves

---

7. George Levine remains the best discussion of the moral implications of Eliot's understanding of "universal law," which Levine likens to that of Mill.

the consequences of their own deeds. Eliot's fiction thus urges on its readers the aspiration incarnated in Dorothea Brooke, who seeks "the freedom of voluntary submission"—submission not to some particular person or institution but ultimately to the operation of moral law generally.

One might frame this paradox in broadly Kantian terms, as stated by an unlikely kindred spirit of Eliot, Oscar Wilde. In effect, one could argue, Eliot is trying to represent what Wilde in *De Profundis* calls "the eternal paradox of human life": to be "entirely dominated by law" and yet at the same time, "to be entirely free" (172). The emphasis of course draws on Christian tradition (John Milton would be another kindred spirit in this emphasis), but in Eliot's secular thought the paradox is elaborated through an ascetic regimen, as Nietzsche so vehemently recognized. In Dorothea's response to "the dead hand," the moral and social tensions informing Eliot's understanding of inheritance are addressed through an ascetic organization of desire. We see in Dorothea how submission to external power can become a strangely exhilarating experience—much as the young Marian Evans realized a powerful sense of liberation in reading Charles Bray's *Philosophy of Necessity*. The experience of being "fettered," as Dorothea thinks of her predicament with Casaubon, in this light becomes an object of desire as well as dread.

Recent criticism of Eliot has tended to shy away from this "embarrassingly intense asceticism," as William Myers rightly calls it (183). Thus Gallagher's brilliant account of the novel celebrates an "erotics of particularization" that she finds exemplified most powerfully in the "metamorphosis" Dorothea undergoes upon learning of her husband's will. In that transformation, Gallagher argues, when Dorothea experiences "the stirring of new organs," the sudden eruption of "new erotic sensation" in her newly recognized sense of longing towards Will Ladislaw, "the idea called 'Dorothea' is reshaped around a sexual and reproductive core, so that the very notion of her 'species' takes on a newly biological meaning" (70–71). In this, she contends, Eliot participates in a large shift within nineteenth-century fiction, "a massive redirection of longing away from disembodied transcendence and towards embodied immanence" (71). But the "implanting of unaccustomed vitals" is a metamorphosis more often realized in Eliot's fiction through suffering, which is far from "disembodied." Hence the insistent evocation of a "dread" frequently experienced as a pain akin to torture, as characters are "yoked" and "fettered" to agonizing forms of shame, disgrace, and humiliation. These are emphatically corporeal experiences: Dorothea, Lydgate, Bulstrode, Casaubon all "shrink" to no avail from the proximity of others, with a sense of alienation that lacerates and burns. Thus Bulstrode contemplates the exposure of his past "as if with the terrible eruption of a new sense overburthening the feeble being" (618–19;

chap. 61). This may be a less alluring immanence than Dorothea's longing for Will Ladislaw, but it is central to the moral psychology of Eliot's fiction. Only through grappling with the burdens one inherits from the past—whether as the "terrific force" of Greek nemesis, in the deeds that cannot be strangled, the consequences that are unpitying, the fetters forged by our own illusions—only thus do Eliot's characters come to an agonizing moral awareness that can be felt as a kind of freedom.

WORKS CITED

Beer, Gillian. *George Eliot*. Harvester, 1986.

Burke, Edmund. *Reflections on the Revolution in France*. Edited by Conor Cruise O'Brien, Penguin, 1986.

Chase, Cynthia. "The Decomposition of the Elephants: Double-Reading *Daniel Deronda*," *PMLA*, vol. 93, no. 2, Mar. 1978, pp. 215–27.

Cross, J. W. *George Eliot's Life as Related in Her Letters and Journals*. Harper Brothers, 1885. 3 vols.

Derrida, Jacques. *Specters of Marx: The State of the Debt, the Work of Mourning, and the New International*. Translated by Peggy Kamuf, Routledge, 1994.

Dickens, Charles. *Hard Times*. 3rd ed., edited by Fred Kaplan and Sylvere Monod, W. W. Norton, 2001.

Eliot, George. *The George Eliot Letters*. Edited by Gordon S. Haight, Yale UP, 1954–6. 7 vols.

———. *Middlemarch*. Penguin, 1994.

———. *The Mill on the Floss*. Penguin, 1985.

———. *Romola*. Penguin, 1996.

Frank, Cathrine O. *Law, Literature and the Transmission of Culture in England, 1837–1925*. Ashgate, 2012.

Gallagher, Catherine. "George Eliot: Immanent Victorian." *Representations*, vol. 90, no. 1, Spring 2005, pp. 61–74.

Graver, Suzanne. *George Eliot and Community: A Study in Social Theory and Fictional Form*. U of California P, 1984.

Hobhouse, Arthur. *The Dead Hand: Addresses on the Subject of Endowments and Settlements of Property*. Chatto & Windus, 1880.

Kucich, John. *Repression in Victorian Fiction: Charlotte Bronte, George Eliot, Charles Dickens*. U of California P, 1987.

Levine, George. "Determinism and Responsibility in the Works of George Eliot." *PMLA*, vol. 77, no. 3, June 1962, pp. 268–79.

Markovits, Stephanie. *The Crisis of Action in Nineteenth-Century Literature*. The Ohio State UP, 2006.

Miller, Andrew. *The Burdens of Perfection: On Ethics and Reading in the Victorian Moral Imagination*. Cornell UP, 2006.

Miller, D. A. *Narrative and Its Discontents: Problems of Closure in the Traditional Novel*. Princeton UP, 1989.

Mulock, Dinah Maria. *John Halifax, Gentleman*. Dent, 1983.

Myers, William. *The Teaching of George Eliot*. Leicester UP, 1984.

Nietzsche, Friedrich. *On the Genealogy of Morals*. Translated by Walter Kaufmann and R. J. Hollingdale, Vintage, 1989.

Nunokawa, Jeff. *The Afterlife of Property: Domestic Security and the Victorian Novel*. Princeton UP, 1994.

Paine, Thomas. *The Rights of Man*. Penguin, 1985.

Rowe, Katherine. *Dead Hands: Fictions of Agency, Renaissance to Modern*. Stanford UP, 1999.

Semmel, Bernard. *George Eliot and the Politics of National Inheritance*. Oxford UP, 1994.

Simmel, Georg. *The Philosophy of Money*. 2nd ed., edited by David Frisby, translated by Tom Bottomore and David Frisby, Routledge, 1990.

Travers, Timothy. *Samuel Smiles and the Victorian Work Ethic*. Garland, 1987.

Wilde, Oscar. *Selected Letters of Oscar Wilde*. Edited by Rupert Hart-Davis, Oxford UP, 1979.

CHAPTER 8

Computation and the Gendering of Gestures

JONATHAN CHENG

BODY STUDIES in general, and scholarship on Victorian literature and culture more specifically, has recently shifted from focusing on heads and faces to a new interest in the representation of hands. This shift to hands raises multiple questions: are they an indicator of manual labor, a discrete space for the projection of different sexualities, a distinguishing trait of a racially segmented human species? While scholars have begun to interpret manual culture from a variety of perspectives, they tend to agree on a particular point. Paying adequate attention to the representation of nineteenth-century hands affords us new ways to configure the familiar outlines of what mattered to the Victorians. Meticulous prose dedicated to the appearance, motions, and sensations of characters' hands, for example, is not merely a stylistic effect in nineteenth-century realism. Parts of Helena Michie's and William Cohen's work treat the ways in which hand gestures are also euphemistic encryptions of Victorian sexuality, providing readers an intimate sense of the period's social discretions.[1] Peter J. Capuano connects physical descriptions of characters' hands

---

1. In Helena Michie's *The Flesh Made Word* (1989), her fourth chapter, "Body, Figure, Embodiment: The Paradoxes of Heroine Description," argues that the hands of fictional women often represent their romantic interests. Michie analyzes how fictional men often seek the hands of women, and she demonstrates how the description of women's hands tends to reflect their attitude towards potential partners. In Cohen's *Sex Scandal* (1997), his second chapter, "Manual Conduct in *Great Expectations*" analyzes the masturbatory imagery of Dick-

with new industrial and scientific developments, allowing readers to reevaluate overarching existential and theological anxieties unique to the era.[2] Similarly, in Aviva Briefel's work, those anatomical depictions can also underscore late Victorian colonial relationships, sensitizing readers to perceived racial differences embedded in a hand's physical attributes.[3] This recent reconfiguration of nineteenth-century body studies unquestionably establishes the importance of the hand's literal and metaphorical dimensions—requiring us to think in new ways about the period's manual culture.

Computational methods are useful for analyzing the hand and its embodied gestures, because quantitative techniques help magnify understated contours of literary history not immediately legible to readers.[4] Let us take a small-scale yet insightful example from Pamela Gilbert's analysis of manual touch in Dickens's *David Copperfield* (1848-9). Positing that Dickens's manual style correlates with an increasing cultural fascination with human hands, the article begins by surveying the number of hands mentioned in novels from the mid-eighteenth to the mid-nineteenth century. In a survey of nine novels from that period, there seems to be a steady increase in the number of hands as we move towards the mid-nineteenth century.[5] That suggestive increase creates an occasion for Gilbert to then further elaborate the historical developments bound up in that trend. In short, the word counts are by no means treated as conclusive. Rather, they allow Gilbert to argue provisionally that more cultural research is needed in order to qualify this observed pattern. We might disagree on what counts as a significant increase or what that escalation signifies, but provisional claims are excellent at creating exploratory occasions out of these latent stylistic patterns.

Similarly, but on a larger scale, this chapter uses computational methods to explore the changing description of characters' hand gestures in 905

---

ens's novel. He argues that the hand becomes immediately available for sexual signification, because it is one of the few uncovered body parts during this period.

2. Capuano's second chapter of *Changing Hands* (2015) thoroughly discusses manual culture as configured by natural theology, with, in particular, a close analysis of Charles Bell's Bridgewater Treatise on *The Hand* (1833) and how the hand gets configured with anxieties about mechanized manufacture.

3. Briefel's *The Racial Hand in the Victorian Imagination* (2015) argues that racial hands are central to understanding colonial relationships during this period. The images of racial hands that were widely distributed are indicative of an effort to configure racial categories and hierarchies.

4. For a thorough discussion about the role of numbers in studying literary history, see Ted Underwood's, "We Don't Already Understand the Broad Outlines of Literary History" (2013).

5. For the exact counts in each novel, see Gilbert.

nineteenth-century novels,[6] with a specific emphasis on investigating the extent that these hand gestures behave as signs of gender. I have reached two conclusions that seem to suggest a progressive story of social development. The first is that characters' hand motions decreasingly behave as a stable sign of gender. Initially, at the end of the late eighteenth century, female and male characters tend to perform a distinct range of hand gestures. However, these exclusive ranges increasingly overlap as we move towards the twentieth century, because several hand gestures become more common to both female and male characters. That overlap might appear to resonate with the chapter's second conclusion, as it occurs around the same time when authors begin writing about the hands of both their female and male characters. At first, male authors tend to write about men's hands and female authors tend to write about women's hands, but this decreasingly becomes the case as we move towards the end of the nineteenth century. In fact, as we move from 1780 to 1880, in novels by both men and women, the representation of men's versus women's hands becomes stunningly close to proportionally even. In short, when authors increasingly write about both men's and women's hands, it seems that their characters' hand motions decreasingly bifurcate into rigid gender categories. This correlation might encouragingly suggest that gender norms were becoming more flexible as authors represented a more diverse range of hands. However, although *characters'* hand motions were becoming less and less stable signs of binary gender in fiction, I will argue that it still remains unclear whether this stylistic trend extends to *lived* gender roles in the broader nineteenth-century milieu. Ultimately, my point is not that there was ever a stable conception of gender, but that stereotypical hand gestures manifest a far larger question about the range of manual agency available to actual men and women of the period.

This chapter adopts a Butlerian concept of gender: as conventional roles that people—real or fictional—were often expected to perform in order to be recognizable as men or women to nineteenth-century readers.[7] And this chapter will explore the extent to which performances of gender surface in characters' hand motions. As Capuano has argued, nineteenth-century depictions of characters' hands "reflect a rapidly changing economic reality that

---

6. This essay will describe the general composition of the corpus. All code and related materials will be made available on GitHub at https://github.com/ChengYJon/CharacterHands.git.

7. As Judith Butler has argued, the construction of gender is the product of actions that express gender. Gender in of itself is neither a concrete nor stable category. See *Gender Trouble* (2006).

only sharpens the lines delineating the separate spheres for each gender" (82). In this industrializing moment, when different forms of manual labor tend to diverge along gendered lines, characters' hand gestures afford further insight into bodily representations of gender identity. To that end, my study measures whether particular gestures tend to be exclusively performed by either female or male characters. And these gestures are recorded as either "feminine" or "masculine," because these categories reflect the overt gender roles emerging in the "separate spheres" ideology which dominates nineteenth-century culture. My study identifies "feminine" and "masculine" gestures according to a list of gendered possessive nouns and pronouns (described further below). And it should be noted that characters' genders are often more complicated than the nouns or pronouns used to signal a particular gender category. This study, for example, might count "her hand laid" or "the woman's hand touched" in the feminine category, but those signifiers can communicate different registers of femininity depending on the context in which these phrases appear. Qualifying each of those registers can be informative, and it would be possible to construct a separate study that accentuates those complex differentials. But this chapter explores what characters' hand motions can tell us about England's rigid configurations of feminine and masculine gender roles. By demonstrating that characters' gestures decreasingly functioned as a stable sign of gender, I will show that even stereotypical gender roles changed in subtle ways over the nineteenth century.

EXTRACTING THE HAND GESTURES OF FICTIONAL MEN AND WOMEN

This chapter models the visibility of men's and women's hand gestures based on a collection of 905 nineteenth-century novels. These works are not strictly confined to the nineteenth century, as their publication dates range from 1782 to 1903. However, the vast majority of the novels were published between the years of 1800 and 1900. Some of these novels were taken from Chadwyck Healey's *Nineteenth-Century Fiction* collection. Others were drawn from a corpus developed at the Nebraska Literary Lab. It should be noted that my evidence represents a canonical sample of the fiction published during this period. And throughout this essay, I will resist portraying this dataset as completely representative of the period's literature. However, it is still worth noting that this is a much larger sample of novels than typically studied in literary scholarship. Furthermore, I will attempt to account for my dataset's sampling biases by comparing my results with that of Google's Ngram Viewer.[8] By contrasting the distribution of men's and women's hand gestures between the two datasets, it will become easier to render the patterns unique to my sample of novels.

To measure the gendered distribution of hand motions across the corpus, I required a tool that could locate those gestures while differentiating the hands of fictional men and women. I used the Stanford Dependency Parser[9] to first restructure each novel for sentence-level analysis. I then used the open-source programming language R[10] to locate the sentences containing certain gendered nouns and pronouns performing a hand motion (discussed in further detail below). The parser is an ideal tool for this kind of analysis, because it records a wide range of words connected to hands in a given sentence: the gendered pronoun governing it, the actions it performs, and the actions of which the hand is an object. In short, the parser does the basic work of finding hands in a given novel, but it also performs the significant task of retaining the various details configuring those hands. This process results in a list of hand motions and the number of times they are performed by men's or women's hands. We can then subset that list to render how those numbers change over each year represented in the corpus. By subset, I mean we can zoom in on a particular hand gesture to see their gendered or historical distribution. This method helps to accentuate which hand motions were stereotypical of male and female characters, and it also sketches how those conventions changed over time.

Measuring the embeddedness of gender in characters' hand motions builds on an emerging conversation about computationally modelling gender in fiction.[11] This discussion has several potential implications for future studies of the Victorian body, as it sets a number of precedents for computational work in the period. Matthew Jockers and Gabi Kirilloff (2016) have analyzed the connection between gender, characters' actions, and genre in a similar corpus of nineteenth-century novels, specifically asking whether gendered characters behave differently across genres. They employed the same Stanford Parser

---

8. For a detailed description of Google Ngram, see https://books.google.com/ngrams/info. For a discussion of the Ngram viewer's relevance to humanities research, see Dan Cohen's "Initial Thoughts on the Google Books Ngram Viewer and Datasets."

9. This is a program that reorganizes tests into sentence-level grammatical structures for quantitative analysis. For a full description of the parser, visit https://nlp.stanford.edu/software/lex-parser.shtml#About.

10. While digital text analysts will use a wide variety of programming languages, R is often chosen because a community of literary scholars and statisticians actively contribute to this language's development.

11. Aside from the articles mentioned here, there is a far more extensive conversation. See Bethany Nowviskie, "What Do Girls Dig?"; Lisa Marie Rhody, "Why I Dig: Feminist Approaches to Text Analysis"; Laura Mandell, "Gender and Cultural Analytics: Finding or Making Stereotypes?"

to demonstrate pervasive trends between conventional gender pronouns and their associated verbs. For example, the Jockers–Kirilloff study found that men in fiction tend to be associated with the verb "taking" while women tend to be associated with the verb "sitting." In conversation with their work, Ted Underwood, David Bamman, and Sabrina Lee (2018) analyze these trends within the context of broader demographic changes in authorship. Looking at English-language fiction from both the nineteenth and twentieth centuries, Underwood, Bamman, and Lee found that fewer women were publishing fiction from 1800 to 1960, yet they found that the language differentiating male and female characters was becoming less rigid over time. They do not suggest that gender categories collapsed during that time, but they discuss the need for further computational research on how gender was increasingly codified in descriptions of settings, material possessions, and bodies.

At this juncture it is important to note that there are some components of my analysis which are reasonably unstable, and would require special attention in future research. First, the list of nouns and pronouns used to detect men's and women's hand gestures is decidedly short of comprehensive. Currently, the words "his," "man's," "brother's," "father's," "husband's," "son's," and "gentleman's" are used to extract the hand motions of fictional men, while the words "her," "woman's," "sister's," "mother's," "wife's," "daughter's," and "lady's" are used to extract the hand motions of fictional women. There are certainly many other nouns that could signal gender (king, queen, butler, maid, etc.), and future work can continually add to that list. But my current list has the benefit of clearly sketching the stereotypical gender categories of characters' hand motions. This also means, however, that my method does not account for significant characters who are referred to by generic nouns. If we consider Frankenstein's creation, for example, this method does not record the actions performed by "the creature's hands." The challenge with these instances is that these nouns do not inherently signal a conventionally gendered identity. A future study would have to manually, or computationally, ascertain the gender of these subjects and see how their gestures alter the results. For a similar reason, this study does not focus on the hands governed by first-person pronouns. When Dr. Seward writes that Dracula "took my hands in one of his, holding them tight," it is difficult for the computer to extrapolate a gender from the pronoun "my" (Stoker 268). Because of the prevalence of first-person narrators who refer to themselves and their hands using first-person pronouns, there are a number of instances which must be necessarily excluded from this study. Further research could, however, see if first-person narrators afford their hands a wider range of verbs and how those results line up with the historical survey developed in this chapter.

Nevertheless, modelling stereotypically gendered hand motions can profoundly affect how one interprets the significance of characters' gestures. Let us take a moment that Kimberly Cox has recently highlighted from Anne Brontë's *The Tenant of Wildfell Hall*.[12] The novel's central narrator, the farmer Gilbert Markham, undergoes various morally developmental episodes in seeking the wealthy Helen Huntingdon's hand in marriage. In one of the relatively intimate scenes, Gilbert notes how Helen "gave me her hand, without turning her head" (Brontë 338). Cox appreciates how this scene is a subtle moment when Helen proactively negotiates how to express her romantic interest while signaling her hesitation. The significance of this interaction requires recognizing how Helen's touch affectively facilitates this interaction. But where we go from there can depend on whether male or female characters tend to give their hand in fiction. If giving one's hand turns out to be associated with fictional men, then we could further investigate whether her gestures gain further significance as appropriating a stereotypically male hand motion. If giving one's hand tends to be performed by fictional women, then we might investigate what details significantly differentiate this moment from a broader historical trend. Either way, the observations produced in this chapter help to complicate existing interpretations of such manual interactions.

The method I am employing, despite its limitations, provides a new way to measure gendered patterns in characters' hand gestures. In order to interpret the significance of gender in the patterns, however, we first have to pose an obvious but important question: To what extent were novelists even mentioning the hand motions of their male and female characters? We know from Capuano's macro-data that hands "appear in nineteenth-century novels more often than any other body part including faces, heads, and eyes" (Capuano 12).[13] And it is certainly informative to know what motions are associated with which gender roles. But we will first want to know *whose* hands were more visible and whether that visibility remains constant over the nineteenth century.

THE DISTRIBUTION OF MEN'S AND WOMEN'S HANDS FROM 1780 TO 1900

While we are working with a canonical sample of novels, this sample can still inform investigations of the nineteenth-century literary tradition. In order

---

12. Cox's argument addresses how previous scholars read into manual touch as either behavioral management or body language. She argues that these approaches do not account for the affective quality of manual intercourse nor their sexual dimensions.

13. Capuano's quantitative survey shows how hands appear about four times as often as any other body part.

to gauge our expectations, we should ask whether scholars already have reasons to predict that either men's or women's hand gestures would feature more prominently in this corpus. Between different academic accounts of literary history, we have plenty of reasons to consider a wide range of predictions. Underwood et al. demonstrated that "there was, in fact, a fairly stunning decline in the proportion of writers who were women, from the middle of the nineteenth century to the middle of the twentieth," and this decline partially suggests that "fiction itself became more attentive to men." The increasing likelihood that the fiction of male writers would be published might lead us to expect that more attention would be given to descriptions of men's bodies.[14] That said, as many literary historians have also demonstrated, the period's development of the separate spheres ideology correlated with a heightened interest in portraying both male and female handiwork. Capuano has demonstrated how England's industrialization coincided with the production of social novels, such as Charlotte Brontë's *Shirley* and William Thackeray's *Vanity Fair*, that were heavily invested in men's and women's manual labor.[15] It would be entirely reasonable to expect that nineteenth-century novels would increasingly feature both men's and women's hands. Outlining these hypotheses puts us in a better position to compare a quantitative history with existing scholarly impressions of gender and manual discourses.

If we predicted that either men's or women's hands featured more prominently, we would have been right or wrong depending on the specific years. As it turns out, both men's and women's hands were more prominent at different historical moments. In Figure 8.1, I have plotted the average proportion of men's and women's hands mentioned for a given year. These proportions were produced by first tabulating the percentage of men's and women's hands for each novel, and then averaging those percentages for each year in the corpus. This produces a model that estimates the changing distribution of men's and women's hands in nineteenth-century novels. The proportion sharply evens out from 1850 to 1875—a surprising trend given that men were being published in fiction more often than women writers during this period.[16] This is after a period, from 1810 to 1850, when men's hand motions tend to be more prominent. This represents a reversal from 1780 to 1810, when women's hands

---

14. Underwood et al.'s survey of 104,000 works of English language fiction primarily demonstrates that books by both men and women were decreasingly characterizing women. What it also confirms, however, is that books by men tend to feature male characterization more prominently and vice versa for books by women. For a visual, see Figure 6 in Underwood et. al.

15. For a thorough discussion about the rise of industrialism, the rigid development of the separate spheres ideology, and manual labor, see chapters 3 and 4 in Capuano's *Changing Hands*.

16. Underwood et al.'s survey also demonstrates that the proportion of fiction books being written by women often drops below 50% from 1850 to 1875. See Figure 2 in Underwood et. al.

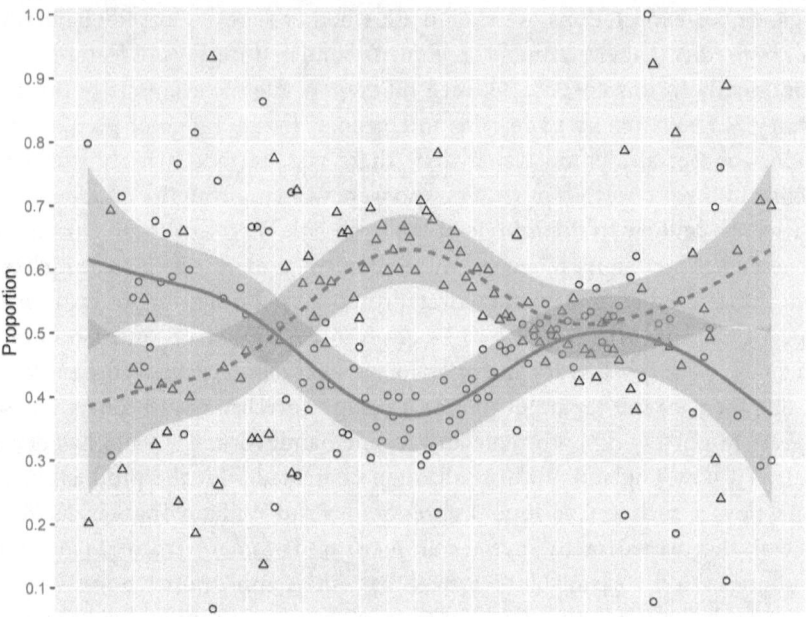

FIGURE 8.1. Distribution of Men's and Women's Hand in Nineteenth-Century Novels

The average proportion of men's and women's hands by year. The circular points represent the proportion of women's hands whereas the triangular points represent the proportion of men's hands for that particular year. The lines are an estimated fit for each gender's data points (dashed for men and solid for women). The shaded area represents the margin of uncertainty in that estimation, meaning the line could also be drawn elsewhere in that region.

are featured to a remarkable degree. These gradual turnabouts are significant, and my analysis will address the literary implications of these trends.

While it is tempting to explain these shifts using what we already know about literary history, we should first investigate the extent to which those shifts are inflected by corpus composition. In other words, *how reliable is the data?* As I have acknowledged above, my corpus reflects a canonical literary tradition long studied in universities, but I am analyzing a much larger sample of novels than is normally considered in literary scholarship. The corpus privileges novels and sometimes overemphasizes male writers. And one way to render the effects of my sample is to contrast these results against those of Google's Ngram Viewer.[17] Their corpus provides a useful point of contrast,

---

17. In a more ideal scenario, I would construct a second sample of nineteenth-century British fiction to compare against my sample of novels. This is a labor-intensive process. Relying on Google Ngram's English Fiction corpus provides a quick check, but it does not make a distinction between American and British English.

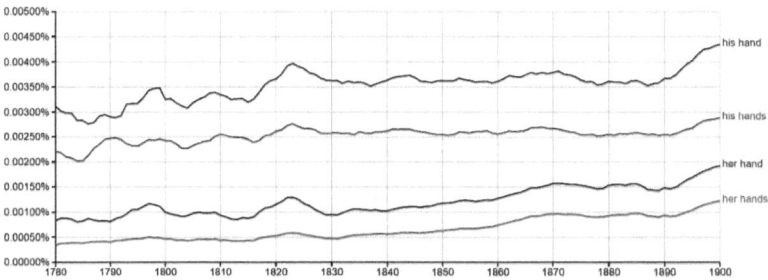

FIGURE 8.2. Possessive Language and Men's and Women's Hands. Google Ngram Viewer.

The frequency of "his hand/s" and "her hand/s" relative to the total number of words per year in Google Books. The low percentages are because Google Ngram calculates a word's frequency relative to the frequency of all words for one particular year.

because it comprises a much wider range of genres as well as a much larger sample size. It is worth noting, however, that Google Ngram's dataset is based on a Google Books project driven by university libraries, so their data will be shaped by the book-buying practices of those academic libraries. In any case, by comparing the previous figure with Google Ngram's distribution, we will have some sense of how our corpus might affect the distribution of men's and women's hands. In Figure 8.2, I have provided the relative frequency of the phrase "his hand/s" and "her hand/s" in the Google Books dataset.

The two datasets overlap in some key ways, but the differences accentuate which portions of the distribution are unique to my corpus of novels. The two models are similar in that men's hands generally receive more attention. However, these models significantly differ between the years 1780 to 1810 and 1850 to 1880, and any trends we observe in characters' hand motions will have to account for the following historical movements. In the former range of years, the hands of fictional women decline from relative prominence. In the latter years, the hands of men and women are almost proportionally equal to each other. In short, the two distributions are similar in that men's hands outnumber the hands of women, but these two trends stand out enough that they merit further analysis.

So how do we explain the declining prominence of women's hands in novels from 1780 to 1810, even though Google Ngram displays women's hands as occurring less often to begin with? One significant factor might be found in the novel corpus's author demographics. If there were, for example, a declining number of women writers in the early years of the corpus, that might partially explain the rapid diminishment of women's hands. That subset of

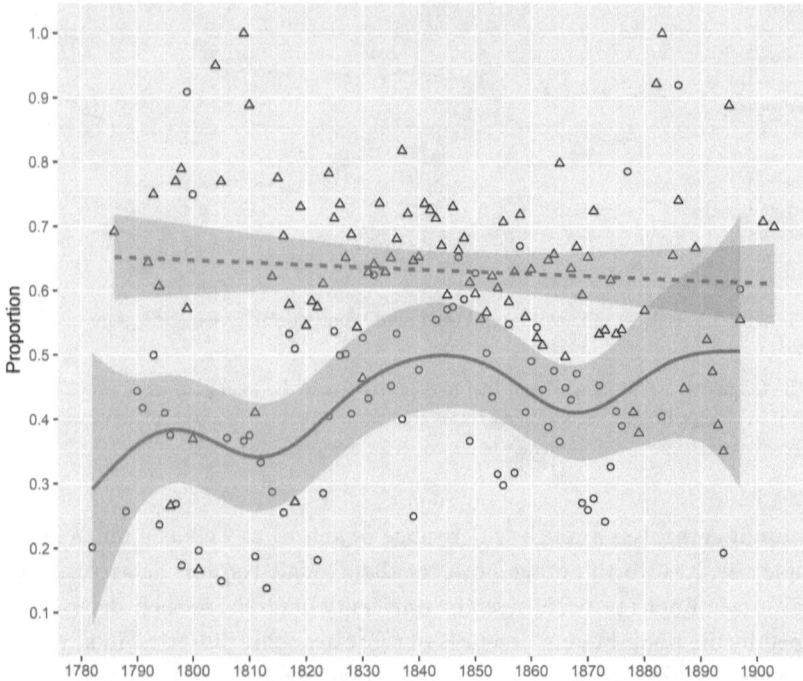

FIGURE 8.3. Average Proportion of Women's Hands in Novels by Men Versus by Women

Average proportion of women's hands that appear in books by men versus by women. The circular points represent the average proportion of women's hands in novels by women. The triangular points represent the average proportion of women's hands in novels by men. The lines are an estimated fit for each gender's data points (dashed for men and solid for women). The shaded area represents the margin of uncertainty in that estimation, meaning the line could also be drawn elsewhere in that region.

the corpus, however, turns out to be relatively equal when it comes to author gender: sixty percent of authors in the 1780s are women, sixty-two percent in the 1790s, and fifty-one percent in 1800s. While there is a slightly decreasing proportion of women writers in the corpus, these demographic changes cannot completely account for the sharp decline of women's hands by 1810.

Those demographic changes would better account for that decline, however, if women writers were simultaneously writing less about the hands of fictional women. The combination of these two factors would help to explain such diminishing representation. In Figure 8.3, I have plotted the average proportion of women's hands featured in novels written by men versus those written by women. This figure is generated by first calculating the proportion of men's to women's hands for each novel. But I separate that data by male and female authors before calculating the average proportion of hands per year. By separating the data by author gender, the plot renders how male and female writers were invested in the representation of men's hands versus women's hands to varying degrees.

As one might expect, women writers tend to write more about women's hands, but there is a quite remarkable decline in that tendency as we move towards the end of the nineteenth century. The proportion of women's hands in books by women declines from roughly seventy percent to about fifty-five percent. This strongly suggests that the diminishing representation of women's hands is partially due to the fact that *female authors were decreasingly mentioning women's hands*. Though it goes beyond the scope of this study, it would be worth seeing if that decline holds up in other bodily discourses. This work could raise a wide range of questions concerning women writers and their changing relationship to the bodies of fictional men and women. For now, though, it is enough to say that the declining prominence of women's hands may be partially explained by the fact that female authors were devoting less space to them.

But how do we explain the nearly equitable distribution of men's and women's hands from 1850 to 1880? If we attempt to answer that question by using author demographics again, we might expect to see an even proportion of men to women writers. But when we look at that range of years, seventy-two percent of the novels are written by men and only twenty-eight percent are written by women. To have an even proportion of men's to women's hands in the novels, despite the author–gender imbalance, is extremely interesting. In order to help account for this occurrence, we should return to Figure 8.3, as there is a subtle shift meriting further discussion. While women are decreasingly writing about the hands of fictional women, *men are gradually writing more about women's hands*. This gradual shift might seem of little consequence, but the corpus leans heavily enough towards male authors that even gradual changes within that demographic would weigh heavily on the overall distribution of hands. In short, the proportion of men's to women's hands stabilizes, partially because male writers increasingly mention the hands of fictional women.

Taken altogether, the trends suggest a thought-provoking historical pattern: *both male and female writers increasingly write about the hands of the other gender.* While Figure 8.3 only shows that female authors wrote less about women's hands, I provide Figure 8.4 to illustrate how they conversely wrote more about men's hands to a remarkable degree.

From 1780 to 1900, the proportion of men's hands in books by women inflates from roughly thirty percent to roughly forty-five percent (with several years where that proportion goes well above fifty percent). On its own, this historical trend complicates Cohen's sense that "For the Victorian reader, the hand would immediately be available as a site of sexual signification" (34). If

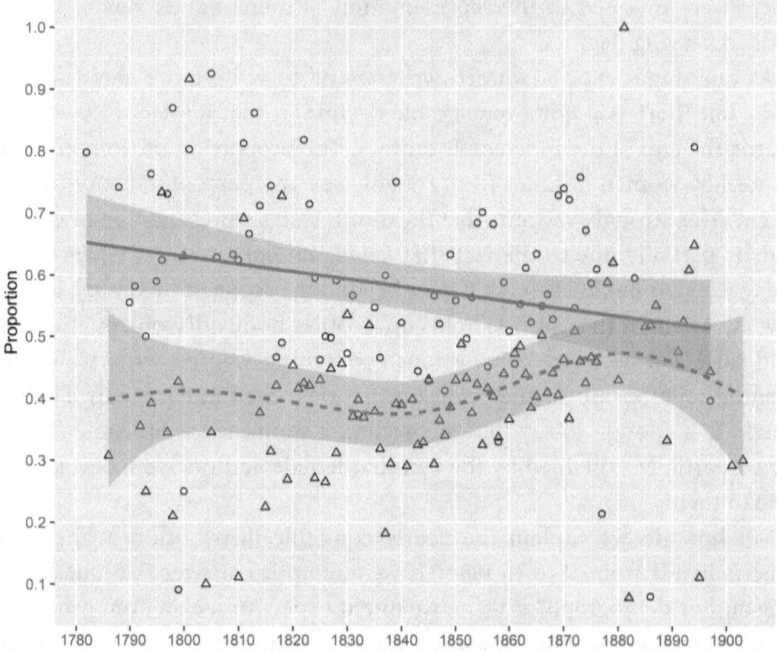

FIGURE 8.4. Average Proportion of Men's Hands in Novels by Men Versus by Women

Average proportion of men's hands that appear in books by men versus by women. The circular points represent the average proportion of men's hands in novels by women. The triangular points represent the average proportion of men's hands in novels by men. The lines are an estimated fit for each gender's data points (dashed for men and solid for women). The shaded area represents the margin of uncertainty in that estimation, meaning the line could also be drawn elsewhere in that region.

both men and women writers gradually start to write about the hands of the other gender, how immediate is Cohen's idea of sexual signification? If this trend extends to other bodily discourses, it would be an important fact about literary history that ties together existing scholarship on Victorian bodies, gender, and sexuality.

While these correlations are suggestive and promising in what they may indicate, more research is required to make any broad claims about Victorian culture. It is certainly tempting to hypothesize that men and women became more comfortable writing about the bodies of the opposite gender. If we wanted to pursue that claim, we could leverage the increasingly even distribution of men's and women's hands in fiction leading up to iconic novels published in the 1850s.[18] But the extent to which literary scholars take these

18. As a matter of fact, my method shows several Dickens novels as having a nearly even distribution of gendered hands, which is remarkable, given how often hands appear in his

subtle shifts in manual characterization as a reflection of deep cultural undercurrents is still up for debate. To what degree should we read these shifts as a sign of changing gender norms, and to what extent do they instead reflect the stylistic developments of particular literary genres? The following section will not attempt to pose any causal arguments, but it will suggest a few possibilities by examining the more stereotypical hand motions of male and female characters. If certain gestures are overwhelmingly performed by one gender over the other, we can then analyze the historical significance of those specific manual discourses.

THE UNEVEN DISTRIBUTION OF HAND MOTIONS AMONG FICTIONAL MEN AND WOMEN

Now that we have a sense of when men's and women's hands tend to appear in the corpus, we can investigate the specific gestures that they tend to perform. However, we have largely taken it for granted that characters' maneuvers will clearly reflect gendered divisions, so we first need to ask a fundamental question: Are there significant gender divisions between characters' hand motions? As addressed earlier, this is a fraught question, because one can qualify that division based on a variety of social or stylistic parameters (genre, nationality, race, etc.). Future research could be conducted to flesh out these variables. We may, however, at least begin to ask broader questions about stereotypical gender binaries: Do fictional men and women tend to perform different hand gestures? And does that tendency change at different points across the nineteenth century?

Quantitative classification methods help explore these questions because they clearly estimate the relative prominence of related categories. These methods are not intended to definitively label gestures as feminine or masculine. Rather, they measure how well notions of gender explain the distribution of characters' gestures. In order to weigh the connection between characters' gestures and gender, we train the computer to develop a stereotypical sense of "feminine" and "masculine" hand gestures. These categories are derived by having a computer observe roughly 14,000 gestures performed by fictional women and about the same number by fictional men. We then observe how accurately the computer can make gender predictions about characters it has not seen, and it makes those predictions solely based on characters' hand gestures. If there is a high percentage of correct predictions, it means

---

novels. *Phineas Finn* has a 50/50 distribution despite 82 gendered hands. *Dombey and Son* has a 52/48 distribution despite having 259 hands. *David Copperfield* has a 52/48 distribution despite having 197 gendered hands.

that the computer was able to observe a strong gendering of characters' gestures, which allows the computer to make accurate predictions based on the data. We would then have reason to believe that characters' hand gestures are at least somewhat structured by a binary notion of gender. This outcome could open new sites for interpretation around seemingly innocuous gestures, because hand motions that seem ubiquitous by the twenty-first century may have been more gendered in the nineteenth century. If the accuracy percentage proves unstable over time, then we would instead argue that gender binaries inconsistently shape characters' gestures. Or rather, that the gendered element of characters' hand gestures is often more than two dimensional.

After training the model on my corpus, the preliminary results suggest that there is a gendered division between characters' hand motions. When presented with a given hand gesture, the machine classifier was able to correctly guess the gesturing characters' gender eighty percent of the time. Because this result was derived from a nearly even sample of men's and women's hand gestures, computational text analysts and statisticians would take this thirty percent improvement over random chance as strongly suggestive. That accuracy is high enough over fifty percent that they would strongly consider whether conceptions of gender were a powerful organizing force. But they would also remind themselves that this is an exploratory study, and these observations should only be taken as statistically significant if the results are reproducible in a separate study. The sheer strength of this trend makes it hard to resist interpreting the literary significance of these results. It is especially easy to achieve eighty percent accuracy and immediately claim that characters' hand motions are concretely gendered over the nineteenth century, but we should first investigate how consistent that accuracy is across each year in the corpus. In Figure 8.5, I have plotted the classifier's average prediction confidence for each year. This measure of confidence can be understood as an estimation of how difficult it was for the computer to generate a gender prediction using a hand gesture. We want to see how that difficulty changes over each year in the corpus, because it helps illustrate the extent that gender binaries consistently structured characters' gestures.

While the classifier is able to correctly predict gender eighty percent of the time, the classifier becomes less and less confident about those predictions. The closer a year gets to fifty percent predictive confidence, the more indicative that the computer struggled to predict whether a male or female character performs a particular gesture. The data is split to show whether the computer has a more difficult time predicting either men's or women's gestures. It is slightly easier for the computer to classify women's hand gestures from 1780 to 1830 and slightly easier to classify men's hand gestures from 1830 to

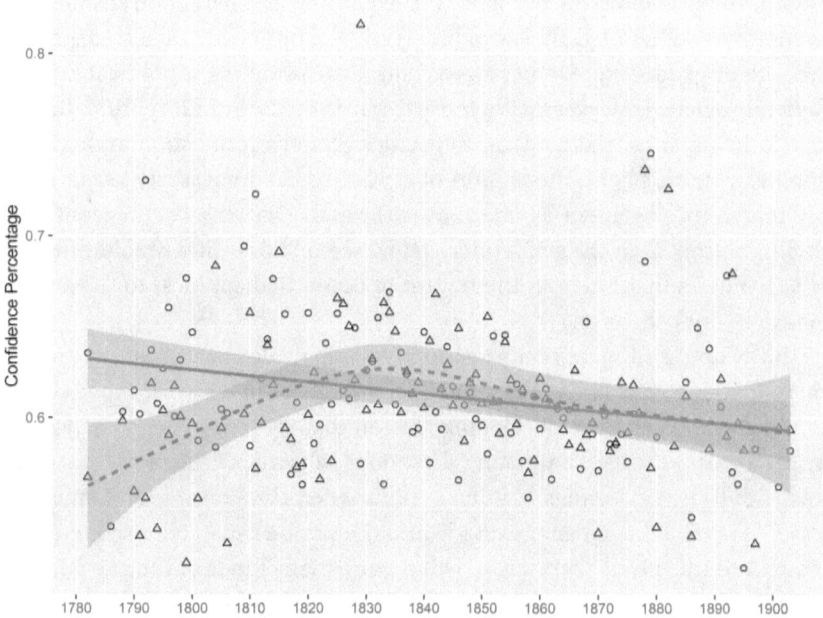

FIGURE 8.5. Confidence of Gender Prediction in Nineteenth-Century Novels

The classifier's confidence in making gender predictions. The circular points represent the classifier's average confidence in predicting women's hand gestures. The triangular points represent the classifier's average confidence in predicting men's hand gestures. The lines are an estimated fit for each gender's data points (dashed for men and solid for women). The shaded area represents the margin of uncertainty in that estimation, meaning the line could also be drawn elsewhere in that region.

1880. Overall, however, they both exhibit a similar historical tendency; while the computer detects a gendered divide between characters' hand motions, it gradually becomes less certain about the rigidness of that division.

That increasing uncertainty is congruent with Nancy Armstrong's argument in the *Cambridge Companion to the Victorian Novel* that the social appeal of rigid gender roles diminishes as we move towards the twentieth century.[19] She posits that early nineteenth-century novels initially tend to depict gender as the harmonious union of stereotypically feminine and masculine qualities—a happy union of gender types that one expects to see at the end of Austenian marriage plots. Armstrong emphasizes how these novels connect gender to a domestic "reproduction that secured the gendered division

---

19. For a thorough introduction to Victorian gender roles as they increasingly interacted with conceptions of sexuality, see Armstrong.

of labor, the perpetuity of property, the expansion of liberal citizenship, and the continuity of an English way of life" (171). The optimistic maintenance and marriage of gender stereotypes were central to sustaining a political fantasy of liberal society. However, as we move towards the twentieth century, turbulence in England's social landscape unsettles gender's connection to domestic happiness: "In this light, the failures of gender-based domesticity became not only increasingly evident as one moves through Darwin's century, but also more significant than the gender norms that seem to pass into obsolescence in the very novels that hold out the reward of domestic happiness to those who manage to obey them" (174).

This is not to say gender norms simply dissipate. Rather, gender's connection to that domestic fantasy becomes increasingly tenuous as we move across the nineteenth century, a developing tension that, in Armstrong's analysis, is already apparent when contrasting depictions of gender in Austen's marriage plots with those of Thomas Malthus's *An Essay on the Principle of Population* (1798). Whether this tension extends into the period's manual discourses, or further into the novels themselves, will require many kinds of social evidence. At any rate, the computer's decreasing confidence about the gendering of gestures might corroborate that hypothesis.

Setting aside broad historical theories for a moment, we can at least begin to investigate the hand gestures themselves. If particular gestures initially appear to be gendered in ways that align with or deviate from scholarly expectations, it could affect how confidently we assert that the gendering of characters' gestures declines over the nineteenth century. So how do we determine which hand motions are initially associated with either fictional men or women? One can computationally approach this question in a couple of different ways. For example, one can only look at sentences when hands are the active grammatical subject of the sentence (e.g., his hand slammed the table / her hands adjusted the picture). The verb "slam" would count as a masculine hand motion, and "adjust" would count as a feminine hand motion. This approach neatly extracts when characters' hands perform a particular action. However, one can also choose to only explore sentences where hands function as the grammatical object of a sentence (e.g., she placed her hands on the table / he enthusiastically took her hand). The verb "place" would count as a feminine hand motion, and the verb "take" would also count as a feminine hand motion on account of her hand being taken.

My approach extracts characters' hand motions, but it also renders how *characters' hands often move as the object of other characters' actions*. There are two advantages to this approach. First, eighty-eight percent of the sentences depicting men's or women's hand gestures grammatically position hands as an object, so this approach accounts for a larger percent of hand motions in these novels. Second, this approach has the advantage of recognizing when characters' hands are passively set in motion. As Gilbert notes, investigating the significance of hands means remembering that "the touching hand enacts the toucher's will, but the sensing hand troubles distinctions between active and passive, between the touching and the touched" (Gilbert). In order to explore the literary history of both the touching and the sensing hand, this study opts for the latter approach. This means that the computer examines each of the sentences where hands are a grammatical object and tallies the verbs configured with men's and women's hands.

The ten verbs the computer identifies as most indicative of feminine hand motions are take, clasp, wring, give, retain, withdraw, bestow, claim, seek, and press. The ten verbs the computer identifies as most indicative of masculine hand motions are rub, pass, strike, thrust, wave, offer, dash, grasp, stay, and try. When the computer attempts to make its predictions about a character's genders, these verbs proved to be the most reliable in making that prediction.

Nineteenth-century novelists, apparently, often depict women's hands as part of 'give' and 'take' interactions. Furthermore, not only are women's hands often given and taken, they similarly are part of scenes where their hands are 'retained' or 'bestowed' and 'withdrawn' or 'sought.' It should be noted that this is a group of six verbs with strong proprietary connotations. Statistics alone will not explain this proprietary gendering of women's hand motions, but we can subset the data to show where these manual interactions emerge in the novels themselves. If we look at the novels that most frequently depict women's hands being given and taken, we find something worth further study. The top three novels are all written by Fanny Burney: *Camilla; A Picture of Youth* (1796), *The Wanderer; or Female Difficulties* (1814), and *Cecilia; Memoirs of an Heiress* (1782).[20]

In these novels, women's hands are physically given and taken often to emphasize various forms of character agency. For example, *The Wanderer*'s protagonist, Juliet, withdraws from Lord Melbury who "from impatience, from curiosity, from charmed interest, and indescribable wonder . . . bent forward, so irresistibly and so palpably to take her hand" (567). This is a familiar scene where taking a woman's hand underscores a threat to her agency, dramatizing the masculinized threat of domineering noblemen. In *Camilla*, however, the eponymous character takes another woman's hand, allowing readers to sense her subtle ability to deftly handle social situations. Camilla increasingly con-

---

20. As we may recall, these appear in Austen's famous defense of the novel in *Northanger Abbey* (1817).

siders her friend, Mrs. Berlinton, a morally questionable "gamestress," and "as soon as they were alone together, Camilla took her hand but without returning its pressure" (833). Camilla mildly takes Mrs. Berlinton's hands, signaling Camila's subtle maneuvering to broach a sensitive subject. This is, of course, not a comprehensive study of women's hands in Burney's novels, but both moments suggest that the give and take of women's hands configures a varied sense of their social autonomy.

This configuration partially aligns with Michie's argument that "Victorian novels are frequently about women's hands: hands that stand for hearts . . . Asking for a hand is an entrance to the female body, the touch of the hand frequently the first touch between lovers" (Michie 98). For Michie, giving or taking a woman's hand is fundamentally about governing access to an entire sexualized female body. She traces the fetishization of women's hands to the broader social fantasy that governing sexual desirability can be handled without overtly saying anything. And Victorian novelists often dramatize the pressures of social decorum through quiet scenes of manual interactions that depict women's hands being given and taken.[21] This is not to say that men's hands are never given or taken, but that women's hands figure more prominently in stories of desirability and discretion. For example, Armstrong highlights this prominence in a reading of Maggie Tulliver's body in George Eliot's *The Mill and the Floss* (1860).

The hand motions of fictional men, however, seem to exhibit a wider range of meanings. There are several ways critics might subset these verbs to emphasize the various contours of literary history. For example, given that men's hands tend to "grasp," "thrust," and "strike," we might reiterate that men's hands often embody the threat of masculinized violence. Grasping hands certainly have several nonviolent connotations, but the image of men firmly grasping onto their victims tends to threaten unspoken forms of harm. One could also underscore how women's hands are often given and taken, even though men's hands are the ones being "offered." The fact that men's hands are frequently offered would presumably suggest that they are also frequently given or taken, but this is not the case. Women's hands are the ones literally given and taken, while men's hands embody a choice to be made by another character—almost as though marriage plots often hinge upon maturing female characters to consider what a man's hand entails. But perhaps one of the more suggestive avenues is the fact that "rubbing" one's hands is predominantly done by male characters. If we further investigate the context of male characters rubbing

---

21. For an analysis of a female character who appropriates so-called "masculine" hand interactions in choreographed social settings, see Capuano's Chapter 4, "Etiquette and Upper-Handedness in Thackeray's *Vanity Fair*," 89–124.

their hands, we see a similar result as with women's hands in Fanny Burney. The top five novels featuring men's hands rubbing are all written by Charles Dickens: *Nicholas Nickleby* (1839), *Martin Chuzzlewit* (1844), *Dombey and Son* (1848), *The Pickwick Papers* (1837), and *The Old Curiosity Shop* (1841).

Readers might associate the image of men rubbing their hands with unsavory characters that are up to little good, and they would often tend to be right. In *Nicholas Nickleby,* parliament members are often depicted rubbing their hands and plotting their political misdeeds. Mr. Gregsbury, for instance, receives a visit from his colleagues in parliament who are suspicious about his voting record. When Gregsbury successfully drives away the suspicious crowd, he "rubbed his hands and chuckled, as merry fellows will, when they think they have said or done a more than commonly good thing" (194). Gregsbury's scheming gesture pretty unambiguously embodies his dubious character. But there are also instances in the novel when it is unclear how the reader should feel about men rubbing their hands. For example, early in the plot, the novel's materialistic antagonist, Ralph Nickleby, banters with his quirky office clerk, Newman Noggs, about a malfunctioning watch. After Ralph concedes to Noggs's hypothesis about the malfunction, Noggs "rubbed his hands slowly over each other: cracking the joints of his fingers, and squeezing them into all possible distortions. The incessant performance of this routine on every occasion . . . [was] among the numerous peculiarities of Mr. Noggs" (24). While this unsettling gesticulation might seem to align Noggs with the novel's more suspicious characters, he will eventually emerge as the protagonist's trusted confidant, leaving the reader to reassess the significance of his incessant behavior. Regardless, when male characters rub their hands, there seems to be an invitation for the reader to reassess the moral alignment of these characters.

So given that fictional men and women initially tend to perform these particular gestures, can we reach any conclusions about the gendering of characters' hand motions? Hard to say. If we take the computer's decreasing confidence at face value, it would seem that the gender division between characters' hand gestures gradually diminishes as we move towards the twentieth century. But if we look at the gestures themselves, there are certainly reasons to discuss how we interpret that decline. For example, it appears that male characters initially tend to "wave" their hands more frequently than female characters. If we feel that it becomes increasingly normal for both female and male characters to wave their hands, then we may feel more confident in concluding that characters' hand motions decreasingly function as a stable sign of gender. This does not seem to be an unreasonable conclusion, especially if we feel that waving one's hand becomes a common social practice. That conclusion might, however, overlook how gender differentiation could be codified in the specific manner one waves their hand. It would be difficult to quantify, but one could certainly argue that there are feminine and masculine forms of waving one's hand (a broad open-body wave versus one more confined to the body). Waving in and of itself may decreasingly function as a sign of gender, but this may have put more of a gendered emphasis on *how* one waves a hand. If we extrapolate from that premise, then we end up with a more robust yet conflicted conclusion. Hand gestures themselves may decreasingly function as a sign of gender, but this may have put more of a gendered emphasis on other aspects of those gestures: the tense of the gesture, adverbs describing the action, physical descriptions of the hand performing the gesture, or subtler forms of gender differentiation.

CONCLUSION

This chapter navigates several forms of evidence that seem to lead towards different literary-historical interpretations. Initially, there seems to be a clear gendered division between characters' hand motions. Women's hands tend to be given and taken, for instance, while men's hands are often rubbing and striking. However, there is also evidence to suggest that characters' hand gestures increasingly function as an unstable sign of gender. While male characters initially wave their hands more often than female characters, for example, fictional women increasingly begin to perform this particular hand gesture as we move towards the twentieth century. That pattern might incline us to assert that gender divisions are gradually diminishing, but waving one's hand can still embody notions of gender through performative variations. The indistinctness of these gender divisions might seem less surprising, however, if we zoom out and look at the shifting behavior of nineteenth-century novelists. Both female and male authors, on average, begin mentioning men's and women's hands to a remarkably proportionate degree, meaning that female authors increasingly write about men's hand gestures and vice versa. It might then make intuitive sense that both fictional men and women would gradually begin featuring a broader range of hand gestures. And, as the Venn diagram of feminine and masculine hand gestures expands, the number of overlapping masculine and feminine gestures would simultaneously increase. We could interpret that growing overlap as a sign of diminishing gender divisions, but we could also argue that there are still gendered performances of gestures within that overlap.

We will not be able to fully reconcile these various historical trajectories in this chapter, but there are clues in Capuano's *Changing Hands* to help historicize why they might be bound up with each other. For example, if gender differentiation is beginning to surface more often through *gendered performances* of commonplace gestures, especially when novelists begin to write about the other gender's hands, then we might have greater context for Capuano's specific point about depictions of female maneuverability in William's Thackeray's *Vanity Fair* (1848). Capuano argues that the protagonist, Becky Sharp, threatens to climb the novel's social order by performing polite hand gestures that camouflage her dominance of routine social rituals:

> Becky's freely gesticulating hand is so frequently the object of Thackeray's narrative and pictorial attention not merely because the hand had become an especially dense transfer point for a whole system of binary oppositions between the sexes at midcentury, but also because it provided a dynamic location for *Vanity Fair*'s unique and overarching concern with the psychic and physical foundations of control in the social sphere. (93)

For Capuano, Becky's hands simultaneously embody anxieties about class and gender. He traces the social efficacy of Becky's manual tactics to a broader anxiety that socially ambitious women would achieve upward mobility, despite the barriers of etiquette, by learning how to *act* like proper society. The point is not to deny overarching concerns about men breaching social decorum. Rather, men's hands figure less centrally to anxieties about social manipulation and maneuverability. Under these historical conditions, it might not actually be so surprising that gender would be increasingly embodied by feminine and masculine variations of commonplace gestures; etiquette discourses often attempt to configure socially elevated notions of gender, such as "gentleman" and "lady," precisely through the proper execution of common hand motions. It is possible that if we separate the gestures of "his hand/s" and "her hand/s" from "the gentleman's hand/s" and "the lady's hand/s," we might be able to render the effects of class in gendered depictions of the body. This is a large enough hypothesis to say that it will require further research.

This chapter also deliberately leaves open significant theoretical questions about embodied notions of gender. Should we take the increasing *range* of men's and women's hand gestures as a loosening of rigid gender categories? Or does the increasing *overlap* between feminine and masculine gestures blur gender distinctions along a spectrum? Or does each gesture exponentially *branch* into a multitude of gendered variations? I don't pretend that my digital methods have answers to these questions. They do, however, provide quantitative patterns for asking these provocative questions while pointing to specific gestures and texts for investigation. In short, quantification creates a context for closely reading into many different kinds of social and literary forms of evidence.

This chapter does not pose any concrete answers to those questions, but it has, I hope, provided several avenues to help explore these questions. Readers are encouraged to return to the ten most frequently used verbs (top of 230) and further explore the gestures that fictional men and women most often perform. Readers are also encouraged to consider how the gendering of those gestures may have changed over the nineteenth century. This chapter briefly provides literary contexts for a small subset of these trends, but it is very likely that there are histories about the gendering of "clasping," "bestowing," and "trying" one's hands—to say nothing of what can be learned through combinations of these gestures.

Statistical models can only tell us so much about the cultural or literary provenances of these stylistic patterns. This chapter provides specific gestures that point to Burney and Dickens novels, because traditional close-reading methods will do a better job of fleshing out those configurations. However, as I have emphasized throughout, there are ways of adjusting the methodology to accentuate perspectival variations on the body's relation to gender. This chapter largely operates under a Butlerian approach, because the notion that gender roles are a performative product aligns well with an analysis of Victorian hand gestures. But, there is also an opportunity to begin imagining what a non-binary model of embodied gender might look like.

WORKS CITED

Armstrong, Nancy. "Gender and the Victorian Novel." *The Cambridge Companion to the Victorian Novel,* edited by Deirdre David, Cambridge UP, 2013, pp. 97–124.

Briefel, Aviva. *The Racial Hand in the Victorian Imagination.* Cambridge UP, 2015.

Brontë Anne, et al. *The Tenant of Wildfell Hall.* Oxford UP, 2008.

Burney, Fanny, et al. *The Wanderer, or, Female Difficulties.* Oxford UP, 2001.

Butler, Judith. *Gender Trouble: Feminism and the Subversion of Identity.* Routledge, 2006.

Capuano, Peter J. *Changing Hands: Industry, Evolution, and the Reconfiguration of the Victorian Body.* U of Michigan P, 2015.

Cohen, Dan. "Initial Thoughts on the Google Books Ngram Viewer and Datasets." *Dan Cohen,* 9 Dec. 2010, https://dancohen.org/2010/12/19/initial-thoughts-on-the-google-books-ngram-viewer-and-datasets/.

Cohen, William A. *Sex Scandal: The Private Parts of Victorian Fiction.* Duke UP, 1997.

Cox, Kimberly. "A Touch of the Hand: Manual Intercourse in Anne Bronte's *The Tenant of Wildfell Hall.*" *Nineteenth-Century Literature,* vol. 72, no. 2, 2017, pp. 161–91.

Dickens, Charles. *Nicholas Nickleby.* Edited by Mark Ford, Penguin Books, 2007.

Gilbert, Pamela K. "The Will to Touch: David Copperfield's Hand." *19: Interdisciplinary Studies in the Long Nineteenth Century,* no. 19, 2014, https://19.bbk.ac.uk/article/id/1626/.

Jockers, Matthew, and Gabi Kiriloff. "Understanding Gender and Character Agency in the 19th Century Novel." *Journal of Cultural Analytics*, 2016.

Michie, Helena. *The Flesh Made Word: Female Figures and Women Bodies.* Oxford UP, 1989.

Shelley, Mary Wollstonecraft Godwin. *Frankenstein, or, The Modern Prometheus: the 1818 Text.* Edited by Nick Groom, Oxford UP, 2018.

Stoker, Bram. *Dracula.* Edited by Diane Mowat, Oxford UP, 2008.

Underwood, Ted. "We Don't Already Understand the Broad Outlines of Literary History." *Stone and the Shell,* 8 Feb. 2013, tedunderwood.com/2013/02/08/we-dont-already-know-the-broad-outlines-of-literary-history/.

———, et al. "The Transformation of Gender in English-Language Fiction." *Journal of Cultural Analytics,* 2018.

PART III

Framing and Staging Hands

CHAPTER 9

The Photographer's Hand

KATE FLINT

HANDS ARE EVERYWHERE in Victorian photographs—embracing people; holding books, resting on a table or chair arm or on a papier-mâché balustrade. They are kept very still; folded in prayer; clasped over the chest in mugshots. Hands gesture; are posed on knees; appear gloved and ungloved. A comforting maternal hand holds the tiny paw of a baby. They are sometimes ghostly, whether made so because they moved during a plate's exposure, or as the result of new imaging technology: the hand of Anna Bertha Roentgen, wife of Wilhelm Roentgen, inventor of the X-ray, emerges in the first, 1895 X-ray image as a set of long, knobbly finger-bones wearing a solid-appearing ring. At worst, hands are significant because they are missing. Images taken in 1904 by the missionary Alice Seeley Harris, using the relatively new, highly portable Kodak camera bore witness to the mutilations carried out in King Leopold's Congo. These were used in lantern slide lectures given by members of the Congo Reform Association in the UK, Europe, and North America.[1]

The hands that most interest me in this essay, however, are not those that belong to the main subjects of a photograph, eloquent though these can be, but are those that bear some relationship to the photographer him or herself, and to the taking and making of a photograph. They are tactile hands, at the

---

1. See the images shown at the exhibition "Brutal Exposure: the Congo" at the International Slavery Museum, Liverpool, 24 January 2014–7 June 2015; Twomey; Briefel 134.

interface of body, brain, and technology. They are hands that, as Sir Charles Bell put it in the Fourth *Bridgewater Treatise*, represent "correspondence with the intellect"; instruments that, for Victorian commentators, could evince the power of intelligent design and/or evolution (148).[2] They may signify individual agency, yet may also be understood as metonymic—that is, as Janet Zandy reminds us in the opening of *Hands*, "human beings reduced to working parts" (1). As she also writes, "Working-class hands are rarely still" (1), and the photographed hand may, even in domesticated industrial labor, move with such speedy, accustomed motion that when captured in a photograph, it's reduced to a blur. This is clearly seen in one of the flashlight photographs taken by the pioneering documentary journalist and photographer Jacob Riis of "Little Susie at her Work," pasting linen onto tin covers for pocket-flasks, "with hands so deft and swift that even the flash could not catch her moving arm, but lost it altogether" (109).

The hand, and touch, have already played an important role in recent photographic history. The very title of Margaret Olin's *Touching Photographs* is a formulation that deliberately brings together the haptic and the affective to support her claim that photographs create community and build relationships: photographs touch by proxy when we are far from those whom we represent; photographs bear testimony to the individual eye of the photographer; photographs themselves have—or have had, until the ubiquity of digital screens—a powerful affective quality when they are held in the hand. Elizabeth Edwards and Janice Hart, too, have discussed the connection between touch and memory when handling albums and individual images, reminding us in *Photographs Objects Histories* of photography's materiality: "a photograph is a three-dimensional thing, not only a two-dimensional image" (1). In turn, these writers are drawing on Geoffrey Batchen's important reminder that photographs have "volume, opacity, tactility and a physical presence in the world" (2). This three-dimensionality may be microscopic, taking the form of chemical deposits on paper, or it may be far more visible through an image's mounting or framing—the physical form through which it enters into social and cultural existence; through which it changes hands. Photographs, Edwards and Hart explain, bear "scars of their use"—torn and creased corners; dirty thumb marks; a central crease caused by constant folding and unfolding; perhaps writing on their backs—all pointing to their literal handling (12–13). But touch, in almost all of the instances that Olin, Edwards and Hart discuss,

---

2. For recent indispensable accounts of Victorian attitudes to hands, see Briefel, esp. 1–26, and Capuano, esp. 1–16, and on Charles Bell 42–53. The *Bridgewater Treatises* constituted eight volumes by different authors that appeared between 1833 and 1840, and that connected natural theology and natural science.

is related to the subjective and personal—to questions of affect and emotion; of erotics and desire; of touch as it lingers in the imagination and in memory. By contrast, I will be relatively literal in my exploration of what happens at the interface of body and photographic technology—that is, although the potential for affect can rarely be banished from photography, I shall largely be concerned with the strictly material.

What follows has three sections. First, I explore the marks of hands that are visible on a final print or negative—marks that supply different types of traces of labor. Second, I discuss how, for much of the nineteenth century, the practice of photography could imprint itself on the physical human hand: the chemicals employed in the darkroom meant that there was considerable scope for corporeal staining. Finally, I look at the role that hands played in late nineteenth-century advertisements for photographic equipment, especially for the new, relatively inexpensive and easy to use box cameras. To consider the role of the hand is a means of understanding the changing relationship of photographic technology and human agency during the long nineteenth century. Focusing on the hand, both as a physical part of an individual and as a synecdoche for photographic work, proves to be an extraordinarily useful means of approaching the conundrum about the interwoven roles of human and mechanical in writing photographic history. What happens, I ask, in the permeable area between the human body and a piece of photographic apparatus?

HANDS IN PHOTOGRAPHS

Stray hands sometimes intrude into a photographic frame. They may belong to the photographer's assistant, for example, when holding an umbrella for shade over the camera, as we see in Julia Margaret Cameron's portrait of the art critic William Michael Rossetti. Of course Cameron could have removed this intrusive hand in the darkroom, but, as she wrote, what might have been an aesthetic "improvement" would also have removed the record of another individual's presence that day, a strange sort of autograph: "I never print out the hand holding the umbrella because I always remember proudly it is [Robert] Browning's hand!!"[3] The errant hand may belong to the photographer themselves: several of Jacob Riis's depictions of tenement life, taken by flash, show the hand that pulled the string attached to the flint that would have ignited the

---

3. Julia Margaret Cameron. Letter to William Michael Rossetti, 23 Jan. 1866, Cameron Correspondence, Harry Ransom Center, Austin, Texas, quoted Kelsey 81.

FIGURE 9.1. Julia Margaret Cameron, *Lady Elcho/A Dantesque Vision*, 1865. Albumen print from wet collodion glass negative. Given by Mrs Margaret Southam, 1941. © Victoria and Albert Museum, London. PH.255-1982. Used with permission.

flash powder sitting in the tray of the flash gun.[4] Such hands as these are part of the record of making a picture. They provide a clear reminder of the technology involved in creating an image: moreover, the hand's presence makes it impossible to think of the camera functioning as any simple prosthesis of the photographer's eye.

---

4. See, for example, Riis's "Ancient Lodger, Eldridge Street Police Station" (1890), and "Bohemian Cigarmakers at Work in Their Tenement" (1889). Both of these images frequently have the errant hand cropped out in reproduction.

Other disembodied hands appear on occasion. Whereas these may not belong to the photographer themselves, they nonetheless are attached to someone in the world outside the frame. They may reach out, as in the case of Cameron's "A Dantesque Vision" (1865)—to touch the rough bark of a tree trunk. Like the more firmly positioned hand that's already supporting the model (Lady Elcho), it invites the spectator to project their own somatic memories of feeling texture onto the scene. In Riis' "Ready for Sabbath Eve in a Coal Cellar—A Cobbler in Ludlow Street" (c.1890), there are two very anonymous hands holding a shovel on the right of the image, with only a thin sliver of the rest of the body visible. In one further example from Riis, "Black and Tan Dive in Broome St." (c.1890), a disembodied hand reaches out from the shadows to touch the shoulder of the woman in front of him. There are more hands in this image than there are visible owners of them. Such hands as these function as unintentional markers of continuity: that is, they are a part of the social environment that extends beyond that which is made visible in the photograph. These hands disrupt the apparent self-sufficiency of an image that has otherwise been created by the frame, the composition, and the lighting.

More frequent, however, are the smears and smudges—even the fingerprints—that appear on images that have been taken from plates, especially wet plates. It's easy enough to see how they occur, whether through lack of experience in finessing one's movements, or because the whole operation demands that one take caution with the plate's surface. Notoriously, Cameron did not initially understand this. "I began with no knowledge of the art," she wrote. "I did not know where to place my dark box, how to focus my sitter, and my first picture I effaced to my consternation by rubbing my hand over the filmy side of the glass" (Cameron 181). Instructions to amateur photographers make it very clear quite how deftly fingered one needed to be. Take the directives in one transatlantically popular mid-century manual, John Towler's 1864 *The Silver Sunbeam*. After coating the plate with iodized collodion, "It is very easy to ascertain by the touch of the finger on the right-hand corner, whether the film is sufficiently dry or not; if it no longer yields beneath a slight touch, the plate is ready for the next step" (131) —that is, putting it into a sensitizing bath of silver nitrate solution for a few minutes, before you:

> Withdraw it from the bath, seize the right-hand corner between the thumb and finger of the right hand; allow the silver solution to drain off thoroughly into the bath; with a piece of blotting-paper remove all specks of collodion from the back of the plate, taking care not to disturb the collodion along the edges of the plate or on the film side; remove the last drop of silver from the lowest corner, place it in the plate-holder, and close the slide and the shutter. (131)

FIGURE 9.2. Julia Margaret Cameron, *The Neapolitan,* 1866. Albumen print from wet collodion glass negative. Given by Mrs Margaret Southam, 1941. © Victoria and Albert Museum, London. PH.249-1982. Used with permission.

Smear-free perfection demands considerable dexterity, and as Robin Kelsey makes clear in the chapter on Cameron in his *Photography and the Art of Chance,* such technical purity was not one of her priorities. Indeed, he sees the very many glitches—his preferred term—that appear in her work as, if not necessarily deliberate in the first place, representing a commitment on her part to artistic ambitions that transcended the material possibilities of photography. One might also hypothesize the internalization, on Cameron's part, of a Ruskinian belief in the artistic and moral values of imperfection at work here—little as Ruskin himself liked Cameron's photographs.

Moreover, these hand touches may be seen as marks of authenticity. Esther Leslie, paraphrasing Walter Benjamin's "The Storyteller," reminds us in relation to pottery of the coming-together of soul, eye and hand in the production of a true craftsperson. Someone whose work demonstrates that they take an active and creative command over their tools, rather than being used by them, is the sign of a very particular type of authentication. "Fingerprints," Leslie maintains—those left in clay, or, for that matter, on a photographic plate, not those pressed into service for state identification—"Fingerprints and the handprints of the potter are not signatures; such traces differ from the individuating, authenticating autographs of high art" (and they differ too, one might point out, from the mass-produced signatures that appear on studio cartes de visite and that function as a form of advertisement). "Their virtue lies in their hinge with actuality, not their market value" (9).[5] Whereas Cameron was certainly not averse to making money from her photographs, these unretouched smudges, drips and fingermarks attest to the originality of her production; the human hand at work; art, not something mechanical. Defects, as Kelsey puts it, come to signify distinction. The "glitch was a way to spurn this moment of commercialization and connect her practice back to the origins of photography" (72).

Yet for most photographers, "retouching"—that is, the manual alteration of images, the removal of glitches, whether they be stray images of digits or digital traces themselves, or the careful addition of color—was a regular part of production, particularly within the commercial portrait studio. As John Plunkett's entry on "retouching" in the *Encyclopedia of Nineteenth-Century Photography* usefully spells out, "the aesthetics and practices of retouching can be separated into two broad periods. The first is from the early 1850s to the early 1860s. The second is from the 1870s onwards to the end of the century" (1189). The two periods are differentiated both in practical terms, as a result of the changing methods employed, and when it comes to attitudes towards photography as a genre. During the earlier period, photographs themselves were manipulated, especially through careful coloring—a practice that demanded, at best, the precise eye/hand coordination and delicacy of a miniature painter. Although some (like François Arago, secretary of France's Académie des sciences) believed that retouching in the form of added color ruined medium specificity, others perfected retouching the surface of daguerreotypes, adding

---

5. See also Briefel 51–77, for potters' hands and the marks they leave. One might also note that such fingerprints are ungendered and unracialized.

color to clothes and flesh and backgrounds. "Colourists," as Laura Claudet explains, "would make a tracing of the portrait on glass and then a paper stencil was made for each colour. The dry powder colour with gum Arabic was shaken over the stencil or applied with a fine camel-hair brush." The gum arabic was fixed to the plate by breathing on it, or the plate itself might be covered with a thin layer of gum arabic, which was breathed on to make it sticky, and then, with "a fine brush the powder pigment was applied carefully" (322).

When it came to turning out cartes de visite, especially at the less high-end, appearances could be greatly improved by a far less sophisticated manipulation—scratching the surface of a wet plate negative to achieve lights in people's eyes. During the second retouching phase, retouching of the negative became the dominant means of manipulation (although hand-coloring remained popular), especially after the introduction of dry-plate negatives, which were far easier to rework than wet-plate ones. Again, portrait photographs were the most frequent targets for retouching, whether technical imperfections were being cleared up, or a sitter's vanity flattered through the removal of wrinkles, the pulling in of a woman's waistline, or the removal of a double chin. The work was done by using a range of soft lead pencils on the glass negative after it had been covered by a medium (cuttlefish powder, or a simple resin dissolved in turpentine, for example)—a process that needed the same careful hand skills that are possessed by a practiced steel engraver. It also meant learning to see and think in reverse; remembering that working on a negative, black would become white, and that gradations and shadows were always affected by this. Workers were helped by new equipment, including desks with inbuilt lights and reflectors.

The skilled labor of retouching demanded, necessarily, a "light and steady hand," as Joseph Hubert, a photographer from Hackney, and author of *The Art of Retouching* (1891) termed it (26–7). In this deft activity, the retouchers' hands were necessarily at work for commercial ends. When Hubert remarked that "the brain should form a greater motive power than the hand," he had much less in mind artistic choices informed by a finely developed aesthetic sensitivity than pure pragmatism (although some writers recommended that one should consult the techniques of portrait painters when it came to indicating, say, how light from an outside source falls on a face).[6] Writing at the end of the century, he warned against the overuse of graphite pencils, since consumers had wised up to *too* much visible manipulation—even as he advised that there were some areas in which one should make an exception, especially when it came to "ladies' waists . . . You are always safe in cutting off an inch

---

6. See, for example, Barrett 658.

on each side, and in some cases, where corpulence is rather conspicuous, two or more inches will never be missed" (48–49).

During the retouching process, hands themselves came in for particular attention. After eyes, which were routinely brightened up, they were the most frequently retouched part of a likeness. J. P. Ourdan, in *The Art of Retouching* (1880), links their delineation with manual skill: "Few retouchers study the hand at all, and those who do generally dispose of it in a slovenly, sketchy style by which it is not much improved" (66). But practice and care in this area is very desirable: "The hands and arms in ladies' portraits . . . will require to be worked up to subdue the heavy veins, which usually appear more prominent than in nature. The creases on the knuckles should be removed and the luna in nails strengthened. Unless the hands are very small and very well posed they should be always as much subdued as possible" (65). Similarly, Ida Lynch Howe remarks that if "the hand be relaxed and lying without muscular strain" in a portrait, little retouching will be necessary, but if either "the veins or muscles are too much in evidence, or the hand or arm is resting awkwardly, causing a knotted or swollen appearance," some cosmetic remedial work will definitely be necessary (39). If the overall emphasis is on conveying the image of a lady's genteel femininity, it is noticeable, across a range of texts offering advice about photographic retouching, what an important role hands played. They should always be secondary to the face; they should not call attention to themselves, but unmistakably hands—or well-kept hands, rather—were, as we're about to see, very much a badge of respectability.

STAINED HANDS

By the standards of mid-nineteenth-century decorum, Julia Margaret Cameron was herself notoriously messy and disheveled in ways that went way beyond the appearance of her hands. Her great-niece, Laura Troubridge, recalled that she would be "dressed in dark clothes, stained with chemicals from her photography, (and smelling of them, too)" (38). Edith Nicholl Ellison, who as a child on the Isle of Wight also knew Mrs. Cameron, wrote in 1906 that "I can see her now, clad in the never-failing wrapper, stained—as were her hands and eager face—with the chemicals she used in her work" (72–73). Emily Tennyson recollected that when Cameron rather over-dramatically asked the Italian general and nationalist Giuseppe Garibaldi if he would sit for her, he "thought she was a beggar when she kneeled before him, her stained hands upraised" (Ellison 76). She was unsuccessful in obtaining his image.

Discoloration could spread to other parts of the body beside the hands. A cartoon from Cuthbert Bede's humorous *Photographic Pleasures* (1855) introduces the "Lady Mother," anxious that the facial stains resulting from her daughter's use of silver nitrate will render her completely unfit "to be seen at Lady Mayfair's tonight" (opp. 50). This drawing is placed opposite Bede's account of the fictitious

> Miss Dash, who had taken up Calotyping, and had produced some very pretty specimens of her skill, but who was so careless of her nitrate of silver that she was not satisfied with staining her fair fingers and almond-shaped nails, but—a rudely inquisitive fly having probably settled upon her damask cheeks and celestial nose—she must even proceed to rub her face with her stained fingers. The natural consequences ensued. Black stains and spots, like to those which occasionally traverse the face of the sun, appeared on the sacred precincts of her countenance, and not all the Kalydor of Rowland could remove them. She looked like a half-washed Othello at some private theatricals. (50)[7]

Aiming for an easy laugh, Bede's gender assumptions are on full display. He's unsurprisingly disconcerted, therefore, by the idea that a young lady might look upon such stains as a badge of honor; might choose to display them in a non-Shakespearean social performance of her own in which something other than epidermal vanity is at stake:

> Occasionally, indeed, the young lady amateur will, by a freak of fancy, allow the stains to remain on her hands, and will call your attention to them, as you sit beside her at the dinner-table, or lounge with her in the little inner drawing-room, and will point to them proudly—just as an old Peninsular man would point out to you his wounds and scars. I have always remarked, however, that in cases of this kind the young ladies have hands that might have been stolen from the Medician Venus, and that the black stains—like crows on a field of snow—only serve to set off the dazzling whiteness of the rest of the skin; serving them the same purpose as the patches did by their great grandmothers. (52)

---

7. Rowland's Kalydor was a lotion widely marketed from the 1840s onwards, promising to remove "Freckles. Tan, Sunburn, Redness, and Roughness . . . produces soft, fair skin and a lovely delicate complexion." Web. http://www.historyworld.co.uk/advert.php?id=52&offset=150&sort=0&l1=medicines+%26+health&l2 12 Oct. 2018.

Bede's labored humor depended on the ready recognition—at least among the photographers who were the most likely immediate audience for his volume—that silver nitrate was notorious for discoloring fingers and hands. The same held true for the developing fluid known as pyro—pyrogallol acid.[8] This meant that developing their plates in a darkroom, middle-class men and women were involved in an activity that often temporarily marked them with signs of their occupation. Alfred Stieglitz, writing in the *American Annual of Photography* in 1892, called silver nitrate the "hand fiend," claiming that many amateurs disliked using it because the use of this chemical was "equivalent to badly stained hands, which are not easily put into society shape again" (31). He proposed using a pre-prepared kallitype formula instead. Dirty, cracked hands—those markers of manual engagement—until the end of the century and beyond, displayed the traces of leisure activity as well as announcing the work of photographic professionals and darkroom workers. Amateur photographers, like Dick, the protagonist in E. W. Hornung's 1888 photo-comedic short story, "A Spoiled Negative," wore "on [their] hands the stains—not, indeed, of blood, but of some virulent chemical compound far less easy to expunge" (77). What did it mean, we must ask, for middle-class men and women to be involved with a practice that often temporarily marked them with signs of their activity?

Photographic literature regularly expressed anxiety about "digital discoloration"—to borrow a term from the *Photo-Era* (French 328)—and described and advertised numerous tricks and gadgets designed to play to "the solicitude of amateur photographers for the preservation of the immaculateness of their finger-tips," from finger-stalls to india-rubber gloves ("Photography de Luxe" 742). Journals reported on ingenious devices to tilt the developing dish, or to move the developed plate, like Mr. Cowan's "kind of thimble [which] fitted on to the index finger of the right hand, and at the end of the 'thimble' was a spiny protuberance with which you lifted the plate out of the dish" ("Plate-Lifting Devices" 742). Should one's hands *get* stained, though—and as many writers remarked, the means for avoiding this tended to be extremely cumbersome, and hence unappealing to those who worked with photographic development on a frequent basis—a range of remedies was suggested: for silver nitrate's brown deposits, touching the skin with tincture of iodine and then potassium cyanide; a solution of chloride of lime can work effectively on pyro. Bede mentions "cyanogen soap" (50).[9] Even before these remedies were needed,

---

8. Pyrogallic solution was in common use as a developer by the early 1850s: it was previously commonly encountered as a very durable hair-dye. See "Hair-Dye" (314).

9. The soap seems to have been invented in late 1853: see, at any rate, advertisements in *Notes and Queries* and the *Athenaeum* from October 1853. An editorial comment in the

it could help to rub the fingertips with Vaseline or lanoline to fill up pores and cracks; or to dip one's fingers from time to time in a weak solution of sodium sulphite and sulphuric acid. And—so long as one was quick off the mark—soap, water and a nailbrush were often remarked on as being invaluable, as was pumice stone.

Unsurprisingly, discolored hands—inevitably figured as belonging to a white photographer—were racialized, as we saw in that casual reference in Cuthbert Bede to Othello being played in blackface. There's a jokey query raised by Cameron—herself 1/16th Indian—in a letter to Herschel. "When my hands are as black as an Ethiopean Queen," she inquired, "can I find no other means of recovery & restoring them but this dangerous Cyanide of Potassium" (qtd Ford 39).[10] Tanya Sheehan has linked concern about the effects of silver nitrate on skin in the United States with discussion around racial identity, especially around the time of the Civil War, and with what Dr. Norman Bridges termed, in an 1880 lecture, the "hygiene of photography," something that connected the social codes practiced by the professional classes—including studio photographers—with those upheld by those whose patronage they wished to attract (117). One aspect of this was physical hygiene, and maintaining an unpolluted body: in turn, this was frequently associated with the maintenance of racial "purity." This is the context in which Edward Wilson penned a couple of pieces in the *Philadelphia Photographer* in 1866. One of these tells of a toddler who visits her father in his darkroom, and misidentifies what she believes to be a "crock of water" on the floor: it's actually silver nitrate waste solution, and when the photographer returns home, he finds "our little elfin with arms of a dark mulatto color, and her hands of such intense blackness that they should have put to shame a genuine son of Ham" (319–20). Even more derogatory in its invocation of race is an 1910 editorial in the *Professional and Amateur Photographer* penned from Buffalo, New York that castigated the ill-mannered and slipshod proprietor of a photographic gallery for arriving late, "hands so badly stained with pyro that they might easily have been taken for a

---

Photographic News notes that whereas the commercial house that markets this soap keeps its ingredients a secret, "by means of a piece of pumice stone and a lump of cyanide of potassium all the good results attending the use of the cyanogen soap may be effected, at a tenth part of the expense" ("Cyanogen Soap" 11).

10. Letter from Julia Margaret Cameron to Sir John Herschel, 20 March 1864. As Ford goes on to record, "Herschel later warned her 'about your free use of the dreadful poison the Cyanide of Potassium,—letting it run over your hands so profusely.—Pray! Pray! Be more cautious,' and sent his own recipe for cleaning silver salts off her hands" (39).

negro's" ("Chats with the Editors" 356).[11] Such prejudice is, of course, strongly reminiscent of the connotations of Oscar Dubourg's skin in Wilkie Collins's *Poor Miss Finch* (1872): he takes silver nitrate to cure the aftereffects of a serious head injury, which results in a full-body discoloration that renders him, to some, both repulsive and fear-inducing.[12]

More frequent still are the quasi-humorous comments that draw uneasy parallels between stained hands and the marks not of race, but of manual labor—or, at the very least, of failure to adhere to adequate standards of respectability in one's appearance, which amounts to more or less the same thing. Social status was something to be read from someone's self-presentation. An article on "Stained Fingers and How They May Be Avoided" in *Wilson's Photographic Magazine* in 1911 remarks with a certain amount of disdain that, when the author observed fellow members of a photographic society seated around a table, "a large proportion of them revealed the fact that they were photographers by the condition of their hands, especially of their finger tips and nails, which in many cases were badly stained." The remainder of the article is full of instructions about how to keep one's "finger tips unsullied," for "there is no reason," the writer sternly concludes, "why any amateur's finger should show signs of his hobby" (199–201). This sentiment is amplified by an article on "Stained Fingers" in *Camera* that opens "You have noticed, no doubt, that some photographers keep their hands as clean as a debutante's"— although there's more than a hint of a sneer at such fastidiousness, the article goes on to offer some useful hints for cleaning up one's fingers (674). Lest the reasoning should seem paradoxical, we're told that a prime contributor to pyro stains, "strange as it may seem, is cleanliness" (675). If one keeps washing one's hands in the darkroom, the damp skin surface is far more likely to take a stain than is a dry one—so save one's hand washing until the end. Even more pointed in its class-based terminology is an 1892 comment by John Hodges, in a volume explaining how to make lantern slides, that "it is not phenomenal to see a photographer who confines his attention exclusively to gelatin plates with fingers stained like those of a scullery maid who has been engaged in the culinary operation of pickling walnuts" (47).

Notably, all of these comments come from the late nineteenth and early twentieth centuries, when both the serous amateur photographer and the indi-

---

11. Silver nitrate could also play its role in racial masquerade, as we see in the case of Sarah Edmonds, who enlisted in the Union Army under the name Frank Thompson, and then, so as to gain entrance into the Confederate camps as a spy, bought a wig of "negro wool" and stained her skin with silver nitrate so as to pass as an African-American.

12. See Durgan.

vidual who considered themselves an art photographer drew an increasingly sharp distinction between themselves and the commercial practitioner—let alone from those who provided the labor in large-scale photographic establishments.[13] As a writer in the *Photographic News* in 1899 points out, "people who work professionally would not be bothered with plate-lifters and other means for preventing finger-stains" (742), and this extends to those who developed and printed plates and film in commercial establishments. Indeed, Wilfred French records the comment of a photo-finisher who is positively *pleased* to have blackened digits.

> Noticing the deplorable condition of his ten fingers, one day, I suggested to him that he restore them to their normal state, applying the simple remedy recommended by an English worker—first, potassium permanganate and then sodium meta-bisulphate. "What's the use," he replied: "no sooner are my fingers cleaned than they are stained again. Besides, as I go about a good deal, I consider it good advertising. Somebody will make a remark about my stained fingers and, inquiring into the cause, will know that I am a professional photographer. It helps business. Thanks, just the same." (328)

Here, pyro and silver nitrate joined with other chemical health hazards, including cyanide and ammonia fumes in the darkroom. The industrialization of photography is an important and, to date, underresearched (and hard to research) part of the technical history of the medium—one that puts emphasis on the interaction between the human and the chemical. One might well ask what happened to all those poisonous solutions as they were washed into drainage systems and sewers along with a host of other industrial pollutants. Posing this question brings home the fact that technology cannot be considered separately from (and I borrow Jussi Parikka's useful formulation) "a complex ecology of economy, environment, work, and skill." The photographer's hand, stained or otherwise, is inextricably connected not only to the individual body, but to the environment as a whole.

But in terms of immediate and visible impact, it was, above all, the hands of these skilled workers that were vulnerable. Cracks and inflammation from acid could make it impossible to continue working; toning silver prints in a phosphoric acid platinum bath could result first in a "cracking of the skin on the backs of the fingers . . . later on sores are formed on the backs of the fin-

---

13. For the importance of the "amateur" to Victorian photography, and the changing status of this figure, see Seiberling and Boone.

gers and pimples come on the wrists." This repetitive labor distinguishes their contact with developing materials from those for whom photography is a leisure activity, for "in the case of amateurs," we are told, ". . . there need be but little fear of suffering, particularly if the hands be thoroughly washed when the work is finished" ("Poisons Used in Photography" 442).

HANDS AND CAMERAS

The writer of "Poisons Used in Photography," from which I've just quoted, is assuming an amateur who still develops their own plates or film. Yet at the turn of the century, a different type of hand starts to play a role in my argument: the disembodied hand that helps to advertise the new portable cameras—most famously, the Kodak Brownie. These hands have several functions. They give a sense of scale, emphasizing the compact convenience of the new cameras. They are frequently women's hands, again suggesting ease of use, and perhaps modishness—the camera as desirable, and up-to-the-minute accessory. These are generic hands, rather than markers of individuality; they invite us into a somatic identification, imagining that our hands are positioned where the hands are placed in the advertisement, performing the same actions with equal dexterity. A similar role is played by the hands in how-to diagrams.

This apparently simple box camera was known, of course, as the "hand camera." It was valued for its portability—it could be carried to places where it was hard to take a stand camera—as we saw in relation to those missionary photos of mutilation. It could be used to take images inconspicuously in the streets of one's home town. Advertisements marketed it as a fashionable consumer toy; articles touted its appeal to the vacationer. W. H. Burbank wrote an article in the *American Amateur Photographer* for 1890 in which he claimed that the hand camera was "now almost an indispensable part of the outfit of every tourist and summer lounger," and that its popularity "hastens the coming of the time when the whole world will lie within easy reach of one's hand" (327, 328).[14]

Yet with this ease of use came some skepticism. A. Horsley Hinton, editor of the *Amateur Photographer,* remarked in 1899 how the "modern Hand Camera" is, more than anything else, responsible for "the 'fatal facility' of making photographs." He sends it up:

---

14. The "dangers" of the title are the apparent danger that the hand camera poses to art and to the cultivation of artistic feeling.

FIGURE 9.3. Advertising for Folding Pocket Kodaks. 1899. Ellis Collection of Kodakiana. Duke University: K0559. ark:/87924/r43t9fz70. duke:430271. Used by permission.

With perhaps 99 per cent. the Hand Camera is the merest of mere pastimes. My lady buys it with as little—alas, with far less—concern that that with which she buys a new sunshade.

A poodle, a Hand Camera, and a modern novel, are but the armament against *ennui* during a sojourn away from town. The Camera is as harmless as the poodle, and not more aggravating, and is less harmful than the novel. (xix)

In 1908, "A mere man" attempts to claim that women had a manual advantage when navigating the small piece of apparatus:

To reload a Kodak or similar camera with a spool of film is easy, and once the lady owner of a Kodak has been shown how to do it she does it far better than the average man, and far more quickly. The fingers trained to such exquisitely delicate tasks as, for example, knitting and crochet, can manipulate small objects with a neatness which comes only with practice to a man. (Part I 45)

There's an unmissable condescension, of course, in the invocation of these traditional female leisure pursuits, even if they demonstrate enviable dexterity, and what's more, he shows an increasing disdain for women's digital propensities. Whilst claiming that "the same sensitiveness and control of the finger-tips which makes a woman good at knitting and at threading black film papers makes her also good at the task of loading plates into their slides in total darkness" (Part II 36), he suggests that her common sense may be less developed than her fingers. Women rarely, he maintains, have enough

"respect" for the sensitive emulsion of a plate or film or printing paper. It takes her a long time to grasp its extraordinary sensitiveness, not only to light, but to other actions, such as the touch of a finger or the deposit of dust. When a woman takes the packet of plates out of their box in total darkness she will quite calmly feel the film side, and in so doing, however "clean" her hands are, she will be very apt to make a mark which will subsequently show on the negative. A man, contrariwise, puts full trust in the plate marker. (Part II 36).

But Hinton, like others among his contemporaries who saw themselves as "serious" photographers, was far from dismissing this new piece of apparatus out of hand, or treating it as something facile. First, he commends the design and manufacturing skill—invisible manual labor, one might say—that lies behind it. Second, he emphasizes the skill necessary for its successful operation. He draws attention to a perennial problem: the steady hand necessary to avoid camera shake. Other experts, like Walter Coventry, writing two years later in *The Technics of the Hand Camera*, also make the point that "to many persons the hand camera is far from being a toy" (1) because of the remarkable skill and ingenuity shown in its construction. Moreover, as Coventry says, "It is generally recognized that the successful use of the hand camera requires greater skill, as well as a more intimate knowledge of some of the fundamental principles of photography, than is the case with the *stand* camera"—the capacity to estimate distance and establish depth of field, above all (1). And the photographer Alfred Stieglitz adds a further element, patience. In an 1897 piece, "The Hand Camera—Its Present Importance," Stieglitz acknowledges that he was at first dismissive of this apparatus, thinking its use a craze that he compares to bicycling. But he has come, he says, to acknowledge its portable advantages—providing that one can resist the temptation to shoot off all the time, and

> await the moment in which everything is in balance; that is, satisfies your eye. This often means hours of patient waiting. My picture, "Fifth Avenue, Winter," is the result of a three hours' stand during a fierce snow-storm on February 22nd, 1893, awaiting the proper moment. My patience was duly rewarded. (25)

The image shows churned up slush; a horse-drawn cart making its difficult way through the snowy ruts towards the photographer; a couple of other beleaguered vehicles; men frenziedly clearing the sidewalks on either side, and the snow still falling. Compositionally, they are brought together by the carrier's outstretched right arm, turning his laboring cart into a low triangle that, in turn, is just off-center from the inverted wedge-shape of snowy sky formed by the Fifth Avenue buildings.

Anticipating Henri Cartier-Bresson's famous dictum about the photographic importance of the "perfect moment" by some fifty years, Stieglitz is, in effect, restoring the centrality of individuality to photograph-making. What matters, though, is not the workings of the hand, but the combination of eye and brain; the visual certitude that comes with practiced looking, in which the hand (assuming the digits are not too frozen in the snowstorm) is little more than the prosthesis suggested in advertisements. Stieglitz bestows upon the photographer the traditional status of the heroic artist, undergoing physical privations for the sake of his vocation. At the same time, the photograph itself underwent some significant cropping and retouching. It exists in two versions:

in one, we see a broad and bleak expanse of winter street, the dominance of the snow intensified by the removal of the railway ties that were prominent in the cropped version which Stieglitz published with this article—a horizontally framed image that emphasized the dynamics of movement towards the viewer rather than a struggle with the inhospitable elements.[15] He himself was to exhibit different versions of the image in order to illustrate the different effects achieved through photographic editing and retouching.

I have been emphasizing the role of touch and, therefore, of the hand in the history of photographic technology in the long nineteenth century in order to claim that the reduction in its perceived physical importance registers the shifting status of photography. More than this, focusing on the hand—or rather, on the hand/apparatus interface—helps to bring out, very clearly, certain distinctions that are fundamental to the rhetoric of photography's relations to the sphere of technology in the long nineteenth century: above all, the apparent need to discriminate between photography as art versus mechanical reproduction, or as commercial activity versus leisure pursuit. For through paying attention to the material and corporeal aspects of the processes by which photographs come into being, we see a permeable interface of thing and body. This permeability is enhanced beyond recognizing the localized contact zone that touch entails: fingers leave marks, and, in turn, bear the stains of photographic practices. Yet by the end of the century, the intimate imbrication of the hand with amateur photography of various sorts becomes far less conspicuous— at the very least, residual stains become an undesirable mark of slovenliness rather than a badge of serious aesthetic and scientific engagement—or show that one's working in the commercial sphere: trade, not art. More frequently, hands are seen primarily as the tools that carry and operate one's camera, and adjuncts to the more important eye and mind. They are left to twiddle dials and levers or, as the advertisement goes, they just push the button.

WORKS CITED

"A Mere Man." "Ladies and Photography," Part I. *Photography and Focus*, vol. 26, 7 July 1908, pp. 42–45.

———. "Ladies and Photography," Part II. *Photography and Focus*, vol. 26, 14 July 1908, pp. 36–37.

Barrett, Redmond. "The Art of Retouching. Chapter XVI.—Method No. III." *Anthony's Photographic Bulletin*, vol. 22, 14 Nov. 1891, pp. 655–58.

15. For a comparison of these two versions, see https://www.watchprosite.com/photography/-winter-fifth-avenue—1893-by-alfred-stieglitz/1278.1105708.8290413/. Accessed 19 Oct. 2018. Nor, in fact, was this the only image that Stieglitz took that day: another showed the back of the carriage, after it had passed.

Batchen, Geoffrey. *Photography's Objects*. U of New Mexico Art Museum, 1997.

Bede, Cuthbert. *Photographic Pleasures. Popularly Portrayed with Pen & Pencil*. T. McLean, 1855.

Bell, Sir Charles. *The Bridgewater Treatises on the Power Wisdom and Goodness of God as Manifested in the Creation. Treatise IV. The Hand: Its Mechanism and Vital Endowments as Evincing Design*. London, W. Pickering, 1837.

Briefel, Aviva. *The Racial Hand in the Victorian Imagination*. Cambridge UP, 2017.

Burbank, W. H. "The Dangers of Hand Camera Work." *American Amateur Photographer*, vol. 2, 1890, pp. 327–29.

Cameron, Julia Margaret. "Annals of My Glass House." (1874; first published 1889). *Photography in Print*, edited by Vicki Goldberg. U of New Mexico P, 1981, pp. 180–87.

Capuano, Peter J. *Changing Hands: Industry, Evolution, and the Reconfiguration of the Victorian Body*. U of Michigan P, 2015.

"Chats with the Editors." *Professional and Amateur Photographer*, vol. 15, 1910, p. 356.

Claudet, Laura. "Colouring by Hand." *Encyclopedia of Nineteenth-Century Photography*, edited by John Hannavy, 2 vols., Routledge, 2008, vol. 1, pp. 322–24.

Coventry, Walter Bulkeley. *The Technics of the Hand Camera*. London, Sands; New York: D. Van Nostrand, 1901.

"Cyanogen Soap." *Photographic News*, vol. 1, 10 Sept. 1858, p. 11.

Durgan, Jessica. "Wilkie Collins's Blue Period: Color, Aesthetics, and Race in *Poor Miss Finch*." *Victorian Literature and Culture*, vol. 43, 2015, pp. 765–83.

Edwards, Elizabeth, and Janice Hart. "Introduction: Photographs as Objects." *Photographs Objects Histories: On the Materiality of Images*, edited by Edwards and Hart, Routledge, 2004, pp. 1–15.

Ellison, Edith Nicholl. *A Child's Recollections of Tennyson*. New York, E. P. Dutton, 1906.

Ford, Colin. *Julia Margaret Cameron: A Critical Biography*. J. Paul Getty Museum, 2003.

French, Wilfred A. "On the Ground-Glass: Stained Fingers." *Photo-Era Magazine*, vol. 4, 1918, p. 328.

"Hair-Dye." *The Chemical Gazette; or Journal of Practical Chemistry*, vol. 2, 1844, p. 314.

Hinton, A. Horsley. Introductory Chapter. *The Use of the Hand Camera, with Remarks Upon Larger Apparatus*, by Clive Holland, London, Archibald Constable, 1898, pp. ix–xx.

Hodges, John A. *The Lantern-Slide Manual*. London, Hazell, Watson and Viney, 1892.

Hornung, E. W. "A Spoilt Negative." *Belgravia Magazine*, vol. 65, 1888, pp. 76–89.

Howe, Ida Lynch. *The Art of Retouching Systematized*. Chicago, A. C. McClurg, 1908.

Hubert, J. *The Art of Retouching: With Chapters on Portraiture and Flash-Light Photography*. 1891. 7th ed. London, Hazell, Watson and Viney, 1895.

Kelsey, Robin. *Photography and the Art of Chance*. Belknap Press of Harvard UP, 2015.

Leslie, Esther. "Walter Benjamin: Traces of Craft." *Journal of Design History*, vol. 11, 1998, pp. 5–13.

Olin, Margaret. *Touching Photographs*. U of Chicago P, 2012.

Ourdan, J. P. *The Art of Retouching*. 1880. 3rd American ed., New York, E. & H. T. Anthony, 1891.

Parikka, Jussi. "Dust and Exhaustion. The Labor of Media Materialism." *CTheory.net*, 2013, https://journals.uvic.ca/index.php/ctheory/article/view/14790/5665. Web. Accessed 23 Oct. 2019.

"Photography de Luxe." *Photographic News*, vol. 43, 17 Nov. 1899, p. 742.

"Plate-Lifting Devices." *Photographic News*, vol. 43, 17 Nov. 1899, p. 742.

Plunkett, John. "Retouching." *Encyclopedia of Nineteenth-Century Photography*, edited by John Hannavy, 2 vols., Routledge, 2008, vol. 2, pp. 1189–91.

"Poisons Used in Photography—II." *British Journal of Photography*, vol. 52, 9 June 1905, p. 442.

Riis, Jacob. *The Children of the Poor*. Charles Scribner's Sons, 1908.

Seiberling, Grace, with Carolyn Boone. *Amateurs, Photography, and the Mid-Victorian Imagination*. U of Chicago P, 1986.

Sheehan, Tanya. *Doctored: The Medicine of Photography in Nineteenth-Century America*. Penn State UP, 2011.

"Stained Fingers." *Camera*, vol. 24, 1920, pp. 674–75.

"Stained Fingers and How They May Be Avoided." *Wilson's Photographic Magazine*, vol. 48, 1911, pp. 199–201.

Stieglitz, Alfred. "A Simplified Kallitype Printing Process." *American Annual for Photography and Photographic Times Almanac for 1892*, New York, Scovill & Adams, 1891, pp. 31–32.

———. "The Hand Camera—Its Present Importance." *American Annual of Photography and Photographic Times Almanac for 1897*, New York, Scovill & Adams, 1897, pp. 22–31.

Towler, John. *The Silver Sunbeam: A Practical and Theoretical Text-Book on Sun Drawing and Photographic Printing*. New York, Joseph H. Ladd, 1864.

Troubridge, Laura Gurney. *Memories and Reflections*. London, William Heinemann, 1925.

Twomey, Christina. "The Incorruptible Kodak. Photography, Human Rights and the Congo Campaign." *The Violence of the Image: Photography and International Conflict*, edited by Liam Kennedy and Caitlin Patrick, I. B. Tauris, 2014, pp. 9–33.

Wilson, Edward. "Salad for the Photographer." *Philadelphia Photographer*, vol. 3, 1866, 319–20.

Zandy, Janet. *Hands: Physical Labor, Class, and Cultural Work*. Rutgers UP, 2004.

CHAPTER 10

Staged Hands in *Bleak House*

JULIANNE SMITH

THE ROLE hands play in *Bleak House* is crucial. The emphasis on handwriting in the novel is central to the plot, of course, but hands that write/wright are everywhere important. A broad list includes both implied and literal use of hands in connection with Esther's keys, Lady Dedlock's rings, Nemo's pen, Jo's broom, Hortense's gun and Bucket's fat forefinger—useful hands, ornamental hands, laboring hands, threatening hands. Dickens suggests that hands are essential both literally and symbolically; his own hands, for example, write the narrative, and the narrative, in turn, centralizes the writing hand within a cosmos where hands both perform and are on display. In addition, *Bleak House* hands form a significant motif in the book's illustrations, which were a central part of all his novels from start to finish. Though Q. D. Leavis and others assert that, by the time *Bleak House* was published in 1853, illustrations in Dickens's novels lacked the power they held over his earlier readers (344), Dickens's novels continued to be illustrated to the end, and these illustrations were particularly important for the critical role they played in Victorian stage adaptations of his work. For the purposes of this analysis, *Bleak House* illustrations provide a critical link between text and performance, and the gestures they contain focus in various ways on characters' hands and what those hands are doing or indicating as opposed to what the characters—and perhaps the readers/viewers—can or cannot see.

In *Bleak House*, the interplay of hands in Dickens's text and their visual portrayal in illustrations and subsequently in stage adaptations conveys critical information about Victorian bodies. What hands might mean or do is closely allied with the cultural meanings constructed for them; for the Victorians specifically, hand gestures became formally and consciously codified instruments in a system of scientific classification for the stage. Eventually, many actors as well as public speakers learned stylized postures and hand gestures from charts as part of Victorian stage convention from manuals such as Gustave Garcia's *The Actor's Art* (1882) and the *Delsarte System of Oratory* (1888). Alice Batt suggests that these acting manuals were also bought and used by middle-class Victorians as correctives to the body's "innately flawed" ability to "speak or gesture effectively" (170), extending the science of hand gesture into daily life. In addition, hands became literally and metaphorically more significant in the nineteenth century, as Peter Capuano has shown, because they were invested with new meaning by industrialism and Darwinian notions about the body that raised new notions about hands as working mechanisms and markers of humanity itself (2). Capuano argues that handedness often superseded sightedness in new ways that can be traced through "a sudden but sustained spike in representations of hands in British fiction and in English culture more generally" (1), . . .a spike so marked that hands appear in nineteenth-century novels more often than any other body part including faces, heads, and eyes" (12). However, while hands took on new literary and cultural significance and were sometimes governed by gestural stage conventions, they were also in tension with other, less-presentable body parts. Especially in *Bleak House* stage performances, hands were sometimes upstaged by competing appendages, notably feet with all their appeal to mobility and movement as well as a secretive kind of eroticism. Capuano reminds us that, for the Victorians, "the head and the hands were routinely the only two body parts open for inspection" (10), lending them an overt authority to openly convey meaning. With all their dexterity and presentability, hands in *Bleak House* often direct the eye to notice what is hidden, but when Victorian feet were bared as part of the embodied stage spectacle, they brought something normally concealed into plain sight. This unaccustomed sight was fraught with class but also gender infractions and signaled ways social change was afoot. To follow these body parts as they are visualized first for the novel and its illustrations and then for the stage is to trace Victorian anxieties that center on and in the body. In *Bleak House*, bodily disclosures, particularly in the form of pointing fingers and shod or unshod feet, signal incursions across class and gender lines as characters write/wright, gesture toward, look at, see (or refuse to see), and then are "chivvied" or moved on by the inevitable changes wrought by economic and social forces.

Hablot K. Browne ("Phiz") was Dickens's *Bleak House* illustrator and, as Aileen Farrar notes, often a collaborator with artistic input as well (49). Browne establishes the centrality of hands as opposed to eyes starting with the cover of *Bleak House,* where hands structure the chaos at the top of the frame around the title. A central be-turbaned figure flings his hands outward in both directions. He is flanked by two court officials pointing in different directions. All three are vision impaired—two have hats covering their eyes, and one wears glasses. Raying out from these, other blindfolded or vision-impaired figures flee away from the center, hands stretching in opposing directions toward the edges of the page. Other figures at the edges of this scene use their hands to shore up bookshelves or reach out to grab onto others or make protective or self-protective gestures. Michael Steig suggests that this top part of the cover represents "a panoramic game of blindman's bluff, with the Chancery attorneys and officials, appropriately, the 'blindmen,' and a host of terrified men, women, and children their fleeing victims" (133). Steig also notes that this theme of game playing continues at the bottom of the cover, where, in both corner pieces, court officials manipulate human figures as gamecocks or game pieces.

The gaming and other vignettes that frame the *Bleak House* title page display both contemplative and dynamic hands. Some belong to recognizable figures, such as Miss Flite, who feeds birds, and Krook, who writes letters that he cannot read on the wall. There is a law copyist at work (an unromanticized, perhaps drug-addled Nemo) along with the allegorical figures mentioned above who play games of chess and tennis. At the bottom of the page, Browne situates John Jarndyce with his hands shoved in his pockets. Jarndyce's vision is limited though not actually cut off. He gazes downward between his low-slung hat bill and upturned coat collar. He does not look at the urban scene around him, which is crowded with figures, a few of whom point in his direction or upward to the weather vane hovering over him. Taken as a whole, frantic, working, manipulating and pointing hands literally frame the page in these vignettes, suggesting that hands doing predominate over eyes seeing. Stieg posits that the front cover must necessarily have been created with Dickens's detailed involvement given that Browne cannot have read the novel in its entirety when he drew it (132). Close design collaboration between Dickens and Browne seems likely therefore not only because certain motifs and vignettes illustrate scenes not yet written but also because the front cover places unmistakable emphasis on the judicial abuses and clumsy, inhumane legal system that structure the overall narrative in so many ways.

Browne's other illustrations for *Bleak House,* forty in all, accompanied each installment of the novel two at a time and famously featured his new dark plate technique. The ten dark plate illustrations contain much less white space than Browne typically incorporated, giving them a shadowy cast said to reflect the gloomy nature of the novel itself. Three of these dark plates form a critical foundation for the continued focus on handedness in *Bleak House,* not only within the original illustrations but in the novel's afterlife onstage. These three plates not only highlight hands as visual bright spots within the darkness but also literally point to unseen objects, recalling the precedence handedness takes over sightedness on the cover page.

The first plate is called "Consecrated Ground" and features Jo pointing out Nemo's grave to Lady Dedlock. The plate is designed with Jo's pointing finger at the apex of an arrow of light within the darkness. As the two figures stand at the locked cemetery gates, Jo's arm is thrust through the bars, and the shaft of light behind them shapes the outline of a house with Jo's finger at the tip of the overhanging eave. All the light is focused on his pointing finger. Lady Dedlock, whose face is hidden, seems to look in the direction Jo points, and Jo gazes along his arm as well with a hat pulled down partially over his eyes. With eyes half-concealed or hidden, they attempt to discern Nemo's grave in the menacing shadows of the cemetery, but the actual grave is also concealed from the reader, the details of Nemo's inadequate burial perhaps more horrible imagined than realized. Neither the illustration's viewer, nor Jo, nor Lady Dedlock see clearly what is being pointed out. Their hands, however, reveal where the focus of attention is or should be if only sight were more trustworthy.

Dickens narrates this passage in *Bleak House* using a network of eyes and hands, emphasizing the way even looking intently or intentionally conceals information that hands more directly convey as they gesture or make contact with items or human flesh. What Jo sees is a familiar sight to him, so he can look past the horror of the place to see other features; he mentions in his speech, for example, the nearness of Nemo's grave to someone's kitchen window and expresses excitement over the rat disappearing into the ground. Lady Dedlock sees more generally a scene of unfamiliar horror, and she is sickened by it so that everything around her, including Jo, is "hideous" and "loathsome" (202).[1] She expresses fears about contamination by her surroundings and infection from the very stones in the gate's archway. Jo, on the other hand, holds the bars of the cemetery gate and shakes them; he points to the grave and then to a rat and finally to the grave again but this time with his broom.

---

1. Quotations from the novel are from the Norton Critical Edition (1977) throughout.

FIGURE 10.1. "Consecrated Ground" by H. K. Browne. Used with the permission of the Department of Special Collections, Stanford University Libraries.

At the end of this scene, Lady Dedlock removes her glove to give Jo money, and her hand becomes the identifying feature that Jo most remembers; he "silently notices how white and small her hand is, and what a jolly servant she must be to wear such sparkling rings" (201). Though Jo has stared and stared at Lady Dedlock throughout this passage, he will later identify Hortense as Lady Dedlock's imposter because of her hands, though he is unsure about her face. Hands assert their power in *Bleak House* to indicate "unique individual identity" (Capuano 186) and character as well as to reveal true feelings. Just before Lady Dedlock slips away, "she drops a piece of money in [Jo's] hand, without touching it, and shuddering as their hands approach" (202). Dickens substitutes hands for faces here; Lady Dedlock's disgust, for example, cannot be seen in her veiled face, while Jo looks at but does not really see her. Hands convey truths eyes do not see.

The second dark plate that critically highlights hands instead of eyes is called "A New Meaning in the Roman" and portrays the room in Tulkinghorn's house that contains his murdered corpse. A shaft of light from a tall window at the left invades the dark room and shines intently on the area behind the table that conceals the corpse from view. Above, a Roman figure in the painted ceiling points a warning finger downward toward the spot where we imagine but cannot see the corpse is splayed out. Dickens describes this figure as an "Allegory, in Roman helmet and celestial linen, [who] sprawls among balustrades and pillars, flowers, clouds, and big-legged boys, and makes the head ache—as would seem to be Allegory's object always, more or less" (119). A few paragraphs later, Dickens characterizes Tulkinghorn's relationship to the allegorical figure as antagonistic since the figure "stare[s] down at [Tulkinghorn's] intrusion as if it meant to swoop upon him"; Tulkinghorn, in return, refuses to acknowledge the figure's warning finger, "cutting it dead" (120). Tulkinghorn, to his peril, ignores other pointing fingers in the allegory as well. When he refuses to see what they point to, he misses important information as in this passage where the disguised Lady Dedlock walks by Tulkinghorn's house on her way to meet Jo: "From the ceiling, foreshortened Allegory, in the person of one impossible Roman upside down, points . . . obtrusively toward the window. Why should Mr. Tulkinghorn, for such no-reason, look out of window! Is the hand not always pointing there? So he does not look out of window" (199–200). Browne's illustration shows the ironic outcome of Tulkinghorn's antagonism and refusal to look because the Roman figure, who now presides over Tulkinghorn's dead body, points "with far greater significance than he ever had in Mr. Tulkinghorn's time, and with a deadly meaning. For, Mr. Tulkinghorn's time is over for evermore; and the Roman pointed at the murderous hand uplifted against his life, and pointed helplessly at him, from night to morning lying face downward on the floor, shot through the heart"

(586–87). Just as Nemo's gravesite is discreetly hidden in the previous dark plate, Tulkinghorn's body is also present in this illustration but unseeable. The pointing hands in both plates testify to these grisly sights, but eyes cannot discern them.

The third plate in which hands provide a dominant motif across page and stage in *Bleak House* productions is titled "The Morning," which is Lady Dedlock's death scene. After a long night of wandering in cold, wet weather, she has returned to the cemetery gate she visited with Jo in the first illustration above and collapsed on the steps. Whereas the viewer is inside the cemetery looking out in the first illustration, the viewer is outside along with Lady Dedlock in this one. The view beyond the gate is dark and hazy with barely discernable, rickety tombstone shapes. There is nothing to see inside the cemetery because Lady Dedlock is the center of this display. Her body is draped along the steps, face down, and her bonnet conceals any glimpse of human countenance. There is a lamp overhead that achieves a flickering effect by lighting up the scene only in spots. Significantly, two of those spots are Lady Dedlock's hands: one hand lies on the top step touching the very stones she feared infected in the previous cemetery scene; the other hand has been thrust through the gate, arm entwined through the bars. Her final intimacy with this "hideous" and "loathsome" (202) place, as she called it when she visited with Jo, is complete. Her hands are white and small, as Jo has noticed, and passively signal her resignation to her fate. The illustration incorporates many of the details Dickens gives about this scene, even down to Lady Dedlock's "one arm creeping round a bar of the iron gate, and seeming to embrace it" (713). As Esther narrates this scene in the novel, she can "dimly see heaps of dishonoured graves and stones, hemmed in by filthy houses, with a few dull lights in their windows, and on whose walls a thick humidity broke out like a disease" (713). Esther notices the same corruption and infection Lady Dedlock noticed when she visited with Jo, but significantly Esther is unable to identify the figure on the steps correctly. She is taken in by Lady Dedlock's disguise, and, in the text, Bucket and Woodcourt lead her step by step to the correct realization of her mother's identity. They seem to understand that Esther must touch the body to realize who it is when Woodcourt says, "Her hands should be the first to touch her. They have a higher right than ours" (714). Esther describes her realization this way: "I lifted the head, put the long dank hair aside, and turned the face. And it was my mother, cold and dead" (714). Her eyes are easily deceived by appearances, but her hands lead her to the truth.

These three illustrations highlight the way hands function—pointing, touching, feeling, contacting or refusing contact—to testify to the truth but also as more reliable truth-tellers than eyes. Dickens himself apparently tied the three scenes in these illustrations together from the beginning since his working notes from Part 5, the part that includes the chapter with Jo and Lady Dedlock at the cemetery, include this information: "Jo. Shadowing forth of Lady Dedlock at the churchyard. Pointing hand of Allegory—consecrated ground" (Ford and Monod 782). Thus the three illustrations connecting the three deaths, Nemo's, Tulkinghorn's, and Lady Dedlock's, formed a kind of triptych in Dickens's imagination. It is likely that he gave Browne instructions about this connection and thus about illustrating the pointing hands since Nemo and Tulkinghorn are the objects of these gestures in the first two illustrations.

These illustrations are of further interest here because they resonate beyond the frame of the page as the narrative was later rewoven for the Victorian stage. I choose reweaving as an appropriate metaphor for adaptation because the action of reweaving brings in a second and third set of authorial hands, hands that unravel Dickens's plot to illustrate it visually and later reweave it for the stage. Browne's illustrations often provided a bridge between text and performance since one convention of Victorian drama was to end a scene or act with a tableau that recreated the book's illustration. It is not always clear in a play manuscript how strictly or when a tableau taken from Browne may have been portrayed, but it is clear that the scenes Browne illustrated heavily influenced the way *Bleak House* was staged and thus the way that the hands in *Bleak House* remained as crucial on the stage as they were on the page. *Bleak House* stage adaptations tended to highlight a small number of the original illustrations, but two out of the three analyzed above consistently shaped stage portrayals: "Consecrated Ground" (Jo and Lady Dedlock at Nemo's grave) and "The Morning" (Lady Dedlock's death)—though Tulkinghorn's death illustration resonated in more subtle and less consistent ways.

The main body of *Bleak House* stage adaptations happened in the 1870s, just after Dickens's death. By that time, the novel had been in circulation for nearly two decades, and thus the illustrations had been widely disseminated. *Bleak House* became a less-stable narrative in the 1870s because, with Dickens himself out of the picture, playwrights rewove it for the stage and cut out large swaths of characters and subplots. In 1876 alone, there were no fewer than seven versions of *Bleak House* competing for London theatre audiences (Bolton 353–56). It was commonplace for these adaptations to abandon the complexities of Dickens's Chancery Court critique and make *Bleak House* into a story about a fallen woman, Lady Dedlock, or else a story about an orphan; surprisingly, that orphan is not Esther, nor Ada, nor Richard, but Jo. Two of the most popular *Bleak House* plays from the 1870s each posit a different central character as the focus of the narrative. Henry Rendle's play *Chesney Wold*

(1871) takes Lady Dedlock as its center, and J. P. Burnett's play *Bleak House* (1876) centers on Jo, but the same few illustrations from the original novel provide stage motifs that emphasize hands in each play.

Henry Rendle's 1871 play is the impetus for *Bleak House* stage revivals in the 1870s. It appears to be the first staged version in more than a decade and a half (Bolton 352). *Bleak House* had been staged in several different, short-lived productions just after Dickens finished the installments in 1853, but interest in adapting the novel quickly waned. Just after Dickens died in 1870, stage productions of his works fairly exploded (Bolton 349); *Bleak House* participated in this renaissance and, in fact, became one of the most high-profile successes among Dickens's adaptations through the end of the century. Henry Rendle's *Bleak House* debuted on 19 October 1871 at De Bar's Opera House in St. Louis, Missouri.[2] The first review of the play gives its title as *Chesney Wold* ("Theatrical" 239), though it will subsequently be advertised or reviewed under the title *Lady Dedlock and Hortense* as well as *Bleak House*. The play was performed regularly across America as part of famed tragedienne Madame Franziska (Fanny) Janauschek's repertoire through the 1880s. Part of its appeal was that Janauschek played the roles of both Lady Dedlock and Hortense.

Much of Rendle's play is lifted from Dickens, even down to the characters' dialogue. However, the play is also necessarily truncated so that suggestions scattered more leisurely throughout Dickens's text, especially as hands and feet are represented, come into closer contact in Rendle's and exemplify both spoken and unspeakable anxieties. Some of these are suggested in Dickens's text and Browne's illustrations, but others, especially covered or uncovered feet, are particularly pronounced on stage. While hands are treated overtly in the larger *Bleak House* narrative, feet also structure the metaphorical interplay of secretiveness and transgression that make up Dickens's themes, such as the ancestral footsteps on the Ghost Walk that threaten to reveal the Dedlock inheritance of doom. Though elements of literacy and higher-class standing are signaled by handwriting as well as what is handed down or inherited, to have any standing at all—physically and culturally—feet are literally and metaphorically necessary, though not always appropriate to mention or to look at. Rendle's play highlights a hierarchy of limbs—hands vs. feet—to signal the

---

2. Philip Bolton's performance handlist gives the imprecise premiere date of 1871–72 in Cleveland, Ohio, for Henry Rendle's play. But new evidence indicates the play premiered in St. Louis, Missouri, on 19 October 1871. Bolton misspells the playwright's name as Randle and is also uncertain about whether the writer was Rendle or his leading lady Fanny Janauschek. Rendle is definitely the playwright since the Library of Congress shows that he sold his copyright to Janauschek's manager/husband Frederick J. Pillot in 1876. The title listed on the copyright agreement is *Lady Dedlock and Hortense* instead of Rendle's original title given in the manuscript as *Bleak House* or in the first review as *Chesney Wold*.

transgressive body along class lines. Rendle's play opens by juxtaposing feet and hands both literally and metaphorically. Act I, scene 1, begins with Bucket alone onstage, having just seen Hortense in the aftermath of her dismissal from Lady Dedlock's service. He says, "Well, that's about the most extraordinary young woman as ever I see. Is she mad—or what, I wonder? I've seen something of woman's temper afore today, but blow me if I ever see one of them slip her shoes off and go barefoot thro' the damp grass before" (Rendle[3]). Hortense's inappropriate, working-class bare feet identify her as a madwoman and suggest an erotic metaphorical connection not only between revelation and concealment but also between class and moral standing; they introduce the theme of moral violations that are legible on her body given that Victorian fashion concealed almost everything under layers of material. In the novel, Dickens does not say Hortense's feet are bare; he prefers shoeless and does not specify whether or not she wears stockings. Any mention of stockings at all in Dicken's *Bleak House* is connected only with the male sex. Hortense's bare feet are the opening image in Rendle's play, and, juxtaposed immediately with the issue of handwriting, posit both body parts as central to the identity and class issues that trouble the narrative. Bucket's second speech turns immediately to hands and handwriting. He reads aloud a letter from Tulkinghorn asking him to "see the housekeeper [at Chesney Wold] . . . and ascertain if possible the name of the Captain in whose regiment her runaway son served many years ago? When last in Lincolnshire, I was reading an affidavit . . . and Lady Dedlock, catching sight of the handwriting, was startled into unusual emotion. I have a purpose in comparing it with some of that Captain's handwriting, and this housekeeper may help you" (1.i.). Bucket introduces the way hands might signify true identity, and Capuano points out the irony that, in the larger narrative, aberrations in Nemo's supposedly uniform legal hand do not erase but reveal who he is (196–98). While Hortense's aberrant working-class feet identify her as a madwoman, Nemo's aberrant handwriting proves his hidden class identity—his descent from middle-class army officer to drug-addicted pauper.

Feet and hands continue to structure the rest of Rendle's Act I in both literal and metaphorical ways. Hortense uses the metaphor of the "soiled glove" (1.i.). with all its resonances of dirty hands and moral infraction, to describe how Lady Dedlock tosses her aside, a handy metaphor not employed by Dickens. Hands and feet are at issue later in Act 1 when Mrs. Rouncewell narrates the story of the Ghost Walk and mentions how the name and story have been "handed down" (1.i.). The Ghost Walk story brings together the approaching feet of tragedy and issues of heritage and class misconduct. Part of the

---

3. Quotations from Rendle's play are from this source throughout.

tragic misconduct Rendle highlights in Act 1 is seen in the way that lighting and character blocking prepare the audience to already understand that Lady Dedlock and Esther are related in some secret way through inheritance. The stage directions for this scene say that Lady Dedlock's portrait appears in a shaft of light, while Esther is also illuminated in a matching shaft of light upon her entrance into the drawing room where she is juxtaposed with the portrait. Esther subsequently tells Mrs. Rouncewell about her childhood, and when she intones these words from her godmother, "Your mother, Esther, is your disgrace, and you were hers," Lady Dedlock enters behind her in a similar shaft of light. That Lady Dedlock has handed down her physical and moral genetics to Esther is the major visual revelation in Act 1, where the playwright has arranged bodies to emphasize their similarity. The play raises questions about what else has been "handed down" with all the overtones of class and gender infractions. Violations of class standing as well as moral standing might be handed down as the sins of the mothers are visited on their offspring in the *Bleak House* narrative. Meanwhile, the sound of ghostly feet and the piquant suggestion of the bare feet and soiled gloves that mark Hortense's body convey a sense of the plot's sexual secrets.

Hands and feet are featured further when Jo takes Lady Dedlock to Nemo's grave in Act I, scene 3, which is lifted mostly word-for-word from Dickens. The entire scene resembles Browne's "Consecrated Ground" illustration, but there is no indication of a tableau held for any length of time as a static stage picture; however, the scene itself serves as an animated rendering of Dicken's text. The play specifies that this is a dark scene: "The gate of a miserable pauper burying ground. Stone steps in front of gate and a dirty gas lamp burning sullenly under the archway above it" (1.iii.). This description comports with the steps, stone archway and dim lamp of Browne's drawing. The play's dialogue here indicates that Jo points to the grave several times. Though he is connected with the work his hands do as a crossing sweeper, he is also well known in all *Bleak House* narratives to be peripatetic, always being "chivvied" and "moved on." In a scene previous to this, and as Dickens also establishes, Jo represents lower-class characters who are compelled to take to their feet. Though I have not located production photos of Jo in this play, his feet may be bare since many of the surviving portraits of Jo's successors on stage show the actor without shoes or stockings, and, as shall be seen, Rendle's Jo set off a landslide of imitators. In contrast, Browne's illustrations of Jo show him wearing shoes. So once again, the stage offers a bare foot when Dickens does not, a spectacle heightened even more by the fact that Jo was a breeches part almost always played by a young woman. While the play's cemetery scene requires obvious hand gestures that direct the eye as Jo points out Nemo's grave, Jo's feet raise other issues related to both class and gender at the same time. Just as Hortense's bare feet mark her identity in a way that titillates and raises questions about her sanity, Jo's bare feet not only mark his class identity but raise gender issues too, since they plainly implicate the actress in centuries-old inferences about the moral standing of women on stage. Jo's literal hand gestures are undergirded and perhaps overshadowed by the transgressive implications of his bare feet marked by class and erotic spectacle in Rendle's play. While Jo's hands testify to the truth by pointing to obscured objects, his feet insinuate things hidden in plain sight—what is or might be looked at but not seen or openly acknowledged.

Jo's next action on stage is to separate the identities of Lady Dedlock and Hortense in Act 2. Lady Dedlock's and Hortense's hands provide the physical evidence of identity as Dickens imagines them: Lady Dedlock's aristocratic hand is "a deal whiter, a deal delicater, and a deal smaller" (282) than Hortense's working-class one. On stage, however, a hand might be less distinctive to the audience in a large auditorium—and certainly less provocative than bare feet. Rendle does not mention the hand evidence in the play, and Jo identifies Hortense as an imposter because of her French accent instead. Rendle has similarly glossed over the way Dickens has Jo notice Lady Dedlock's hands in the cemetery episode; in the play, Jo says this, "Ain't she a jolly servant jist to wear such sparkling rings"—but nothing more. In addition, hands might be unexceptional on stage, having become artfully stylized to express meaning through charted gestures, so Lady Dedlock's hands, much less her body, do not provide much stage spectacle. In contrast, Jo's body, revealed physically as it is by ragged clothing and bare feet, is spectacular in a way that Lady Dedlock is not because she is under wraps, concealing her identity under clothing, gloves, veil and presumably shoes while Jo's body is more compelling and secretively legible, a female hidden in plain sight because masquerading as male. The class and gender issues staged here turn on tensions between hands and feet and suggest working-class female bodies are openly revealed but not appropriate to acknowledge while the hidden bodies of the duplicitous aristocracy are not for vulgar display at the same time the world looks to them as powerful models.

Rendle's play goes on to highlight the hand's centrality to the *Bleak House* narrative in other places however. At the end of Act 3, Tulkinghorn's death at the climax of the play features hands prominently though in a different way from Browne's illustration. Tulkinghorn enters his death chamber because he has forgotten his gloves. Though there is no indication that he puts them on, gloves are clearly on his mind as something necessary and not to be left behind on this sinister night he describes as "a very quiet night, as still as death ... The stillest night I ever knew" (3.i.). The concealment gloves provide, especially in a detective story in which hands are a prominent motif, suggests that gloves have a psychological function; they will not protect against death and danger per se but may play the role of talisman, a comforting correctness—an ordering of one's affairs—against the unknown lurking in the dead of night. When he picks up his gloves, a note in the prompt script says "music change to hurry" (3.i.). The lighting cues just previous show that the drawing room is in half-light, but double underlined in red are the words "Calcium up full" (3.i.) as Tulkinghorn begins the speech above. Calcium light, or limelight, was glaringly bright when focused, and as Michael Booth notes, "Spectacle effects of any kind would have been almost impossible without it" (87). Tulkinghorn's gloves are the cue for musical urgency in this scene, but the murderer's hands and not Tulkinghorn himself are the reason for the limelight, which both reveals and conceals the murderer's identity: "One side of the window L. H. is stealthily pushed back. The creeping foliage outside drawn away. A female hand and pistol appears. SHOT FIRED" (3.i.). Hortense's hand alone is starkly highlighted and becomes a gendered metonym—a "female hand"—for her transgressive body already established at the outset by her bare feet. Rendle wants to maintain the ambiguity about whether Hortense or Lady Dedlock is the shooter, so while the murderess's deadly hand is prominently featured, it is not a strong marker of a single identity. Since Janauschek famously played both roles, her hand cannot differentiate the characters and may explain why Rendle, contrary to Dickens, downplays this feature when Jo tries to identify Hortense in her Lady Dedlock disguise. Rendle wants to conceal the murderess's identity at the same time he reveals the female transgression the hand evokes. Because of this deliberate ambiguity, the female hand does double duty, representing both women. The play's audience does not identify the difference between Lady Dedlock and Hortense on hand evidence alone just as Jo does not. At the deadly climax of the play, this single female hand becomes the main actor, identifying the guilty secrets of both transgressive females.

The final act reestablishes the importance of hands by reasserting and repositioning the way fingers are pointed. Though Rendle has retained the centrality of Jo pointing at Nemo's grave in Act 1, which is staged almost entirely as Browne's illustration, Sir Leicester replaces Tulkinghorn as the object being pointed at by accusatory fingers late in the play. In Act 4, scene 1, Bucket reveals Lady Dedlock's past and arrests Hortense, leaving Sir Leicester briefly alone on stage. He deals with his grief and bewilderment by saying, "What are these stranger's fingers pointing at me and tearing the fibres of my heart? Through her, my bride, my wife—whom I cannot bear to think of cast down from the high place she has graced so well" (4.i.). As in the novel, Sir

Leicester forgives, but he is cast in a much larger role in the play's final scene. Lady Dedlock dies in his arms as he paraphrases Richard's dying words in the novel, urging her not to succumb to death but to "Begin the world, begin the world anew" (3.iii.). Lady Dedlock's final words in the play complete Richard's last speech in the novel when she sobs, "Not this world, O not this! The world that sets this right" (763).[4] Here, Sir Leicester is pointed out, like Tulkinghorn, at the apex of his tragedy, brought about by refusing to truly see Lady Dedlock. Since he is part of the aristocracy whose titles are handed down through generations, his powerful class standing is of the utmost importance in the play's final tableau, where he not only holds the body of the fallen woman but also pronounces his forgiveness. So Rendle has taken from both Dickens's novel and Browne's illustration the suggestion of accusing fingers pointed at Tulkinghorn and turned them to point directly at the highest representation of entrenched class power. Though Tulkinghorn exerts his power in the novel because he represents the power and corruption of the courts that Rendle deemphasizes, Sir Leicester takes over the representation of power in the melodrama where class issues are more polarized and predominate. The fingers pointing at Sir Leicester are imagined but are certainly a part of the motif of hands established in the *Bleak House* narrative and illustrations.

However, Jo's bare feet are present in Lady Dedlock's death scene in the play as well. As will become more apparent shortly, Jo is an upstart stage character in 1870s *Bleak House* productions. Rendle's play gives Jo an important but not a central role, focusing as it does on Lady Dedlock. Jo is treated as a background character subordinate to the play's main action and the Dedlock tragedy. Though he is a tragic figure, he remains merely a serviceable and perhaps ornamental one. Jo's death, regarded by many of *Bleak House*'s first readers as a particularly fine part of Dickens's narrative, does not happen in Rendle's play. Instead, Jo is a peripheral witness to Lady Dedlock's demise in the final scene, the blocking sketch of which is preserved in the manuscript. Jo is at the far edge stage right. Esther, Lady Dedlock, and Sir Leicester form a tight grouping stage left, presumably huddled closely on the cemetery steps where Sir Leicester holds Lady Dedlock in his arms since the stage directions say that he raises her. The blocking specifies that Lady Dedlock is between Esther and Sir Leicester, but the lighting cue on the page opposite this dia-

---

4. The prompt script for Rendle's play belonged to Fanny Janauschek. In this script, the only known copy since the play was never published, only Janauschek's line cues are given though everyone else's speeches appear in full. Thus there is no record of Lady Dedlock's entire speech since it appears only as . . . world that sets this right." But given Rendle's pattern of regularly incorporating Dickens's own words, it is safe to speculate that Rendle put the rest of Richard's dying words into Lady Dedlock's mouth. The manuscript is available online through the Houghton Library at https://iiif.lib.harvard.edu/manifests/view/drs:52278493$15i.

logue says, "Moonlight full on Madame Janauschek" (4.iii.). So Jo stands at the far edge of the scene outside the shaft of light just as he stands on the edge of the play's plot and the edges of society as well. Perhaps his bare feet are now concealed by the darkness, but those feet have been center stage in conscious and unconscious ways. The finger of light that reveals Lady Dedlock's repentance, punishment, and forgiveness leave Jo standing in perpetual obscurity, upstaged by the events important to his betters. Yet his feet as a spectacle have made their mark, suggesting the impact of the working classes is often hidden in plain sight. Though Jo is shunted aside in Rendle's plot, he does not really move on and lives to assert his primacy in subsequent and even more popular stage productions of *Bleak House* to come.

When Rendle's play toured in America as part of Madame Janauschek's increasingly high-profile repertoire, it landed in San Francisco in 1875. There, a young British actress with considerable sex appeal named Jennie Lee had been making a splash in soubrette roles that "captured at once all the young men in San Francisco, who became instantly the ardent adorers of her voice, her singing, her dancing, her figure, her acting, and most all, possibly, of a certain *espièglerie* which defies definition, but makes her one of the most fascinating little ladies that ever looked across the footlights to set the susceptible youngsters in a blaze" ("Footlight" 1). She was chosen to play the part of Jo opposite Madame Janauschek, and the result was unsettling for Madame but propitious for Jennie Lee. Lee apparently played the bit part so effectively that she stole the show from Janauschek. Playwright Dion Boucicault, who was also in San Francisco at the time, saw Lee play this part and told her husband, playwright J. P. Burnett, that he must write a *Bleak House* adaptation that "make[s] Jo *the* part" (qtd. in Morley 177). He did, and it was the making of both Burnett's and Lee's livelihoods. While Rendle's version toured primarily in America, Burnett and Lee took their show to London and created a *Bleak House* spin-off craze that would seem almost unbelievable if we were not as modern audiences already used to the explosion and fizzling out—the viralization—of trendy entertainment. In the summer and fall of 1876, plays featuring Jo as the focus of the *Bleak House* narrative were everywhere. As many as seven of these adaptations played simultaneously or contiguously in London alone that summer. Burnett's play subsequently toured globally, and Jo became Lee's signature role, a part she played regularly into the 1890s ("Miss Jennie" 19).

Burnett's play, titled *Bleak House* in the manuscript but subsequently advertised only as *Jo* or sometimes *Poor Jo*, premiered in London at The Globe Theatre on 21 February 1876, and reviewers were bowled over. Lee's style and use of her broom were much remarked upon and imitated, so there must have been something distinctive in the way Lee deployed her hands in some signature sweeping gesture. The catalog of theatrical gestures that stylized acting in the first part of the century appears to be part of the mix for plays in the 1870s since Burnett's play makes it particularly clear that stylized gestures of despair (hand to brow, for example) occupy a regular place in the stage directions. But naturalism, imagined as an untrained and unsophisticated working-class paradigm, likely crept into Lee's style since reviewers remarked upon it so often and specifically as effective and realistic (Fitzgerald 247–48).

Jennie Lee's portrayal of Jo in the 1870s created a radical shift in the *Bleak House* narrative. Though Jo had often been cited as one of the most effective/affective characters in the novel, he seems to have been considered a minor character by both Dickens and Browne. Jo dies about two-thirds of the way through the novel, and he is only portrayed in three illustrations: once on the title page; once in Browne's "Mr. Chadband 'improving' a tough subject"; and once, of course, in the "Consecrated Ground" illustration discussed at length above. Though Jo's death in the novel evoked much contemporary comment from readers and reviewers, it apparently was not considered central enough to illustrate, unlike both Tulkinghorn's and Lady Dedlock's deaths. Burnett's adaptation rewove the *Bleak House* narrative to feature Jo as the central part, while the Dedlock plotline lurks in the background. Subsequently, Jo's death dominates most Victorian stage adaptations after 1876 largely inspired by Burnett's success.

Burnett foregrounds the way hands function both literally and metaphorically in his play, while suppressing overt references to feet in spite of—or perhaps because of—the physical presence of Lee's bare feet on stage shown in extant photographs. Burnett mentions hands 41 times; oppose this number to Rendle's mention of hands 23 times and Burnett nearly doubles down on the way hands might potentially structure his play. Burnett's references to hands often pick up threads of social critique that highlight Jo's working-class status. Though hands are literally central to working-class livelihoods, the metaphorical use of hands far outweighs their literal qualities as markers of class identification in this play. For example, hands are often featured as instruments of economic exchange, though money, in the end, is not of lasting value and slips through needy fingers.

The play begins with imagery and dialogue connecting handwriting to hands and marking literacy as belonging to an upper-class world beyond Jo's ken, though the scene ends with an exchange of comic hand gestures that are legible to the illiterate Jo. Act 1 begins at the "inkwich" where a book is handed to witnesses to kiss before testifying. This act of veneration signifies the value of the written, sacred text as a moral and cultural authority.[5] Snagsby, the second to testify after Tulkinghorn, turns immediately to the way Nemo's identity is invested in his hands alone:

> I have ascertained he was in arrear with his rent; that may have depressed him. I know no more where he came from than I know who inhabits the moon. . . . As to his connections—if a person were to say to me—"Snagsby, here's twenty thousand pounds down, ready for you, in the Bank of England if you'll only name one of 'em." I couldn't do it, sir. . . . About a year and a half ago, to the best of my belief, when he first came to lodge at the rag and bottle shop—he came into our place one morning after breakfast . . . [and] produced a specimen of his handwriting. . . . He gradually fell into job work at our place. That's the most I know of him, except that he was a quick hand—and a hand not sparing of night work; and that if you gave him—say five and forty folios on Wednesday night, you would have it brought home on Thursday morning—I don't think he slept much; and perhaps—not to put too fine a point on it—didn't sleep at all! (Burnett 1.i.)[6]

This speech is a combination of quotation and paraphrase (and a bit of original invention) from Dickens's text. It begins with the economic context in which work must be performed (to pay rent) and then pivots to the mode of handwork/handwriting that begins to stand in for Nemo himself. Instead of a body, he is "a quick hand . . . a hand not sparing of night work." The way money changes hands for those who must work for it is implied in this speech that then culminates in the displacement of identity onto the hand itself—and the hand alone in Nemo's case. Part of Nemo's relentless tragedy is that his literate, middle-class hands betray him; they neither save his life nor the life of the woman he loved since it is his handwriting that provides the pivotal evidence that eventually destroys both Lady Dedlock and himself. Literacy provides Nemo work, but it does not save him from poverty. This is the working-class conundrum at the center of capitalism, and Nemo's middle-class expectations are thwarted by the exigencies of life with all its cultural and sometimes self-inflicted complications.

---

5. Burnett does not specify the book is a Bible. British plays were subjected to official censorship for decency by the Lord Chamberlain's office up until the Theatres Act of 1968. The Lord Chamberlain often censored religious language in play scripts since the stage had long been considered too irreligious for sacred references.

6. Quotations from Burnett's play are from this source throughout.

Jo's illiteracy, in contrast, provides comedy in the midst of tragedy, but, as in Dickens, is meant to critique an increasingly polarized economic system. Jo's famously reproduced testimony comes next in the "inkwich" scene, and his entrance provides the first tableau moment in the play. Jo[7] enters to his own special music, described as tremolo and repeated when he is onstage. The stage directions say, "Joe's Music accented Enter Joe, Door in Flat R. A picture formed" (1.i.). There is no indication of what this picture consists of, and there is no correspondence to Browne's work, which illustrates nothing from the Sol's Arms inkwich. But as the scene continues with Jo's testimony rendered more or less as in Dickens, it closes with a double exchange of secrecy involving literal and metaphorical handedness: Snagsby gives Jo "half a crown" and then signals that he is to be discreet about this gift by putting his finger to his nose; Jo returns the signal, and then they repeat this exchange once more for comic effect. Snagsby's charity, mostly secret from Mrs. Snagsby, forms part of an underground economy of exchange. When money changes hands here, it is behind hands or underhanded, and the theatrical hand gestures between working-class characters are not of the stylized sort addressed by middle- or upper-class notions of appropriate hand gestures learned from acting manuals. Here, hands send messages between characters of the same class who agree to keep their exchanges between themselves, secret from the characters around them though, for the sake of effective critique, they are legible to the audience at the same time as they are legible to Jo.

Act 1 ends with the "Consecrated Ground" scene in which Jo shows Lady Dedlock Nemo's grave. There are few details to indicate how closely the stage set might have resembled Browne's illustration. Burnett calls for an "Exterior of the Potter's Field Burial Ground. Moonlight. C. Rail. Gates fastened" (1.v.). But the scene specifies that Jo points, so his hand gesture is directive and structures Lady Dedlock's gaze if not the audience's. Lady Dedlock removes her glove to give Jo money, and Jo comments in an aside on her "small white hand all covered with sparkling rings" (1.v.). Money changes hands overtly here and across class lines, as opposed to the exchange between Snagsby and Jo. Lady Dedlock tells Jo, "Hold out your hand" (1.v.). Her sparkling rings suggest an ostentatious giving, and, as in Dickens, she gives Jo "more money than you ever had in your life" (1.v.). She then tells him to point to the grave again and slips away. Lady Dedlock manipulates Jo, commanding Jo's use of his hands and rewarding him for his compliance. She does not enjoin him to secrecy about the cemetery visit itself, trusting that her aristocratic secrets are

---

7. In Burnett's manuscript, he spells the name Jo with an "e" more often than not, as do many other *Bleak House* adaptors.

not legible to Jo. So in Act 2, Jo freely admits to taking a woman to the cemetery and identifies Hortense as not being Lady Dedlock based on her hands. Hands are thus strongly established as class identifiers in regard to their color (whiteness), ornamental properties, delicacy, and access to lots of cash that can be exchanged overtly.

Throughout the play, Jo gets handed money, as he also does in the novel. Up until the final scene, the amounts he is given are mentioned in the play text, though not always in the dialogue. By the time Jo is on his deathbed, he has received a pound and a half from various sources. This amount would have seemed generous to Burnett's first audiences though it sounds little to us today. Jo does not become rich, but he does have enough resources to get by on for some time. Those who hand Jo money are the very rich—Lady Dedlock, who gives him a windfall all at once—and the working classes—Snagsby and Bucket, who together give him at least half as much as Lady Dedlock does. As charity goes, the working-class characters display open-handed generosity though often covertly; Lady Dedlock could clearly have done more. From Lady Dedlock, the money is for services rendered. From those in the working classes, especially Snagsby and Bucket, the money is given when they are most moved by Jo's plight and, especially for Bucket, as a way to acknowledge Jo's human suffering. Poignantly, Snagsby keeps thrusting unknown amounts of money into Jo's hand in the final scene as Jo lays dying, even though it is clear that money cannot help him.

Jo's death scene is structured by other hands as well. Bucket has been characterized in earlier scenes, as in Dickens's text, as not afraid to manhandle his subjects, and he pokes, prods and physically bullies both Snagsby and Jo into submission. Bucket undergoes a change of heart, however, and it is he who confesses his heartlessness in the final act and does the most to help Jo, even caring at the last for Jo's eternal soul; Jo dies repeating the Lord's prayer after Bucket (instead of after Woodcourt as in the novel). The penultimate scene opens with Bucket binding the wounds of domestic abuse for Jenny, the bricklayer's wife, inflicted by the "large heavy hands" that have "misused" her so (3.ii.). Bucket sets out here "to see if I can't help that wound to heal" (3.ii.), with all the resonances eventually of healing both physical wounds and moral abuses. Though Bucket has had a hand in Jo's demise as the chief mover in denying Jo residency on the streets of London, he spends the last two scenes repenting in such a way that the final prayer encompasses, perhaps, his own sins as well as Jo's. Bucket has had heavy hands in other ways too, hands that represent the power of the law to act without the heart to sympathize. Bucket's character arc occurs in Dickens as well, but it is magnified in the stage version by replacing the middle-class characters crowded around Jo when he dies at Mr. George's gun range with only the working-class characters, chiefly Snagsby, Bucket, and Jenny, in the play. Though the scene is played out publicly on a street, the street is in Tom-all-alones and becomes a private and class-bound spectacle. The final speeches themselves call attention to the mishandling of the very poor with overt references to the use of hands:

> JOE: Thankee, sir. It's turned wery dark. Is there any light a' comin'?
> BUCKET: (Softly.) It is coming fast, Joe.—Joe, my poor fellow.
> JOE: I hear you, sir, in the dark, but I'm a gropin'—a gropin'—let me catch hold of your hand.
> BUCKET: (Very softly.) Joe, can you say what I say?
> JOE: (Very feebly.) Anythink as you say, sir.
> BUCKET: (Uncovering, all do the same.) "Our Father—"
> JOE: "Our Father"—yes, that's wery good, sir.
> BUCKET: "Which art in Heaven—"
> JOE: "Art in Heaven"—Is the light a' comin, sir?
> BUCKET: It's close at hand.
> JOE: (Moonlight has fallen on his face—he pauses—smiles—mutters gladly.) I'm movin on. (Falls back dead in Bucket's arms. [Music.] Music swells out forte.) (Slow Drop.) Finis. (3.iii.)

Eyes and hands are significantly juxtaposed in this scene. Though Jo looks for light, he relies on his hands to grope his way through this experience. Bucket's reply lines up with this metaphor when he reassures Jo that the light is "close at hand." Hands both begin and end the final act of this play as Bucket's hands perform the physical atonement of healing Jenny's wound and then the spiritual atonement of holding Jo's hand as he dies. The dialogue here is taken mostly from Dickens, where the healing hands are those of the middle-class Allan Woodcourt. So the shift from cross-class to working-class spectacle in the play shuts out the more well-heeled characters from participation in this redemption. The world of the story dwindles down to the privacy of working-class pathos where the witnesses are those who are closer to or even across the poverty line that is hidden in plain sight on a disreputable street in the middle of prosperous London. Seeing poverty as a theoretical problem to throw money at is one thing; reaching hands across the poverty line in intimate ways and at the most important moments is reserved for the working classes in this play.

Burnett mentions feet only a few times and mostly with sinister connections. The incident that sets off the action in Rendle's play, Hortense's bare feet, does not even occur in Burnett's. Jennie Lee, who became so iconic playing

FIGURE 10.2. "Jennie Lee as Jo in *Bleak House*" by unknown photographer, circa 1876. NPG Ax7679. © National Portrait Gallery, London. Used with permission.

Jo that her photograph in costume became a collectable, definitely played this part in bare feet. Burnett's text, though, does not call attention to this fact. Feet are covert body parts that Burnett refers to directly only four times alongside two mentions of footsteps. Burnett's references to feet are all connected with secrecy, guilt, pain or death itself, and both references to footsteps connect to Lady Dedlock at moments she fears exposure. The well-heeled Lady Dedlock stands in stark contrast to Jo's naked heels, which, as a feature of poverty, mark Jo's class identity and, as a feature of gender, may have increased Jennie Lee's private, erotic appeal as an actress playing a transgressive role. Though Jo's handedness is treated overtly, the transgressive implications of his bare feet are covert, private, and unmentionable. The tensions between the abundance of active, working-class hands and the poverty of feet, though they are nakedly present on the stage, highlights another way the economic metaphor shifts when Jo's under-class plot in Burnett's play displaces the Dedlock upper-class plot in Rendle's play.[8]

Bleak House illustrations and adaptations rewove Dickens's critical themes as these interpretations shaped new meanings from the threads of his original text. Visual illustrations framed *Bleak House* for its reading audiences, and later theatrical adaptations staged it for even bigger, international audiences since Rendle's and Burnett's plays toured widely. Dickens's establishment of hands as a powerful motif from the start of his novel dominated the subsequent framing and staging of *Bleak House,* while his oblique references to feet, colored by Victorian restraint, signaled fraught discourses about appropriate looking and seeing, as well as making exchanges, across class lines. On stage, performances employed Dickens's motifs established in the *Bleak House* text and visualized in Browne's illustrations, where hands testify to identity in various ways and force the unreliable eye to witness important details. However, the stage also employed feet in a provocative counterpoint discourse, expressing complex and sometimes unspeakable anxieties about class and gender hidden in plain sight.

WORKS CITED

Batt, Alice. "From Page to Parlour: Gestures Toward a Victorian Middle Class." *Victorians Institute Journal,* vol. 24, no. 1, 1996, pp. 161–94.

Bolton, H. Philip. *Dickens Dramatized.* G. K. Hall, 1987.

Booth, Michael. *Theatre in the Victorian Age.* Cambridge UP, 1991.

Burnett, J. P. *Bleak House.* 1876, British Library, Ms 53162 B. Lord Chamberlain's Collection.

Capuano, Peter J. *Changing Hands: Industry, Evolution, and the Reconfiguration of the Victorian Body.* U of Michigan P, 2015.

Dickens, Charles. *Bleak House: A Norton Critical Edition.* Edited by George Ford and Sylvere Monod, Norton, 1977.

Farrar, Aileen. "Charles Dickens and Hablot K. Browne: Cross-Narrative and Collaboration in *Bleak House.*" *Victorians: A Journal of Culture and Literature,* vol. 122, 2012, pp. 36–50.

---

8. Since Rendle was an American and Burnett a British playwright, other cultural vectors might also be at work. Rendle wrote for an American stage with less censorship. So the American adaptation may have been freer to use language that acknowledged certain body parts on stage.

Fitzgerald, S. J. Adair. *Dickens and the Drama*, Scribner's, 1910.

"Footlight Flashes." *San Francisco Chronicle*, 28 June 1874, p. 1. ProQuest Historical Newspapers.

Ford, George, and Sylvere Monod, editors. "Dickens' Working Plans." *Bleak House: A Norton Critical Edition*, by Charles Dickens, edited by Ford and Monod, Norton, 1977, pp. 777–99.

Leavis, Q. D. "The Dickens Illustrations: Their Function." *Dickens the Novelist*, by F. R. and Q. D. Leavis, Chatto & Windus, 1970, pp. 332–71.

"Miss Jennie Lee." Obituary. *The Times*, 5 May 1930, p. 19. The Times Digital Archive.

Morley, Malcolm. "*Bleak House* Scene." *The Dickensian*, vol. 49, 1953, pp. 175–82.

Rendle, Henry. *Bleak House*. 1871. Robert J. Preston, Prompter & Copyist, California Theatre, San Francisco, 1875. Harvard University, Houghton Library, MS Thr 261, http://nrs.harvard.edu/urn-3:FHCL.HOUGH:23185551.

Steig, Michael. *Dickens and Phiz*. Indiana UP, 1978.

"Theatrical Record." *The New York Clipper*, 28 Oct. 1871, pp. 238–39. *Center for Research Libraries Global Resources Network*, https://dds-crl-edu.lib.pepperdine.edu/ crldelivery/16638. Accessed 17 Feb. 2018.

PART IV

∼

Manual Exceptionalism in Later Victorian Literature and Culture

CHAPTER 11

Handling Private Dramas of Class and Gender in Anthony Trollope's *The Duke's Children*

DEBORAH DENENHOLZ MORSE

In *Changing Hands: Industry, Evolution, and the Reconfiguration of the Victorian Body,* Peter J. Capuano contends that "at the unique moment when the hand was being superseded by machinery and stripped of its status as a supposedly God-given appendage, it also emerged in the Victorian practical consciousness as a primary locus for a new set of fictionalized identities that are quite removed from, but that nonetheless recapitulate anxiety provoked by new industrial and scientific relations" (13). His chapter on Becky Sharp's (literally) manipulative behavior in *Vanity Fair* establishes a new bar for analyzing the intimate and often high-stakes bodily rituals that make up social interactions at midcentury. This chapter extends the vein of such interpretation, but focuses on an author who possesses perhaps the finest grasp on the embodied choreography of genteel interaction—particularly as it occurs during the last quarter of the nineteenth century.

When Trollope wrote *The Duke's Children* from May to October 1876, the terms of gender and social class rights and obligations were urgently discussed in the public arena. The previous decade's 1867 Reform Act had extended the franchise to some working-class men, and The Matrimonial Causes Act 1857 followed by The Married Women's Property Act 1870 had incrementally expanded the legal rights of married women. Supporters of women's rights continued to agitate for greater autonomy over married women's property as well as for female suffrage, while the struggle over universal male suffrage begun in the 1830s by the Chartists urged more comprehensive voting rights for working-class males. When Trollope revised his novel in April and May of 1878,[1] England was on the cusp of even more far-reaching social change with the 1882 Married Women's Property Act and the 1884 Third Reform Act. This public agitation and the ensuing uncertainties about traditional social class and gender roles deeply influence *The Duke's Children*. Among the major Victorian novelists, Trollope draws the most sustained portrait of England's upper classes in the High Victorian era; he is known both for the dense social fabric of his novels and their intricate representation of consciousness.

Trollope's most expansive portrayal of the Victorian ruling class is in his urban Palliser chronicle. *The Duke's Children,* the final novel of the series, is imbued both with Trollope's Liberal reformist sympathies and with his lifelong love of the theater, as he explicitly represents tableaux in which hands explore the altering boundaries of caste and gender in the wake of rapid social reforms.[2] Trollope's depiction of England's political upper crust emerges in his characters' pervasive attempts to express and distinguish gradations of emotion specifically through their hands, which are staged as the bodily appendages that must negotiate the swift-changing manners and mores of this society in the century's later decades. These intimate theatrical interludes of intense emotion expressed by the haptic punctuate Trollope's seemingly leisurely fiction, the dramatic genre marked by touch interspersing the novel at key textual moments. Indeed, one might argue that Trollope constructs *The Duke's Children* around intense ritual moments of touch that fuse drama and novel.

In *The Duke's Children,* the haptic especially marks gradations of loss and connection—in particular between lovers, but also between family members and between friends. The novel begins: "No one, probably, ever felt himself to be more alone in the world than our old friend, the Duke of Omnium, when the Duchess died." This sentence is both solemn and intimate, assuming longtime acquaintance and affection among the narrator, the character of the Duke, and the reader of the novel, familiarity accrued from the previous Palliser novels. Trollope's opening sentence introduces the narrative focus not only upon intimacy but also upon loss and isolation, particularly in relation to the Duke, an intensely private figure who has always found it difficult to express emotion through touch, a man Trollope's narrator describes in *The Prime Minister* as "in manner . . . as dry as a stick" (483). In later sections of the novel, loss and isolation are also explored in relation to the intelligent,

---

1. For Trollope's writing and revision of *The Duke's Children,* see Amarnick and Egremont ix–xxv.

2. See my *Reforming Trollope* for an expansive consideration of Trollope's reformist fiction.

articulate London beauty Lady Mabel Grex and the bluff, presumptuous Major Tifto, companion in Silverbridge's youthful horseracing pursuits. This loneliness and desolation is in tension throughout the narrative with the successful marriage plots of the young Pallisers, Silverbridge's with the dazzling American heiress Isabel Boncassen and Mary Palliser's with the handsome, ambitious scion of lesser Cornish gentry Francis Tregear.

The Duke's slow reconnection with life is marked by symbolic, intimate scenes in which the embodied hand dramatizes his incremental acceptance of more progressive ideas about gender and social class. Trollope's final Palliser novel might indeed be inscribed with E. M. Forster's later epigraph to *Howards End,* "Only Connect"—connect the highest tier of the peerage with Isabel, granddaughter of an American dockworker and Tregear, younger son of a Cornish squire; connect diminished male privilege to female empowerment for greater equality between the sexes; connect the past with the present and the future; and most of all, connect the isolated Duke to his children after the death of Glencora. He is determined to help direct the lives of the now grown sons and daughter he had previously left mostly to Glencora's loving care.

The Duke is therefore pleased with his elder son and heir's invitation to dine at his club, the Beargarden, where the first of the novel's intimate rapprochement scenes featuring the embodied hand occurs. The Duke has not been in a London club for fifteen years, but he is glad to have an intimate dinner with his son. Silverbridge and the Duke have been listening to speeches in Parliament—where for now, they sit on opposite benches—and they walk from thence to the Beargarden. This context is significant; the Duke has been dismayed by his son's choice to run as a Conservative for the borough of Silverbridge rather than as a Liberal in the Palliser tradition. Yet the warm affection and respect between the son and the father is evident throughout the scene. The Duke is gracious not only to Silverbridge's great Cambridge friend Tregear, who is (arrogantly, as the Duke thinks) asking for Mary Palliser's hand in marriage, but also to the crass, forward Major Tifto, Silverbridge's horseracing chum, of whom he is more than a bit ashamed. After their meal, the father and son chat over coffee in the library, and the Duke characteristically tries to educate his son about his responsibilities:

> "I should be glad to see you marry early," said the Duke, speaking in a low voice, almost solemnly, but in his quietest, sweetest tone of voice. "You are peculiarly situated. Though as yet you are only the heir to the property and honours of our family, still, were you married, almost everything would be at your disposal. There is so much which I should only be too ready to give up to you!"

> "I can't bear to hear you talking of giving up anything," said Silverbridge energetically.
>
> Then the father looked round the room furtively, and seeing that the door was shut, and that they were assuredly alone, he put out his hand and gently stroked the young man's hair. It was almost a caress,—as though he would have said to himself, "Were he my daughter, I would kiss him." "There is much I would fain give up," he said. (171)

This tableau of near-maternal tenderness as the Duke urges marriage and domesticity undermines the male bastion of the "Beargarden," a name suggestive of a primitive male playground. The Duke makes certain that his uncharacteristic gesture is private—"the father looked round the room furtively . . . they were assuredly alone"—before he ventures his gentle stroking of Silverbridge's hair in "almost a caress," a gesture the narrator compares to a kiss bestowed upon a daughter. Both father and son are for a moment feminized in this private space, which allows an intimacy that has apparently heretofore not been possible to them. The Duke's gesture enacts a drama of family affection in which Glencora's influence upon the Duke seems manifest. His emphasis upon renunciation, upon his wish to "give up" the accoutrements and responsibilities of his position to his son elicits an authentic protest from the generous Silverbridge. While he touches his son's head, the courtly, old-fashioned Duke expresses his desire with the archaic locution "would fain," bespeaking tender care in its poetic unfamiliarity.[3] The Duke's wish to see his beloved son not only happy but responsible is evident. Perhaps even this early on in the novel, the Duke hopes that his son's wife might be a kind of emotional surrogate for Glencora—as it turns out she will be.

A dramatic scene featuring the embodied hand indeed occurs between Silverbridge's affianced bride, Isabel Boncassen, and the Duke. Isabel is not the wife the Duke would have chosen for his son, but Silverbridge has moved past his desire for his childhood friend, the London society beauty Lady Mabel Grex, and now desires the quicksilver Isabel, supple in both mind and body, whose beauty is more vibrant—and who, moreover, loves Silverbridge. He cleaves to his love for Isabel despite Mabel's melodramatic blandishments at the Palliser retreat Matching and the Duke's anger at Silverbridge's change of heart after confiding his hopes of making Lady Mabel his wife. The Duke much prefers the English daughter of an earl—even if that peer of the realm is the vicious Lord Grex—to American Isabel, daughter of a distinguished statesman and scholar. But Silverbridge chooses for himself, and the Duke

---

3. See especially Markwick 182 for a good discussion of this scene.

ultimately finds he must accept his son's decision to take Isabel's hand in marriage.

The passages between Isabel and the Duke are prefaced by a scene between the Duke and Silverbridge that also significantly features the embodied hand. The father at last succumbs to his son's plea: "What am I to say, sir? . . . When I love the girl better than my life . . . ?" The Duke declares in exasperated response: "My opinion is to go for nothing,—in anything!" However, the father realizes that as he has consented to Silverbridge's marriage, he should try to be more gracious and loving: "'However, perhaps we should let that pass,' said the Duke, with a long sigh. Then Silverbridge took his father's hand, and he looked up into his face" (450). Although the father is chagrined at not being able to influence Silverbridge's decision, he respects his son, with whom he desires not only amity but loving concord. Silverbridge in turn communicates his own understanding of how much this yielding costs the Duke with both touch and gaze, palpably demonstrating his sympathy, respect, and love for his father.

The Duke's acceptance of Isabel herself, marked by a literal grasp of her hand, is done thoroughly and with genuine love in perhaps the most beautiful private tableau scene of the novel. In this set piece, the Duke blesses Isabel as Silverbridge's chosen wife as well as his own daughter. This meeting occurs in the Duke's room in his London residence, Carlton Terrace, soon to be Silverbridge and Isabel's home; the Duke thus welcomes Isabel into his own private physical space, as he will then allow her into the innermost recesses of his heart, making both her own. He thinks that "it was not simply that she was to be the wife of his son,—though that in itself was a consideration very sacred . . . But this girl, this American girl, was to be the mother and grandmother of future Dukes of Omnium—the ancestress, it was to be hoped, of all future Dukes of Omnium!" (454).

In this scene, the Duke speaks in a more personal language than we have heard him use in the entire novel, words signifying his intention to be a second father to Isabel:

> "Then hear it from me. You shall be my child. And if you will love me you shall be very dear to me. You shall be my own child,—as dear as my own. I must either love his wife very dearly, or else I must be an unhappy man. And she must love me dearly, or I must be unhappy."
> "I will love you," she said, pressing his hand. (456)

This passage, with its promises of love, begins a ceremony echoing the sacrament of marriage in which the Duke places Glencora's ring upon Isabel's finger:

> It was a bar of diamonds, perhaps a dozen of them, fixed in a little circlet of gold. "This must never leave you," he said.
>
> "It never shall,—having come from you."
>
> "It is the first present that I gave to my wife, and it is the first that I give to you. You may imagine how sacred it is to me. On no other hand could it be worn without something which to me would be akin to sacrilege." (457)

Having long resisted the intrusion of American Isabel into his family, the Duke now thoroughly embraces her as his daughter in a sacred ritual that aligns Isabel with the Duke's beloved Glencora and recalls his own betrothal and marriage. His commitment to Isabel becomes entire, as he bestows the precious ring he has most likely removed from Glencora's dead finger[4] and places it on the warm flesh of Isabel, consecrating her as his daughter. Silverbridge later tells Isabel, "I did not think he ever would have parted with that . . . She wore it always. I almost think that I never saw her hand without it. He would not have given you that unless he meant to be very good to you" (458). In a reversal of mortmain as the dark clutching of the past upon the present that Katherine Rowe discusses in *Dead Hands*, the once vivacious Glencora seems reembodied through the Duke's touch of brilliant Isabel's hand, as she now wears the ring that symbolizes devotion to Glencora's husband and son.[5]

This scene reconciles past, present, and future for the mourning Duke. In the very moment the Duke remembers his devotion to Glencora, he is thinking as well of Isabel's marriage to Silverbridge, and of the future children that will likely be born of their union. "Do not keep him long waiting," he beseeches Isabel. Her newly ringed finger, with its circlet of gold and bar of diamonds symbolizing eternal love, is a sign of regeneration for the Duke himself. He literally takes Isabel by the hand and figuratively marries her to the Pallisers. In performing this gentle ritual, he immerses himself imaginatively in the future of his family, visioning Isabel's body as the bearer of his own descendants, while honoring his love for Glencora, whose body he promised to worship in their wedding vows, the body that gave birth to his son Silverbridge, to whom Isabel will be united in marriage. This interlude with

---

4. This solemn, heartrending act can only be imagined, and is a part of what John Sutherland called the "unnarrated hinterland" of the Victorian novel. In a reading of this essay, the distinguished Trollopian Margaret Markwick first remarked upon Sutherland's term as a description of this imagined past scene.

5. Rowe cites the famous fifth section of *Middlemarch*, "The Dead Hand," among the writing that delineates a legacy that must be "resisted . . . as when Dorothea gives up Casaubon's property to marry Will" (117). See Morse, *Women* for a reading of Isabel as Glencora's surrogate daughter.

Isabel is necessary for the Duke's emotional progression not only because of all the pain in his relationship with Glencora when she was alive, but also since her death, as his mourning reveals her own unsettled desires, her own wish that her daughter marry for love rather than status and financial security, as she herself was forced to do.[6] In response to the Duke's enactment of a private sacred ritual, Isabel promises to love him in words echoing the marriage vow—"I will love you"—augmenting the covenant with manual pressure upon the Duke's hand.

A further dramatic scene of conciliation represented by the embodied hand occurs when the Duke has at last accepted Mary's marriage with Tregear after many months of angry resistance to a man he wrongly fears may be disturbingly similar to his beloved Glencora's first love, Burgo Fitzgerald.[7] The Duke holds a dinner party for the two engaged couples and the Boncassens, Isabel's parents. He still finds his son-in-law "distasteful" (472), although he has come to respect him more than when he first thought of him only as "the younger son of a little county squire" (41). Tregear is a Member of Parliament now, and he has acted honorably throughout his courtship with Mary; the Duke realizes that his judgment is impaired in this regard because of his own erotic history with Glencora joined with class prejudice, and "that the pride that had been wounded was a false pride" (472). Thus, "before the dinner was over, he made a great effort":

> "Tregear, he said,—and even that was an effort, for he had never hitherto mentioned the man's name without the formal Mister,—"Tregear, as this is the first time you have sat at my table, let me be old-fashioned, and ask you to drink a glass of wine with me."
>
> The glass of wine was drunk, and the ceremony afforded infinite satisfaction to at least one person there. Mary could not keep herself from some expression of joy by pressing her finger for a moment against her lover's arm. He, though not usually given to such manifestations, blushed up to his eyes. (472)

The ancient ritual of host and guest has a sacred resonance, although the Duke inwardly is bemoaning his daughter's choice of husband, and "he was not able to bring himself into harmony with this one guest, and was almost savage to him without meaning it" (472). The Duke intends this gesture to be magnanimous, and he certainly views it as performed in a spirit of self-sacrifice,

---

6. Herbert argues the opposite, that the Duke does not change, in a significant resistance to the conversion narrative.

7. This history is discussed in McMaster, *Palliser Novels* and Morse, *Women*.

but it remains a resolutely secular ritual, not a Eucharist. The one significant effect it has is registered on the bodies of the lovers, instigated by the long-suffering Mary's hand, as she "could not keep herself from some expression of joy by pressing her finger for a moment against her lover's arm," whereupon he "blushed up to his eyes," the public ceremony and private touch of his beloved's hand combining to produce his blush, "although not usually given to such manifestations." Despite the other dinner guests' interpretation of the Duke's gesture as "solemn rather than jovial" and their realization that "an act of reconciliation had been intended" (472), the lovers experience the wine-drinking ritual more viscerally, represented by Mary's touch of her affianced husband, who registers her now licensed manipulation upon his own body. This connection between the touch of a hand and a blush of the face—here erotic, elsewhere a sign of embarrassment—is another significant feature of Trollope's exploration of the haptic.

A final important reconciliation in the novel is that between the Duke and Mrs. Finn, a rapprochement that is represented by their joined hands. In the process of reconnecting with life after Glencora's death, the Duke has unjustly separated himself from her closest friend, Mrs. Finn, a wealthy Viennese widow who has married the Irish country doctor's son and Liberal politician Phineas Finn. The Duke convinces himself that Mrs. Finn has acted dishonorably in relation to Mary's secret engagement to Tregear, when in truth Glencora sanctioned the lovers' union. Mrs. Finn has acted with the utmost probity, as she has done throughout her relationship with the Duke and his family; she is a figure the Trollope scholar Shirley Letwin calls "the most perfect gentleman in Trollope's novels" (74). The devoted reader of the Palliser Novels will recall the description in *Phineas Finn* of the "very fair" (423) jeweled hand of Madame Max Goesler that arouses the old Duke's desire in that novel; years later, that same elegant hand in *The Duke's Children* is penning sternly eloquent letters demanding an apology from that late besotted old Duke's nephew, the current Duke of Omnium.

The representation of Madame Max's hands in the earlier Palliser novels is essential for understanding both her firmness in putting pen to paper in letters that argue for justice from the Duke, and for fully appreciating her reconnection to him in the final novel of the series. Ultimately Mrs. Finn must forgive the Duke for his unjust censure in a quietly dramatic scene in which this least effusive of men must take her by the hand as a gesture that is the second stage—and the only public manifestation—of his apology to this most staunch Palliser family friend.

In *Phineas Finn,* the early attraction between Madame Max and Phineas is represented perhaps as much through the embodied hand as through their intimate conversation. "You are full of life," Madame Max assures Phineas, and "as she spoke, she had hold of his hand" (362). She offers him money, speaking in French, because even this sophisticated woman is "blushing and laughing as she spoke,—almost stammering in spite of her usual self-confidence" (362) as she tells him that she would like to support his next election campaign since he is in need of money and she is wealthy:

> He still was holding her by the hand, and he now raised it to his lips and kissed it. "The offer from you," he said, "is as high-minded, as generous, and as honourable as its acceptance by me would be mean-spirited, vile, and ignoble. But whether I fail or whether I succeed, you shall see me before the winter is over." (362)

Madame Max needs to speak in the more familiar and intimate French as well as sustain the physical manual connection with Phineas in order to express her willingness to give him wealth. She is still young and beautiful—and an eligible widow—and Phineas, the man she loves, is pursuing the lovely heiress Violet Effingham. Even the socially adept, cosmopolitan Madame Max is embarrassed by what might be taken as her forwardness; her touch is accompanied by a blush, communicating her erotic feelings toward Phineas. However, Phineas is also generous, and he is grateful for his intimate friend's offer rather than feeling embarrassed by it. Madame Max's proffering of her riches in order to help Phineas make his way in London politics elicits the first kiss between these future lovers and spouses: Phineas's spontaneous kiss of Madame Max's hand.

Most memorably, Madame Max offers herself in marriage to Phineas by stretching out her right hand to him in a dramatic gesture that defies gender and social class expectations. She is lonely, despite her social position, her exquisite dinner parties, and her beautiful Park Lane house, and yet she has refused the marriage offer of the old Duke of Omnium even though it would give her tremendous social elevation, because she does not love him. Madame Max offers money again to the impecunious Phineas so that he can stay in London politics:

> "It is because you are a woman, and young, and beautiful, that no man may take wealth from your hands."
> "Oh, it is that!"
> "It is that partly."
> "If I were a man you might take it, though I were young and beautiful as the morning?"

> "No;—presents of money are always bad. They stain and load the spirit, and break the heart."
>
> "And specially when given by a woman's hand?"
>
> "It seems so to me. . . .
>
> . . . I can do more than a man can do for a friend. You will not take money from my hand?"
>
> "'No, Madame Goesler;—I cannot do that."
>
> "Take the hand then first. When it and all that it holds are your own, you can help yourself as you list." So saying, she stood before him with her right hand stretched out towards him. (538)

Although Phineas is sorely tempted by Madame Max's beauty and friendship as well as by the political power that her money would bring when he takes her outstretched hand, he has not yet decided what to do. He is engaged to Irish Mary Flood Jones, and he remembers his betrothal even while holding Madame Max's hand, finally telling her that "it cannot be as you have hinted to me" (539).[8] Madame Max instantly withdraws not only her hand but her entire body from his presence, and he is left alone to contemplate what might have been with Madame Max, as well as his faithfulness to Irish Mary.[9]

The history between Madame Max and Phineas is consummated at the end of *Phineas Redux*, when the two meet again at Matching, the Palliser country home. Madame Max has travelled all over Eastern Europe in search of the evidence that exonerates Phineas from the charge of murdering Mr. Bonteen, and he knows the full extent of her faith in him. Their love is mutual, and he is free of romantic entanglement, as poor Mary has died in childbirth before Phineas returns to London. Phineas has not seen Madame Max since his vindication, after which he is distrustful of the world. Now he is reentering the worlds of politics and love. This is the wonderful description of his erotic reunion with Madame Max:

> He did not speak, but walking across the room to the window by which Marie Goesler stood, took her right hand in his, and passing his left arm round her waist, kissed her first on one cheek and then on the other. The blood flew to her face and suffused her forehead, but she did not speak, or resist him, or make any effort to escape from his embrace. As for him, he had no thought of it at all. He had made no plan. No idea of kissing her when they should meet had occurred to him till the moment came. (vol. 2, p. 302)

---

8. In Simon Raven's well-known 1974 BBC television adaptation, Mary is pregnant.
9. See Morse, *Women* for a reading of this scene that focuses upon the body.

Phineas's spontaneous gesture of gratitude and love begins with his taking of her hand—the same hand she offered him in marriage at the close of *Phineas Finn* years before. Now he is symbolically plighting his troth to her by grasping her hand before circling his arm around her waist and kissing each cheek, manifesting both his feelings as a lover and as an intimate friend. Madame Max recognizes his erotic touch with her blush. Phineas's manual connection to Madame Max signals his reconnection to a world that he feels has betrayed him in believing that he could be a murderer. She has always known that he was innocent, and she has been not only loyal but heroic in asserting his innocence and actually discovering the evidence to prove it. Now this sensitive, loving man and this generous, brave woman touch hands that will soon join in a successful marriage of equals—but also of outsiders not born into the ruling English classes. As the great Trollopian Robert Polhemus states, Phineas's gesture might "seem almost nothing, and yet it is everything. In it Trollope sees the grace, the emotional intensity, the poise, and the will to communion and love on which civilization depends" (185).

In *The Duke's Children*, we are insistently made aware of the Duke's withdrawal of the hand of friendship from Mrs. Finn, who has been a great and unselfish friend to the Pallisers. Readers of the previous Palliser novels are aware that as Madame Max Goesler, she refused the hand of the old Duke of Omnium—thus making Silverbridge safe as the heir—and remained the old Duke's stalwart friend until his death; she will not accept his legacy of the Omnium diamonds, worth a fortune; in order that Adelaide Palliser, first cousin to the current Duke, be allowed to marry the lackadaisical Gerard Maule, Madame Max bequeaths £25,000 she has previously refused to acknowledge as another part of her legacy from the old Duke of Omnium; and she was a wise and affectionate friend to Glencora until her death. She has been honorable in advising Mary as well, but the Duke must blame someone for what he views as his daughter's inappropriate choice of husband—and he cannot bear to blame his late wife. Moreover, Glencora's blessing of Mary's lover stirs misgivings in the Duke about his wife's marital happiness, and makes him wonder if she grieved over her own early love, Burgo Fitzgerald, another handsome man like Mary's Francis Tregear.

The entire argument between the Duke and Mrs. Finn takes place through letters—an intimate genre often represented in Trollope's fiction. Their correspondence negotiates social class and gender dynamics through the letter writing hand, as the Duke must come to respect this Viennese, possibly Jewish woman not born into the English aristocracy.[10] He alleges

---

10. Because of the uncertainty surrounding Mrs. Finn's Jewish heritage, I will not engage with the possibility of the racialized hand so fascinatingly discussed in other contexts by Aviva Briefel.

the betrayal of the family trust vested in Mrs. Finn, and she writes an impassioned and closely reasoned defense against his accusations that begins "now I will plead my case" (98). The Duke responds physically as well as mentally to her letter, which he reads "with tingling ears, and hot cheeks, and a knitted brow" (99). Eventually the Duke rather grudgingly writes an apology, "feeling that it was ungracious . . . all the favors had been from her to him and his" (146–47).

Trollope represents the fervent dialogue between the Duke and Mrs. Finn in handwritten letters that express their histories and their states of mind. The hands that write these missives are assumed rather than described, but the consummation of the Duke's apology is written on his body and on the body of Phineas, Mrs. Finn's husband, when they meet inadvertently in Switzerland. This encounter, marked by the male friends' embarrassed blushes, culminates with the Duke's desire to join his hand to Mrs. Finn's in a gesture of friendship and contrition—while he is both literally and figuratively hat in hand: "Both the Duke and Phineas blushed . . . The Duke stood with his hat off waiting to give his hand to the lady" (265). After this haptic reconciliation, Mrs. Finn finally convinces the Duke to accept Tregear for the happiness of his beloved daughter: "In thus performing your duty to your order, would you feel satisfied that you had performed that to your child?"[11] The Duke, greatly moved, responds: "all that you have troubled yourself to think and feel in this matter, and all that true friendship has compelled you to say to me, shall be written down in the tablets of my memory" (420).[12] He imagines his mind as a Decalogue-like written record, sacred text that is explicitly "written down" by the same hand that months before wrote in anger.

There is a tension in *The Duke's Children* with this narrative of reconnection, however, that is most prominent in the stories of Tregear's first love Lady Mabel Grex and Silverbridge's racing partner Major Tifto. The increasing isolation of both figures occurs in scenes in which representations of the hand are central in defining their losses in relation to gender and social class demarcations. The first of these scenes occurs early on in the novel, when Silverbridge fancies himself in love with the "young beauty" (61) Lady Mabel Grex.

> "I am not chaffing now in recommending that you go to work in the world like a man."

---

11. The best discussion of this scene remains Juliet McMaster's in *Trollope's Palliser Novels*.
12. See the unpublished essay by Alexa Kelly for another interpretation.

... Now in her energy she put out her hand, meaning perhaps to touch lightly the sleeve of his coat, meaning perhaps not quite to touch him at all. But as she did so he put out his hand and took hold of hers.

She drew it away, not seeming to allow it to remain in his grasp for a moment; but she did so, not angrily, or hurriedly, or with any flurry. She did it as though it were natural that he should take her hand and as natural that she should recover it.

... "If you will say that you care about it, you yourself, I will do my best." As he made this declaration blushes covered his cheeks and forehead.

"I do care about it,—very much, I myself," said Lady Mabel, not blushing at all. (107–8)

This scene foreshadows what keeps Silverbridge and Mabel apart: she has a secret love, Francis Tregear, whom she sent away because she thought wisdom lay in marrying for wealth and status. Mabel cannot quite initiate touching Silverbridge even though "she was sure that she liked him" (108). She knows the forms of courtship, but her heart is not in them; while Silverbridge blushes with emotion, she remains unblushing, a reversal of gender expectations. Mabel is experienced with love's tragedy, while Silverbridge lives in the realm of comedy.

The staged hand in two scenes where Silverbridge offers Mabel an heirloom ring presages her unwillingness to marry him. Mabel asks him to "give me that ring off your finger," at which he "at once took it off his hand" (232), nearly proposing to her despite Mabel's characterization of their relation as "real friends" (233). Despite her discouragement, Silverbridge insists on sending Mabel the ring; when she tries to give it back, he refuses it, and she leaves the valuable jewelry on the bench between them, a ring that will never be on Mabel's finger. No wonder Silverbridge is drawn to beautiful, vivacious Isabel, who plays badminton with him for hours and afterwards dances with him that same evening:

"Of course I shall stay now," he said, and as he said it he put his hand on her hand, which was on her arm. She drew it away at once. "I love you so dearly," he whispered to her, "so dearly."

"Lord Silverbridge!"

"I do. I do. Can you say that you will love me in return?"

"I cannot," she said slowly. "I have never dreamed of such a thing. I hardly know now whether you are in earnest."

"Indeed, indeed I am."

> "Then I will say good-night, and think about it . . ."
> When he went to his room he found the ring on his dressing-table. (256)

While Isabel and Silverbridge's love progresses toward their marriage at the novel's end, Mabel remains alone, a static, isolated figure.[13] In her last interview with Tregear, the discussion of their past love elicits her cry: "Oh Frank, Frank! . . . rising to her feet and stretching out her hands as though she were going to give him back all those joys" (492). The forlorn gesture of Mabel's empty outstretched hands is reinforced at the chapter's close, when she tells Tregear: "'Go now, and do not touch me' . . . He came to her . . . to take her hand as he parted from her. But she, putting both her hands before her face, and throwing herself on to the sofa, buried her head among the cushions" (493). Mabel has finally realized, as she later tells Silverbridge, that "to the end of time, I shall love Frank Tregear" (464). Her outstretched empty hands early on in the scene segue to hands barricading her face at the scene's close; both gestures dramatize the bereft future in which she will never again lovingly touch any man.

A quite different version of alienation from the haptic is represented in Major Tifto's narrative. While Mabel is the daughter of an earl, Tifto is a social hanger-on whose position is due to his knowledge of horses: "He was, without doubt, one of the best horsemen in England . . . there were some who considered that they had suffered unduly under his hands in horse dealings" (42). His star is in the ascendant as the novel opens: "Now, at this very moment, was the culmination of the Major's life. He was Master of the Runnymede Hounds, he was partner with the eldest son of a Duke in the possession of that magnificent colt, the Prime Minister, and he was a member of the Beargarden" (44). Silverbridge's disaffection with Tifto begins with the young lord's reneging on his spontaneous invitation to his turf comrade to come down with him to the hustings at the borough of Silverbridge. Tifto accuses Silverbridge of "throwing me over" (91) and plans revenge. Silverbridge's dislike of Tifto increases with the Major's inebriated intrusion into the room at the Beargarden where the Duke and Silverbridge are having an intimate conversation, and the young lord reproves Tifto. The Duke quietly lets Silverbridge recognize that "you can gain nothing by his companionship" (177), after which the son "is thoroughly sick of Major Tifto" (179). The culmination of the Tifto story occurs when he purposely lames their horse The Prime Minister just before the Leger race, whereupon Silverbridge owes £70,000 in gambling debts and

---

13. See McMaster, *Palliser Novels* and Morse, *Women*, for the seminal and still most thorough discussions of Mabel's character.

must ask his father for the money. The Duke has of course been the prime minister of England, and the nail driven into the racehorse's foot in part symbolizes an injury to the Duke and to all he represents of Englishness.

However, this calamity is the occasion of Silverbridge's accession to manliness, which has been slowly taking place throughout the book.[14] In their scene of confrontation, the emphasis is upon the Duke's tenderness toward his remorseful son and his strong desire for him to be morally worthy, emotions expressed by the Duke's hands lovingly touching Silverbridge, his tactile response making his forgiveness of his prodigal son complete. After Silverbridge sobs "so that he could hardly speak," and promises that he has given up horseracing, the turf, and Major Tifto forever, "the father came up to the son and put his arms round the young man's shoulders and embraced him" (293). This warm gesture, so uncharacteristic of the restrained Duke, marks his further reentry into the world after his period of mourning for Glencora. Silverbridge, with his good heart and his impetuosity, has been Glencora's son—but now he is also the Duke's son, with an increasingly "steady manliness" (261). His integrity as well as his good looks and lively wit mark Silverbridge as the son of both Glencora and the Duke, dramatized by the haptic, the Duke's warm, forgiving embrace of his beloved son.

In contrast, Tifto's downfall and isolation has something of the Shakespearean about it, echoing Falstaff removed from Prince Hal's good graces when he becomes Henry V. The Shakespeare-loving Trollope revises that drama in a scene of forgiveness between Silverbridge and Tifto that features both their hands.[15] Silverbridge thinks "he almost owed some reparation to the wretched man,—whom he had unfortunately admitted among his friends, whom he had used, and to whom he had been uncourteous" (475). Silverbridge "would not shake hands with him, but could not refrain from offering him a chair" (475):

> . . . Silverbridge sat with his hands in his pockets trying to look unconcerned. "But if you've got it here, and feel it as I do,"—the poor man as he said this put his hand upon his heart,—"you can't sleep in your bed till it's out. I did that thing that they said I did." (475)
>
> . . .
>
> "Then why couldn't you let the horse alone?"

---

14. Amarnick discusses this character development as it is represented in the original manuscript of *The Duke's Children*, now published under Amarnick's editorship.

15. For Trollope's vast knowledge of both Renaissance and Jacobean drama, see especially Epperly, Harvey, Coyle, and Osborne.

"I was in their hands. And then you was so rough with me! So I said to myself I might as well do it;—and I did it."

"What do you want me to say? As far as my forgiveness goes, you have it." (476)

By the close of this long scene, both Silverbridge and the reader sympathize with Tifto, who finally "burst out into a paroxysm of tears and sobbing" (478). Silverbridge realizes that he "could not take the man into partnership again, nor could he restore to him either the hounds or his club,—or his clean hands. Nor did he know in what way he could serve the man, except by putting his hand into his pocket,—which he did" (478). Tifto "ultimately became an annual pensioner on his former noble partner, living on the allowance made him in some obscure corner of South Wales" (478). Instead of Henry V's final rebuke to Falstaff—"I know thee not, old man"—Silverbridge listens to his previous companion's confession of wrongdoing and forgives him. Moreover, although he does not take Tifto by his hand literally, he does provide him a handout upon which Tifto can live—albeit in isolation. The passages throughout this dramatic scene are riven with images of hands, from Silverbridge's refusal to shake hands as the interview begins with his hands in his pockets, through Tifto's melodramatic hand upon his heart as he confesses he was "in their hands," to Silverbridge's biblical metaphor "clean hands," unstained by sin[16] or the more secular idea of criminal actions, and his eventual decision to "put his hand into his pocket" to give Tifto money (476).

While the novel banishes Tifto to South Wales and isolates Mabel with her lady's companion Miss Cassewary—"two old maids together!" (487)—*The Duke's Children* closes with the weddings of Isabel to Silverbridge and of Mary to Tregear. Although in the very midst of these celebrations the Duke "was reminding himself of all that he had suffered" (505), he has also accepted a new order in which American Isabel Boncassen and untitled Francis Tregear are a part of the Palliser family. The Duke pronounces upon Tregear in the final line of the novel, spoken to Silverbridge: "But now I will accept as courage what I before regarded as arrogance" (505). Indeed, in the original manuscript version of *The Duke's Children*, The Duke thinks, "Who knows. He may yet live to be a much greater man than his father-in-law. I am certainly very glad that he has a seat in Parliament" (784n542).[17] The Duke has recon-

---

16. See for instance Psalms 24:3–4, King James Bible: "Who shall ascend into the hill of the LORD? or who shall stand in his holy place? / He that hath clean hands, and a pure heart; who hath not lifted up his soul unto vanity, nor sworn deceitfully."

17. For a fuller context, see the recent edition of the original manuscript, edited by Steve Amarnick.

nected with the world through his love for his children, and theirs for him, and he has decided to yield to the younger, late Victorian generation's more flexible and progressive ideas about social class and gender—a process represented throughout the novel with great beauty in dramatic scenes featuring the embodied hand.

WORKS CITED

Amarnick, Steve. "Trollope at Fuller Length: Lord Silverbridge and the Manuscript of *The Duke's Children*." *The Politics of Gender in the Novels of Anthony Trollope: New Readings for the Twenty-First Century*, edited by Margaret Markwick, Deborah Denenholz Morse, and Regenia Gagnier, Aldershot, UK and Burlington, VT, Ashgate Press, 2009, pp. 193–206.

Briefel, Aviva. *The Racial Hand in the Victorian Imagination*. Cambridge UP, 2015.

Capuano, Peter J. *Changing Hands: Industry, Evolution, and the Reconfiguration of the Victorian Body*. U of Michigan P, 2015.

Coyle, William. "Trollope and the Bi-Columned Shakespeare." *Nineteenth-Century Fiction*, vol. 6, no. 1, June 1951, pp. 33–46.

Egremont, Max. Introduction. *The Duke's Children*, by Anthony Trollope, edited by Steven Amarnick, Everyman's Library / Alfred A. Knopf, 2017, pp. ix–xxviii.

Epperly, Elizabeth. *Anthony Trollope's Notes on the Old Drama*, English Literary Studies 42, U of Victoria P, 1988.

Harvey, Geoffrey. "Trollope's Debt to the Renaissance Drama." *Yearbook of English Studies*, vol. 9 (Theatrical Literature Special Number), 1979, pp. 256–69.

Herbert, Christopher. "Trollope and the Fixity of the Self." *PMLA*, vol. 93, no. 2, Mar. 1978, pp. 228–39.

Kelly, Alexa. "Allusions to *Hamlet* and Complexities of Character in Anthony Trollope's *The Duke's Children*." Unpublished essay.

Letwin, Shirley. *The Gentleman in Trollope: Individuality and Moral Conduct*. Palgrave Macmillan, 1982.

Markwick, Margaret. *New Men in Trollope's Novels: Rewriting the Victorian Male*. Aldershot, UK and Burlington, VT, Ashgate P, 2007.

McMaster, Juliet. *Trollope's Palliser Novels: Theme & Pattern*. London and Basingstoke, Macmillan, 1978.

Morse, Deborah Denenholz. *Reforming Trollope: Race, Gender, and Englishness in the Novels of Anthony Trollope*. Aldershot, UK and Burlington, VT, Ashgate P, 2013.

———. *Women in Trollope's Palliser Novels*. Ann Arbor and London, UMI Research P, 1987; London, Boydell & Brewer, 1991.

Osborne, Hugh. "Shakespeare, William." *The Oxford Reader's Companion to Trollope*, edited by R. C. Terry, Oxford UP, 1999, pp. 479–80.

Polhemus, Robert. *The Changing World of Anthony Trollope*. U of California P, 1968.

Rowe, Katherine. *Dead Hands: Fictions of Agency, Renaissance to Modern*. Stanford UP, 1999.

Terry, R. C., editor. *The Oxford Reader's Companion to Trollope*. Oxford UP, 1999.

Trollope, Anthony. *The Duke's Children*. Edited by Steven Amarnick, Everyman's Library / Alfred A. Knopf, 2017.

———. *The Duke's Children*. Edited by Katherine Mullin and Francis O'Gorman, Oxford UP, 2011.

———. *Phineas Finn*. Edited by Simon Dentith, Oxford UP, 2011.

———. *Phineas Redux*. Edited by John C. Whale, with an Introduction by F. S. L. Lyons. Oxford UP, 1983.

———. *The Prime Minister*. Edited and with an Introduction by David Skilton. Penguin, 1994.

CHAPTER 12

Reading by Hand

Oscar Wilde and the Body in the Archive

DANIEL A. NOVAK

IN HIS 1915 VOLUME *Contemporary Portraits,* Frank Harris, who would publish his entertaining if unreliable[1] biography of Oscar Wilde in the following year, recounts his first meeting with Wilde and the first time he shook his hand:

> His appearance was not in his favour; there was something oily and fat about him that repelled me. Of course, being very young I tried to give my repugnance a moral foundation; fleshy indulgence and laziness, I said to myself, were written all over him . . . He shook hands in a limp way I disliked; his hands were flabby; greasy; his skin looked bilious and dirty . . . His appearance filled me with distaste . . . I think most people felt it, and because it is a tribute to the fascination of the man that he should have overcome the first impression so completely and so quickly . . . His talk soon made me forget his repellant physical peculiarities (90–91; 92).[2]

---

1. Merlin Holland calls for a reevaluation of Harris's work, which is usually dismissed as "nowhere reliable" ("Biography and the Art of Lying"), 6.

2. A similar version of this description appears in his biography of Wilde (*Oscar Wilde* 53–55). Harris appeals to photographs (both material and metaphorical) as a way of describing Wilde's personality: "I may now try and accentuate a trait or two of these photographs, so to speak, and then realise the whole portrait by adding an account given to me by Oscar himself" (17); or, "Oscar himself only completed these spirit-photographs by what he told me of his life at Trinity" (24); "The 'Green Carnation,' which was a photograph of Oscar as a

FIGURE 12.1. Photograph of Oscar Wilde. *Contemporary Portraits* by Frank Morris, 1915. William Andrews Clark Memorial Library, UCLA. Used by permission.

Despite framing his moralistic interpretation of Wilde's hand as a sign of youthful naiveté, his emphasis on the widespread "repugnance" Wilde's body inspired seems to encourage rather than discourage the sense that "fleshly indulgence and laziness . . . were written all over him." The image paired with Harris's description hardly represents the repulsive creature conjured by him, but this gap only reinforces the idea that to truly *know* Wilde is to touch his hand—a hand literally oozing with the "distasteful" and "dirty" desires that

---

talker and a caricature of his thought" (106) See also Smigiel: "He was, or made himself to be, monstrous. He would be darker. Fatter. Strange. Oily. Perverse. He wore Dorian's portrait as his mask; he approached the table with Salome's hunger. He gorged himself and rolled bout in the remains. He meant to be a foul thing. He would not hide indulgence" (211).

had, in the not-so-distant past been the subject of public scandal. What is striking, however, is that Harris conjures a strict separation between what is written on Wilde's body and his seductive speech. Wilde's brilliant talk, and by extension his writing, has the power to make him forget Wilde's hand.

Since Wilde's death, however, readers have longed for that touch—longed to connect what Harris separates: Wilde's handwriting and his living hand. The literary-theoretical enterprise of Wilde studies has been particularly concerned with being in touch with Wilde's body and desires through his writings. Critics have routinely turned to Wilde's texts in an effort to uncover and discover their author, and books with titles like *The Unmasking of Oscar Wilde*, *The Secret Life of Oscar Wilde*, and *The Man Who Was Dorian Gray* still being produced after over 100 years of searching (Pearce; McKenna; McCormack).[3] According to Joseph Bristow, it was not until the late 1980s and 90s that Wilde criticism truly shifted "from Wilde's actual body to his textual corpus" ("Memorializing" 320). Nevertheless, for many readers, Wilde's work (both in manuscript and print) still promises to provide an experience of what Jules Law calls "(im)mediation"—a virtual connection to Wilde's body and mind, a "fantasy of transcending mediation" (976).

I want to stress at the outset that I am not deriding this kind of reading as naïve or insufficiently theoretical. Leah Price of course has reminded us how, for the Victorians, reading was a highly embodied experience (*How to Do Things; What We Talk About*). But critics like Rita Felski, Jennifer Felissner, and others have also worked to theorize transtemporal approaches to literature, arguing that we need different models to attend to and account for our own affective responses to texts that have a "busy afterlife" (Felski 580)—to account for the way texts reach out and touch us not only from the past but *in* the present. As Felski puts it, "their temporality is dynamic, not fixed or frozen; they speak to, but also beyond, their own moment, anticipating future affinities and conjuring up not yet imaginable connections" (580).[4] That "busy afterlife" is also more complicated than it appears to be in much of the work that explores the relationship between a Victorian past and twenty-first-century present. Megan Ward has recently theorized what she calls "the historical middle," the long period between then and now (that is, most of the twentieth century)—a period even presentist approaches have ignored. Ward suggests that we can and should look to this period as a site for alternative

---

3. As Jerusha McCormack argues of *Dorian Gray*: "it was written—and once written, inscribed its text with a kind of fatality. He had written the script for his own life even while, in writing it, he precipitated the events which were to lead to his downfall" ("Wilde's Fiction(s) 112). See also Gomel on "the hall of mirrors that is Wilde scholarship" (79).

4. See also Fleissner, "Is Feminism a Historicism?" and Harris, *Untimely Matter*.

models with which to understand and reframe nineteenth-century ideas, even and especially when those models may not have survived into the present (7–8).[5]

Nor, I would argue, are such modes of reading in opposition to the spirit of Wilde's philosophy and approaches. As much as we think of Wilde in terms of his efforts to question traditional notions of authorship and originality, as well as the link between the artist and art work, at times, Wilde modeled and dramatized different approaches to reading in novels, letters, and reviews—approaches that echo the drive for connection with the author's hand and body. For example in a letter to John Keats's niece Emma Speed on Keats's "Sonnet in Blue," he writes "now I am half enamoured of the paper that touched his hand, and the ink that did his bidding" (*Complete Letters* 157).[6] Wilde extends this approach from manuscript to printed texts when he reviews William Henley's poems and claims that "it seems as if one could put one's hand upon the singer's heart and count its pulsations" (*Complete Works* vol. 7, pp. 112–13).[7] He would return to this trope a year later in *The Portrait of Mr. W. H*: "I felt as if I had my hand upon Shakespeare's heart, and was count-

---

5. I don't have space to explore the complex and wide-reaching methodological effects of Ward's deceptively simple formulation. Most relevant to this discussion is the way her approach has the potential to transform what constitutes both historicism and presentism.

6. Wilde met her during his North American tour, and Speed gave Wilde an early draft of "Answer to a Sonnet Ending Thus." For more on the links between Keats, the late nineteenth-century reevaluation of Romanticism, the Pre-Raphaelites, Thomas Chatterton, and the "male incarnated beauty" Wilde associated with both Chatterton and Keats, see Bristow and Rebecca N. Mitchell, *Oscar Wilde's Chatterton* (290).

7. "A Note on Some Modern Poets," originally published in *The Woman's World*, December 1888. Wilde himself talked about biography in similar terms: most often, Wilde complains that biographies focus far too much on trivial details and not enough on the poet or artist. In "Two Biographies of Keats," Wilde argues that "to a certain degree this is, no doubt, inevitable nowadays. Everybody pays a penalty for peeping through keyholes, and the keyhole and the backstairs are essential parts of the method of the modern biographers" (187); "Two Biographies of Keats," *Pall Mall Gazette*, 27 September 1887 (*Complete Works* vol. 6, pp. 187–89). However, it is less the violation of private space or even private desires ("the keyhole and the backstairs") that concerns Wilde, and more the way in which "modern biography" makes "the great mistake of separating the man from the artist . . . When Mr. Rossetti writes of the man he forgets the poet, and when he criticises the poet he shows that he does not understand the man. His first error, as we have said, is isolating the life from the work" (187–88). In *De Profundis*, Wilde concedes that this violation is inevitable: "I forgot that every little action of the common day makes or unmakes character, and that therefore what one has done in the secret chamber one has some day to cry aloud on the house-tops" (101). For more examples where Wilde condemns biographies for concentrating on trivial details, see "A Cheap Edition of a Great Man" (on Dante Gabriel Rossetti), *Pall Mall Gazette*, 18 April 18 1887 (*Works* vol. 6, pp. 146–49) and "Great Writers by Little Men" (particularly his criticism of Hall Caine's biography of Coleridge), *Pall Mall Gazette*, 28 Mar. 1887 (*Complete Works* vol. 6, pp. 134–37).

ing each separate throb and pulse of passion" (*Complete Short Stories* 124).[8] These accounts of what we might call the tactile erotics of reading by hand are reminiscent of the language *Dorian Gray* uses to describe the erotics of influence—the way Lord Henry's seductive philosophy "had touched some secret chord that had never been touched before, but that he felt was now vibrating and throbbing to curious pulses" (21).[9] Or one might recall the aural pleasure Gwendolyn experiences through the "music" in the name Earnest, which "produces vibrations" (*Importance of Being Earnest* 263).

If we can think of these modes of reading as constituting a kind of expanded time and space in which we shake hands with an author's ghost, this idea took literal form early in Wilde's afterlife—cultural and otherwise.[10] Hester Travers Smith published her *Psychic Messages from Oscar Wilde* in 1923, a text that purported to be Wilde's meditations on death and contemporary literature (he has nasty things to say about Ulysses and the production of his own plays). To prove their authenticity, she reproduced facsimiles of Wilde's handwriting alongside the writing of a medium communicating with Wilde's spirit.[11] While as Elisha Cohn has argued, *Psychic Messages* represents authorship as highly mediated and echoes Wilde's own reputation as a "champion of artifice" (Cohn 475). I am more interested in the fantasy that animates the project to begin with, a desire for Wilde's hand and handwriting to reach readers from beyond the grave—a fin-de-siècle, spiritualist version of Keats's "This Living Hand."[12] Lest you think my language extravagant, such a desire took visual form in a book by Wilde's fortune teller, Mrs. Robinson. In her 1911 edition of *The Graven Palm*, she reproduced a photograph of a cast taken of

---

8. See also Wilde's expanded version of *Mr. W. H.*, where the narrator marvels at the response to the Sonnets—"A book of Sonnets, published nearly three hundred years ago, written by a dead hand and in honor of a dead youth, had suddenly explained to me the whole story of my soul's romance" (*Complete Works* vol. 8, p. 251).

9. For more on the relationship between the embodied hand and modes of reading, see Capuano's *Changing Hands* and Briefel's *Racial Hand*.

10. Felski usefully differentiates New Historicism's professed desire to speak with the dead from its tendency toward "diagnosis" rather than "dialogue" (577). See also Goldberg who has argued that "New historicism, insofar as it is still practiced, is virtually indistinguishable from old historicism" (ix–x). See also scholars who have critiqued the way in which the rise of New Historicism has produced a fetishization of the archival object, such as Knapp and Pence or Freshwater.

11. See Gomel. Gomel shows that *Psychic Messages* sparked a serious debate over the authenticity of the messages between those who believed in their authenticity (like Arthur Conan Doyle, who wrote that Wilde's "brain is at the back of it") and those who thought they were fraudulent like C. W. Soal (74).

12. See Najarian for a reading of "This Living Hand," the posthumous audience, and same sex desire.

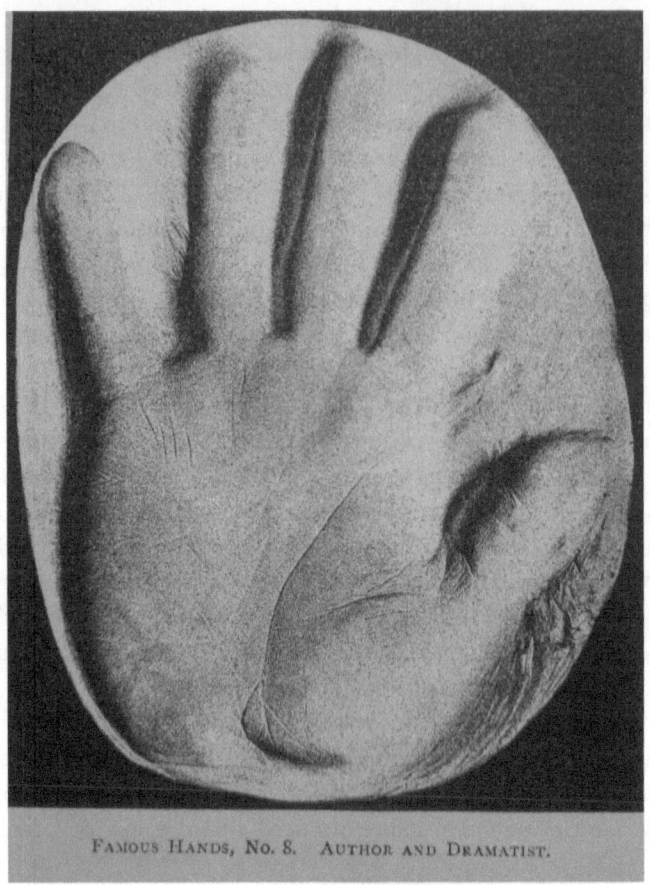

FAMOUS HANDS, NO. 8. AUTHOR AND DRAMATIST.

FIGURE 12.2. *The Graven Palm; a Manual of the Science of Palmistry*, by A. Robinson. New York: Longmans & Green Co., 1911, p. 350.

Wilde's hand, perhaps made during his visit days before the opening of his first trial.[13]

During this session, Robinson famously and erroneously prophesied a "complete triumph" (*Complete Letters* 636). Neil Bartlett reconstructs this visit in his play *In Extremis*, recasting her error as itself a "triumph" of prediction, when viewed in a different time frame: "listen very carefully to what I am going to say; I told him I saw a great triumph. . . . Well, was I lying?" (Bartlett 52). Instead of exposing his past life, his immediate future, and its ultimate

---

13. The caption only reads "author and dramatist," but in his *Oscar Wilde Chronology*, Page identifies the hand as Wilde's (61).

tragedy, for Bartlett, Wilde's hand had inscribed on it the future of Wilde's posthumous reception and the "triumph" of his legacy. That legacy is still in the process of being written and revised. With this in mind, one can read the cultural and critical focus on Wilde's embodied textual past neither as a naïve form of historicism nor as simply about the past. On the contrary, as Felski argues, "pastness is part of who we are, not an archaic residue, a regressive force, a source of nostalgia, or a return of the repressed" (578). Or as Bruno Latour puts it, the "past is not surpassed but revisited, repeated, surrounded, protected, recombined, reinterpreted, and reshuffled" (75).

I mentioned Keats's "This Living Hand" because it is perhaps the most famous literary touchstone for thinking about the conflation of hand and handwriting, but also because it serves as a way of thinking about the strange temporality of literary posterity. As Brooke Hopkins puts it, the poem "seems to have been written from the grave" (35). The final gesture—"see here it is— / I hold it towards you"—potentially participates in both present and future; "it" is either the hand of the present (the "here" and now) or the hand (and text) encountered in the future. As Andrew Bennett argues, for the Romantics, this "posthumous life of writing" is "itself inscribed in the originary moment of reading" (9-10). In conjoining present and future, writing and reading, Keats's "Living Hand" offers a theory of literary reception and even of the archive—the future site in which the hands of authors and the hands of readers meet in "earnest grasping."

Though Wilde would not have read Keats's fragment (it wasn't published until 1898), he turns again and again to Keats when writing about literary posterity and "the posthumous life of writing" in poems like "On the Sale by Auction of Keats' Love Letters" (1885)—a poem to which he also refers in *De Profundis,* comparing himself to Keats in an attempt to shame Douglas for having published some of their correspondence. In his first published prose work, "The Tomb of Keats" (1877), he complains of the inadequate physical monument to Keats and appeals to his still vital legacy.[14] Even more pertinent is a lesser-known poem entitled "Bittersweet Love" (the original Greek title is ΓΛΥΚΥΠΙΚΡΟΣ ΕΡΩΣ) published in his first volume of poetry (1881), in which Wilde links Keats to a fantasy of lasting poetic fame, and in which the speaker imagines grasping Keats's "living hand" in an atemporal afterlife. If he was not

---

14. The essay ends with a poem, in which Wilde alludes to Keats's epitaph, "here lies one whose name was writ in water" and his poem *Isabella* as he promises to sustain Keats's legacy: "Thy name was writ in water on the sand, / But our tears shall keep thy memory green, / And make it flourish like a Basil—tree"; *Irish Monthly* 5, July 1877, 476–8 (*Complete Works* vol. 6, pp. 11–13; qtd at 13). See Najarian 19. For more on Wilde's "passion for Keats" (139) and relationship to late nineteenth-century constructions of Romanticism, see Bristow and Mitchell.

"made of common clay" the speaker argues, he would have "sat within that marble circle where the oldest bard is as the young ... Keats had lifted up his hymeneal curls from out the poppy-seeded wine, / With ambrosial mouth had kissed my forehead, clasped the hand of noble love in mine" (*Complete Works* vol. 1, p. 126, ll.1, 11, 13–14). Ultimately a poem about the failure to achieve literary fame or even to write at all, it ends with the speaker choosing love over work: "I have made my choice, have lived my poems, and, though youth is gone in wasted days, / I have found the lover's crown of myrtle better than the poet's crown of bays" (p. 127, ll. 29–30).[15]

Wilde returns to this poem in the same letter to Emma Speed from which I quoted earlier—where Wilde is "half enamoured of the paper that touched [Keats's] hand."[16] Already conflating Keats's hand with his writing, he refigures this grasping of hands in terms of a grasping of texts. Wilde slightly alters the lines about Keats: "In my heaven he walks eternally with Shakespeare and the Greeks, and it may be that some day he will lift 'his hymeneal curls from out his amber gleaming wine, with ambrosial lips will kiss my forehead, clasp the hand of noble love in mine.'" In the letter Wilde transforms a love embraced at the expense of writing into both a love *for* the materiality of writing and an eroticized version of literary fame. As part of this effort, he introduces figures who don't appear in the poem (which only names Dante and Keats). "Shakespeare and the Greeks" situate both Keats and Wilde not only within "the marble circle" (p. 126, l. 11) of artistic immortality but also within a queer pantheon, made up of figures he will famously invoke during his trials in his defense of "the love that dare not speak its name."[17] In recasting his own poem about the failure to shake hands with the literary canon, touching Keats's hand and touching his text becomes a way of imagining Wilde's own literary and sexual immortality, even if it takes the form of a highly mediated, uncertain, and hoped-for future.[18]

---

15. In a final irony, however, there is no existing manuscript of this poem. See Bristow and Mitchell on the way in which this line represents Keats as "a fantasized erotic object" (138).

16. Even this phrase echoes Keats's "Ode to a Nightingale": "I have been half in love with easeful death." Thanks to Elsie Michie for this suggestion.

17. See Dowling. Najarian notes that Wilde associates Keats with St. Sebastian in "The Grave of Keats," where he "metaphorically associated Keats, the doomed poet, with the man attracted to his own sex" (19). See also Craft on the same-sex erotic charge of the hand (56).

18. When at the end of *De Profundis* Wilde instructs Douglas not to write anything "false or counterfeit" when he (finally) writes to him, Wilde compares himself to Keats once again, quoting from his sonnet "If by Dull Rhymes our English must be Chained": "It is not for nothing, or to no purpose, that in my lifelong cult of literature I have made myself 'Miser of sound and syllable, no less / Than Midas of his coinage'" (210).

Not only does *Dorian Gray* invoke a similarly queer "marble circle" in describing Basil's love for Dorian (a love "as Michelangelo had known, and Montaigne, and Winckelmann, and Shakespeare himself"), but it is also the text to which critics return again and again to think through the relationship between sexuality and embodiment, as well as between Wilde and the sexual landscape of the 1890s (Sedgwick; Craft; Cohen). A wonderful symptom of this association is the cover of Broadview's 1998 edition of *Dorian Gray* (see this cover at https://broadviewpress.com), which encourages us to read both Dorian's body and the text as a whole through the hand. Rather than depicting the portrait or a close-up of Dorian's painted face, the cover offers a detail of Michelangelo's David—his right hand to be specific. If we are to judge this book by its cover, the edition suggests that the novel is essentially about Dorian's hand not his face, and that the key to the novel's sexual secrets can be found in the hand. After all, not only is the historical David an important figure in the long history of same-sex desire, but so is Michelangelo. More important, what the cover quietly alludes to is that both David and Michelangelo appear in Wilde's famous courtroom defense: "a great affection of an elder for a younger man as there was between David and Jonathan . . . such as you find in the sonnets of Shakespeare and Michelangelo" (Hyde 201). Like Wilde's own reference to "Shakespeare and the Greeks" in his letter to Emma Speed, in its concise allusion, the cover suggests that to read Wilde's hand is to read the history of homosexuality from the Bible to the twentieth century.

Dorian Gray is also bound up thematically and historically with the problem of reading the body or the hand. Indeed, as Richard Kaye has pointed out, passages excised from the original *Lippincott's* manuscript show that it highlighted the erotic potential of Dorian's hand even more than the printed version.[19] The fantasy of illegibility that forms the premise of *Dorian Gray* is only

---

19. "Several critics have noted the ways in which Wilde toned down the homoerotic dimension when he revised the magazine version for the book edition. In fact, the impulse to render less explicit the erotic dynamic between Lord Henry, Basil, and Dorian informed Wilde's choices even before Dorian Gray appeared in magazine form. From the manuscripts located in the Morgan it is clear that Wilde while was composing the *Lippincott's* text he sought to render Basil's infatuation with Dorian less explicit. Thus in Chapter I of the Morgan manuscript, Wilde initially included a sentence in which Basil recounts a declaration of intimacy on Dorian's part as Basil paints a landscape. 'It is one of the best things I have ever done. And why is it so? Because, while I was painting it, Dorian sat beside me and as he leaned across to look at it, *his lips just touched my hand. The world becomes young to me when I hold his hand. . . .*' (emphasis added). In the printed *Lippincotts* edition, the lines after "beside me" are stricken, so that Dorian remains an object of beauty, not an emotionally expressive friend with whom Basil maintains a physically intimate relationship. In a sense, Dorian is increasingly aestheticized—as opposed to eroticized—over the course of Wilde's revisions, adding to a sense that Wilde's novel often aestheticizes the homoerotic" (personal communication).

made necessary by the assumption, fear, or even fantasy, that (in Basil's words) "sin" really *is* "a thing that writes itself across a man's face" (143). But in *Dorian Gray* (even in the 1891 edition of the novel), hands often appear in the context of bodily identification and its failure and help to complicate the relationship between the body and reading, legibility and sexuality, surface and secrecy. In Basil's speech about the legibility of sin, his specific example focuses on the hand in ways reminiscent of Harris's description of Wilde: "Somebody—I won't mention his name . . . came to me last year to have his portrait done . . . I refused him. There was something in the shape of his fingers that I hated. I know now that I was quite right in what I fancied about him" (143). While contemplating Dorian's hands after the murder of Basil, the narrator suggests that "those finely-shaped fingers could never have clutched a knife for sin" (167). The promise of *Dorian Gray* of course is that this escape from legibility is only temporary—that a wider public than the reader will have access to the picture's embodied secrets, sexual and otherwise. Yet the novel complicates the assumption that touching Dorian's (or Wilde's) hand will provide knowledge of any secrets. Even before the ending, when Basil gets a rare glimpse, what he sees in the painting is the trace of his own hand—his "handiwork," and his signature "in long letters of bright vermillion" (146, 149). And, as a range of critics like John Paul Riquelme, Christopher Lane, and others have noted, the ending remains "enigmatic" and Dorian's identity unrecognizable (Riquelme 627; Lane 943).[20] The final words of the novel refer to the rings on Dorian's fingers as the only identifying features: "It was not until they had examined the rings that they recognized who it was" (213). Illustrated editions of *Dorian Gray* often end with an image of a solitary, disembodied, and bejeweled hand, emphasizing not how much we finally learn from Dorian's hand, but how little. While the final scene of the novel returns Dorian's "real" body to him, that body is still illegible and unrecognizable—"withered, wrinkled, and loathsome of visage" (213). What isn't shown in these editions, but what remains, is the picture—an object of and for the archive, an image Basil tells

---

20. Riquelme reads the novel in terms of Pater's aesthetics, the Gothic, and fin-de-siècle painting. He argues that "In addition to this odd ultimate brushstroke in the novel's mythic surface, which resists explanation, other details of the ending remain enigmatic. We still do not know where we stand in relation to the darkness and the light. There is no vanishing point and no orienting perspective" (627). Lane argues that "Dorian's death cannot clarify who he really is because death marks the full meaning of his identification only by its disparity with what the narrative and public forced him to become. By retaining this secret to its end, the narrative represents the truth of Dorian Gray by default and misrecognition; this 'truth' issues precisely from his struggle to excoriate the meaning of his desire" (943). On the other hand, Cohen argues that "in the end, Dorian's corpse becomes the surface that records his narrative, liberating Dorian in death from the consciousness divided between experience and representation that had marked his life" (810).

us from the beginning cannot be displayed. While the painting and its closet act as a kind of archive—a site where past, present, and future meet—Dorian's living body is itself "a walking museum of strange curious and rare artifacts" (Frankel 28). In the end, the painting survives both in the world of the novel and in the form of the book itself, waiting to be read and reread in the future.

In a sense, the publication history of *Dorian Gray* reinforces both this association with hands and an orientation toward the future. The novel was originally published in an issue of Lippincott's that featured an article by Wilde's friend and expert on cheiromancy (or palm reading) Edward Heron-Allen.[21] Wilde asked Heron-Allen to read his son Cyril's palm soon after his birth (*Complete Letters* 177).[22] And after the publication of "Lord Arthur Saville's Crime"—Wilde's darkly humorous story in which the palm reader who sees murder on Lord Arthur's hand is himself killed at the end to fulfill the prophecy—Wilde wrote to him in October of 1887 suggesting that, if he published the story in the US he would have him "write a short preface on the cheiromancy of the story!" (*Complete Letters* 209). Though published together, it seems as if *Dorian Gray* and "The Cheiromancy *of Today*" could not be more different. Heron-Allen's work details exactly how to read the body's open secrets and its future, both of which it gives up at the touch of a hand. In a description that echoes Harris's account of shaking Wilde's "limp" hand with which I began, he notes "the instinctive observation of which renders every one, to a certain extent, a Cheiromant,—I allude to hand-shaking . . . Has not every one experienced the feeling . . . of repulsion and discomfort which comes over one when one is given what a recent essayist calls 'a hand like a cold haddock'" (Heron-Allen 19). If *Dorian Gray* is largely devoted to escaping such tactile legibility—if touching Dorian's hand is *not* to "know" him—we might better understand the novel as postponing indefinitely when and how the hand and body are read.

---

21. See Lorang, who notes that the conjunction of the essay and the novel "allows one to read the hands of the characters in the novel" (26). She also notes Heron-Allen's celebrity status in the US, established during a lecture tour in 1887.

22. Wilde wrote to Heron-Allen asking whether he would "cast the child's horoscope for us? . . . My wife is very anxious to know its fate, and has begged me to ask you to search the stars" (12 June 1885; *Complete Letters* 177). Despite Wilde's faith in palm reading, he mocks spiritualism in a review of Stuart Cumberland's *The Vasty Deep*. Wilde begins by suggesting that fiction allows us all to be clairvoyants, by "reading a novel backwards" (509): "some of us may think that there is very little use in exposing what is already exposed and revealing the secrets of Polinchinelle, no doubt there are many who will be interested to hear of the tricks and deceptions of crafty mediums, of their gauze masks, telescopic rods and invisible silk threads, and the marvelous raps they can produce simply by displacing the *peroneus longus* muscle!"; "A Thought-Reader's Novel," *Pall Mall Gazette*, 5 June 1889 (*Complete Works* vol. 7, pp. 224–26).

In a way, "Lord Arthur Saville's Crime" is the inverse of *Dorian Gray*. Instead of a fantasy of illegibility (or the displacement of legibility away from the body), bodies are entirely readable and secrets always open (at least to the right reader). "Could it be that written on his hand, in characters that he could not read himself, but that another could decipher, was some fearful secret of sin, some blood-red sign of crime?" (*Complete Short Stories* 10).[23] Lord Arthur, who is betrothed to a woman (appropriately) named "Sybil" (like *Dorian*'s Sybil Vane), has his palm read at a party by a cheiromantist named Mr. Podgers. Lord Arthur's future is so horrible and so spectacularly visible that Podgers becomes completely pale and refuses to tell what he has seen. With a little incentive (and money) Podgers reveals what he has seen, which is simply "murder." Sybil, however, is no *sibyl* and cannot read her future husband's future. For her sake, Lord Arthur decides to get the murder out of the way, but his efforts fail; his second cousin dies not of his poison bon-bon but rather of natural causes, and the exploding clock he sends to his uncle only gives off amusing little explosions. Instead, Lord Arthur solves his problem by murdering Mr. Podgers himself, when he comes upon him by chance on a bridge and throws him over. Reading the wrong palms, it appears, can be fatal.[24]

But the story also suggests that interpretation acts as a circular and self-fulfilling prophecy, finding only what it places there in the first place.[25] Despite this, the story doesn't seem to concern itself with whether the knowledge gained from the body is true, but rather what to *do* with such knowledge. While Carolyn Lesjak argues that Lord Arthur misreads the prophecy as a "duty" and fails to see that "its meaning is merely provisional, occasioned by the expectations of fortune telling," Lord Arthur's solution to his dilemma sug-

---

23. See Gagnier, *Idylls*, who argues that "unlike Dorian, who cannot just act but refers himself to a work of art as conscience, Savile simply commits the murder and marries the girl . . . That is, Savile is a practical man of action . . . The effete, aristocratic Dorian, on the other hand, permits Wotton to dominate him" (63).

24. Neil Bartlett links Wilde and Lord Arthur Saville through what he reads as "the idea of Fate, of Doom" that "haunts" Wilde's work: "Wilde's own fiction even seems sometimes to predict with fatalistic accuracy his own destiny; Lord Arthur Saville, in a short story written eight years before Wilde met Mrs. Robinson, becomes a criminal precisely because of his superstitious belief in the predictions of a palmist who he meets at a party" (8–9). In the play, we are not present on the night of Wilde's visit to Mrs. Robinson, but rather at a reenactment staged by both of them after their death, giving them the opportunity to tell the audience both what they said and what they wished they had said. In one of these asides, Mrs. Robinson makes it clear that her version of palm reading echoes the circularity of reading and writing in "Lord Arthur Saville's Crime." Reading Wilde's palm she admits that she "didn't know" that Queensberry's allegations were really true: "I didn't know, no one did. If I had known, if I had known whose hand I was holding—well, I am sure I would have read different things in it" (38).

25. Critics, however, have read Lord Arthur's embodied "secret" as (yet another) "encoded representation" of (Wilde's) homosexuality. See Gurfinkel.

gests a more complicated theory of how the body is written and read (190). In one sense, critics have responded to Lady Windemere's claim at the end of the story that Podgers "was a dreadful impostor" and associate her fluid faith with Wilde's flippant tone: "He was a dreadful impostor. Of course, I didn't mind that at all, and even when he wanted to borrow money I forgave him, but I could not stand his making love to me. He has really made me hate cheiromancy. I go in for telepathy now. It is much more amusing" (32). Yet, for Lord Arthur, it isn't nearly as obvious that Podgers is a fake, and he adamantly defends cheiromancy at the end of the story. Sybil warns Lady Windemere that "it is the only subject that Arthur does not like people to chaff about. I assure you he is quite serious over it" (32). Taking seriously Lord Arthur's "seriousness" about cheiromancy, however, we arrive at a different definition of authenticity and interpretation. After all, Podgers's reading ends up being accurate. But it can only be fulfilled with the death of the (palm) reader, who is also in a sense a writer who plots his own demise. Ultimately, the story ties the accuracy of reading to the reader–writer's afterlife.

I want to close with a glance at Wilde's own "living hand," his text written, if not from the grave, then "from the depths"—*De Profundis*—a text written for the future and destined for the archive. The manuscript was sealed in the British Museum for 60 years, and still today, one can only view the original document if one can prove that a published facsimile will not suffice.[26] Despite the fact that *De Profundis* is a heterogeneous document that crosses several genres, critics have most often read it as a letter—whether (as Ellmann suggests) a "love letter . . . one of the greatest, and the longest, ever written," as a letter without an "audience" (as Regenia Gagnier argues), or as a letter addressed to future ages (Ellmann 484; Gagnier, "Wilde" 27).[27] As a letter, *De Profundis* holds out the promise of all letters—a touch of the "real" self, along with a chain of hands that stretch across space and time: the hand of the writer touching the paper, the hand of the recipient who (like Wilde describ-

---

26. See Holland, "*De Profundis*: The Afterlife of a Manuscript." Ross deposited the manuscript after Douglas claimed it as his property in 1909. Ross had published excerpts in 1905 explicitly leaving out references to Douglas. In 1912 Arthur Ransome published excerpts not in Ross's 1905 edition and Douglas sued for libel. After the trial, the manuscript was returned to its archive. In order to prevent Douglas from publishing a copy of the manuscript in the US, Ross sent a copy to the US and printed 16 copies for purposes of copyright. Fifteen of the books were sent back to England, while the sixteenth was put on sale for $500 in a showroom in New York and bought by someone who still remains anonymous. According to the British Library, the MS (Add MS 50141 A) is a "Highly Restricted manuscript" and readers can only gain access to it under special circumstances and with the permission of the relevant curator (personal communication, 29 Oct. 2019).

27. Gagnier is one of the few who calls *De Profundis* "perhaps Wilde's greatest work of art" ("Wilde" 27).

ing Keats's manuscript) treasures the trace of that hand, and finally, the many hands of unauthorized (or authorized) readers.

Wilde's main focus, however, is on his posthumous reception. Certainly, he imagines the possibility of a *living* legacy, famously asserting that "I was a man who stood in symbolic relations to the art and culture of my age . . . Few men hold such a position in their own lifetime, and have it so acknowledged . . . With me it was different" (151). Yet early on he admits the challenge of controlling that legacy: as he notes, Queensberry's "version" of his life "has now actually passed into serious history" (139). Describing the document to his friend and literary executor Robert Ross, he argues that "Some day the truth will have to be known: not necessarily in my lifetime or in Douglas's: but I am not prepared to sit in the grotesque pillory they put me into, for all time."[28] He both hopes to reclaim his legacy after death and knows how little control he will have over what kind of "symbol" he will become. And it is precisely this process of *becoming* that *De Profundis* both anticipates and continually postpones. As a letter to and for the future, Wilde's hand and handwriting doesn't give us access to the "truth" of his desires, identity, or body, let alone certain years of his life. It doesn't even tell us who Wilde hopes we will think he was, but rather what he will become and continue to become in the "posthumous life of writing." Made and remade in the strange temporal space of the archive,[29] Wilde's hand embodies what Michel Foucault defines as the essence of the archive. It is not just a static past embodied in texts ("the sum of all the texts that a culture has kept upon its person as documents attesting to its own past"), nor simply "the institutions, which, in a given society, make it possible to record and preserve those discourses that one wishes to remember and keep in circulation. On the contrary . . . *it is the general system of the formation and the transformation of statements*" (128–30 [emphasis in original]). But Wilde's own still-living hand also captures what David Halperin describes as "the possibility of a *queer* politics"—one "defined not by the struggle to liberate a common, repressed, preexisting nature but by an ongoing process of self-constitution and self-transformation" (122). Or, as Wilde puts it in *De Profundis,* "what lies before me is my past" (161).

---

28. Letter to Robert Ross, April 1, 1897 (*Complete Letters* 780).
29. On "the archive's multiple temporalities" temporalities, see Ward and Wisnicki. Focusing particularly on the Imperial archive, Ward argues that recent work in and on archives has understood the work of the archive not only as engaging with or reacting to the past, but as spaces to "imagine new futures" and as "sites of futurity" (202).

WORKS CITED

Bartlett, Neil. *In Extremis: A Love Letter*. London, Oberon Books, 2000.

Bennett, Andrew. *Keats, Narrative and Audience: The Posthumous Life of Writing*. Cambridge UP, 1994.

Briefel, Aviva. *The Racial Hand in the Victorian Imagination*. Cambridge UP, 2015.

Bristow, Joseph. "Memorializing Wilde: An Explosive History." *Journal of Victorian Culture*, vol. 5, no. 2, 2000, pp. 311–22.

———, and Rebecca N. Mitchell. *Oscar Wilde's Chatterton: Literary History, Romanticism, and the Art of Forgery*. Yale UP, 2016.

Capuano, Peter J. *Changing Hands: Industry, Evolution, and the Reconfiguration of the Victorian Body*. U of Michigan P, 2015.

Cohen, Ed. "Writing Gone Wilde: Homoerotic Desire in the Closet of Representation." *PMLA*, vol. 102, no. 5, pp. 801–13.

Cohn, Elisha. "Oscar Wilde's Ghost: The Play of Imitation." *Victorian Studies*, vol. 54, no. 3, 2012, pp. 474–85.

Craft, Christopher. *Another Kind of Love: Male Homosocial Desire in English Discourse 1850–1920*. U of California P, 1994.

Dowling, Linda. *Hellenism and Homosexuality in Victorian Oxford*. Cornell UP, 1994.

Ellmann, Richard. *Oscar Wilde*. Penguin, 1987.

Felski, Rita. "Context Stinks." *New Literary History*, vol. 42, 2011, pp. 573–91.

Fleissner, Jennifer. "Is Feminism a Historicism?" *Tulsa Studies in Women's Literature*, vol. 21, no. 1, 2002, pp. 45–66.

Foucault, Michel. *The Archeology of Knowledge*. Translated by A. M. Sheridan Smith, Pantheon Books, 1972.

Frankel, Nicholas. *Masking the Text: Essays on Literature and Mediation in the 1890s*. High Wycombe, Rivendale P, 2009.

Freshwater, Helen. "The Allure of the Archive." *Poetics Today*, vol. 24, no. 4, 2003, pp. 729–58.

Gagnier, Regenia. *Idylls of the Marketplace: Oscar Wilde and the Victorian Public*. Stanford UP, 1986.

———. "Wilde and the Victorians." *The Cambridge Companion to Oscar Wilde*, edited by Peter Raby, Cambridge UP, 1997, pp. 18–33.

Goldberg, Jonathan. *Shakespeare's Hand*. U of Minnesota P, 2003.

Gomel, Elana. "Oscar Wilde, *The Picture of Dorian Gray*, and the (Un)Death of the Author." *Narrative*, vol. 12, no. 1, 2004, pp. 74–92.

Gurfinkel, Helena. "'Each Man Kills the Thing He Loves.'" *Oscar Wilde: The Man, His Writing, and His World*, edited by Robert N. Keane, AMS P, 2003, pp. 168–71.

Halperin, David. *Saint Foucault: Towards a Gay Hagiography*. Oxford UP, 1995.

Harris, Frank. *Contemporary Portraits*. Methuen, 1915.

———. *Oscar Wilde*. New York, Caroll & Graf, 1992.

Harris, Jonathan Gil. *Untimely Matter in the Time of Shakespeare*. U of Pennsylvania P, 2009.

Heron-Allen, Edward. *A Manual of Cheirosophy: Being a Complete Practical Handbook of the Twin Sciences of Cheirognomy and Cheiromancy by Means Whereof the Past, the Present, and the Future May Be Read in the Formations of the Hands.* London, Ward, Lock, 1885.

Holland, Merlin. "Biography and the Art of Lying." *Cambridge Companion to Oscar Wilde*, edited by Peter Raby, Cambridge UP, 1997, pp. 3–17.

———. "*De Profundis*: The Afterlife of a Manuscript." *Oscar Wilde: The Man, His Writings, and His World*, edited by Robert N. Keane, AMS P, 2003, pp. 251–67.

Hopkins, Brooke. "Keats and the Uncanny: 'This Living Hand.'" *Kenyon Review*, vol. 11, no. 4, Fall 1989, pp. 28–40.

Hyde, H. Montgomery. *The Trials of Oscar Wilde.* Dover, 1962.

Knapp, James A. and Jeffrey Pence. "Between Thing and Theory." *Poetics Today*, vol. 24, no. 4, 2003, pp. 642–43.

Lane, Christopher. "Framing Fears, Reading Designs: The Homosexual Art of Painting in James, Wilde, and Beerbohm." *ELH*, vol. 61, no. 4, 1994, pp. 923–54.

Latour, Bruno. *We Have Never Been Modern.* Harvard UP, 1993.

Law, Jules. "Being There: Gothic Violence and Virtuality in Frankenstein, Dracula, and Strange Days." *ELH*, vol. 73, no. 4, 2006, pp. 975–96.

Lesjak, Carolyn. "Utopia, Use, and the Everday: Oscar Wilde and a New Economy of Pleasure." *ELH*, vol. 67, no. 1, 2000, pp. 179–204.

Lorang, Elizabeth. "Dorian Gray in Context." *Victorian Periodicals Review*, vol. 43, no. 1, Spring 2010, pp. 19–41.

McCormack, Jerusha. *The Man Who Was Dorian Gray.* St. Martin's Press, 2000.

———. "Wilde's Fiction(s)." *Cambridge Companion to Oscar Wilde*, edited by Peter Raby, Cambridge UP, 1997, pp. 96–117.

McKenna, Neil. *The Secret Life of Oscar Wilde.* Basic Books, 2003.

Najarian, James. *Victorian Keats: Manliness, Sexuality, and Desire.* Palgrave, 2002.

Page, Norman. *Oscar Wilde Chronology.* G. K. Hall, 1991.

Pearce, Joseph. *The Unmaksing of Oscar Wilde.* London, Harper Collins, 2000.

Price, Leah. *How to Do Things with Books in Victorian Britain.* Princeton UP, 2012.

———. *What We Talk About When We Talk About Books: The History and Future of Reading.* Basic Books, 2019.

Riquelme, John Paul. "Oscar Wilde's Aesthetic Gothic: Walter Pater, Dark Enlightenment, and The Picture of Dorian Gray." *Modern Fiction Studies*, vol. 46, no. 3, Fall 2000, pp. 609–31.

Robinson, Mrs. A. *The Graven Palm.* London, Edward Arnold, 1911.

Sedgwick, Eve Kosofsky. *Epistemology of the Closet.* U of California P, 1990.

Smigiel, Frank. "Wilde's Monstrosity." *Oscar Wilde: The Man, His Writing, and His World*, edited by Robert N. Keane, AMS P, 2003, pp. 203–13.

Ward, Megan. *Seeming Human: Artificial Intelligence and Victorian Realist Character.* The Ohio State UP, 2018.

———, and Adam Wisnicki. "The Archive After Theory." *Debates in the Digital Humanities*, edited by Matthew K. Gold and Lauren F. Klein, U of Minnesota P, 2019, pp. 200–204.

Wilde, Oscar. *The Complete Letters of Oscar Wilde*. Edited by Merlin Holland and Rupert Hart-Davis, Henry Holt, 2000.

———. *The Complete Short Stories*. Edited by John Sloan, Oxford UP, 2010.

———. *Complete Works of Oscar Wilde*, vol. 1, "Poems and Poems in Prose." Edited by Bobby Fong and Karl Beckson, Oxford UP, 2000.

———. *Complete Works of Oscar Wilde*, vol. 6, "Journalism Part I." Edited by John Stokes and Mark W. Turner, Oxford UP, 2013.

———. *Complete Works of Oscar Wilde*, vol. 7, "Journalism Part II." Edited by John Stokes and Mark W. Turner, Oxford UP, 2013.

———. *Complete Works of Oscar Wilde*, vol. 8, "The Short Fiction." Edited by Ian Small, Oxford UP, 2017.

———. *The Importance of Being Earnest and Other Plays*. Edited by Peter Raby, Oxford UP, 1995.

———. *The Picture of Dorian Gray*. Penguin Books, 2000.

CHAPTER 13

Hands in Hardy and James

J. HILLIS MILLER

MY PRIMARY professional commitment is to literary study. I have long been fascinated by the crucial references to hands in literary works, as well as in "real life." A good example of the former is the description of Dorothea Brooke's hands at the opening of George Eliot's *Middlemarch*: "They were not thin hands, or small hands; but powerful, feminine, maternal hands." That sentence gives the reader, at the start of the novel, a strong sense of just what Dorothea was like. In contemporary "real life," scornful references to Donald Trump's small hands are used to admirable effect by his denigrators to indicate what a small and weak personality he is, how unfit to be President of the United States. How can he "make America great again" if he has tiny hands?

This present essay, however, is about the role of hands in work by Thomas Hardy and, more briefly, in Henry James's fiction. My context is the general cultural role of hands in literature in English as I discuss it and as it makes up an important part of Peter J. Capuano's magisterial and comprehensive *Changing Hands: Industry, Evolution, and the Reconfiguration of the Victorian Body*.[1]

---

1. I make use in this present essay of a lecture on "Hands in Hardy" given some years ago at Yale. A different version of that essay was published as "Hands in Hardy" in *The Ashgate Research Companion to Thomas Hardy* (2010), edited by Rosemarie Morgan. I also use in this present essay a revised form of a brief discussion of hands in Henry James's *The Wings of the Dove* that was published by *Critical Inquiry* as "What Do Stories About Pictures Want?" I am grateful for permission to reuse this material in revised form.

Let me add, however, a demurrer. Just since I wrote the essays referred to in footnote one, the human situation in the United States and globally has changed markedly. Our situation has altered enough toward imminent danger to make me wonder whether I can in conscience devote time to writing an essay on something so relatively marginal as "Hands in Hardy and James."

Four features of that present-day context are salient.

I. Global warming is accelerating, with and ineffective attempts to stop it. Climate change has already led to widespread disasters, such as recent fires all over California, Oregon, and Washington, as well as elsewhere around the world; sub-zero temperatures mixed with unusually warm weather in New England brought about by the melting of Arctic Ice; more frequent and more devastating hurricanes (like the one recently that so damaged Puerto Rico or the one that glanced by Hawaii in August 2018; the one coming ashore in the Carolinas as I revise this essay on September 14, 2018); glaciers melting worldwide, and so on. A truly terrifying essay presenting the latest information about global climate change was published in the April 2018 issue of *Scientific American*: Jennifer A. Francis, "The Arctic is Breaking Climate Records, Altering Weather Worldwide." A refrain of this essay, as of many others by scientists these days about climate change, is, "Oh, this is happening faster than we thought it would." Scientists have tended to underestimate the feedback effect. Arctic ice melts. The melt water absorbs heat rather than reflecting it as ice does, and so the warming process occurs even faster. We are, many scientists think, on the way, probably irreversibly, to widespread extinction of plant life and animal life, both on land and in the sea. This extinction may quite likely include, some scientists anticipate, the human species, good old *homo sapiens*, that sapient and self-destructive creature. No more literature then, and no more hands with which to write literary works.

II. A major transformation of the dominant media from print to digital is happening globally with amazing rapidity. Though many people worldwide will go on reading printed literature for a long time, huge numbers of people now primarily use digital programs and gadgets rather than reading print literature. They live with smartphones in their hands and with eyes "glued" to their screens, as if these devices were part of their bodies, prostheses. Mostly such people are not even reading print literature in its rapidly proliferating e-text form. They are playing video games, or "texting," or using Facebook, or tweeting, or watching an online film. Print literature is being greatly marginalized as a result.

When I have lectured in China about this or that work of Western literature, Henry James's *The Portrait of a Lady*, for example, people in my audience inevitably want my judgment of the film made from the book. Never mind the printed book. It is the film that matters to them. Print literature counts less and less in many people's lives, even in the lives of those who come to hear me lecture about print literature. This casts much doubt on my claim in my book with Ranjan Ghosh, *Thinking Literature Across Continents* (2016), that you can learn from print literature how to spot lies in the media, for example, in Trump's tweets. Recommending that procedure is of no use if so few of our citizens read such works as *Othello* or *Middlemarch* any longer. We need to use new forms of what I call "rhetorical reading" to understand what is going on in specific examples of those new media, for example, Jane Campion's film of *The Portrait of a Lady* or the rhetoric of video games. We need look at the new digital media, including Trump's tweets, through literary-critical eyes, as kinds of transmuted "writing."

III. A marked shift has recently occurred back from global thinking to nationalist thinking. Partly this is a result of fear and anxiety brought about by thinking globally, for example, the renewed fear these days of civilization-destroying nuclear war. Trump keeps threatening that. Better not to think globally, such people may think. We need to worry primarily about our own country's survival. Part of Donald Trump's spurious appeal has been his grandiose promise to "Make America Great Again," though his actions have instead made America weaker, less and less a true democracy. The Trump administration is almost as great a danger to the United States and to civilization worldwide as is climate change. Scott Pruitt, once Trump's head of the Environmental Protection Agency, turned it as much as he could, into the Environmental Destruction Agency. Trump's Secretary of Education, Betsy DeVos, is bent on replacing American public education with unregulated for-profit private schools. She wants, moreover, to use Federal money to arm schoolteachers and make schools into battlegrounds. Her original proposed reason for this was the truly surrealist idea that schoolteachers need guns to protect themselves and their students from grizzly bears! It is a great embarrassment, and more than an embarrassment, to live in a country that was once a great democracy, and is now ruled by liars, frauds, and downright criminals, such as, a while ago, Paul Manafort, Michael Cohen, and still in 2019 Trump himself. The United States is rapidly becoming just another banana republic.

One major factor that has made this possible, in my view, is the rise of the new media's power to erase the distinction between truth and lie. Many people apparently think that if it is on Fox News or in Facebook it must be true news not fake news.

IV. In the years since my earlier work on hands in literature and culture was written, much change has occurred and is occurring in colleges and universities, at least in the United States. These changes have tended to weaken and marginalize the study and teaching of literature and literary theory in our schools, colleges, and universities. Partly these changes have been a result of the shift from print to digital. What is the point of having big departments of English and of foreign languages if students no longer show up to take the courses they offer? Partly these changes have been the result of a lack of interest in the humanities generally, as well as a downright fear of them by our conservative politicians, voters, and right-wing media. A Pew Research Center national poll conducted in the United States on June 8–18, 2017 discovered that more and more Republicans think colleges and universities have a negative effect on the country. The number was by that time an astonishing 58%, up from 45% a year earlier. Republicans and the media that support them do not like it, I suppose, that colleges and universities are teaching climate change and evolution, as well as scientific method and critical thinking generally, with their rigorous standards of proof.

Republicans also have a well-founded suspicion that the teaching of critical thinking as part of higher education might lead people to understand and then put in question the manipulation of the new media to promulgate lies. Trump's tweets are an example. Such lies include climate change denial and the false assertion that the recently new United States tax law is good for the middle and working classes. That law in fact transfers over a trillion dollars in the United States to make the very rich richer. Such transfer is already being used to justify denying benefits like Social Security and Medicare to the rest of us. No money left to pay for it, they are already saying, nor money for more or less free mass higher education that is available in countries like Norway for those who qualify for it by scholastic accomplishment.

All these amazingly rapid cultural and technological changes will not keep me from fulfilling my promise to write an essay on hands in Hardy and James. I want, however, to begin by stressing that the contexts for doing that have changed markedly in the last few years. Nevertheless, as Peter J. Capuano has forcefully argued in his *Changing Hands,* hands still continue to matter both inside and outside of literature. The rest of this essay explores just one small area in this immense display of hands in literature and life: the function of hands in Thomas Hardy's and Henry James's work. This will be done in the context of an account of the many and complicated idiomatic uses of the words "hand" or "hands" in everyday English and American speech. These tend to stress the way the use of hands tends to be intentional, a matter of will or agency, as in "I took her by the hand." I hope my readers will take for granted that I by no means myself use all these idioms and strongly detest the sexist ones.

HANDS IN HARDY

Why do I use the motif of hands as a way of getting a handle on Hardy? For one thing, representations of gesture speech and other references to hands are frequent in Hardy's work.

Second, I am mindful of Jacques Derrida's persuasive demonstration, in *Le toucher, Jean-Luc Nancy*, that human hands, in their ability to touch and manipulate inanimate objects, the body of another living thing or person, and themselves (as when my right hand touches my left hand), are, in the Western philosophical tradition from Aristotle through Maine de Biran to Husserl, Heidegger, and Merleau-Ponty, in one way or another taken as an essential feature of human beings, *homo sapiens*. Having and using hands, this powerful tradition claims, distinguishes human beings from the other animals. Derrida coins the word *humainisme*, "humanualism," to name this tradition. (*Main* means "hand" in French.)

Third, so many ordinary idioms in English use "hand" in literal or figurative fashion that, so I hypothesize, what is most distinctive, singular, about a given writer may be identified by way of his or her manipulation of hand idioms. Saying this presupposes that the singular, the special, is what matters most in a given writer, just as Hardy, in "The Dorsetshire Laborer," argues that it is a mistake to think of all rural laborers as fitting one stereotyped "Hodge." Each farm worker, says Hardy, is "somehow not typical of anyone but himself."[2] Thomas Hardy too is somehow not typical of anyone but himself. That includes his use of hands in his work.

A fourth and final reason for my hand-reading is a somewhat contrarian desire to approach Hardy widdershins, rubbing his writings against the grain of the text, so to speak. A novel by Hardy like *The Mayor of Casterbridge* is so visibly visual in orientation, so cinematic, that many passages almost read like an elaborate scenario for a film. *The Mayor* is presented from the perspective of a somewhat detached spectator who sees what anyone who was there might have seen, often as a kind of spy, voyeur, or invisible looker-on seeing from the outside in or from the inside out. Hardy's work depends so much on seeing that to approach his fiction and his poems by way of their references to that premier organ of touch, the hand, seems perverse. My hypothesis, nevertheless, might be phrased as a particular form of speech act, a wager: "I bet an investigation of how Hardy uses the word 'hand' will bring into the open what is most distinctive about his writing." Whether I win or lose this bet remains to be seen.

---

2. See 168–71 for the context of this claim.

Here is a more or less random collection of everyday idiomatic expressions in English using "hand."[3] I myself by no means use all of them, either in speech or in writing, and I deplore the many sexist ones. I have added three examples from Heidegger's German for good measure. The *American Heritage Dictionary* gives a whole small-type column of various definitions and usages of the word "hand," for example, "hand and glove," "hand over fist," and "hands down." That entry is followed by no less than fifty-five compound words using "hand," such as "handcraft," or "handmade," or "handyman." Clearly the semantic sleight-of-hand of the word "hand" is impressively intricate. We could hardly speak for long without using one or more of these words. People say, "Let's shake hands on it," when patching up a quarrel, or "I give you my hand on it," when making a promise or sealing a contract. The French say, according to Jean-Luc Nancy, "*'Touchez là!' pour conclure un accord ou pour terminer un différend.*"[4] That is the way grain sales are concluded by Henchard, in Hardy's *The Mayor of Casterbridge*, before Farfrae comes along and changes that to the indirection, the prosthetic technicity, of a paper contract.

People say I am "touched to the heart" by something or other, but heart and hand are connected by the idea that the third finger of the left hand is "heart in hand."

People say I "put my hand on my heart" when swearing allegiance or when making a solemn promise. I may also solemnize an oath or sanctify it by swearing with my hand on the Bible, for example, when in the witness box I promise to tell the truth, the whole truth, and nothing but the truth, so help me God. A member of the United States House of Representatives, Keith Ellison, the first Muslim in that august body, gave offense by suggesting that he might take the oath of office with his hand on the *Qur'an* rather than on the Bible.

"Give that fellow a hand" is an invitation to a round of applause by clapping hands. It is extremely odd, when you think of it, to say I can *give* my hand. Surely that is a gift that is taken back in the moment of giving, except, perhaps, when you say, "I'd give my right hand for it," though I never heard of anyone who actually did that.

A famous Zen koan says: "This is the sound of two hands clapping." Clap! "What is the sound of one hand clapping?" Dickens's Pip, in *Great Expectations*, was "brought up by the hand." When I need help, I say, "Please give me

---

3. The list is borrowed from another, related, essay, "Touching Derrida Touching Nancy," a chapter in my *For Derrida* (2009).

4. Nancy 55.

a hand." We play a hand of cards, or deal someone a hand. We say, "Fate has dealt me a losing (or winning, usually losing) hand." The heroine in melodramas says to the hissing villain, "Unhand me, sir!" I ask: "How can I get a handle on Hardy's use of hands?" People say: "Don't you lay a hand on me," or, "He didn't lay a hand on me." "I'll see if I can lay my hands on it," is a promise to look for something you have misplaced. Spiritual power passes from person to person by a "laying on of hands," as in the biblical story of Isaac's blind blessing of Jacob rather than Esau, the younger son in place of the elder. The thief or policeman says, "Hands up!" A "handmade" object of manufacture, a piece of handwork, for example, handmade lace, is often assumed to be better than a machine-made one. People say, "Please hand me the salt." The "Get Ready Man," in James Thurber's story, walks around with a sandwich-board that says, "Get ready! The end of the world is at hand."

Martin Heidegger, notoriously, makes use of some German idioms using *Hand* in *Sein und Zeit*. He speaks of the way something is *zur Hand*, "to hand," and he makes a crucial distinction between material objects that just happen to be there, *vorhanden*, present-at-hand, and other things, such as tools, that are for man's use, prepared by man for manipulation by human hands. These are *zuhanden*, "ready-to-hand."

A wonderfully specific passage near the beginning of Hardy's *The Mayor of Casterbridge* gives a list of such ready-to-hand farm implements as they were offered for sale in Casterbridge shop windows:

> Scythes, reap-hooks, sheep-shears, bill-hooks, spades, mattocks, and hoes at the iron-monger's; bee-hives, butter-firkins, churns, milking stools and pails, hay-rakes, field-flagons, and seed-lips at the cooper's; cart-ropes and plough-harness at the saddler's; carts, wheel-barrows, and mill-gear at the wheelwright's and machinist's; horse-embrocations at the chemist's; at the glover's and leather-cutter's, hedging-gloves, thatchers' knee-caps, ploughmens' leggings, villagers' pattens and clogs. (32)[5]

The hyphens here indicate the inherence of these man-made objects in the use for which they were intended, while the apostrophes indicate the way these shopkeepers make by hand what they sell, in that inversion of making and made that distinguishes even the most primitive manufacture. One must make a tool to make a tool, use one stone to chip away another stone to make it a spear-head or a flint scraping tool. A "hay-rake" is for raking hay, while

---

5. This edition is the American version of the Wessex Edition.

"the saddler's" is a shop where cart-ropes and plough-harnesses are made by means of other hand-tools, and then sold.

To continue my list of hand idioms. A woman "gives her hand in marriage," as in Thomas Hardy's *The Hand of Ethelberta*. We say that someone who is good at fixing things is "handy." A servant of all trades is a "handyman." We "manhandle" something into place. Of an errant child who was corrected, we say, "His parents took him in hand." A used article, often clothing, that you receive from an older sibling, or from your parents or grandparents, or from some older relative, is called a "hand-me-down." Often a hand-me-down is a relic of the dead. "The back of my hand to you" is an insult, like thumbing one's nose, which, as Joyce puts it, means "KMRIA," or "Kiss my royal Irish arse." I have elsewhere discussed kisses, though not of the "arse."[6]

"Hand" in the sense of idiosyncratic handwriting style is one item in this tangled, interlaced multitude, which includes manipulation of things with the hands, hand gestures, or hand signs—pointing, waving, clapping, "thumbs up" (or down), and so on—as well as hands touching, as in the touching last lines of *Paradise Lost* describing Adam and Eve after the fall. They have been exiled from Paradise into the thorny wilderness of Eden. Nevertheless they walk hand in hand, as earthly fallen lovers still do, hand touching hand in a way that is almost a self-touching. Derrida, in *Le toucher,* comments at length on Nancy's linguistic "invention," *se toucher toi,* touching myself touching you. That is what Milton's Adam and Eve do. The tangle of idioms is not quite the same in French. We do not say, as the French do, "*maintenant,*" literally "holding in the hand," for "now," but we do say "maneuver," "manage," "manufacture," "maintain," and "maintenance," all words that contain the Romance word for "hand," whereas "hand" itself is Germanic in origin.

It will surprise no one to be told that the word "hand" and combined forms of it appear often in Hardy's work. I count nine times in the 4486 words of the first chapter of *The Mayor of Casterbridge*: "the hand that was passed through the basket strap"; "she became pretty, even handsome"; "hands of Time and Chance"; "little business remained on hand"; "a wave of the hand"; "a good experienced hand in my line"; "Seizing the sailor's arm with her right hand"; "with her hands on her hips"; "that remained on hand." Perhaps that is no more than a statistical average. As I have indicated, it is hard for an English-speaker to talk for long without using the word.

---

6. See Miller, *Literature as Conduct,* 30–83.

The first chapter of Henry James's *The Wings of the Dove,* for example, contains thirteen "hands," out of 6340 words, but several of them are in the word "handsome," and all but three of the rest are metaphorical idioms like "take in hand": "She was handsome"; "take in hand"; "placing a hand on his arm"; "the humble hand that assuaged him"; "it gave him pleasure that she was handsome"; "Poor Marion might be handsome"; "Standing before her with his hands behind him"; "slipping his hands into his pockets"; "she'll 'do' for you handsomely"; "wholly in your aunt's hands"; "her handsome quiet face"; "I'll wash my hands of you"; "take you in hand." Not surprisingly, James's prose is more abstract or figurative, as in "wholly in your aunt's hands," whereas four of Hardy's "hands" are literal ones, in 30% fewer words. James tells the reader primarily about the feckless Mr. Croy's hands, while Hardy names Henchard's hands, Susan's hands, and the furmity woman's hands. He tends to take note of his characters' hands.

It would be a long path to follow the adventures of the word "hand" through all Hardy's work. An example is *The Hand of Ethelberta,* in which the "hand" in the title names not just the hand that Ethelberta gives in marriage, but the power she displays to manipulate the people around her. This handpower is the true subject of this early comic novel by Hardy. One more example is the ironic scene at the end of *Tess of the d'Urbervilles* in which Tess's sister 'Liza-Lu and Tess's erstwhile beloved, Angel Clare, walk sadly away hand in hand before and after seeing, from a mile away, in another cinematic notation, the black flag raised that indicates Tess has been hanged: "'Justice' [has been] done, and the President of the Immortals, in Aeschylean phrase, [has] ended his sport with Tess."[7] Before seeing the flag, the narrator says, "They moved on hand in hand, and never spoke a word, the drooping of their heads being that of Giotto's 'Two Apostles'" (TD 448). Then, after seeing the black flag, "The two speechless gazers bent themselves down to the earth, as if in prayer, and remained thus a long time, absolutely motionless: the flag continued to wave silently. As soon as they had strength they arose, joined hands again, and went on" (TD 449). The irony is that 'Liza-Lu and Angel bend down to the earth only "*as if* in prayer" (my italics). The ending unmistakably hints that, grief-stricken as they are, they walk away to a happy married life together. Another irony in *Tess* lies in the reference to Giotto's (really Spinello Aretino's) fresco fragment of what used to be called "Two Apostles." Hardy would have seen this painting in the National Gallery, for which it was bought in 1856. To compare Tess to a heroine of Greek tragedy is hardly compatible

---

7. Thomas Hardy, *Tess of the d'Urbervilles,* 449, henceforth TD, followed by the page number.

FIGURE 13.1. Two Haloed Mourners (1587–95), by Spinello Aretino. National Gallery, London. Used by permission from Art Resource, New York.

with comparing her to the crucified Christ being mourned by two haloed apostles with their heads bowed in mourning. Though both analogies are at least ironically implied, they to some degree cancel one another out.

Hardy can hardly be blamed for thinking the fresco is by Giotto, since that was the original ascription, nor for not knowing that the fresco fragment is now called "Two Haloed Mourners," taken from a larger fresco of the "Burial of Saint John the Baptist" formerly in the chapel of Vanni Manetti in the Carmine, Florence. The spectator can hardly help admiring the rakish angle at which the mourners wear their haloes. That the mourned person is John the Baptist, not Christ, is a further irony, and that the mourners are not "apostles" is yet another irony that somehow, like the other ironies, reinforces the incongruity of the comparison of Tess to central figures in the Greek and

Christian traditions. The whole scene is a kind of masquerade or playacting. Finally, Hardy's two mourners are walking hand in hand, while the two hands in the fresco are those of the left-hand mourner who is clasping his hands together in prayer or in grief. Of the two forms of *se toucher toi,* touching you and touching myself as other, Hardy names my hand touching the hand of the other, and being touched in return, while Spinello shows my left hand touching my right hand and being touched in return, narcissistically, by my own hand. Did Hardy misremember or did he mis-see the painting and take that left hand as the right hand of the nearest mourner? It is impossible to know, but one can see why Hardy was moved by it, and referred to it.

I turn now to a brief discussion of hands in Hardy's poetry. As one might expect, Hardy's poems are continuous in theme and stylistic texture with his fiction, including his use of the word "hand," but differences exist. The poems, like the novels, focus on "satires of circumstance," as the title of one book of Hardy's poems puts it: crossed fidelities, missed appointments, ironic incongruities of intention and knowledge. An example is "The Workbox," in which the newly married young "joiner" makes his wife a loving gift, a workbox fashioned out of the same piece of wood of which he had made the coffin for a man who, though the bridegroom did not know it, had been the person his new wife really loved and who had died of love for her.[8]

The word "hand" functions in the poems, as in the novels, to express these connections without connection, as, for example, in an early poem in *Wessex Poems,* dated 1866, "Her Dilemma." In this poem a young woman lies to her dying suitor, "so wan and worn that he could scarcely stand," when, "holding long her hand," "he softly said," "Tell me you love me!" (CP 13). She does not love him at all, but cannot bring herself to hasten his death by telling him the truth, perhaps partly because of the intimacy that hand-holding indicates. It is not easy to hasten the death of someone who is "holding long my hand."

I am more interested, however, in a thematic strand using hands that is threaded through Hardy's poems, especially the latest ones. I am thinking of the many ghost poems and of the ghostly hands in many of them. I have space here to discuss only one of these.

---

8. Thomas Hardy, *Complete Poems,* 397–8, henceforth CP, followed by page numbers. Years and years ago, I heard Dylan Thomas read this poem, along with other poems by Hardy. That powerful reading has remained in my mind, along with what Thomas said about Hardy's poems in general: "I like the bus that Hardy misses more than the bus other poets catch."

The ghost hands in Hardy's poems are usually detached from any body, even a ghostly one. They are presented just as hovering disembodied ghostly hands. Even if you could touch them you would not be put in touch with the whole body of the dead person. The effect of the phantom hands in these wonderful poems is moving, powerful, and strange. One such poem is "Old Furniture," from *Moments of Vision and Miscellaneous Verses* (1917). In this poem the speaker says:

> I see the hands of the generations
>   That owned each shiny familiar thing
> In play on its knobs and indentations,
>   And with its ancient fashioning
>   Still dallying:
>
> Hands behind hands, growing paler and paler,
>   As in a mirror a candle-flame
> Shows images of itself, each frailer
>   As it recedes, though the eye may frame
>   Its shape the same. (CP 485–86)

The reader will see the strange and uncanny effect of presenting the hands alone, hovering in spectral affection over each knob and indentation of the old furniture. How can they seem so alive, when they are dead hands, spectral hands, and hands, moreover, detached from their bodies? The effect of these lines is uncanny in the technical Freudian sense of the return of something familiar, something seen before that nevertheless ought not still to be there. The "hands behind hands" are not synecdoches for the whole bodies and persons of those who handled the old furniture, or if they may be called synecdoches they are of an exceedingly peculiar species of that figure. The effect of Hardy's locution is, rather, to suggest that even when the people who "owned" these hands, as parts of their bodies proper, were alive, it was the hands rather than the whole volitional embodied person which were at play on the furniture's knobs and indentations. It was the fingers that of their own accord were and are "dancing" "on this old viol." It was a "foggy finger" that of its own accord set the clock (CP 486).

Here, as in all such poems by Hardy, the material object or the material place survives. Those survivors occasion the spectral return of those who touched the objects or who were once present at the place they now haunt. For Hardy, as for Yeats, though in a specifically Hardyesque way, that is, without the apparatus of Yeatsian theory, what has once happened never ceases to go on happening. This occurs as long as the place and some material substance, such as the old furniture in this poem, still remain. They remain there for those who have eyes to see these twice-spectral specters, impalpable hands without even apparitional bodies.

I claim to have won my bet. I have shown that trying to get in touch with the motif of hands is a good way to get a handle on what is going on in Hardy. I also claim to have shown that though Hardy's fiction and his poetry are differently figured regions of the same whole cloth, nevertheless the uses to which hands are put are significantly different in each case. Even so, the poems, in presenting examples of disincarnated hands, hands floating in the air, so to speak, hands that are untouchable and that cannot touch, bring into the open the more figurative failure to touch or to be touched that is at the center of such a novel as *The Mayor of Casterbridge*.

HANDS IN HENRY JAMES

In one of the greatest scenes in Henry James's *The Wings of the Dove*, Milly Theale, the dying, orphaned, fathomlessly rich American heiress who inadvertently brings devastation, through her very goodness, to all those around her, is led by Lord Mark to see a painting by Bronzino in the great country house of Matcham, where both are guests.[9] Lord Mark and all the other guests say the Bronzino remarkably resembles her.[10] "But the likeness is so great," says Kate Croy. "Yes, there you are, my dear, if you want to know. And you're superb."[11] A significant feature in James's account, however, is that Milly herself does not see the likeness. She does not recognize herself, or, at least initially, "know" herself, in the portrait: "I wish I could see the resemblance," says Milly. When Lord Mark says, "It's down to the very hands," Milly replies, "Her hands are large, . . . but mine are larger. Mine are huge." "But you're a pair

---

9. I mistakenly said in *Literature as Conduct* (220) that Matcham is Lord Mark's house. That is not the case. Matcham belongs, rather, to unnamed persons who are described by the narrator, speaking here for Milly, as part of the general "infusion" of "*appointed* felicity" in which Milly basks: "the honored age of illustrious host and hostess, all at once so distinguished and so plain, so public and so shy" (19:208–9). This is important because Lord Mark, aristocrat though he is, is impecunious. He needs to marry money, if he can, hence his proposal to Milly, who has lots.

10. I have discussed this scene from a different perspective and in the context of a fuller reading of *The Wings of the Dove* in "Lying Against Death, *The Wings of the Dove*," *Literature as Conduct* 184, 220–21.

11. Henry James, *The Wings of the Dove*, 19:223. Henceforth identified by chapter and page number.

FIGURE 13.2. Lucrezia Panciatichi (1539–45), by Agnolo Bronzino. Uffizi Museum, Florence. Used by permission from Scala/Art Resource, New York.

[like a pair of hands?]," Lord Mark continues. "You must surely catch it." Milly replies "I don't know—one never knows one's self" (19:222).

The painting James had in mind, though he never mentions it by name, must be the great portrait, said to be of Lucrezia Panciatichi, painted by Agnolo Bronzino in 1540, now in the Uffizi in Florence.[12]

---

12. The identification was made by Allott. She observes that James most likely saw the painting on one of his visits to Florence. The first visit was in 1869, when James's cousin Minny Temple, the supposed "original" of Milly Theale, lay dying back in the United States. Anderson discusses Milly Theale's encounter with the Bronzino at 178–88.

I say "said to be of Lucrezia Panciatichi" because of course nothing in the painting itself verifies that identification. We are dependent on external performative testimony, even if the name were inscribed on the painting itself, which is not the case. Somebody has to say, "I swear this is a portrait of Lucrezia Panciatichi," and we have to take their word for it. So far as I know, no other paintings of this great lady exist with which to compare Bronzino's painting. The woman herself, the ultimate verification, is long since dust, as Milly is painfully aware. People in general, I, for example, are prone not to recognize themselves in portraits, even in photographs, though the camera never lies. Everyone else says, "It is you to the life, a spitting image," but you say, "Do I really look like that? I can't believe it." The subject of the portrait or photo is blind to the resemblance, even though most people see themselves in the mirror every day.

Lucrezia Panciatichi's subjectivity is exposed by being embodied, materialized in paint. It exists in its embodiment, as in the hands that are so beautiful and so beautifully painted. Those hands, however, are unmistakably provocative. They are an exposure, even an indecent exposure, for example, in the way the first and second fingers of the left hand resemble miniature legs, Baubo-like legs.[13] Baubo, in Greek mythology, consoled Demeter for the loss of Persephone by lifting her skirts and exposing her vulva. Lucrezia Panciatichi's exposed hands echo in miniature what the viewer can guess is the look of her legs hidden under the red skirt. But Bronzino's painting of his subject's face is itself an exposure. The spectator of this great portrait has the obscure feeling that he or she is seeing something that ought not to be seen. At least that is the way I feel. Milly Theale certainly reacts that way when she sees the Bronzino in *The Wings of the Dove*. Tears obscure her sight. Looking at the Bronzino, even at a reproduction like the one I give, the spectator is perhaps led to reflect that just as Milly by looking at the portrait of Lucrezia Panciatichi not only was made a mirror image of that figure, as everyone says she is, but also was put in the position of Bronzino himself when he looked hard at his model in order to paint her or when he looked at the direct gaze of the painted Lucrezia staring back at him from his masterwork, moving his eyes back and forth from the model to the wooden panel on which he was painting her image. In a further reflection, the spectator may realize that he or she is in turn placed not only just where Milly Theale was when she gazed through her tears at the Bronzino, and where Henry James was when he pre-

---

13. Peter J. Capuano mentions to me in this connection: "Helena Michie's work in *The Flesh Made Word: Female Figures and Women's Bodies* where Michie avers that 'the [female] hand is in itself a synecdoche for more obviously sexual parts of the body . . .'" (98).

sumably saw the painting in the Uffizi, but also in the position of Bronzino himself when he painted the figure, as well as in our position now when we look at a reproduction, another drawing out into the open, a re-pro-duction.

Peter J. Capuano has in his *Changing Hands* brilliantly shown how hands still matter for us in literature and in life. This is true in spite of the tremendous historical, class, and technological changes that have taken place in the last couple of centuries in Europe, America, and globally. These have immensely changed the way hands are used these days, just as that use changed markedly in the course of the nineteenth century, even though we still use hands to caress and embrace one another. Now, however, we more and more use hands to type on keyboards, to play video games, to press buttons, not to wind cranks or to manipulate machinery directly. We now mostly wash dishes in a dishwasher, not by hand in a kitchen sink. To do those things we need quite different forms of manual dexterity and strength from the ones required, for example, to write a manuscript by hand or, for that matter, to type on a manual typewriter. Nevertheless hands still matter greatly for us human beings, quite differently for different people in different countries and different "life positions."

WORKS CITED

Allott, Miriam. "The Bronzino Portrait in Henry James's *On the Wings of the Dove*." *Modern Language Notes*, vol. 68, no. 1, 1953, pp. 23–25.

Anderson, Charles R. *Person, Place, and Thing in Henry James's Novels*. Duke UP, 1977.

Capuano, Peter J. *Changing Hands: Industry, Evolution, and the Reconfiguration of the Victorian Body*. U of Michigan P, 2015.

Hardy, Thomas. "The Dorsetshire Laborer." *Personal Writings*, edited by Harold Orel, U of Kansas P, 1966.

———. *The Mayor of Casterbridge*. Anniversary Edition, New York and London, Harper & Brothers, 1920.

———. *Tess of the d'Urbervilles*. New Wessex Edition, Macmillan, 1974.

———. *Complete Poems*. Edited by James Gibson, Macmillan, 1976.

James, Henry. *The Wings of the Dove*. Reprint of New York Edition of 1907–9, Augustus M. Kelley, 1976.

Michie, Helena. *The Flesh Made Word: Female Figures and Women's Bodies*. Oxford UP, 1987.

Miller, J. Hillis. "Hands in Hardy and James." *The Ashgate Research Companion to Thomas Hardy*, edited by Rosemarie Morgan, Ashgate, 2010, pp. 505–16.

———. *Literature as Conduct*. Fordham UP, 2005.

———. "Touching Derrida Touching Nancy." *For Derrida*, by Miller, Fordham UP, 2009, pp. 245–305.

———. "What Do Stories About Pictures Want?" *Critical Inquiry*, vol. 34, no. 5, 2008, pp. 59–97.

———, and Ranjan Ghosh. *Thinking Literature Across Continents*. Duke UP, 2016.

Nancy, Jean-Luc. *Noli me tangere*. Paris, Bayard, 2003.

AFTERWORD

The Well Spoken Hand

HERBERT F. TUCKER

AN ESSAY like this one can default to a pat on the back. The afterword is an academic genre that ordinarily entails a more or less summary retrospect, saying again with some difference of emphasis what the harder-working essays before it have said better already, alone and in concert. Of such duties here I am relieved (in every sense) by the care with which the volume editors have performed them up front, both in the usefully detailed account of each chapter that their introduction supplies and in a sequential arrangement of chapters that lets the strands of argument spun out in each knit up a broader fabric of reflection on the Victorian ubiquity and polyvalence of discourses of the hand. The tensile strength of that result frees me to act here as a first responder, modeling the kind of handoff that a book of this kind aspires to make to others at work in the field, who will carry its initiatives forward along lines it lays out.

The brief consideration of poems in the two immediately preceding chapters—and there only, unless I've missed someone else's very fleeting glance—provides a late opening that I might explore further now. When Daniel Novak cites a Keats fragment and J. Hillis Miller discusses a Hardy lyric, they do so in pursuit of larger arguments of their own. But I am arrested by the quintessential instantiation that verse itself offers of what remains a leading theme within *Victorian Hands* as a whole: the embodiment of language. For it is in poetry above all, where the weight and music and pattern of words become crucial, that language not only represents a world but enacts it. When the editors outline our joint project as "taking this period's fascination with hands seriously, which is to say taking them literally and metaphorically at their word" (Introduction), they point to a semiotic juncture that, while it facilitates Victorian writing of many kinds, poetry's distinctive foregrounding of the signifier is especially well suited to clarify.

"I kiss my hand / To the stars . . . // Kiss my hand to the dappled-with-damson west" ("The Wreck of the Deutschland," 33–37): Hopkins's courtly moue pays to the changing mortal beauty of nature a characteristic homage of hail and farewell. And the act goes beyond mere indication of a phenomenon external to its observer. Like everything that deeply mattered to Hopkins, the inscape of evening "must be instressed, stressed" (39), taken as a pulse in the body through what this poem inaugurated as "sprung rhythm": a radically organic versification wherein the arithmetic of metered syllables yielded to the elastic calculus of felt stress itself. Kissing one's hand *means* something, to be sure, as it executes a Victorian gestural code of the social sort extensively illuminated in, for example, the foregoing essays by Pamela K. Gilbert and Jonathan Cheng (chapters 4 and 8). But when the gesture is prosodically incorporated, it also *does* something. The vocalic inner rhyme of "hand" with "dappled" and "damson," the more distant but still audible match of "kiss" with "stress" (each word moreover doubled, and at each occurrence rhythmically stressed) pluck the blown kiss out of the intellectual air and plant it in the sensorium of poet and reader alike. That enjambed, *a*-rhyming "hand" at the end of the first line hovers right where *Victorian Hands* has shown Victorian hands hovering: in the "place where humans have negotiated the relation between their language and their material being all along" (Introduction), with the leverage that is imparted to such negotiation by verse's manifold charter to materialize language and make a poem not just mean but be.

Imagery of the hand leaves prints all over *In Memoriam*, which scholarship has long detected, and which recent scholarship (Lanestedt and Landow; Sanders; Craft) has linked in subtle ways with the intense manual eroticism that contributors to this volume concur in associating with the Victorian hand's accessibility, gloved or bare, during an era that kept most body parts well under wraps. The loss of Arthur Hallam leaves Tennyson during the initial portion of this long elegy clutching so at vacancy that nature itself appears phantasmal, "A hollow form with empty hands" (3.12). But in time the friend's hand that, repeatedly felt for, is repeatedly not there effects with excruciating slowness what Tamara Ketabgian might call "its own prosthetic replacement" (chapter 2). The disabled, groping orthodoxy of the poet's "lame hands of faith" (55.17) eventually gives way to the different ministrations of literature. In reading "The noble letters of the dead"—letters inscribed, that is, by Hallam's hand while alive, and quickened again by the survivor who reads its scripted traces—Tennyson finds that "word by word, and line by line, / The dead man touched me" (95.24–35), with a haptic intelligibility like that Deborah Morse senses in Trollope's novels (chapter 11), but here with the intensity of lyric. When at last "in my thoughts with scarce a sigh / I take the pressure of thine hand" (119.11–12), it hardly matters any more whether the means of contact are chiromantic, chirographic, or (per Aviva Briefel's chapter 5) spiritualist. The poet writes under a "pressure," comparable to Hopkins's "stress," that it is his to shape; and, as the unstopped flow of "sigh" into "I" suggests, it emerges out of a sorrow as profound as selfhood. "Out of darkness came the hands / That reach through nature, moulding men" (124.3–4): consolation that lasts can arise only from a no less lasting melancholy. If those craftsman-like man-molding "hands" stretched forth at the end of the line are ultimately supernatural, their mediate tool remains Tennyson's writing hand, clasped in Hallam's written hand, and bound together in manuscript's industrial prosthesis, the published book.

Curiosity about the deed of artistic making sustains in Robert Browning's many-handed oeuvre a pattern of steady reference to the hand as double agent. The Victorian hand's treacherously liminal situation "between self and non-self, subject and object, body and tool" (Sue Zemka, chapter 6) finds corroboration in this poet's dramatic monologues, all of which variously permute the subject/object relation by conveying a character's inside and outside stories at one stroke. This compounded creation is regularly thematized when, in monologues spoken by artists, the pictorial or musical hand assumes a life of its own (Ower; Sussman). Thus in "Andrea del Sarto," much as the painter's enervated sex life has dwindled down to holding hands with his faithless wife ("Your soft hand is a woman of itself, / And mine the man's bared breast she curls inside," 21–22), a like personification of the hand governs how he thinks about the practice of his art, through "hand and eye and something of a heart" (224)—and in that order too. If weak-heartedness is Andrea's complaint, in art as well as marriage, he finds twin compensations in the remarkable facility of his hand. For one thing, he finds commissioned work so easy and profitable that, with his "hand kept plying" (161), he can "Finish the portrait out of hand" (236) and ensure domestic solvency; for another thing, and a subtler, he can make of his hand a scapegoat for the betrayal of his higher calling as a major artist. "This low-pulsed forthright craftsman's hand of mine" (82) has played the part of an enabler within Andrea's system of interlocking erotic, artistic, and commercial dependencies: "forthright" after the sinister fashion of honest,

honest Iago, the personified hand is a tool that long ago got the upper hand of its master and now runs the whole show.

The artful hand's status as more than a tool is reinforced by the quasi-autonomous way it uses tools itself, at what Kate Flint designates as "the hand/apparatus interface" (chapter 9). For Andrea these include "pencil" (60) and "chalk" (196). For "Abt Vogler (After he has Been Extemporizing upon the Musical Instrument of his Invention)," the tools are the keys on the playing board of his orchestrion or chamber organ. In recounting his performance Vogler speaks always of the instrumental "keys" (2, 10, 41, 91), never of his own body; "finger" and "hand" are terms sparingly reserved for that divine agency to which his monologue nevertheless boldly likens the improviser's inspired construction of an elaborate but temporary musical edifice. "Here is the finger of God, a flash of the will that can" (49), Vogler claims of his jazzy touch for rococo riffing; and he claims this godlike power for the musician in craft terms, "That out of three sounds he frame, not a fourth sound, but a star" (52). That God remains the "Builder and maker . . . of houses not made with hands" (66) pointedly underscores the fallible human maker's reliance on manual labor, which in this instance includes not only the improvisation of the music but the invention of the instrument that makes it possible.

"All through my keys that gave their sounds to a wish of my soul, / . . . / All through music and me!" (41–42). Brokering this collaboration between tool and soul, art and artist, is the unnamed hand, which can do the performer's bidding to realize a wish in art only because it has a will, and a resourceful mind, of its own. So David Sudnow reports after his apprenticeship in keyboard jazz in *Ways of the Hand*: "the body's own appreciative structures serve as a means of finding a place to go" (13). Witness also, from the other side of the liaison, Heidegger on the relation of brainwork to handwork: "Every motion of the hand in every one of its works carries itself through the element of thinking . . . All the work of the hand is rooted in thinking"; "We have called thinking the handicraft *par excellence*" (Heidegger 16, 23; see also Capuano 237–39 and Jackson 123–26). The continuum along which both intellectual memory and muscle memory reside defines a gamut of ideation on which the practiced artistic imagination does its thinking. "I can do with my pencil what I know, / What I see, what at bottom of my heart / I wish for" (60–62): that's Andrea del Sarto again, and in saying it he emerges again as one member of a team, in effect the spokesman for his silent partner, his right hand's right-hand man. Elsewhere, the lessoning of an art student's hand by trial and error in the sketching of a hand—and thereby the moral education of the artist—furnishes the occasion of another Browning poem less well known, "Beside the Drawing Board," the eighth lyric in "James Lee's Wife" (1864).

In the Victorian era the figure of the hand becomes a locus "where the constitutive primacy of language over material being, or vice versa, is not only impossible to decide—its impossibility is a heartbeat that runs through the whole" (Introduction). Having provided a few samples taking the pulse of this undecidability within the body of poetic language, let me conclude by calling attention to nineteenth-century developments that made of the hand not just a semiotically ambiguous topic but a signifier in the most elementary sense. The first of these is the long incubation of what we now know as British Sign Language, which emerged in the later eighteenth century under Thomas Braidwood's tutelage as a hybrid of fingerspelling with manual and other signing, and was by the turn of the nineteenth century established in schools for the deaf. Braidwood's was a gestural language indeed: a uniquely evolving blend of those orthographic, indexical, and iconic features which I have admittedly asserted some rhetorical license to claim for the poetic handlers just discussed. ("Indexicality" and "iconicity" are respectively the terms for deixis and embodiment in the semiotics of Charles Sanders Peirce, who does not appear to have taken an interest in sign language for the deaf, but whose language philosophy undergirds aspects of sign language theory today, and arose concurrently with the ramification of both BSL and its very different transatlantic counterpart, the French-based American Sign Language.) Indexicality and iconicity were present in BSL's early avatars with a combined force that mustn't be denoted "literal," yet that committed interlocutors of the deaf to, as our volume editors have put it in another context, taking them "literally and metaphorically at their word." To be fluent in BSL was to shuttle back and forth between reference and performance at the speed of thought, and with a wave of the hand. Given the evolving object-subject-verb syntax of BSL, at even a sheerly grammatical level the language apparently played out the agential ambiguity that this book has repeatedly discovered in the hand's discursive brokerage.

Following decades of pedagogical development and practical application, towards the *fin de siècle* a rising international tide of standardization placed BSL at risk, until in 1893 oralism—the mainstreaming of deaf students into hearing culture—became official educational policy when Parliament passed the Elementary Education (Deaf and Blind Children) Act. This discouragement of manual language among the deaf coincided, ironically, with a boom in manual language among the general public. From mid-century the French performance coach François Delsarte taught and tabulated a system of physical postures and manual gestures that by the 1890s were well known to actors, vocalists, orators, and dancers across the anglophone world as expressive enhancements of live delivery. Evidently Delsarte trusted to live delivery in his teaching as well, since like Socrates he left formulation of the gestural method in book form to his successors. Here was a teacher, one infers, who talked a lot with his hands. He must have done so in loyalty to an intuition that the medium was the message, especially when medium and message alike were the expressive body, and that in a lyceum or an auditorium the grace notes and diacritics of that medium lay in the expressive flourishes of the performing hand.

Or, we might add, in an artist's studio, or a dining room. Wilde wrote *The Picture of Dorian Gray* just as the Delsarte wave was cresting in the fashionable world, and its most tellingly dramatic moments occur, not at the theater with Sybil Vane, but in the intimacy of the salon with Lord Henry Wotton. Lord Henry makes it his business from the first to entrance Dorian with dialectics of the senses and the soul, whose intellectual content is the sangfroid of paradox but whose medium of transmission is orchestration of the voice and hands, Delsarte's method trimmed to drawing-room scale. Dorian falls under a spell wrought by the older man's understated, inexplicit, yet fluently suggestive prestidigitation:

> There was something in his low, languid voice that was absolutely fascinating. His cool, white, flower-like hands, even, had a curious charm. They moved, as he spoke, like music, and seemed to have a language of their own. (ch. 2)

The charm of this manual idiolect is, in marked contrast to sign language like Braidwood's—but as with all really potent charm—inherently unintelligible. That Lord Henry's hands betoken homoerotic seduction, and beckon with aristocratic allure, nobody will deny. But they mean more than that, precisely because they signify less. What they bespeak is extravagance as such.

That's one reason these eloquent hands persist unmentioned into a chapter that Wilde added between his novel's journal publication in 1890 and the book that appeared a year later. The new chapter 3 records Lord Henry's charmed reflection on the charm he casts on Dorian—"Talking to him was like playing upon an exquisite violin. He answered to every touch and thrill of the bow"—and, near the close, caps with another instrumental image a sequence of verbs figuring the conversational brilliance of impromptu monologue as sublimed manu-logue. Look, Dorian, no hands:

> He played with the idea, and grew willful; tossed it into the air and transformed it; let it escape and recaptured it; made it iridescent with fancy, and winged it with paradox . . . He charmed his listeners out of themselves, and they followed his pipe, laughing.

"You know more than you think you know," says Lord Henry right before the paragraph first quoted, "just as you know less than you want to know." That difference between articulation and intimation, between cognition and desire, creates the surplus reserve of the well spoken hand. It implies—and by the end of the story brings about—far more than even Lord Henry can foreknow.

WORKS CITED

Capuano, Peter J. *Changing Hands: Industry, Evolution, and the Reconfiguration of the Victorian Body.* U of Michigan P, 2015.

Craft, Christopher. "'Descend, and Touch, and Enter': Tennyson's Strange Manner of Address." *Genders*, vol. 1, 1988, pp. 83–101.

Heidegger, Martin. *What Is Called Thinking?* Translated by Fred D. Wieck and J. Glenn Gray, Harper and Row, 1968.

Jackson, Sarah. *Tactile Poetics: Touch and Contemporary Writing.* Edinburgh UP, 2015.

Lanestedt, Jon, and George P. Landow on *The Victorian Web*: http://www.victorianweb.org/authors/tennyson/im/hand.html.

Ower, John. "The Abuse of the Hand: A Thematic Motif in Browning's 'Fra Lippo Lippi.'" *Victorian Poetry*, vol. 14, 1976, pp. 135–41.

Sanders, Charles R. "Tennyson and the Human Hand." *Victorian Newsletter*, vol. 11, 1957, pp. 5–14.

Stebbins, Genevieve. *The Delsarte System of Expression.* New York, Werner, 1886.

Sudnow, David. *Ways of the Hand: The Organization of Improvised Conduct.* Harvard UP, 1978.

Sussman, Herbert. "Browning's 'Fra Lippo Lippi' and the Problematic of a Male Poetic." *Victorian Studies*, vol. 35, 1992, pp. 185–211.

Warman, Edward Barrett. *Gestures and Attitudes: An Exposition of the Delsarte Philosophy of Expression, Practical and Theoretical.* Boston, Lee and Shepard, 1892.

CONTRIBUTORS

JAMES ELI ADAMS is Professor and Director of Graduate Studies in the Department of English & Comparative Literature at Columbia University. He is the author of *Dandies and Desert Saints: Styles of Victorian Masculinity* (1995) and *A History of Victorian Literature* (2009), as well as numerous articles and chapters, most recently "Dickens's Theatre of Shame" in *Reading Victorian Literature: Essays in Honour of J. Hillis Miller*, ed. Julian Wolfreys and Monika Szuba (Edinburgh UP, 2019). "The Dead Hand" is part of an ongoing project on constructions of inheritance in nineteenth-century literature and culture.

KAREN BOURRIER is Associate Professor of English at the University of Calgary. Her research interests include Victorian literature and culture, disability studies, the digital humanities, and women's writing. She is the author of *The Measure of Manliness: Disability and Masculinity in Mid-Victorian Fiction* (U of Michigan P, 2015) and *Victorian Bestseller: The Life of Dinah Craik* (U of Michigan P, 2019).

AVIVA BRIEFEL is Professor of English and Cinema Studies at Bowdoin College. She is the author of *The Deceivers: Art Forgery and Identity in the Nineteenth Century* (Cornell UP, 2006) and *The Racial Hand in the Victorian Imagination* (Cambridge UP, 2015), and coeditor of *Horror After 9/11: World of Fear, Cinema of Terror* (U of Texas P, 2011). She is currently writing a book on the material culture of Victorian spiritualism.

PETER J. CAPUANO is Associate Professor of English, a Faculty Fellow in the Center for Digital Research in the Humanities at the University of Nebraska, and a federated faculty member of the University of California's Dickens Project. He is the author of *Changing Hands: Industry, Evolution, and the Reconfiguration of the Victorian Body* (U of Michigan P, 2015). He is currently finishing a monograph on Charles Dickens's body language.

JONATHAN CHENG is a graduate student at the University of Nebraska-Lincoln, researching nineteenth-century British novels with a focus on Computational Literary Studies and distant reading methods. His dissertation project uses machine learning methods to model changes in characterization. A recent article in *Cultural Analytics*, "Fleshing Out Models of Gender," elaborates a wide range of gradual changes in the physical description of fictional men and women in 15,000 novels since the 1850s.

KATE FLINT is Provost Professor of Art History and English at the University of Southern California. Her work is in the cultural history of the long nineteenth century, and is both interdisciplinary and transatlantic. Her most recent book is *Flash! Photography, Writing and Surprising Illumination* (Oxford UP, 2018); she has previously published *The Transatlantic Indian 1776–1930* (Princeton UP, 2008); *The Victorians and The Visual Imagination* (Cambridge UP, 2001) and *The Woman Reader, 1837–1914* (Oxford UP, 1993). Currently, she is working on a project that links contemporary and Victorian artistic and literary treatments of the natural world in order to discuss the scales and temporalities through which we understand ongoing environmental damage.

PAMELA K. GILBERT is the Albert Brick Professor of English at the University of Florida, and has published widely in the areas of Victorian literature, cultural studies, gender, and the history of medicine. She is the author of *Victorian Skin: Surface, Self, History* (Cornell UP 2019), *Cholera and Nation* (SUNY P, 2008), *The Citizen's Body* (The Ohio State UP, 2007), *Mapping the Victorian Social Body* (SUNY P, 2004), and *Disease, Desire and the Body in Victorian Women's Popular Novels* (Cambridge UP, 1997). She has edited collections entitled *Imagined London* (SUNY P, 2002) and the *Companion to Sensation Fiction* (Blackwell, 2011), and has edited a teaching and scholarly edition of Rhoda Broughton's novel *Cometh Up as a Flower* (Broadview P, 2010). She has also co-edited *Beyond Sensation: Mary Elizabeth Braddon in Context* (SUNY P, 1999, with Marlene Tromp and Aeron Haynie), and is co-associate editor of the *Blackwell Encyclopedia of Victorian Literature* (2016).

TAMARA KETABGIAN is Professor of English at Beloit College. She is author of *The Lives of Machines: The Industrial Imaginary in Victorian Literature and Culture* (U of Michigan P, 2011) and various essays and articles on nineteenth-century literature, science, and technology. She is working on a book project entitled *Contrivance: Faith, Persuasion, and Technology in Victorian Scientific and Literary Culture*.

J. HILLIS MILLER is Distinguished Research Professor of English and Comparative Literature Emeritus at the University of California at Irvine. He has published many books and essays on nineteenth- and twentieth-century literature and theory. *An Innocent Abroad: Lectures in China* appeared in 2015 (Northwestern UP). It gathers fifteen of the more than thirty lectures Miller gave at various universities in China between 1988 and 2012. Since then he has published several more books, some collaboratively. These include not only his book with Ranjan Ghosh, *Think-*

ing Literature Across Continents (Duke UP, 2016), but also: with Tom Cohen and Claire Colebrook, *Twilight of the Anthropocene Idols* (Open Humanities P, 2016); in Chinese: *Selected Writings of J. Hillis Miller,* ed. Wang Fengzhen (Beijing: China Social Sciences Press, 2016); *Lektüren—Interventionen: Literature und dei Zeichen der Zeit. Ausgewählte Studien,* gathered, introduced, and translated by Monika Reif-Hülser (Open Humanities P, 2016); *First Sail,* a documentary film made by Dragan Kujundzic (2016). Miller is a Fellow of the American Academy of Arts and Sciences and a member of the American Philosophical Society.

DEBORAH DENENHOLZ MORSE is the inaugural Sara E. Nance Eminent Professor of English at The College of William & Mary. She has written two monographs on Anthony Trollope, *Women in Trollope's Palliser Novels* (U of Rochester P, 1987) and *Reforming Trollope* (Ashgate, 2013), and is the lead editor of the *Routledge Research Companion to Anthony Trollope* (2016, with Margaret Markwick and Mark Turner) as well as co-editor of *The Politics of Gender in the Novels of Anthony Trollope* (2009, with Margaret Markwick and Regenia Gagnier). She has published multiple essays on the Brontës, and is a part of the Cambridge University Press *Complete Works* editorial team. She has co-edited four Brontë volumes, including *The Blackwell Companion to the Brontës* (2016), and is currently completing a monograph entitled *Brontë Violations.* Additionally, she continues to publish in Animal Studies since her co-editorship of *Victorian Animal Dreams* (2007) with Martin Danahay, most recently in the Cambridge volume *Animals, Animality, and Literature* (2018) and, with Martin Danahay, she has co-written a chapter on Animals and Animality for *The Routledge Handbook of Victorian Literature* (2019).

DANIEL A. NOVAK is Associate Professor of English at the University of Alabama. He is author of *Realism, Photography, and Nineteenth-Century Fiction* (Cambridge UP, 2008), and co-editor with James Catano of *Masculinity Lessons: Rethinking Men's and Women's Studies* (Johns Hopkins UP, 2011). He has published essays in *Representations, Victorian Studies, Novel, Criticism,* and other venues. The essay in this volume is part of a book project entitled *Specters of Wilde,* which focuses on the beginning of Wilde studies in the early twentieth century.

JULIANNE SMITH is Professor of English at Pepperdine University in Malibu, CA. Recent publications have focused on Charles Dickens and Victorian theatre, with such works in print as an article in *Nineteenth-Century Theatre and Film* titled "*Bleak House* on London's East End Stage, 1853: George Dibdin Pitt and Dickens at the Royal Pavilion Theatre" (2014) and an essay in Ashgate's Victorian Studies Series titled "Victorian Drama in the 1850s and the Transformation of Literary Consciousness" (*Victorian Transformations: Genre, Nationalism and Desire in Nineteenth-Century Literature,* ed. Bianca Tredennick, Farnham, Ashgate, 2011, 79–94.) She also has an essay in *Teaching Victorian Literature in the 21st Century: A Guide to Pedagogy* titled "Teaching the 'Forgotten' Genre: Victorian Drama" (Palgrave, 2017).

HERBERT F. TUCKER holds the John C. Coleman Chair in English at the University of Virginia. There he edits the Victorian series for the University Press and serves as associate editor of *New Literary History.* He has published books on Browning, Tennyson, and the British epic poem between the French Revolution and the First World War; has edited volumes by sundry hands on Tennyson, literary criticism and pedagogy, and Victorian literature and culture; and has published many essays and reviews. His scansion website *For Better for Verse* will offer readers of this collection practice in counting syllables and stresses on their fingers.

SUE ZEMKA is Professor of English at the University of Colorado where she specializes in Victorian literature and culture, the novel, temporality, media history, and religion. She is the author of *Victorian Testaments: The Bible, Christology, and Literary Authority in Early-Nineteenth-Century British Culture* (Stanford UP, 1998) and *Time and the Moment in Victorian Literature and Society* (Cambridge UP, 2012). Her current project, provisionally entitled *Lives of the Hand*, approaches the hand as a vehicle of humanist critique and reimagining.

INDEX

ACT, 112, 113, 126
Actor's Art, The (Garcia), 197
Adam, James Eli, 11
Adam Bede (Eliot), 140, 143n6
"Adventure of the Engineers Thumb, The" (Doyle), 58
aesthetics, 12, 58, 177, 193, 248n20
Afterlife of Property, The (Nunokawa), 135
agency, 8, 47, 150, 176, 177; human, 16, 41, 112, 129
Alexander, Christine, 59–60
All in the Dark (Le Fanu), 9, 97, 99, 103
All the Year Round, 77, 86
American Amateur Photographer (Burbank), 189
American Annual of Photography, 185
American Photographer, 189
amputations, 23, 36, 37, 44, 45, 57, 58, 63, 67–68; manual, 7, 54, 56, 59
Apartment Stories (Marcus), 103
Arago, François, 181
Aretino, Spinello, 264, 266; painting by, 265 fig. 13.1

Aristotle, 9, 21, 74–75, 260
Armadale (Collins), 77, 78
Armstrong, Nancy, 163–64
Art of Retouching, The (Hubert), 182
Art of Retouching, The (Ourdan), 183
Ashley, Lord (seventh earl of Shaftesbury), 36, 36n2, 38, 44, 45, 48; Bright and, 47, 48, 50, 50n1; criticism by, 48n13; Dodd and, 38, 38n4, 46, 50
Ashworth, Edmund, 48, 48n13, 49, 50n17, 51
Ashworth, Henry, 48, 48n13, 49, 50n17, 51
Austen, Jane, 164, 165n20

Babbage, Charles, 25, 26
Bain, Alexander, 77, 77n4
Baker, William, 86
Ball, Charles, 123
Ballou, Adin, 93
Bamman, David, 153
Bann, Jennifer, 98, 103
Bartlett, Neil, 244, 245, 250n24
Bartrip, P. W. J., 23
Batchen, Geoffrey, 176

Batt, Alice, 197

Bede, Cuthbert, 184, 185, 186

Bell, Acton, 60

Bell, Currer, 60

Bell, Ellis, 60

Bell, Karl, 90

Bell, Sir Charles, 6, 7, 20, 21, 22, 23–24, 26–27, 110, 176, 176n2; mechanical contrivances/hand and, 25–26; Royal Society and, 19

Bell's Treatise, 19–20, 21, 22, 24, 25–27, 28, 31, 34, 176, 176n2

Benjamin, Walter, 181

Bennett, Andrew, 245

"Beside the Drawing Board" (Browning), 276

bigamy, 55, 60, 64, 68

Binney, Thomas, 131

"Bittersweet Love" (Keats), 245

"Black and Tan Dive in Broome St." (Riis), 179

Blackstone, William, 75, 76, 79, 84, 85

Blackwood's Edinburgh Magazine, 27, 29, 61

Bleak House (Burnett), 210–11, 213n7

Bleak House (Dickens), 13, 197, 198–99, 204, 205, 206, 209, 217; hands and, 196, 203; illustrations for, 198, 201, 202

Bleak House (Rendle), 204, 207, 210

body, 1, 155, 166, 176, 197; disabled, 39–40; dismembered, 62; hand and, 37–44, 96; photographic technology and, 177; scholarship on, 160; spectral, 102, 104

Book of the Hand, The, 92

Booth, Michael, 208

Boucicault, Dion, 210

Bourrier, Karen, 8

Braddon, Mary Elizabeth, 98

Brahmins, 115, 117, 118, 119, 124

Braidwood, Thomas, 277, 278

brain, 176; hand and, 110, 276

Bray, Charles, 145

Bridges, Norman, 186

Bridgewater Treatise (Bell), 19–20, 21, 22, 24, 25–27, 28, 31, 34, 176, 176n2

Briefel, Aviva, 9, 10, 54, 57, 108n1, 118, 149, 149n3, 231n10

Bright, John, 44, 49, 50n17; Ashley and, 47, 48, 50, 50n17; on factory system, 47–48

Bristow, Joseph, 241

Bronstein, Jamie L., 22

Brontë, Anne, 92n5, 154

Brontë, Branwell, 61–62

Brontë, Charlotte, 30n5, 56, 56n2, 58, 59, 60, 60n5, 61, 62, 63, 64, 92n5, 100, 155

Brontë, Duke of, 58, 60

Brontë, Patrick, 60

Bronzino, Agnolo, 268, 269n12, 270, 271; painting by, 269, 269 fig. 13.2

Browne, Hablot K., 13, 201, 202, 203, 206, 207, 208, 211, 213, 217; Dickens and, 198–99; illustration by, 200 fig. 10.1

Browning, Robert, 15, 97, 177, 275, 276

Buckley, Daniel, 22

Burbank, W. H., 189

Burke, Edmund, 11, 130, 144

Burman, S. B., 23

Burnett, J. P., 13, 204, 210–11, 212n5, 212n6, 213, 214, 215, 216, 217, 217n8

Burney, Fanny, 165, 166, 167, 170

Caldwell, Janis McLarren, 32

Cambridge Companion to the Victorian Novel (Armstrong), 163

cameras, 175, 178; advertisements for, 189, 190 fig. 9.3; hand and, 189, 191–93

Cameron, Julia Margaret, 177, 179, 181, 186, 186n10; hands of, 183; photo by, 178 fig. 9.1, 180 fig. 9.2

Camilla: A Picture of Youth (Burney), 165

Campion, Jane, 258

Capuano, Peter J., 2, 3, 6, 7, 14, 54, 56, 154, 168, 169, 205, 256–57, 259, 270n13, 271; on Audley, 73n1; hand descriptions and, 148–49, 150–51; on hand/head, 57; on hand/machinery, 221; on hand/visibility, 41; handedness and, 197; manual culture and, 149n2; social novels and, 155

Carlisle, Janice, 43–44

Carlyle, Thomas, 21

Cartier-Bresson, Henri, 192

Carver, Stephen, 99

Caught in the Machinery (Bronstein), 22

Cecilia; Memoirs of an Heiress (Burney), 165
Changing Hands: Industry, Evolution, and the Reconfiguration of the Victorian Body (Capuano), 149n2, 168, 172, 221, 256–57, 259
charity, vocation and, 48–51
Chartists, 61, 222
Chase, Cynthia, 144
cheiromancy, 249, 251
Cheng, Jonathan, 11, 12, 274
Chesney Wold (Rendle), 13, 203–4, 204n2
chirognomy, 57, 92, 93
chiromancy, 92, 93, 249
Christian Lady's Magazine, The, 30
class, 13, 197, 205, 206, 207, 217; hands and, 57, 214
Claudet, Laura, 182
Clever Woman of the Family, The (Yonge), 58
Cohen, Michael, 247, 248n20, 258
Cohen, William, 148, 148–49n1, 159–60
Cohn, Elisha, 243
"Cold Embrace, The" (Braddon), 98
Collins, William Wilkie, 8, 9, 10, 74, 76–77, 78, 83, 84, 84n6, 85, 86, 86n7, 87, 87n9, 107, 109, 112, 115, 116, 117–20, 119n3, 124, 187; action of, 73; allegory of, 121; manual-centrism and, 123; method of character of, 11; "scissor-and-paste" method of, 120n4
colonialism, 121, 123, 149, 149n3
Coningsby (Disraeli), 33, 34
"Consecrated Ground" (Browne), 199, 200 fig. 10.1, 203, 206, 211, 213
Contemporary Portraits (Harris), 239
Contemporary Portraits (Morris), photo from, 240 fig. 12.1
Coventry, Walter, 192
Cox, Kimberly, 65, 154, 154n12
Crouzet, Francois, 20
culture, 4, 6, 19, 41, 197, 252; changes in, 259; hands in, 2, 258–59; industrial, 51; machine, 37, 48, 50; manual, 148, 149, 149n2; Victorian, 15, 56, 115n2, 148, 160; wound, 40, 51

Daniel Deronda (Eliot), 132, 136, 144

Dante, 246
D'Arpentigny, Casimir Stanislas, 93
Darwin, Charles, 110, 111, 164
data, 2, 11, 151, 152, 152n8, 154, 157; gender, 158–59, 160, 163
Davenport Brothers, 102
David (Michelangelo), 247
David Copperfield (Dickens), 149, 161n18
Davis, Lennard, 51
De Profundis (Wilde), 14, 145, 242n7, 245, 246n18, 251, 251n27, 252
dead hand, 2, 108n1, 128, 129, 133, 137, 141, 267
"Dead Hand, The" (Collins), 117–20, 133
Dead Hand, The (Hobhouse), 137
Dead Hands: Fictions of Agency, Renaissance to Modern (Rowe), 2, 226
Defoe, Daniel, 120–22
Del Sarto, Andrea, 275, 276
Delsarte, François, 277–78
Delsarte System of Oratory (Garcia), 197
Derenzy, George Webb, 59
Derrida, Jacques, 4, 5, 6, 132, 260, 263
desire, 15, 132, 177, 247, 279
DeVos, Betsy, 258
Dickens, Charles, 13, 30n5, 77, 82, 86, 115, 130, 160, 167, 170, 197, 202–3, 205, 206, 209n4, 211, 212, 213, 214, 215, 261; Browne and, 198–99; death of, 203, 204; hands and, 201, 217; illustrations and, 196; manual style of, 149; masturbatory imagery of, 148–49n1
disability, 36, 37, 38, 39–40, 44, 48, 49, 51, 54, 55, 57, 59, 60n5, 61n6; heroism and, 8; literary, 43; medical model of, 56; as signifier, 41
discourses, 1, 39, 155, 273; bodily, 159; cultural, 41; evolutionary, 19; industrial, 19, 28–34; religious, 19; scientific, 19
dismemberment, 22, 42, 43, 44, 45, 110, 124
Disraeli, Benjamin, 33
Dodd, William, 7, 8, 23, 26, 45n9, 47, 48, 50n16; Ashley and, 38, 38n4, 46, 50; Bright and, 50n17; as charity case, 49; on co-operative body, 40; disability of, 39, 51; dismemberment of, 42–43, 44; hands and, 40, 41, 42; life story of, 36, 38, 45; social allegory and, 41; Ten Hours

Debate and, 47; Victorian factory and, 37; wound culture and, 40
Dombey and Son (Dickens), 161n18, 167
"Dorsetshire Laborer, The" (Hardy), 260
Doyle, Arthur Conan, 243n11
Duke's Children, The (Trollope), 13, 221, 222, 222n1, 228, 231, 235n14, 236

Echiridion: or A Hand for the One-Handed (Derenzy), 59
economic life, 23, 129, 132, 150–51
Economy of Machinery and Manufactures (Babbage), 25
education, 44, 258, 259, 276, 277
Edwards, Elizabeth, 176
Elementary Education (Deaf and Blind Children) Act (1893), 277
Eliot, George, 11, 132, 133–34, 136, 137, 142n3, 143n5, 143n6, 146, 166, 256; dead hand and, 128; dialectical inwardness of, 142n4; ethics of, 129; inheritance and, 145; men of maxims and, 141–42; moral agents of, 140–41, 144; moral authority and, 133; moral psychology of, 129, 140; nemesis and, 141; Nietzsche and, 143, 144, 145; universal law and, 144n7
Elliotson, John, 115, 116
Ellison, Edith Nicholl, 183
Ellison, Keith, 261
Ellmann, Richard, 251
Encyclopedia of Nineteenth-Century Photography (Plunkett), 181
erotic, 62, 122, 142, 177, 217, 243, 246n17
Esdaile, James, 115–17
Essay on the Principle of Population, An (Malthus), 164
Evans, Marian, 145
exceptionalism, 3, 5, 14, 21
Experimental Investigation of the Spirit Manifestations (Hare), 49

Factory Act (1833), 24, 42n6
"Factory Cripple," 36, 37, 43, 44, 48, 49, 51
factory fiction, 28–34
factory system, 7, 29, 37, 45, 47–48
"Factory System, The" (Wilson), 27

Factory System Illustrated, The (Dodd), 37, 38, 39, 40, 41, 45, 47, 51
Farrar, Aileen, 198
Felissner, Jennifer, 241
Felski, Rita, 241, 245
"Fifth Avenue Winter" (Stieglitz), 192
fingerprints, 57, 181, 181n5
fingers, 96, 191, 261, 267; accidents involving, 41; discoloring, 185, 188; mechanical, 28; missing, 23, 58; moving, 115–17
fingerspelling, 277
Flint, Kate, 12, 276
Forster, E. M., 223
Foucault, Michel, 1, 252
Francis, Jennifer A., 257
Frank, Catherine, 129
Frankenstein (Shelley), 20
Fraser's Magazine, 61
Freedgood, Elaine, 20n3, 40
French Revolution, 75, 77, 86
French, Wilfred A., 188

Gagnier, Regenia, 46, 50, 250n23, 251, 251n26, 251n27
Gallagher, Catherine, 32, 32n6, 129, 141, 142n4, 145
Garcia, Gustave, 197
Garibaldi, Giuseppe, 183
Gaskell, Elizabeth, 61
Gaskell, Peter, 21
gender, 8, 11, 13, 57, 151, 207, 216, 217, 231, 232, 237; author, 158–59; categories, 153, 169; differentiation, 168–69; domestic reproduction and, 163–64; gestures and, 152, 154, 162, 163, 164, 167, 168, 170; hands and, 57, 160–61n18, 169; infractions, 197, 206; notions of, 150, 160, 168, 169, 170, 197; prediction, 162, 163, 163 fig. 8.5; rights, 221; signs of, 150, 168
gender roles, 150, 154, 163, 163n19, 170; feminine/masculine, 151; stereotypical, 151
Genealogy, 144
"George Eliot: Immanent Victorian" (Gallagher), 129
gestures: commonplace, 162, 169; feminine, 151, 154, 162–63, 164–65, 168, 169; gen-

dered, 152, 154, 162, 163, 164, 167, 168, 170; hand, 14, 148, 149–50, 151–54, 155, 162–70, 175, 197, 211, 213; masculine, 151, 154, 162, 164, 165, 166, 168, 169

"Get Ready Man" (Thurber), 262

Ghosh, Ranjan, 258

ghost stories, 97, 98, 99, 100, 103

"Ghost Stories of the Tiled House" (Le Fanu), 93, 98, 99, 103

Ghost Walk, 204, 205–6

Gilbert, Pamela K., 8, 9, 149, 165, 274

Giotto, 264, 265

God, 26, 31; hand of, 33, 87; "Machinery Question" and, 33; moral law of, 29

Graven Palm; a Manual of the Science of Palmistry, The (Robinson), 243–44, 244 fig. 12.2

Graver, Suzanne, 134, 141

Great Expectations (Dickens), 261

Hallam, Arthur, 274, 275

Halperin, David, 252

Hamilton, Lady, 55, 59, 60, 67; Nelson and, 62–63, 66

hand: authorial, 44; average proportion of, 158 fig. 8.3; definitions of, 259, 260, 261; disembodied, 189, 268; displaced, 42; distribution of, 154–61; gendered, 57, 160–61n18, 169; ghost, 103, 267; instrumental/symbolic, 108; invisible, 108; literal, 109, 110; loss of, 22, 44, 58; mangled, 23, 27; materiality of, 99, 100–101; men's, 150, 155, 156 fig. 8.1, 157, 157 fig. 8.2, 158, 159, 160, 160 fig. 8.4, 165, 168, 169; physical, 12, 149; semi-visible, 107–10, 113, 122; sensory apparatus of, 24; shaking, 94, 96; social/thematic role of, 42; spectral, 98, 99, 102; spiritual, 78, 97; stained, 183–89; women's, 150, 155–56, 155n4, 156 fig. 8.1, 157–58, 157 fig. 8.2, 158 fig. 8.3, 159, 160, 165, 166, 168, 169; writing, 44, 196; writing about, 155–60

Hand, The (Bell), 6, 19, 20, 20n2, 22, 25, 27

"Hand Camera—Its Present Importance, The" (Stieglitz), 192

Hand of Ethelberta, The (Hardy), 263, 264

handedness, 6–7, 11, 197, 199

Hands (Zandy), 176

handwriting, 45n8, 196, 211, 263

handyman, 261, 263

Hansard's Parliamentary Debates, 30, 36n1

haptic, 13, 14, 65, 110, 114, 122, 123, 176, 222, 228, 232, 234, 235, 275

Hard Times (Dickens), 30n5, 130, 131

Hardy, Thomas, 256, 259, 266n8; fiction of, 266, 267, 268; hands in, 256n1, 257, 260–68

Harris, Alice Seeley, 175, 239, 241, 248, 249

Harris, Frank, 239, 239n1, 239n2

Hart, Janice, 176

Hazlitt, William, 118

Healey, Chadwyck, 151

Hegel, G. W. F., 9, 76n2, 83, 85; Aristotle and, 74–75; Hobbes and, 75–76; individual freedom and, 75–76; Locke and, 75–76, 76n3

Heidegger, Martin, 4, 5, 260, 261, 262, 276

"Heideggerian Hand" (Derrida), 5

Helen Fleetwood (Tonna), 29–30, 31, 32, 33, 34, 38

Henley, William, 242

"Her Dilemma" (Hardy), 266

Herbert, Christopher, 123, 227n6

heroism, 55, 58, 59, 63, 122, 131

Heron-Allen, Edward, 249, 249n21, 249n22

Hershel, Sir William, 122

Hill, Jen, 61

hinges, human, 37–44

Hinton, A. Horsley, 189, 191

Hobbes, Thomas, 76

Hobhouse, Arthur, 134, 137, 138, 139

Hodges, John, 187

Holmes, Martha Stoddard, 40, 48, 56

Home, Douglas, 95–96, 97, 103; séance and, 91, 95, 98

homosexuality, 247, 247n19, 250n25

Hopkins, Brooke, 15, 245, 274

Hornung, E. W., 185

House by the Church-yard, The (Le Fanu), 99

Howards End (Forster), 223

Howe, Ida Lynch, 183

Howitt, William, 95

Hubert, Joseph, 182
Hughes, Thomas, 57
Hume, David, 77
Husserl, Edmund, 4, 5, 260

Ideas Pertaining to a Pure Phrenology (Husserl), 4
identity, 47, 92, 129; class, 216; collective, 132; English, 11, 144; gender, 151, 153; hands and, 33, 44; working-class, 50
images, 58, 96, 97, 109, 120n4, 122, 125, 149n3, 175, 176, 178n4, 179, 189, 236; alteration of, 181; making, 12; visual, 123
imagination, 8, 20n3, 140, 177, 203; artistic, 276; British, 58, 61; moral, 129
In Extremis (Bartlett), 244
In Memoriam (Tennyson), 274
Incidents in My Life (Home), 95–96
India Mutiny, 11, 109, 122, 124
individualism, 50n15, 123, 139; photography and, 192
industrial question, 7, 22–27
industrialism, 27, 155, 155n14, 197
inheritance, 11, 74, 84, 130, 134, 137 141, 145, 204, 206; burdens of, 128, 129; cultural, 144; legal, 133; national, 132, 136; power of, 131
intention, 4, 8, 9, 74, 77, 85, 112, 119, 121, 122, 225, 266; expressing, 78; individual, 80, 87
Isabella (Wilde), 245n14

James, Henry, 14, 98, 256, 256n1, 259, 269n12; hands in, 257, 268–71
"James Lee's Wife" (Browning), 276
Janauschek, Fanny, 204, 204n2, 208, 209n4, 210
Jane Eyre (Brontë), 8, 54, 55, 57, 58, 61, 68, 92n5, 129; filmic adaptations of, 56
"Jennie Lee as Jo in *Bleak House*" (unknown), 216 fig. 10.2
Jockers, Matthew, 152, 153
John Halifax, Gentleman (Muloch), 131
Johnson, Mark, 47, 131
Jowett, Benjamin, 48, 49n14, 50n17
Joyce, James, 263

jugglers, 107, 117, 118, 120

Kanner, S. Barbara, 30
Kaye, Richard, 247
Keats, John, 242, 242n6, 243, 246n15, 246n16, 246n18, 252, 273; hand of, 246; legacy of, 245n14; living land and, 245; Wilde and, 245–46, 245n14, 246n17
Kelsey, Robin, 180–81
Ketabgian, Tamara, 7, 8, 274
"Key to all Mythologies, The" (Casaubon), 138
King, Katie, 90
Kirilloff, Gabi, 152, 153
Kovačević, Ivanka, 30

labor, 176, 177, 189; hand, 21, 57; manual, 21, 148, 151, 155, 187, 191
Laboring Classes of England, The (Dodd), 44, 46, 46n10
Lady Dedlock and Hortense (Rendle), 204, 204n2
Lady Elcho/A Dantesque Vision (Cameron), 178 fig. 9.1, 179
Lane, Christopher, 248
language, 2, 155n14; hand and, 277; poetic, 277; possessive, 157 fig. 8.2
Laqueur, Thomas, 22, 37
Latour, Bruno, 112, 245
Law, Jules, 241
Le Fanu, Sheridan, 93, 97, 98, 99, 101, 102; fiction of, 10, 103, 104
le mort main, 128
Le toucher, Jean-Luc Nancy (Derrida), 260, 263
Leavis, Q. D., 196
Lee, Jennie, 210–11, 215
Lee, Sabrina, 153
legacy, 3n1, 57, 134, 144, 226, 231, 245; Foucauldian, 2; living, 252
Leopold, King, 175
Lesjak, Carolyn, 250
Leslie, Esther, 181
Letwin, Shirley, 228
Life of Nelson (Southey), 61, 62
"Lily Hart" (Brontë), 59

Lippincott's, 247, 247n19, 249
literature, 154–55, 156, 257; hands in, 258–59; photographic, 185; Victorian, 56, 73, 108n1, 148; working-class, 22
"Little Susie at her Work" (Riis), 176
Lloyd, William, 23
Locke, John, 9, 75, 76, 76n2, 83, 84
"Lord Arthur Saville's Crime" (Wilde), 14, 249, 250
Louis Napoleon, Emperor, 96
Lutener, William, 24
Lytton, Lady, 84

Macaulay, Thomas, 125
Mace, Rodney, 61
machinery, automatic, 21, 22, 26
"Machinery Question," 20, 27, 29, 33
Maine, Sir Henry, 137
Maine de Biran, 5, 260
Maker's hands, 24, 25
Malthus, Thomas, 164
Manafort, Paul, 258
manual activity, 6, 10, 13, 15, 26, 110
manual-centrism, 109, 119, 121, 122, 123
manual grasping (*greifen*), 5
manual intercourse, 65, 154, 154n12
manufacture, 29, 32, 39, 42, 262, 263; automatic, 25, 28, 33–34; mechanized, 19, 22, 149n2
Manufacturing Population of England (Gaskell), 21
Marcus, Sharon, 103
Markovits, Stephanie, 140, 143n5
Married Women's Property Act (1870), 221
Married Women's Property Act (1882), 222
Martin Chuzzlewit (Dickens), 167
Martineau, Harriet, 115
Marx, Karl, 28, 76, 76n3
Matrimonial Causes Act (1857), 221
Matus, Jill, 77
Mayor of Casterbridge, The (Hardy), 260, 261, 262, 263, 268
McAleavey, Maia, 64
McCorristine, Shane, 100, 103

Memoir of Robert Blincoe, A (Brown), 22, 37
Merleau-Ponty, Maurice, 4, 5, 260
mesmerism, 115, 115n2, 116, 117
metaphors, 6, 26, 39, 74, 100, 109, 125, 203, 205, 215, 236; dead, 65, 107; economic, 217; living, 1; manual, 9, 10, 107
Michael Armstrong, Factory Boy (Trollope), 30n5, 37
Michelangelo, 247
Michie, Helena, 148, 148n1, 166, 270n13
Middlemarch (Eliot), 11, 128, 129, 133, 134, 137, 140, 141, 142, 256, 258
Mill, John Stuart, 9, 76, 76n3, 84, 85
Mill on the Floss, The (Eliot), 57, 132, 141–42, 143, 143n6, 166
Miller, D. A., 108, 136
Miller, J. Hillis, 14, 273
Milton, John, 145
Mitchell, David, 41, 43, 43n7
Moments of Vision and Miscellaneous Verses (Hardy), 267
Montaigne, 247
moonstone, 11, 110–13, 121; deposit of, 122–26
Moonstone, The (Collins), 10, 68, 109, 110, 111, 112, 113, 119, 120, 122; colonialism and, 123; composing, 120n4; figural association in, 125; hands of, 107–8, 126; Indian subplot of, 124; plot of, 117
Morgan, Michelle, 92, 92n4
"Morning, The" (Browne), 202, 203
Morse, Deborah Denenholz, 132, 274, 275
mortmain, 128, 134
"Mr. Sludge, the Medium" (Browning), 97
Muloch, Dinah, 131
mutilation, 11, 109, 110, 123, 124, 125, 175, 189
Myers, William, 140n2, 143, 143n6, 145

Nancy, Jean-Luc, 5, 261, 263
Napoleonic Wars, 8, 57, 58, 59, 60, 61
Narrative of the Experiences and Sufferings of William Dodd, a Factory Cripple (Dodd), 22, 37, 38, 45, 46n10, 47, 50n16, 51; personal respect and, 50; social/political impact of, 43–44
narratives: causal, 46; fundamental structures of, 143; humanitarian, 22, 37; trauma, 123

National Review, 93, 98
Natural Theology (Paley), 20
Neapolitan, The (Cameron), 180 fig. 9.2
Nelson, Horatio, 8, 55, 56, 58, 61, 98; adultery of, 63, 64; biographical poem of, 62; Hamilton and, 62–63, 66; heroism of, 63; injuries of, 59, 61n6, 62, 67; Napoleonic Wars and, 68
nemesis, 140, 141, 142, 146
"New Meaning in the Roman, A" (Browne), 201
Nicholas Nickleby (Dickens), 167
Nietzsche, Friedrich, 143, 144, 145
Nineteenth-Century Fiction (Healey), 151
Northanger Abbey (Austen), 165n20
Novak, Daniel A., 14, 273
Nunokawa, Jeff, 135
Nussey, Ellen, 61

O'Connor, Erin, 39, 57
Old Curiosity Shop, The (Dickens), 167
"Old Furniture" (Hardy), 267
Olin, Margaret, 176
Oliver Twist (Dickens), 129
On Liberty (Mill), 76, 76n3, 83
"On the Disposition of Property to Public Use" (Hobhouse), 137
"On the Sale by Auction of Keats' Love Letters" (Wilde), 245
"On the Subject of Endowments and Settlements of Property" (Social Sciences Association), 134
"Only Connect" (Forster), 223
Origin of Species, The (Darwin), 27
Othello (Shakespeare), 258
Ourdan, J. P., 183

Paine, Thomas, 130, 144
Paley, William, 20
palmistry, 57, 92, 249, 249n22, 251
palpable, 93–97, 94n6, 98
Panciatichi, Lucrezia, 269, 270; painting of, 269 fig. 13.2
Paradise Lost (Milton), 263
Parikka, Jussi, 188

Peirce, Charles Sanders, 277
perfection, manual, 22–27
Personal Narrative of the Outbreak and Massacre at Cawnpore (Sheppard), 124
Philadelphia Photographer, 186
Philosophy of Manufactures (Ure), 28, 29
Philosophy of Money (Simmel), 132
Philosophy of Necessity (Bray), 145
Philosophy of Right, The (Hegel), 74, 75
Phineas Finn (Trollope), 161n18, 228–29, 231
Phineas Redux (Trollope), 230
Photo-Era (French), 185
Photographic News, 186n9, 188
Photographic Pleasures (Bede), 184
Photographs Objects Histories (Edwards and Hart), 176
photography, 12–13, 176, 189, 191; amateur, 179, 188n13; body and, 177; cropping and, 192; hands and, 175, 177–83, 193; hygiene of, 186; individuality and, 192; principles of, 192; retouching and, 181, 183, 192, 193
Photography and the Art of Chance (Kelsey), 180–81
phrenology, 3, 3n1
physiognomy, 3, 3n1, 118
Pickwick Papers, The (Dickens), 167
Picture of Dorian Gray, The (Wilde), 14, 15, 241n3, 243, 250, 278; premise of, 247–48; publication history of, 249
Pionke, Albert, 86
Plunkett, John, 181
poetry, 15, 131, 245, 246, 266, 268, 273–74
"Poisoned Meal, The" (Collins), 86
Polhemus, Robert, 231
politics, 73, 229; law and, 74; queer, 252
Poor Jo (Burnett), 210
Poor Miss Finch (Collins), 187
Portrait of a Lady, The (Campion), 258
Portrait of a Lady, The (James), 257
Portrait of Mr. W. H. (Wilde), 14, 242, 243n8
poverty, 135, 212, 215, 216, 217
"Power, Wisdom, Goodness of God as manifested in the Creation" (Bell), 19
Price, Leah, 241

Prime Minister, The (Trollope), 222
Professional and Amateur Photographer, 186
Pruitt, Scott, 258
Psychic Messages from Oscar Wilde (Smith), 243, 243n11
puffy hand, revenge of, 97–104

Racial Hand in the Victorian Imagination, The (Briefel), 10, 92, 149n3
rapping, 90, 97, 100, 101
"Ready for Sabbath Eve in a Coal Cellar—A Cobbler in Ludlow Street" (Riis), 179
Rear-Admiral Horatio Nelson (unknown), 62
Reflections on the Revolution in France (Burke), 129–30
Reform Act (1867), 221
Rendle, Henry, 13, 205, 206, 207, 208, 209, 209n4, 211, 215, 217, 217n8; play by, 203–4, 204n2, 210
responsibility, 112, 125; abrogation of, 110; questions of, 110
rhetoric, 28, 29, 31, 85, 86, 193, 258, 277
Rights of Man, The (Paine), 130
Riis, Jacob, 176, 177, 179
Riquelme, John Paul, 248, 248n20
Robinson, A., 244; work of, 244 fig. 12.2
Robinson Crusoe (Dafoe), 122
Roentgen, Anna Bertha, 175
Roentgen, Wilhelm, 175
Roman Law (Maine), 137
"Romance of Certain Old Clothes, The" (James), 98
Romola (Eliot), 141
Ross, Robert, 251n26, 252
Rossetti, William Michael, 177, 242n7
Rousseau, Jean-Jacques, 75
Rowe, Katherine, 2, 100, 101, 108n1, 128n1, 137, 226, 226n5
Ruskin, John, 40, 181
Ryan, Vanessa, 77

Sadler, Michael, 24, 30
Samuel, Raphael, 20
Schaffer, Talia, 55, 66, 67
Science of the Hand, The (D'Arpentigny), 93

séance, 10, 90, 91, 91n3, 94, 95, 97, 98, 99, 101, 102
Sedgwick, Eve Kosofsky, 247
Seeley, John, 110
Sein und Zeit (Heidegger), 262
Semmel, Bernard, 132
sentimentality, 48, 91, 93, 123
Sermon on the Mount, 63, 64
sexuality, 114, 148, 159–60, 163n19
Shakespeare, William, 21, 242, 246, 247
"Shakespeare and the Greeks," 246, 247
Sheehan, Tanya, 186
Shelley, Mary, 34
Shelley, Percy, 4
Sheppard, W. J., 124
Shirley (Brontë), 30n5, 155
"Signs of the Times" (Carlyle), 21
silver nitrate, 179, 184, 185, 188; discoloration and, 187, 187n11
Silver Sunbeam, The (Towler), 179
Simmel, Georg, 128, 132, 136
"Sir David Baird Discovering the Body of Tipu Sultan" (Wilkie), 122
Smith, Hester Travers, 243
Smith, Julianne, 13
Smith, Samuel, 23–24
Snyder, Sharon, 41, 43, 43n7
Sobchak, Vivian, 41, 41n5
social class, 13, 222, 229, 231, 232, 237; barriers of, 7–8; rights, 221
Social Sciences Association, 134, 137
"Sonnet in Blue" (Keats), 242
Southey, Robert, 61, 62
Spanish Gypsy (Eliot), 140
Spectator, The, 47, 63, 111
Specters of Marx (Derrida), 132
Speed, Emma, 242, 242n6, 247
spirit-hands, 9, 91, 93, 94, 96, 98, 99, 101; detachment of, 97; fictiveness of, 97; isolation of, 95; materialization of, 102
Spiritual Magazine, 96
spiritualism, 9, 10, 90, 92, 94, 95, 96, 97, 98, 99, 101; ghosts of, 93; history of, 90n1; narratives of, 103, 104; repetitions of, 103

"Spoiled Negative, A" (Hornung), 185
"Stained Fingers" (*Camera*), 187
"Stained Fingers and How They May Be Avoided" (*Wilson's*), 187
Steig, Michael, 198
stereotypes, 150, 161, 260; Asian, 107, 118; gender, 151, 152, 153, 154, 163, 164
Stieglitz, Alfred, 185, 193, 193n15
"Storyteller, The" (Benjamin), 181
Sudnow, David, 276
Sutherland, John, 120n4, 226n4
Sweet, Ryan, 58

tactile, 4, 64, 65, 92, 93, 94, 96, 113, 175, 235, 243, 249
Tale of Two Cities, A (Dickens), 77, 86n8
Technics of the Hand Camera, The (Coventry), 192
technology, 176; changes in, 259; imaging, 12, 175; photographic, 177, 178, 193
Ten Hours Debate, 47, 49n14
Ten Hours Factory Act (1847), 36, 36n2, 38, 48n13
Ten Hours Movement, 43, 49, 50
Tenant of Wildfell Hall, The (Brontë), 92n5, 154
Tennyson, Alfred Lord, 15, 274, 275
Tennyson, Emily, 183
Tess of the d'Urbervilles (Hardy), 264
texture, 96, 118, 179, 266
Thackeray, William, 155, 169
Thinking Literature Across Continents (Ghosh), 258
Third Reform Act (1884), 222
"This Living Hand" (Keats), 243, 243n12, 245
Thurber, James, 262
Tom Brown's Schooldays (Hughes), 57
"Tomb of Keats, The" (Wilde), 245
Tonna, Charlotte Elizabeth, 29–33, 37–38
touch, 6, 8, 14, 24, 25, 73, 75, 76, 78–79, 80, 82, 93, 94, 98, 119, 166, 177, 179, 202, 222, 225; erotic, 231; hand and, 5, 65, 87, 176, 226, 228, 229, 240, 260; manual, 82, 149, 154, 154n12; memory and, 176; power of, 9, 113, 117; sense of, 114, 191, 193

Touching Photographs (Olin), 176
Towler, John, 179
"Triumph of Mind over Body" (Brontë), 62
Trollope, Anthony, 13, 221, 222, 222n1, 223, 228, 231, 274; drama and, 235n15
Trollope, Frances, 30n5, 37, 235
Trump, Donald, 256, 258, 259
Tucker, Herbert F., 14–15
Twilight of the Gods (Nietzsche), 143
"Two Apostles" (Giotto), 264
Two Haloed Mourners (Aretino), 265 fig. 13.1

Underwood, Ted, 153, 155, 155n14, 155–56n16
Ure, Andrew, 28, 29, 33n7, 39, 40

Vanity Fair (Thackeray), 155, 169, 221
Victoria, Queen, 68
Victorian Economy, The (Crouzet), 20
vocation, charity and, 48–51
voice: prosthetic, 44–48; public, 45, 47
Vrettos, Athena, 77

Wallace, Alfred R., 115
Wanderer; or Female Difficulties, The (Burney), 165
Ward, Megan, 241, 242n5
waving, 82, 114, 165, 167, 168, 263, 264, 277
Ways of the Hand (Sudnow), 276
Wellington, Duke of, 58, 61
Wessex Poems (Hardy), 266
What Is Called Thinking (Heidegger), 5
White, Colin, 66
Wilde, Oscar, 14, 145, 239–40n2, 240 fig. 12.1, 241n3, 242n6, 242n7, 243n8, 243n11, 245, 251n27, 278; afterlife of, 243; biography of, 239; death of, 241; focus of, 251–52; hand of, 241, 243–44; homoerotic and, 247n19; homosexuality of, 250n25; Keats and, 245–46, 245n14, 246n17; palm-reading and, 249, 249n22; philosophy of, 242
Wilkie, David, 122
Williams, Kate, 59
Williams, Raymond, 31
Wilson, Edward, 186
Wilson, John, 27, 29

Wilson, Kathleen, 62
Wilson's Photographic Magazine, 187
Wings of the Dove, The (James), 256n1, 264, 268, 270
Winter, Alison, 94
Woman in White, The (Collins), 9, 73, 76–77, 78, 84, 86
"Workbox, The" (Hardy), 266
Wounded Soldiers of Industry, The (Bartrip and Burman), 23

writing, 14, 15, 196, 252, 274; prosthetic, 44–48
Wuthering Heights (Brontë), 100, 101

Yeats, William Butler, 267
Yonge, Charlotte, 58

Zandy, Janet, 176
Zemka, Sue, 10, 11, 44, 58
Zlotnick, Susan, 32

www.ingramcontent.com/pod-product-compliance
Lightning Source LLC
Chambersburg PA
CBHW020639230426
43665CB00008B/242